TONY REES

RARE ROCK

A Collectors' Guide

BLANDFORD PRESS
POOLE · DORSET

First published in the UK 1985 by Blandford Press
Link House, West Street, Poole, Dorset, BH15 1LL

Compilation copyright © 1985 Tony Rees

Distributed in the United States by
Sterling Publishing Co., Inc.,
2 Park Avenue, New York, N.Y. 10016

British Library Cataloguing in Publication Data

Rees, Tony
    The encyclopedia of rare rock.
    1. Rock music—Discography
    I. Title
    016.7899'12454   ML156.4.R6

ISBN 0 7137 1513 8

Typeset by Poole Typesetting (Wessex) Limited

Printed in Great Britain by Butler and Tanner,
Frome and London

CONTENTS

FOREWORD

Record collectors need only two tools to ply their hobby: money and discographies. The first determines the size of the collection, the second determines the scope. While this book offers no advice in acquiring funds to help you pursue the 'elusive disc', it should help to fill a gap that's long needed filling.

Until *Rare Rock,* there have been only two general discographies of true merit. Terry Hounsome's *New Rock Record* stands as the best source going for finding out artists' LP output; this is complemented by the hard-to-find *Bootleg Bible* (Babylon Books) which lists artists' illegal output. Supplementing both are the discographies that are sometimes incorporated in individual artists' biographies, and – if the performer is popular enough to justify it – individual discographies such as those cataloguing the works of Bob Dylan, the Beatles, and other top musicians. But none of these have covered the grey area in between the legitimate commercial releases and the bootlegs.

The 'grey area' consists of those legitimately-produced but commercially unobtainable promotional items, and the obtainable 'limited editions' which disappear from the shops within days of release. Many of these items are merely 'packaging', differing only from the marketed version in appearance or format. However, what makes some oddities so desirable are the musical variations that *do* appear from time to time, like edited or extended versions, alternate takes, or even songs which are otherwise unavailable.

Rare Rock lists and identifies as many of these items as its author has unearthed. Because record companies don't like to talk about past promotional output, the task could only be accomplished by scouring the trade magazines, collectors' publications, classified ads, and catalogues. It is by no means complete, for hardly a day goes by without some long-lost acetate or flexi-disc appearing. What Tony Rees has compiled is a listing of the lesser known artifacts of several hundred artists – both major stars and cult figures – to help collectors learn about or identify items they may want or need.

This is a book for the vinyl junkie, the music lover who wants to have everything associated with his or her favourite performer. To foil the greedy, those parasites who when they see the gleam in your eye ask £25 or $50 for something worth a tenth of that, Tony has refused to put a value on the items listed.

6

Rare Rock is also, to use a much-maligned sentiment, a labour of love. Who but the truly dedicated would go through every page, every line of *Goldmine* to find new items? For years I, and others, have relied on Tony for information or verification, be it a catalogue number or the confirmation of a rumoured release's existence. Now, instead of loose sheafs of paper crammed with information, I have a bound tome at my fingertips. It will pay for itself in the first month as my 'phone bill diminishes.

I've waited a long time for this; thanks, Tony.

Ken Kessler
Assistant Editor
Hi-Fi News & Record Review

ACKNOWLEDGEMENTS

My special thanks are due to Andrew for letting me raid his collection. Also to Ken Kessler for not only setting the wheels in motion, but putting them on the right track – so thanks also to all those nice people at Blandford Press.

This book is dedicated to all those still looking for the platters that matter. Also to mum!

INTRODUCTION

A number of terms are used to identify just what type of rarity an item may be, some categories of which are vague enough to cause confusion. The following explains the terms as used in *Rare Rock*.

Acetates   Aluminium discs of various sizes (7, 10 or 12 inch) with a thin coating of shellac or vinyl. These discs are not pressed like regular vinyl issues. Instead, they are individually cut by the master cutter as a 'pre' test pressing to give directions as to how the final cut should go. As such, each acetate is unique, and acetates constitute some of the rarest items in the whole field of record collecting. Incredibly fragile, they are only good for a few playings. Their desirability stems from the fact that they often bear no musical resemblance to the final release; in some cases, acetates may be the only existing source for a particular song or performance (e.g. certain Beatles' takes for *Strawberry Fields* unless you have got access to the master tape.

Errors   Strictly the province of the hard-core; some discs become collectable because a flawed batch was released and then withdrawn. Typical are misprints on the label or sleeve, or the pressing of the wrong song on the A or B side. (e.g. an early US Beatles single spelled the name 'Beattles').

Promos   These are LPs, singles, or tapes given to DJs, reviewers, or retailers, often differing in packaging only from the product in the shops. Most common are 'white labels' in place of the printed label, often unadorned or with handwritten identification. Promo items usually bear the phrases 'for promotion only' or 'not for sale' as the only identification proving it as a non-commercial issue. A recent trend has been to send standard, shop-type releases with the sleeve stamped or defaced (cut corner) to prevent re-sale. Of more interest are promos with musical differences, like 12 inch singles with extended versions or extra (often live) cuts. As they're quite desirable, bootleggers find great inspiration from promos. (e.g. *'Elvis Costello Live at El Mocambo'* from CBS Canada has been bootlegged).

Radio Show Albums   Made by special production companies, these can be either lengthy interviews or live concerts. They're sent out to the various radio stations syndicating a particular programme, and offer up to an hour's worth of otherwise unobtainable material. BBC specials have appeared on disc for airing abroad, and most of the US networks have series which appear on disc, like NBC's *The Source*. Again, a prime target of the bootleggers.

Test Pressings   These are blank label copies made to check sound quality at the pressing plant. Some oddities do appear, but the desirability is more cosmetic than musical.

Withdrawn Items Along with 'Errors', some items are removed from sale because of a change of heart in either the artist or the record company. Occasionally, a few reach the shops, the most famous being the Beatles' 'Butcher Sleeve', which was withdrawn because Capitol thought it was in bad taste. It's now selling for a small fortune. *(Note* Just as bootleggers go for the music, so do some go for counterfeiting rarities with only artwork as their appeal. Beware of copies of items like the 'Butcher Sleeve' which was withdrawn only because of its cover. It's easier to counterfeit a photograph than a vinyl stamping).

The items in *Rare Rock* that were commercially available all fall under the heading of 'Limited Editions', which is, unfortunately, a relative term. In the loosest sense, a limited edition is one that will not reappear after the initial batch has been sold, unlike normal releases which can remain in the companies' catalogues:

Audiophile Discs These are ultra-high quality pressings on pure, virgin vinyl, often with different or better packaging. As most come from smaller companies licensing the LP from the original label, audiophile pressings are limited by the contract. Mobile Fidelity, for example, presses no more than 200,000 copies per title for world consumption, and their UHQR releases are numbered editions of 5,000.

Coloured vinyl Just what it says, and strictly a packaging manoeuvre. Numbers vary; strictly for completists.

Double singles These twin-packs often appear with the initial shipments of a new single, the second 'free' single usually containing two otherwise unavailable tracks. Typically, expect runs of 10,000 copies.

Packaging Picture sleeves, free posters and other giveaways, gate-fold sleeves, or whatever unique package an art department can create usually only appear with initial runs. Again, a non-musical rarity.

Picture Discs Often unplayable because of the manufacturing process, the same remarks apply as per 'packaging'.

Re-issues: Although most re-issues are straight catalogue items, some – especially boxed sets – are severely limited. Often these offer special packaging and rare material, like the free EP in the Beatles EP boxed set.

There are, of course, many other sources for rarities, and two in particular crop up often in *Rare Rock*.

Flexi-discs These are an ideal 'giveaway' as they're cheaper to produce than 'hard' singles, as they contain less than half the vinyl. Usually only good for a few plays, some do offer rare material and as such are worth acquiring. The most famous (and valuable) are the flexis given to members of the Beatles Fan Club at Christmas, which have since been bootlegged many times. (See appendix for a listing of the flexis that came free with *Flexi-Pop* magazine).

Juke Box EPs These special American issues, often containing six tracks on a 7 inch disc, appear in unique sleeves though they offer no musical rarities.

Rare Rock contains oddities up to mid-1984, focussing mainly on rock, with a bit of crossover from R & B, early Rock 'n' Roll, and other forms. To the best of my knowledge and ability, it's accurate, but room for doubt exists regarding certain items that may be little more than wishful thinking on some collector's part. If you have any additions or corrections I may incorporate in future editions, please contact me.

Tony Rees

ALBUMS, EPs, SINGLES, FLEXIS AND CASSETTES

The recordings are listed in date order under the name of the group or artist.

Abba

British singles

Ring Ring First mix/*Watch Out* Epic EPC-1793. 1973.
Ring Ring Second mix/*Rock 'n' Roll Band* Epic EPC-2452. 1974.
The Winner Takes It all/Elaine Epic twelve-inch EPC 13-8835. 1980. This was released in a very limited edition gatefold pop-up sleeve.
Lay All Your Love On Me Epic one-sided promo EPCA-1456-DJ. 1980. This was one of the first records to chart as a twelve-inch single only, so for radio purposes a seven-inch single was made.

British albums

Gracias Pour La Musica Epic EPC-86123. 1980. It's a tradition for internationally known artists to record foreign language versions of their hits. You'll see many of these throughout the book. Abba were no exception, recording many of their hits in different tongues (like English for example!). This album is a collection of their Spanish recordings.
Super Trouper Epic PACHBH-22. 1980. This was issued as a highly collectable boxed set edition complete with a book and poster.
The Best Of Abba Reader's Digest, number unknown. 1983. A three-album boxed set edition.
The Singles, The First Ten Years Epic ABBOX-1. 1983. This was a limited edition boxed set with the double album appearing as two picture discs with a book.

American singles

Dancing Queen Same on both sides. Atlantic twelve-inch promo DSKO-81. 1976.
The Name Of The Game Long and short versions. Atlantic promo 3449. 1977.

Voulez Vous 5:08 and 3:45 versions. Atlantic seven-inch promo 3609. 1979.
Voulez Vous 5:08 and 3:45 versions. Atlantic twelve-inch promo PR-202. 1979.
A Man After Midnight 4:45 and 3:35 versions. Atlantic promo 3652. 1979.
Chiquitita (English version)/*Lovelight* Atlantic 3629. 1979.
Chiquitita (English version) Long and short versions. Atlantic promo 3629. 1979.
Chiquitita (Spanish version)/*Lovelight* (English version) Atlantic 3630. 1979.
Chiquitita Combined English and Spanish versions. Atlantic acetate. 1979.
This only got as far as a ten-inch acetate, and was never released.
Lay All Your Love On Me/On and On/Super Trouper Atlantic twelve-inch promo, number unknown. 1980.
Lay All Your Love On Me Re-mix. Disconnet Records twelve-inch, number unknown. 1980. This was given to club DJ's only, so only a handful would have made their way into collectors' shops. This is extremely rare.
Happy New Year Same on both sides. Atlantic promo PR-380. 1980.
The Visitors Long and short versions. Atlantic seven-inch promo 4031. 1981.
The Visitors Long and short versions. Atlantic twelve-inch promo PR-329. 1981.
When All Is Said And Done Same on both sides. Atlantic twelve-inch promo DM-308. 1981.
The Visitors Re-mix. Hot Tracks Records twelve-inch, number unknown. 1983. This rarity was specially re-mixed for the gay disco market.

American albums
Abba Radio Station Sampler Atlantic promo PR-300. 1977. A compilation.
Billboard Sound Of 77 Radio Series (Dated 16.12.77). This was also issued in double album format with Olivia Newton John on album two (same date).
The Magic Of Abba K-Tel NU-9510. 1978. A limited edition TV-advertised album.
Voulez Vous Atlantic SD-16000. 1979. A special mail order version was made for Columbia House.
Robert W. Morgan Radio Series, number 794. (Dated 24.11.79).
Robert W. Morgan Radio Series, number 802. (Dated 3.5.80).
Robert W. Morgan Radio Series, number 812. (Dated 27.6.81).
A Collection Of Hits Atlantic promo PR-432. 1982. This was made to promote the 'greatest hits' collection.

Odds and sods
Ring Ring/Ah Vilka Tider Both sung in Swedish. Swedish Polar POS-1171. 1973.
Ring Ring/Wer Im Wartesaal Der Heive Steht German Polydor 2040 105. 1973.
Music People At Eurovision EP. UK CBS-Epic promo 2283. 1974. This various artists EP features Abba's *Waterloo*.
Waterloo (sung in German)/B side unknown. German Polydor 2040 116. 1974.
Waterloo (sung in French)/B side unknown. French Vogue 103104 and Canada Atlantic 40003. 1974.

Ring Ring   Swedish Polar POLS-242.   1973.   This album features tracks which haven't appeared in Britain or America.
Honey Honey   German Polydor 2344 122.   1974.   Another album with rare tracks.
Music For UNICEF   UK Polydor 2335 214.   1978.   This album features a live version of *Chiquitita* recorded in New York for a charity concert.
Slipping Through My Fingers   Japan Coca Cola/Discomate one-sided seven-inch picture disc 0590.   c.1980.
Slipping Through My Fingers   Japan Coca Cola/Discomate album, number unknown.   c.1980.   Pressed on red vinyl.
Arrival   Japan Nautilus Audiophile pressing, number unknown.   1981.
The Singles Collection 1972-1982   Country of origin and label details unknown. 1983.   A 27 single boxed set with a free single. *Waterloo* sung in French/sung in German.

In addition to these there are many solo albums by the two girls, as well as records they have produced for other people, etc.

ABC

Before changing their name to ABC in 1981 they had been VICE VERSA and had cut at least two singles in Britain:
Music Four   EP.   UK Neutron Records PX-1092.   1980.
The 1980 EP   UK Neutron Records NT-003.   1980.

The above two Vice Versa records are extremely hard to find as they were only local independent releases. To confuse matters at the time there was another band at the same time called Vice Versa, apparently from Holland, who released one single *Stilyagi* on Dutch BBR Records in 1980.

The band ABC who appeared on the *Honky Tonk Demos* album on UK Oval Records isn't Martin Fry's band either.

British singles
All Of My Heart   Edited.   Neutron one-sided promo NTXDJ-104.   1982.
The Look Of Love   Re-mix.   Same on both sides.   Neutron twelve-inch promo NTXDJ-103.   1982.   This was later given a full release in a limited edition.
Beauty Stab   Sampler.   Neutron promo flexi MADDOX-1.   1983.

American singles
The Look Of Love   Long and short versions.   Mercury twelve-inch promo 4023. 1982.
Poison Arrow/All Of My Heart   Mercury twelve-inch promo MK-230.   1982.
Poison Arrow   Re-mix/B side unknown.   Mercury twelve-inch 811 329-1.   1983. This re-mix hasn't been released in the UK.

AC/DC

British singles

Girl's Got Rhythm   Atlantic one-sided promo SAM-113.   1979.   A one track sampler from their EP.

Shake A Leg/Have A Drink On Me   Atlantic K-11600.   1979.   A mispress. The A side should have been *You Shook Me*. Only a hundred were made.

For Those About To Rock   Edited.   Atlantic one-sided promo K-11721.   1981.

For Those About To Rock   Full version.   Atlantic one-sided twelve-inch promo SAM-143.   1981.

British albums

AC/DC/MAX MERRITT   BBC Transcription Service disc 139797.   1976.   One side each. Both are live.

Highway To Hell   Atlantic K-50628.   1979.   Original white label copies came with a different proof cover to the released version.

Japan Tour '81   Atlantic promo picture disc SAM-155.   1981.   This is not a live album, but a compilation.

American singles

Back In Black   Long and short versions.   Atlantic promo 3787.   1980.

AC/DC Live In Germany   EP.   Atlantic twelve-inch promo, number unknown. 1980.

Let's Get It Up/Snowballed   Atlantic twelve-inch promo PR-419.   1981.

For Those About To Rock   5:42 and 3:50 versions.   Atlantic promo 4029.   1981.

Nervous Breakdown   Plus two others.   Atlantic twelve-inch promo, number unknown.   1983.

Flick Of The Switch   Same on both sides.   Atlantic twelve-inch promo PR-557. 1983.

American albums

Live At The Atlantic Studios   Atlantic promo LAAS-001.   1977.   A great live album. Beware of counterfeits.

The AC/DC Special   NBC-Source Radio Series, number 24.   1980.   A three album set.

Flick Of The Switch Interview Album   Atlantic promo PR-562.   1983.

Odds and sods

Powerage   Australian EMI-Albert Productions, number unknown.   1977.   This has *Rock 'n' Roll Damnation* instead of *Cold Hearted Man* on the UK copy.

Dirty Deeds Done Dirt Cheap   Australian EMI-Albert Productions, number unknown.   1978.   The Aussie version has *R.I.P.* and *Jailbreak* instead of *Rocker*

14

and *Love* which are on the British edition.

Jailbreak   EP.   German Atlantic promo PRO-171.   1977.

AC/DC   French Atlantic, number unknown.   1979.   This is a three album box set with *Dirty Deeds Done Dirt Cheap, High Voltage* and *Powerage*. Also included is an EP with *Soul Stripper, Baby Please Don't Go* and *Jailbreak*.

AC/DC   Australian EMI-Albert Productions, number unknown.   c.1982. A six-album boxed set with a free one-sided twelve-inch single *Cold Hearted Man* and an iron-on transfer.

AC/DC also have some rare material on the *Albert Archives* album on Australian EMI-Albert Productions.

Adam and the Ants

British singles

Zerox/Physical   Do It DUN-8.   1979.   Mispress. The B side should have been *Whip In My Valise*.

Car Trouble   Do It one-sided twelve-inch promo WHAT-1.   1979.

Goody Two Shoes/Red Scab   CBS A-2367.   1982.   Early promo copies were apparently credited to Adam And The Ants instead of Adam Ant.

ANTS   Flexipop 004   (Lyntone LYN-9285).   1981.

American singles

Antmusic/Dog Eat Dog/Kings Of The Wild Frontier   Epic twelve-inch, number unknown.   1980.   Withdrawn, but test pressings exist.

Dog Eat Dog   Same on both sides.   Epic twelve-inch promo AS-906.   1980.

Antmusic   Same on both sides.   Epic twelve-inch promo 48-01061.   1980.

Los Rancheros/Physical   Epic twelve-inch promo AS-973.   1981.

That Voodoo   Other side unknown.   Epic twelve-inch promo, number unknown. 1981.

Antmusic/ANTS   Epic, number unknown.   1981.   Withdrawn, but test pressings exist.

Hello I Love You/Goody Two Shoes/Desparate But Not Serious   Epic twelve-inch promo AS-1556.   1982.

American album

Kings Of The Wild Frontier   Epic NJE-37033.   1981.   This version has *Physical* and *Press Darlings* instead of *Making History*.

Odds and sods

THE MANEATERS   *Nine To Five*   UK EG EGO-8.   1982.   This was Adam and Toyah taken from the *Jubilee* soundtrack album, originally recorded in 1977. They just appear on this A side.

The Adverts

British singles

No Time To Be Twenty One/New Day's Dawning Anchor ANC-1051. 1978. Withdrawn on Anchor, but then issued on their own Bright label.
Gary Gilmore's Eyes/B side unknown. Butt, number unknown. 1981. Possibly withdrawn.

British albums

Crossing The Red Sea With The Adverts Bright BRL-201. 1978. Also pressed in a very limited edition red vinyl run.
Gary Gilmore's Eyes was added to the Butt label re-issue in 1981.

Odds and sods

The Roxy, London, WC 2 UK Harvest SHSP-4069. 1977. This includes *Bored Teenagers* recorded live.

Aerosmith

American singles

Dream On 4:28 and 3:25 versions. Columbia promo 3-10278. 1973.
Kings And Queens 4:46 and 3:46 versions. Columbia promo 3-10699. 1976.
Chip Away The Stone Live and studio versions. Columbia promo 3-10880. 1978.

American albums

Get Your Wings Quad mix. Columbia CQ-32847. 1974.
Pure Gold From Rock 'n' Roll's Golden Boys Columbia promo AS-187. 1975. A boxed set of their first three albums.
Robert W. Morgan *Profiles In Rock* Radio Series (Dated 12.4.80)
King Biscuit Radio Show (Dated 29.6.80)
The First Decade Columbia promo, no number. 1982. An eight album boxed set.

British singles

Dream On 4:28 and 3:25 versions. CBS promo 4000-DJ. 1976.
Rats In The Cellar/Walk This Way/Same Old Song And Dance/Dream On CBS promo AS-1. 1976. Made to promote their first UK tour.

A second promo EP, AS-2, was also made, but I don't know the tracks.

Odds and sods

Sgt. Pepper . . . USA RSO/UK A & M. 1977. They appear on this album.

After the Fire

British singles

80 F Epic promo XPR-104. 1980. This is a four-track white label sampler from the unreleased version of the *80 F* album.
Love Will Always Make You Cry/Every Mother's Son Epic EPC-8394. 1980. Withdrawn.
ATF Live EP. CBS test pressing, number unknown. 1982. Recorded at the Rainbow Theatre in London, but never released.

British albums

Signs Of Change Rapid Records RR-001. 1978. Issued on their own label, this album escaped in 1978 and was quickly deleted.
80 F Epic, number unknown. 1980. This album was recorded, mixed and sequenced, but CBS turned it down. ATF re-recorded the whole thing, and this was the version eventually released. White label cassettes of the first version exist, which is just as well because it's much better than the released version. The *80 F* EP mentioned earlier has excerpts from this unreleased mix.
Batteries Not Included CBS 85135. 1982. The original sleeve for this was scrapped and was eventually released with another number. So it's possible that this withdrawn version may have a different track listing. (Also, this band may have made it in Britain if CBS hadn't mucked about so much!)
Der Kommissar CBS 25227. 1983. There are two different versions of this album. The second version, released about six months after the first, has some alternate mixes.

Altered Images

British singles

Happy New Year/Real Toys/Leave Me Alone Flexipop 14 (Lyntone LYN-10795). 1982.
Pinky Blue Sampler EP. Epic promo XPS-141. 1982.
Little Town Flirt/BAD MANNERS/*Yakety Yak* A & M promo, number unknown. 1982.

British album

Bite Epic cassette EPC40-25413. 1983. This contains five extra tracks.

Odds and sods

Party Party Film soundtrack. UK/USA A & M. 1982.
Jive Wire UK NME cassette 002. 1982. This has a re-mix of *Happy Birthday*.

Jon Anderson

Before joining YES he had already cut two singles under the name HANS CHRISTIAN ANDERSEN:
Never My Love   UK Parlophone R-5676.   1967.
Mississippi Hobo   UK Parlophone R-5698.   1967.
The B sides are unknown on both of these recordings.

American singles
Some Are Born   Same on both sides.   Atlantic twelve-inch promo PR-376.   1980.
Heart Of The Matter   Long and short versions.   Atlantic promo 3795.   1980.
All In A Matter Of Time/Olympia   Atlantic twelve-inch promo PR-449.   1982.

American albums
An Evening With Jon Anderson   Atlantic promo PR-285.   1976.   Made to promote the *Olias Of Sunhillow* album.
Rolling Stone Guest DJ Radio Series, number 20.   c.1981.
King Biscuit Radio Series   (Dated 12.9.82). A live show.

Odds and sods
THE WARRIORS   *You Came Along/Don't Make Me Blue*   UK Decca F-11926.   1964.
Anderson was with this band. This is also available on the *Hard Up Heroes* album on Decca.
Fundamental Frolics   UK BBC REB-435.   1982.   Anderson plays live on this.
MIKE OLDFIELD   *Crisis*   UK/USA Virgin.   1983.   Anderson sings lead on one track *In High Places*.

The Animals

British singles
I'm Crying/B side unknown.   Columbia export issue, number unknown.   1964.
Mama Told Me Not To Come/See See Rider   Decca F-12502.   1966.   This was withdrawn. The A side was replaced with *Help Me Girl*.

British EP
I Just Wanna Make Love To You   Graphic Sound Records ALO-10867.   1963.
This rare independent release was limited to 500 only and was sold in pubs and clubs. It was re-issued by Decca in 1966 as *In The Beginning There Was Early Animals* and in a new sleeve.

British albums
Love Is   MGM CS-8104.   1968.   A single album version.
Love Is   MGM 2619 002.   1971.   This time it was given it's full double album status.

Ark IRS cassette CS-70037. 1983. This tape version has one extra track, *No John No.*

American singles

MGM Celebrity Scene MGM promo MGM-CS-115. 1966. A box set of five singles.
Monterey Long and short versions. MGM promo K-13868. 1967.

American albums

The Best Of The Animals MGM-Capitol Record Club SKAO-90622. c.1969.
Burns Media Radio Series. 1977. Made for their *Before We Were So Rudely Interrupted* re-union album.
Rolling Stone Continuous History Of Rock 'n' Roll Radio Series, number 53. c.1981.
Ark IRS cassette CS-70037. 1983. This has an extra track *No John No.*

Odds and sods

Get Yourself A College Girl USA MGM SE-4273. 1966. This film soundtrack has two new Animals tracks, *Blue Feeling* and *Around And Around.*

Argent

British singles

Hold Your Head Up EP. Epic 7062. 1972. A three track EP with the full version of the main track. It played at 33rpm and came with a colour picture sleeve.
Hold Your Head Up Edited. Epic one-sided promo EPC-9135-DJ. 1972. This 45rpm single was made to promote the above EP.

British album

In Deep Quad mix. Epic Q-65475. 1974.

American singles

THE ZOMBIES *Imagine The Swan/Conversation Of Floral Street* Date ZS7-1644. 1969.
THE ZOMBIES *If It Don't Work Out/Don't Cry For Me* Date ZS7-1648. 1969.

These two singles are apparently Argent using The Zombies' name at the insistance of CBS, who owned Date Records.

ARGENT *Liar/Schoolgirl* Date ZS7-1659. 1969. Their first rare release.
God Gave Rock 'n' Roll To You 6:45 and 3:20 versions. Epic promo 5-10972. 1973.

American album

In Deep Quad mix. Epic EQ-32195. 1974.

Joan Armatrading

British albums

Talk Under Ladders A & M promo SAMP-12. 1981. This is an excellent album with interviews and demo material. Made to promote the *Walk Under Ladders* album.

American album

Live At The Bijou, Philadelphia, 1977 A & M promo SP-8414. 1977. A promo only, live album.

Odds and sods

Interview and music. German *Musik Express* magazine flexi. 1981.

Asia

British single

The Smile Has Left Your Eyes/Lying To Yourself/Midnight Sun Geffen twelve-inch GEF-TA-3836. 1983. A very limited red vinyl pressing.

British album

Alpha Geffen cassette GEF40-25508. 1983. This has an extra track *Daylight*.

American singles

Heat Of The Moment 3:50 and 3:25 versions. Geffen promo GEF-50040. 1982.
Only Time Will Tell/Here Comes The Feeling Geffen twelve-inch promo PROA-1042. 1982.
Sole Survivor Long and short versions. Geffen promo 7-29871. 1982.

American albums

Asia Geffen promo Quiex II pure vinyl pressing GHS-2008. 1982.
Westwood One Radio Series, number 82-19. (Dated 10.5.82).
NBC Source Radio Series, number 82-22. (Dated June 1982).
NBC Source Radio Series (Dated 20.12.82).
Alpha Geffen promo Quiex II pure vinyl pressing, number unknown. 1983.

Kevin Ayers

British single

Sing A Song In The Morning EMI-Disc acetate. c.1971. This acetate has Syd

Barrett, but the finished, released, version has Syd mixed out. This may have had the last recorded appearance of Barrett.

Bad Company

British singles
Deal With The Preacher   Island one-sided promo BCDJ-1.   1976.
Desolation Angels   Sampler and Alan Freeman interview.   Swansong twelve-inch promo, number unknown.   1980.

American single
Burning Sky   5:10 and 3:28 versions.   Swansong promo SS-70112.   1976.

The Barbarians

American single
Hey Little Bird/You Gotta Understand   Joy 290.   c.1964.   A rare local label release. Beware! Brown vinyl counterfeits exist.

The Beach Boys

American singles
Surfin/Lau   X Records 301.   1961.   Withdrawn due to possible confusion with an RCA subsidiary with the same name *X Records*.
Surfin/Lau   Candix 301.   1962.   Most of these were promo only.
Surfin/Lau   Candix 331.   1962.   Its final release.
Spirit Of America/Boogie Woogie   Capitol Custom promo, number unknown (Dated 16.11.63). Made especially for KFWB radio.
Salt Lake City/Amusement Park USA   Capitol Custom PRO-2936/7.   1964. Made for Downtown Salt Lake City Stores.
Sunflower   Radio Spots.   Reprise-Brother PRO-442.   1970.
Child Of Winter/Suzie Cincinnatti   Brother RPS-1321.   1974.   Withdrawn.
Here Comes The Night   Vocal and instrumental versions.   Caribou blue vinyl twelve-inch promo AS-557.   1979.
Here Comes The Night   4:28 and 3:18 versions.   Caribou promo ZS9-9026.   1979.
Here Comes The Night Medley   Disconnet 10.   1979.   This is an extremely rare twelve-inch featuring a medley of Beach Boys oldies based around the *Here Comes The Night* track and only given to club DJ's.
Lady Lynda   3:58 and 2:59 versions. Caribou promo ZS9-9030.   1979.

What's It All About? Radio Series   MA-1790 (507-8).   1979.   The Rolling Stones were on the other side.
What's It All About? Radio Series/BARBARA MANDRELL   593-4.   1980.

American EP's

Ten Little Indians and *Little Miss America*/RAY ANTHONY   2-tracks.   Capitol promo PRO-2186.   1963.
Surfer Girl   Capitol juke box issue SXA-1981.   1963.
Shut Down. Number Two   Capitol juke box issue SXA-2027.   1963.
Brian Wilson Introduces Excerpts From 'Beach Boys Concert'   Capitol promo PRO-2754/5.   1964.
The Beach Boys Today   Capitol juke box issue DU-2269.   1965.
The Best Of The Beach Boys   Capitol juke box issue SU-2545/LLP-189.   1966.
The Beach Boys Party   Capitol promo SPRO-2993/4.   1966.
All Summer Long   Capitol Playtape, number unknown.   1967.
Surfer Girl   Capitol Playtape, number unknown.   1967.
Surfin' Safari   Capitol Playtape, number unknown.   1968.
The Best Of The Beach Boys   Capitol Playtape, number unknown.   1968.
Pet Sounds   Capitol Playtape, number unknown.   1968.
Wild Honey   Capitol Playtape, number unknown.   1968.

American albums

All Summer Long   Capitol ST-2110.   1965.   Early copies credit the track *Don't Back Down* as *Don't Break Down* on the sleeve.
The Beach Boys Concert and *All Summer Long*   Capitol reel to reel Y2T-2370. 1966.
The Beach Boys DeLuxe Set   Capitol TCL-2813.   1968.   A rare thirty-six track, three-album boxed set.
Stack O' Tracks   Capitol Record Club DKAO-82893.   c.1968.
Smiley Smile   Capitol ST-2580.   1968.   Withdrawn and re-issued on Brother ST-9001 about a week later.
The Best Of The Beach Boys   Capitol Record Club DT-502545.   c.1968.
The Best Of The Beach Boys   RCA Record Club R-123946.   c.1968.
Smiley Smile   Capitol Record Club ST-82891.   c.1969.
The Best Of The Beach Boys Volume 3   Capitol Record Club SKAO-80133.   1971.
Good Vibrations   Capitol Record Club ST-80422.   1973.
American Summer   RCA Record Club R-233593.   1973.
Endless Summer   Capitol Record Club SVBB-511307.   1975.
Surf's Up   Asylum-RCA Record Club, number unknown.   c.1975.   A real oddity.
Robert W. Morgan Radio Series (Dated 12.8.79).
Creative Radio Series   c.1980.   A four album set of music and interviews.
Live At The Spectrum, Philadelphia, 18-4-80   CBS promo two ten-inch open reels. 1980.   This concert lasted one and three quarter hours.
Twenty Years Of Good Vibrations   Surf City Radio Series (Dated 5.7.81).   A three album set.

Retrorock Radio Series, number 8231. 1982. Recorded in L.A. in 1963 and New Jersey in 1969.

THE BEACH BOYS/MARVIN GAYE *Sounds Of Solid Gold* Radio Series, number 2. 1982.

THE BEACH BOYS/QUEEN *Sounds Of Solid Gold* Radio Series, number 24. 1982.

British singles

Then I Kissed Her/B side unknown. Capitol export issue, number unknown. 1966.

Don't Go Near The Water/Student Demo Time Stateside SS-2194. 1970. Promo copies came with a picture sleeve.

Suzie Cincinnatti/Child Of Winter Reprise K-14411. 1976. Withdrawn, but promo copies exist.

Twenty Golden Greats Marketing sampler. EMI promo PSR-402. 1976. This has some hilarious sales talk as well as *Good Vibrations* in mono and an embarrassing Carl Wilson interview.

British albums

The Beach Boys UK Capitol promo, number unknown. 1966. A tour sampler.

The Beach Boys Interviews Caribou promo XPR-1204. 1980. A fascinating interview album, and probably their last decent interview together. Only 200 were made.

Odds and sods

Surfin/Lau German Ariola 45-441. 1962. This picture sleeve rarity has an alternate take of the A side. (A £200 item in 1984).

Capitol Silver Platter Service USA Capitol promo PRO-3123. 1964. This album has a Brian Wilson interview and *In My Room* (lasting 4:18).

THE SURVIVORS *Pamela Jean/After The Game* USA Capitol 5102. 1964. A pseudonym release.

Capitol Silver Platter Service USA Capitol promo PRO-3133. 1964. This has a whole side of *The Beach Boys Christmas Album*.

ANNETTE *Monkey's Uncle/How Will I Know* USA Vista/UK HMV. 1964. This has The Beach Boys on backing vocals.

Here's To Veterans Radio Series, number 67. USA. 1964. This was made by The Veterans Administration and featured Brian Wilson introducing *Ten Little Indians* and *Surfin' USA* among others. Side two was taken up by Henry Jerome.

The Beatles vs. The Beach Boys USA Capitol ST-2125. c.1965. I honestly don't know if this really exists.

Programming Aids From Capitol USA Capitol promo PRO-2743/4. 1965. The Beatles are featured on this as well.

Capitol Silver Platter Service album. USA Capitol promo 255/6 (Dated Sept. 1967). This contains a five-minute interview with Brian Wilson talking about *Smiley Smile*.

Bluebirds Over The Mountain/Never Learn To Love Dutch Capitol, number unknown. 1968. This Dutch single featured an alternate mix of the A side.

Celebration At Big Sur UK/USA Ode 70 records. 1971. A soundtrack album to a West Coast 'Woodstock' type festival at which The Beach Boys appeared. A single was also taken from the album *Wouldn't It Be Nice*/other artist. USA Ode 70 records 66016. 1971.

Good Vibrations From London USA More Music Radio Series 0317922 (Date unknown). This has The Beach Boys among others, probably live.

The Beach Boys Ballad Medley/B side unknown. Japan Capitol, number unknown. 1981. A follow up to *The Beach Boys Medley*.

Holland German Reprise REP-54008. 1973. Early German Pressings included an extra track *We Got Love*. This was taken off later copies.

Crawdaddy Magazine interview album, number 6-77. USA. 1977. This features a 23-minute interview with Brian Wilson.

The Beat

British singles

Tears Of A Clown/Ranking Full Stop Two Tone TT-6 1979. Initial copies came with a paper label design, while later copies came with the more familiar plastic label in silver.

I Confess/Sole Salvation Go-Feet FEET-16. 1982. The first few thousand copies came with a free single *Door To Your Heart/Save It For Later/Mirror In The Bathroom* all live.

British album

What Is Beat? Go Feet BEAT-6. 1983. Initial copies came with a free album of re-mixes. This was also included on the cassette version.

American singles

In the USA this group was known as THE ENGLISH BEAT.

Too Nice To Talk To Re-mix and two others. Sire twelve-inch promo PROA-988. 1979.

Save It For Later/Sole Salvation IRS twelve-inch promo SP-70964. 1982.

American albums

THE ENGLISH BEAT/THE GO GO'S. NBC Source Radio Series. 1981.

THE ENGLISH BEAT/THE PSYCHEDELIC FURS. NBC Source Radio Series. 1982.

THE ENGLISH BEAT BBC College Concert Series. (Dated 23.1.83)

Odds and sods

LENNY HENRY *I Am a Mole/The O.K. Song* UK Jet, number unknown. 1981. The Beat play back-up band on this.

Dance Craze Soundtrack. UK Two Tone TT-5004. 1981. Live tracks here.

The Beatles

British singles

Love Me Do/P.S. I Love You Parlophone 45R-4949. 1962. The original 1962 pressing came with a red label, but the 1963 re-press had the more familiar black label. When the record was re-issued in 1972 the album version of the song was used as EMI, bless them, had lost the master tape of the A side.

Please Please Me/Ask Me Why Parlophone 45R-4983. 1963. Again, the red label graced the first few thousand, but was changed to black when the red ran out.

All You Need Is Love/Baby You're A Rich Man Parlophone R-5620. 1967. Early copies don't credit the *Our World* TV show on which the song was recorded.

Strawberry Fields Forever/Penny Lane Parlophone R-5570. 1967. The first 20,000 came in a colour-picture bag.

Hey Jude to *Let It Be* The promo copies of these Apple singles were actually pressed with Parlophone labels. They were green with black print and a large white 'A' on side one. The word 'Parlophone' was in large black type at the top instead of the usual pound sterling symbol.

The Beatles' Rock 'n' Roll Medley EMI promo one-sided PSR-401. 1976. This was made to promote the *Rock 'n' Roll Music* compilation.

So far there have been three singles boxed sets:

The Beatles' Singles Collection, 1962-1970 Parlophone/Apple BS-24. 1976. The box for this set was green and white to match the single sleeves. The twenty-four singles fitted into two compartments alongside each other, while the lid was a flip top. Unfortunately, the box was made of fairly thin cardboard, so it wasn't very strong. The singles ran from *Love Me Do* through to the then newly released *Yesterday,* all in similar sleeves.

The Beatles' Collection Parlophone/Apple, no number. 1977. This boxed set was much stronger as not only were the singles arranged in one row, but tougher card was used in its construction. Designwise it was a black box with a new gold logo 'The Beatles' Collection' on the front. This time the flip top was held in place by a metal hinge which was fine until it rusted! The singles in this set ran from *Love Me Do* through to *Back In the USSR,* again all in the green and white sleeves. The black box was re-issued in 1978 with an extra single *Sgt. Pepper's Lonely Hearts Club Band* in a proper picture sleeve. Both versions of the black box were mail order only, available through EMI's World Record Club.

The Beatles' Singles Collection Parlophone/Apple BSC-1. 1982. This is the most common singles boxed set and was made to accompany the already existing album and EP boxed sets. It was also timed to co-inside with EMI's under-whelming 'It was twenty-years ago today' promo campaign. This box was royal blue with a gold insignia 'The Beatles' Singles Collection' on the front with phony autographs below. That awful metal hinge remained, but it had the added bonus of a leaflet of chart information, release date, etc. The blue box ran from *Love Me Do* through to *The Beatles' Movie Medley.* The real distinction of this set was that for the first time all the British singles appeared in picture sleeves. Both *Strawberry Fields Forever* and *Let It Be* were re-printed with their original sleeves, but the others were in what I consider to be horrible new sleeves, with no thought to period graphics, etc. However, EMI had made a few foul-ups with this box. The version of *All You Need Is Love* used was the shorter album take rather than the original single version. Apparently, this has now been rectified. Also some copies of the *Get Back* single have Wings *I've Had Enough* on the B side instead of *Don't Let Me Down*.

The Beatles' Singles Collection Parlophone/Apple export issue BCSP-1. 1982. This version is basically the same as the regular version, but it includes the *Love Me Do* picture disc as a bonus.

Love Me Do/P.S. I Love You Parlophone 45R-4949. 1982. Some early copies credit the publishers as Ardmore and Beechwood Ltd. instead of MPL Communications.

Love Me Do single version/album version/*P.S. I Love You* Parlophone twelve-inch 12R-4949. 1982. Early copies came with a black bag with a 'Special Limited Edition' sticker. Later copies were given the benefit of a picture bag.

Export singles

If I Fell/Tell Me Why Parlophone DP-562. 1965.
Yesterday/Dizzy Miss Lizzy Parlophone DP-563. 1965.
Drive My Car/Michelle Parlophone DP-564. 1965.
Hey Jude/Revolution Parlophone DP-570. 1968.
All You Need Is Love/Baby You're A Rich Man Parlophone, number unknown. 1968.

These export issues went to places like India, Australia, New Zealand, possibly the USA, and many other countries. I don't know if the mixes are any different on these.

Acetates

There are many acetates in existence: in fact, every single, EP and album was cut as an acetate at some time or another, but those with which I'm dealing here are discs which feature rare material or obscure cuts. It's difficult to speculate how many of these discs were actually cut, but you're only likely to see them at auction houses like Sotheby's. Even then only the very rich or very devoted would be able to afford them. Average prices for a playable disc would range from about £150 to £300 in 1984. Any that turn up at local record fairs are, as likely as not, bootlegs made on modern day EMI-Disc acetates. The following are some of the more tasty items that have turned up in the sales over the last few years.

THE QUARRYMEN *That'll Be The Day/In Spite Of All The Danger* This was in the possession of Leon Duff until Paul McCartney tried to buy it from him. Ownership is now in dispute. It was recorded in 1958 in Liverpool and is thought to be the only copy in existence. The B side was written by George Harrison.
THE BEATLES WITH WALLY *Fever* Arnstick Records. c.1961. This came to light through Philip Norman's book *Shout!* It featured Lu Walters on vocals and was recorded in a recording booth at Hamburg railway station. It was cut there and

Beatles rarities
Top row (left to right) *Oui* magazine free single; Red vinyl Dutch Fan Club single.
Middle *Sing A Song With the Beatles LP*.   Bottom (left to right) *Timeless 2½* interview
pic disc; Promo-only *Beatles Movie Medley* (back of pic sleeve).

then at 78rpm and appeared on the Arnstik label. A re-cut of this disc was made sometime later playing at 45rpm, but this time with *Summertime* on the B side.

Some Other Guy Philips recording studio. 1961. Recorded in London.

How Do You Do It EMI-Disc. 1962.

Some Other Guy Blank label, but made by Granada TV in 1962 to publicise a show featuring The Beatles in September 1962. This had Ringo on drums and apparently 400 copies exist – so where are they?

Bad To Me DJM Publishing one-sided disc TEM-1687/8. c.1963.

One And One Is Two DJM Publishing one-sided disc. c.1963. This was made by The Beatles for use by Billy J. Kramer, but it was eventually recorded by The Strangers.

You're Gonna Lose That Girl Alternate take. EMI-Disc. 1964.

Taxman EMI-Disc metal disc (2:37) (Dated 7.6.66)

As this exists as an acetate can we assume that someone considered this as a possible single?

Strawberry Fields Forever (Take six. The 'slow' version). EMI-Disc. 1967. This also appeared on the *Strawberry Fields* bootleg NEMS CLUE-9 in 1982.

Strawberry Fields Forever Take seven. EMI-Disc. 1967.

Fool On The Hill Alternate take. EMI-Disc. 1967.

Magical Mystery Tour Soundtrack acetates. EMI-Disc. 1967. This is a set of several discs including *Shirley's Magic Accordian* and *Aerial Instrumental* which weren't on the EP or album sets.

Not Guilty Apple Custom. 1968. This is a one-sided metal plate of a George Harrison song left off *The White Album*.

Hey Bulldog/All Together Now DJM Publishing. 1968.

I Want You, I Need You EMI-Disc. c.1969. This is noted as being one song on one acetate, but on the *Rough Notes* bootleg there are two songs from the 1969 sessions. *I Want You* was an *Abbey Road* song, while the other is un-released.

Get Back First single mix. EMI-Disc or Apple Custom. 1969. This was given to Kenny Everett to play on *The Radio One Club* Radio Show, but when the record reached the shops a week later it was a different mix.

The Beatles Get Back Withdrawn album. EMI-Disc or Apple Custom. 1969. In Britian this only exists as an acetate in its finished form. Promo vinyl copies were never pressed. However, in 1983, a brilliant finished copy appeared in promo form, allegedly from EMI-Electrola in Germany. It came complete with the original front cover and explanatory note from Apple PR man Peter Brown. However, with this pressing two things gave the game away. One is that the back cover was not the original with the Tony Barrow liner notes. The second is that the note from Peter Brown has the New York address of Apple, 1800 Broadway. So what we have here is a bootleg, but a really clever one. Ten out of ten Klaus!

Let It Be Alternate. EMI-Disc or Apple Custom eight-inch disc. 1969.

Goodbye DJM Publishing one sided, no number. 1969. A solo demo made by Paul for Mary Hopkin.

These, of course, are just the ones we know about!

Flexi discs

Everybody by now should know of the famous fan-club flexies, so I won't bother going into details, but there are some other nice flexis which aren't so well known.

The Sound The Stars Lyntone LYN-995. 1966. Given away by *Disc And Music Echo*. As well as The Beatles it features Pete Townshend, The Hollies and many others.

1962-1970 World Record Club, number unknown. c.1977. Made to plug the red and blue albums through mail order.

The Beatles' Collection Lyntone LYN-SF-165. 1978. Made to promote the album boxed set and it came with a poster.

The Beatles' Singles Collection Lyntone LYN-SF-1291. 1977. Made to promote the black boxed set of singles from the World Record Club. This also came with a poster.

The Beatles' Box Lyntone LYN-8982. 1980. Made to promote the World Record Club eight album boxed set.

British EP

The Beatles' Golden Discs Parlophone GEP-8899. 1963. To be perfectly honest, your guess is as good as mine as to whether this exists. It turned up in a 'wants list' in a collectors' magazine a couple of years ago. Now, this is where things become confusing. Initial pressings of their second EP *The Beatles' Hits* had *The Beatles' Golden Hits* on the label, but the numbers don't match up! Can anyone put us out of our misery?

British albums

Please Please Me EMI-Disc acetate, number unknown. 1963. This early acetate version has the track *Keep Your Hands Off My Baby* which didn't appear on the finished version.

Please Please Me Parlophone mono PMC-1202. 1963. This album was not released in stereo until a few months later. The original mono copies have a black label with gold type. Beware of more recent counterfeits!

Sgt. Pepper's Lonely Hearts Club Band Parlophone PMC/PCS-7027. 1967. Initial copies came with a red and white inner sleeve.

The Beatles Apple PMC/PCS-7067-8. 1968. The original copies had the sleeve openings at the top instead of at the sides. They also had plain black inner sleeves.

From Then To You. The Beatles' Christmas Album Apple Lyntone LYN-2153/4. 1970. A collection of their Christmas singles.

The Beatles At The Hollywood Bowl Parlophone promo EMTV-4. 1977. Promo copies came as a boxed set.

1962-1966 Apple red vinyl PCSPR-717. 1978.

1967-1970 Apple blue vinyl PCSPB-718. 1978.

Abbey Road was issued in green, *Let It Be* was issued in white and *Magical Mystery Tour* was in transparent yellow vinyl. All are from 1978.

The Beatles' Rarities Parlophone PSLP-261. 1978. This was given away with an album boxed set and was without liner notes on the back.

The Beatles' Box World Record Club SM-701/8. 1980. This eight-album boxed set was a mail order only release. It contained a few treasures like the single version of *Love Me Do,* and American promo version of *Penny Lane.*

Early Years. Volume Two Phoenix PHX-1005. 1981. There are two different versions of both volumes of this set. *Volume One* had a red border on the cover of the first version, and this was missing on the re-issue a few months later. The second volume had a blue border on the first issue, but it also changed on the second issue. There is, however, one other major difference on volume two. The first version, with the blue border, credits a track *You Ain't No Friend,* but in reality it's the Carl Perkins song *Matchbox.* This error was amended on the second issue.

The Beatles' Greatest Hits Parlophone EMTVS-34. 1982. This was to be a TV advertised double album set, but it was withdrawn. Instead, we got what I consider to be the ghastly *Twenty Greatest Hits* album. White label test pressings of the original double album are in existence.

The Beatles At The Beeb BBC Transcription Service CN-3970. 1982. This is the March 1982 broadcast version. There may be another set for the December 1982 version. This magnificent album would probably set you back at least £300. (1984)

Export albums

Something New Parlophone CPCS-101. 1965. This has the familiar black and yellow label design.

The Beatles (White Album) Parlophone PCSJ-7067/8. 1968. This was probably made for export to South Africa.

Something New Apple CPCS-102. 1974.

The Beatles' Second Album Apple CPCS-103. 1974.

Beatles VI Apple CPCS-105. 1974.

Hey Jude Apple CPCS-106. 1974. This is the easiest export album to find. Does CPCS-104 exist?

The Beatles' Mono Collection Parlophone BMC-10. 1982. This consists of the ten re-issued mono albums in a red box with no freebie. The packaging has a similar design to the blue stereo box, with gold lettering. Some copies may have been re-imported into Britain.

American singles

TONY SHERIDAN AND THE BEAT BROTHERS *My Bonnie/The Saints* Decca 31382. 1961. Their first American release was on Decca, who had the USA rights to the German Polydor label. Promo copies had pink labels.

THE BEATLES *Please Please Me/Ask Me Why* Vee Jay 498. 1963. Their first USA Parlophone release mis-spelt their name.

I Want To Hold Your Hand/I Saw Her Standing There Capitol 5112. 1963. Some copies of the picture sleeve don't chop George's head off at the top!

Ain't She Sweet/Nobody's Child Atco 45-6308. 1964. Some copies don't credit 'vocal by John Lennon' on the label.

It's The Beatles Interview disc. Capitol promo PRO-2548/9. 1964. The sleeve is a black and white copy of the *Meet The Beatles* sleeve. It is an open-ended interview with questions on the back cover. This disc has a black label with silver print, a small-album-sized hole and plays at 33rpm. The music included was *I Want To Hold Your Hand, This Boy* and *It Won't Be Long*. It was put together by Jack Wagner.

Open-ended interview. Capitol promo PRO-2598/9. 1964. Similar story to the above, but I don't know what the sleeve's like. The tracks *Roll Over Beethoven, Please Mister Postman* and *Thank You Girl* are included.

Can't Buy Me Love/You Can't Do That Capitol 5150. 1964. Apparently some copies were pressed on yellow vinyl. Along with an ultra-rare picture sleeve, this is their rarest USA single release.

Ain't She Sweet/Nobody's Child Atco 45-6301. 1964. Another rare picture sleeve. Beware of more recent pirated red vinyl copies with black and white photo sleeves. The original sleeves showed the four mop tops.

I'll Cry Instead/I'm Happy Just To Dance With You Capitol 5234. 1964. The A side of this single is supposed to contain an extra verse.

You Can't Do That Capitol Custom pressing promo RB-2637/8. 1965. This was made for radio station KFWB *Music City KFW Beatles*.

The Beatles Introduce New Songs Capitol promo PRO-2720. 1965. Side one has John Lennon introducing Cilla Black's *It's For You,* and on side two Paul McCartney introduces Peter and Gordon's *I Don't Want To See You Again*.

Penny Lane/Strawberry Fields Forever Capitol promo P-5810. 1967. This yellow label promo has an extra trumpet riff at the end of *Penny Lane*. Beware of counterfeits.

The Ballad Of John And Yoko/Old Brown Shoe Apple Pocket Disc 2531-P. 1969. A four-inch mini-disc.

Let It Be Dialogue single. Apple/ABKCO promo, no number. 1970. A one-sided disc. Again, counterfeits are widely available.

Helter Skelter Mono and stereo versions. Capitol promo P-4274. 1976.

Helter Skelter/Revolution Capitol 4274. 1976. This was going to be the single from the *Rock 'n' Roll Music* album, but was withdrawn. Apparently the promo mentioned above does exist.

Girl/You're Gonna Lose That Girl Capitol 4506. 1977. This was taken from the *Love Songs* compilation, but was withdrawn. Legal and counterfeit picture sleeves are in circulation. also doing the rounds are counterfeit yellow and red vinyl copies without picture sleeves, but with the proper purple labels with the *Love Songs* logo at the top.

Girl Mono and stereo versions. Capitol promo P-4506. 1977. This is probably the only legal version in existence as copies never made it to the stores.

The Beatles' Movie Medley/Fab Four On Film Capitol B-5100. 1982. Withdrawn. The B side caused legal difficulties. It was a six-and-a-half minute interview with Paul, George and Ringo about the making of the movie *A Hard Day's Night,* probably taken from the promo interview album.

The Beatles' Movie Medley/Fab Four On Film Capitol yellow vinyl promo PB-5100. 1982.

The Beatles' Movie Medley/Fab Four On Film Capitol twelve-inch promo SPRO-9758/9. 1982. This has a black sleeve with the *Movie Medley* logo on the front.

Like Dreamers Do/Love Of The Loved Backstage, number unknown. 1982. Made for the French *Oui* magazine.

Like Dreamers Do/Three Cool Cats Backstage promo picture disc. 1982.

Memphis/Love Of the Loved Backstage promo picture disc. 1982.

Take Good Care Of My Baby/Crying Waiting Hoping Backstage promo picture disc. 1982. These three were made to promote the Decca tapes album *Like Dreamers Do*.

Timeless 2½ Silhouette, number unknown. 1983. This oddly-named interview picture disc was limited to one thousand copies.

Flexi discs

All My Loving/You've Got To Hide Your Love Away Evatone red vinyl square shaped. No number. 1982. Made to promote *1962-1966*.

Magical Mystery Tour/Here Comes The Sun Evatone blue vinyl square shaped. No number. 1982. Made to promote *1967-1970*.

Rocky Racoon/Why Don't We Do It In The Road Evatone clear vinyl square shaped. 1982. Made to promote *The Beatles* (White album). All three of these were attached to a photo card.

American EP's

Meet The Beatles Capitol juke box issue SXA-2047. 1964. *(It Won't Be Long, This Boy, All My Loving, Don't Bother Me, All I've Gotta Do* and *I Wanna Be Your Man)*.

The Beatles' Second Album Capitol juke box issue SXA-2080. 1964. *(Thank You Girl, Devil In Her Heart, Money, Long Tall Sally, I Call Your Name* and *Please Mister Postman)*.

Something New Capitol juke box issue SXA-2108. 1964. Track details unknown.

Meet The Beatles Capitol Playtape, number unknown. c.1967.

The Beatles' Second Album Capitol Playtape 0575. c.1967.

Beatles '65 Capitol Playtape 0654. c.1967.

The Early Beatles Capitol Playtape, number unknown. c.1967.

Beatles VI Capitol Playtape, number unknown. c.1967.

Yesterday And Today Capitol Playtape, number unknown. c.1967.

Rubber Soul Capitol Playtape, number unknown. c.1968.

Magical Mystery Tour Capitol Playtape, number unknown. c.1968.

American albums

First of all, I'll deal with their Capitol Record Club issues. Dates are unknown.

Meet The Beatles ST-82047.

Something New ST-82108.

Rubber Soul ST-82442.

Yesterday And Today ST-82553.

Revolver ST-82576.

In The Beginning, Circa 1960 Polydor records (Capitol Record Club) SKAO-93199.

The best of the rest

Introducing The Beatles Vee Jay LP-1062 mono/SR-1062 stereo. 1963. This version included the tracks *Love Me Do* and *P.S. I Love You*.

Introducing The Beatles Vee Jay LP-1062. 1964. This re-issue made to cash in on their Capitol success deleted the above tracks, but included *Please Please Me* and *Ask Me Why* instead.

The Beatles And Frank Ifield On Stage Vee Jay LP-1085. 1964. There are two different sleeves for this. The first, and most common, is a cartoon of an old man and was sub-titled *Jolly, What!* (patronising!) The second version has a drawing of the Beatles. Actually, only four Beatles' tracks appeared on this album, and none of them are live as the sleeve suggests.

A Hard Day's Night Interview album. United Artists promo SP-2359. 1964. This featured Paul, George and Ringo talking about the making of their first, and best, movie. Side one featured a half-hour of music and interview, while side two offered another half-hour of interview. A script was also included.

A Hard Day's Night Fifteen radio spots. United Artists promo SP-2362. 1964. This had all the adverts for both the movie and the album to which United Artists had the rights.

Beatles VI Capitol ST-2358. 1965. Some early copies have a different track listing on the back cover.

United Artists Present Help! United Artists promo, number unknown. 1965. Probably a radio spots album.

Sgt. Pepper's Lonely Hearts Club Band Capitol SMAS-2653. 1967. Some early stereo copies have *Good Morning, Good Morning* in mono by mistake.

Abbey Road Apple SO-383. 1969. Some early copies don't credit *Her Majesty* on the sleeve.

The Beatles' Christmas Album Apple SBC-100. 1970. This has a different cover from the British version.

The Beatles. Volumes 1 and 2 TV Products, number unknown. c.1973. This may be a pirate, similar to the *Alpha Omega* set from Audio Tape.

The Beatles Adam VIII, number unknown. c.1974. This was the same company that released the John Lennon *Roots* album in 1975. As that was withdrawn, this may have had a similar fate.

The Beatles' Second Album Apple ST-2080. Early '70s. Some copies have Fleetwood Mac's *Bare Trees* pressed on side two by mistake.

Rarities Capitol SPRO-8969. 1979. This was given away with the American album boxed set. Although this album was pressed in the USA, the boxed set was British. This has the same track listing as the regular 'butcher sleeve' rarities album, but this original freebie version had a different sleeve. It showed lots of tasty memorabilia. This cover was copied later and was used on the *Collectors' Items* bootleg.

Rarities Capitol SN-12009. 1980. Withdrawn. This was to be released in Capitol's $5.98 budget line and had the same sleeve as the British version.

Reel Music Capitol promo yellow vinyl SV-12199. 1982. A thousand numbered copies were pressed on yellow vinyl.

The Beatles Talk Down Under PVC records promo, number unknown. 1982. This is a special radio play version, possibly edited.

Like Dreamers Do Backstage BSR-1111. 1982. A three-album set of the Decca tapes and a Pete Best interview in picture disc format, as well as a white vinyl Decca tapes album.

Like Dreamers Do Backstage BSR-2201. 1982. This double-album version has the two picture discs.

In addition to all these picture disc issues there was also a glut of coloured vinyl albums in the late seventies as there was in the UK:

Sgt. Pepper . . . Capitol SXEB-11840. 1978. Multi-coloured.

The Beatles' Tapes PBR 7005/6. 1978. This is the American version of the Polydor David Wigg interviews in red and blue vinyl.

The Beatles (White album) Capitol SEBX-11841. 1978. White vinyl.

1962-1966 Capitol SEBX-11842. 1978. Red vinyl.

1967-1970 Capitol SEBX-11843. 1978. Blue vinyl.

Love Songs Capitol SEBX-11844. 1978. Gold-yellow vinyl.

Reel Music Capitol promo SV-12199. 1982. Gold-yellow vinyl.

The Silver Beatles Backstage promo AR-30003. 1982. Silver vinyl, limited to four hundred.

Odds and sods
Singles

The Girl I Love/B side unknown. USA Quest 101. Date unknown. Don't panic! This is not the Fab Four, but an American doo-wop group with the name, The Beatles.

Just Seventeen/B side unknown. South Africa Parlophone, number unknown. 1963. This is *I Saw Her Standing There* re-titled.

I'll Get You USA Swan one-sided promo S-4152-1. 1963. It's possible that Swan at one time must have considered this as the A side instead of *She Loves You*.

She Loves You/I'll Get You USA Swan S-4152. 1963. Some copies have a small album-sized hole instead of the more regular juke box size.

Please Please Me/From Me To You USA Vee Jay 581. 1964. Some copies have an oval label design on one side, and the bracket label design on the other side.

The Beatles at Miami USA WQAM promo 560. 1964. An interview single.

Yeah Yeah Yeah/B side unknown. Uraguay Odeon 2097. 1964. Uraguay decided to go for the punchline rather than the real title *She Loves You.*

Komm Gib Mir Deine Hand/Sie Leibt Dich Germany Odeon 22671. 1964. The A side take excludes the handclaps which are found on all album versions. In addition, the picture sleeve mis-titles the B side as *Sie Leibt Mich (She Loves Me).*

She Loves You/I'll Get You Greek Odeon, number unknown. 1964. Pressed in opaque blue vinyl.

Miami Exclusive USA Tiger Radio promo WQ-1096. 1964.

The Murray The K Interview USA Fairway promo KRRNP-1021. 1964.

The Tom Clay Interview (Remember we don't like them . . . we love them!) USA IBBB promo 97436. 1964.

WHB Radio Interview   USA Damon acetate.   1964.

Interview at the Hilton Hotel. Germany *OK* magazine flexi.   c.1965.   The dialogue is in both English and German.

All You Need Is Love/Baby You're A Rich Man   French Odeon F-0103.   1967. These are supposedly alternate takes of both songs.

Intervista Con I Beatles   Italian Apple promo DPR-108.   1968.   This was a part of a four-single set made by Italian EMI to promote Apple's first three singles. A similar set was made in Britain, *Our First Four,* but it didn't include this interview disc. Kenny Everett interviewed The Beatles at Abbey Road during rehearsals for the *White album* sessions. Side one starts with John Lennon's peculiar rendition of *Cottonfields* and then, for me, it's downhill all the way as the five of them try to be funny. A British EMI-Disc acetate, lasting thirteen minutes, exists. (This is a ten-inch one-sided disc). In the early '80s clear vinyl copies, complete with picture sleeves, started appearing. As always, the bootleggers had been at work.

The Beatles' Collection   UK Lyntone LYN-9657.   1978.   This was made to promote the French album boxed set and has French commentary. The French box is green and includes *Magical Mystery Tour* instead of *Rarities.*

Roll Over Beatles   German Polydor, number unknown.   1978.   Made for a Beatles' convention in Cologne and limited to 500 numbered copies. The tracks were *Mein Bonnie* (German introduction)/*Cry For A Shadow* both in stereo.

*My Bonnie/Mein Bonnie/Sweet Georgia Brown/*RINGO STARR   *Just A Dream/*CREAM *Badge/*ROGER DALTREY *Giddy*   Sweden Polydor 2230 114.   1982. Limited to 500 only.

Thank You Members   Dutch red vinyl fan club issue BFR-1978/1983.   1983. Limited to 500, this includes messages to their Dutch fan club.

HAWKWIND   *Silver Machine/*THE BEATLES   *Ask Me Why*   UK United Artists UPP-35381.   1983.   This picture disc edition had a mis-pressed B side.

Paul Talks About Sgt. Pepper   Dutch Apple BFR-001.   Date unknown.   This gold vinyl flexi was issued by the Dutch fan club.

What's It All About?   Radio Series.   USA.   Number 43 (MA-1137).   Date unknown.

EP's

The Beatles And Tony Sheridan   German Polydor record club issue 76586.   Date unknown.

The Beatles Love Songs   Spanish EMI promo only, number unknown.   1977.

Albums

The Beatles' American Tour With Ed Rudy   USA RPN 11.   1964.   Original copies come with a booklet, whereas the more recent counterfeits don't.

Capitol Silver Platter Service   USA Capitol promo PRO-3134.   1964.   This includes an interview with John and Paul as well as *A Hard Day's Night* (7:41 in total).

The Beatles vs. The Beach Boys   USA Capitol ST-2125.   1964.   Does this really exist?

Collier '64 In Sound   USA RPI records promo.   1964.

Cadbury Special   Australia Cadbury's, number unknown.   1964.   A one-sided interview album, some of which later appeared on *The Beatles Talk Down Under* album in 1982.

Collier '65 In Sound   USA RPI records promo.   1965.

Beatles Blast In Stadium. Described by Fans   USA Audio Journal records, number and date unknown.

Here's To Veterans   Radio Series.   USA Veterans' Administration 1406.   c.1965. Paul McCartney introduces Beatles' songs on side one, while actor Phil Harris takes up side two. Each side lasts 14:30 and is in mono. This album was also used by AFN, number 72196.

A Hard Day's Night Before Christmas   USA Evatone ten-inch double album flexi disc set, number unknown.   Date unknown.

Sing A Song With The Beatles   USA Tower SKAO-5000.   1965.   This isn't The Beatles but Capitol session musicians, led by Jimmy Haskell, playing the backing tracks to various hits. Included in the gatefold sleeve are lyrics and chord figures.

Abbey Road   German Apple, number unknown.   1969.   This has the full version of *Her Majesty,* with the missing chord.

Let It Be   Canadian Apple boxed set SOAL-6351.   1970.   This boxed set edition is very similar to the British version.

Earth News   Radio Series (Dated 7.8.78, 21.8.78 and 28.8.78).   From America, as are the following radio series albums.

The Ultimate Radio Bootleg Volumes 3 & 4   Polygram promo 2-121.   c.1981. This includes excerpts from American radio stations of the sixties with a Beatles' interview from 1964.

Rolling Stone magazine Radio Series, number 21-22.   (Dated Nov. 1981). This show is based on the early Beatles.

The Story Of The Beatles   Economic Consultants.   (I don't know who they are!)

Rock Years   Radio Series.   A double-album set.

From Liverpool To Legend   RKO Radio.   A fifteen-album set.

The Rolling Stone Continuous History Of Rock 'n' Roll Radio Series.   A three-album set with three sides of the Beatles and three sides of other British invasion acts.

The Story Of The Beatles   Ten-album boxed set.

THE BEATLES/DEEP PURPLE   Sounds Of Solid Gold, number 27.   1982.

The Beatles At The Beeb   London Wavelength three-album set.   1982.

The Beatles' Story   Rolling Stone magazine special interview. (Dated 2.9.82).   A three-album boxed set.

Rolling Stone magazine *Rock Years* Radio Series.   1982.   A six-album set.

The Beatles' Story   Label details unknown.   1982.   A ten-inch radio show LP.

Rock 'n' Roll Never Forgets   Westwood One Radio Series.   1982.   A five-album set.

Full details on these radio show albums are difficult to obtain as they are so rare.

Meet The Beat   German Polydor fan club ten-inch album J-74557.   Date unknown.

Magical Mystery Tour And Other Splendid Hits   Australian World Record Club issue S-4574.   Date unknown.   A mail order only album.

The Complete Works Of The Beatles Japan EMI-Toshiba, no number. 1980. The ultimate package. Made to commemorate the 25th anniversary of the co-operation of the two companies it consisted of 69 albums (that's 80 including the doubles), all in special boxed sets mounted in a special wooden rack. This set also included solo albums on Apple-EMI. I don't know how many were made, but they certainly couldn't mass-produce an item like this one.

British open reels

These were either 2-track mono or four-track stereo tapes. All played at $3\frac{3}{4}$ ips.
Please Please Me Parlophone TA-PMC-1202 mono. TD-PCS-3042 stereo.
With The Beatles Parlophone TA-PMC-1206 mono. TD-PCS-3045 stereo.
A Hard Day's Night Parlophone TA-PMC-1230 mono. TD-PCS-3058 stereo.
Beatles For Sale Parlophone TA-PMC-1240 mono. TD-PCS-3062 stereo.
Help! Parlophone TA-PMC-1255 mono. TD-PCS-3071 stereo.
Rubber Soul Parlophone TA-PMC-1267 mono. TD-PCS-3075 stereo.
Revolver Parlophone TA-PMC-7007 mono. TD-PCS-7007 stereo.
A Collection Of Beatles' Oldies Parlophone TA-PMC-7016 mono. TD-PCS-7016 stereo.
Sgt. Pepper . . . Parlophone TA-PMC-7027 mono. TD-PCS-7027 stereo.

Up until this release all the open reels had been housed in five-inch square cardboard boxes with four-inch reels. With the release of *The White Album* all tapes came in square clear plastic cases with an inlay card similar to that of cassettes.

The Beatles Apple DTA-PMC-7067/8 mono. DTD-PCS-7067/8 stereo. (For some reason the cassette number is PCS-4501).
Yellow Submarine Apple TA-PMC-7070 mono. TD-PCS-7070 stereo.
Abbey Road Apple TA-PMC-7088 mono. TD-PCS-7088 stereo.
Let It Be Apple TA-PMC-7096 mono. TD-PCS-7096 stereo.

The dates on all of these are the same as the regular vinyl releases. The last two albums, of course, were not released in mono on vinyl album, so it's possible that the mixes were different. The overall sound quality of these open reels was fairly good on the whole, with some cut on the highs. How well the tapes have survived after twenty years or so has to be assessed. Most of them should playback fairly well, with the minimum of dropouts, if used, and stored, correctly. All the sleeve designs on the tapes were very similar to their vinyl counterparts.

American open reels

The American versions were much more complicated, working with different speeds and spool sizes.

This is a selection to give you some idea:
Meet The Beatles Capitol Z2-2047 mono, Z4-2047 stereo. This was re-issued in the late sixties as Y1T-2047 stereo ($3\frac{3}{4}$ ips on a 5-inch reel).
BEATLES *VI* Capitol-Muntz 4CL-2358 mono.
The Early Beatles and *Beatles '65* Double play. Capital Y2T-2365 stereo.

Beatles VI and *Something New*   Double play.   Capitol Y2T-2382 stereo.

Help!   Capitol L-2386 mono.

Rubber Soul and *The Beatles' Second Album*   Double play. Capitol Y2T-2467 stereo.

Yesterday And Today   Capitol Y1T-2553 stereo ($3\frac{3}{4}$ ips on a five-inch reel). This did not come with the butcher sleeve.

Revolver   Capitol ZT-2576 ($7\frac{1}{2}$ ips on a seven-inch reel) stereo.

Sgt. Pepper . . .   Capitol Y1T-2653 ($3\frac{3}{4}$ ips on a seven-inch reel) stereo.

Magical Mystery Tour   Capitol Y1T-2835 ($3\frac{3}{4}$ ips on a seven-inch reel) stereo.

The Beatles   (White album)   Apple Y2WB-101 ($3\frac{3}{4}$ ips probably on a seven-inch reel) stereo.   This has the four colour photos on the front cover.

Let It Be   Apple/United Artists L-3401.   Probably stereo.   If United Artists made this then they must have made an open reel for *A Hard Day's Night.*

The obvious advantage of the open reel is that you don't have the usual problems associated with vinyl discs, i.e. scratches, pops, clicks, warpage and so on. The main reason that the open reel format didn't last longer was the introduction of the compact cassette and the eight-track cartridge. With these formats there is no messy threading of the tape. Also, of course, the machines were much smaller than the large open reels and they were easier to operate. Many people still have open reels today, even though no record companies make pre-recorded tapes anymore. Who's for a revival?

Audiophiles

The only way to get a near perfect copy of an album nowadays is to buy an audiophile pressing. This usually consists of cutting the master plate at half speed, taken from the best available master tape, and then pressing the record on thick, and flat, pure vinyl. Obviously this is an expensive process, but people who can afford state-of-the-art hi-fi can usually afford up to £15, or its equivalent, for an audiophile.

The best Beatles' audiophiles have come from the Japanese/American co-op Mobile Fidelity Labs.

Abbey Road   MFSL-1-023.   1981.   This limited edition (200,000 world-wide) came in a gatefold sleeve.

Magical Mystery Tour   MFSL-1-047.   1981.   As above.

The Beatles   (White album)   MFSL-2-072.   1982.

In 1983 Mobile Fidelity issued a beautiful boxed set of the Beatles' UK albums from *Please Please Me* to *Let It Be* (bypassing *Oldies But Goodies).* The box was wooden, with a black cloth finish, and gold insignia on the side. Instead of the ugly flip-top lid on the British version, this box opened up at the front with the unhooking of a metal clasp. The sleeves used were not the originals, but photos of the original master tape in its tatty-looking box, with a list on the inside of who had used the tape for copying, i.e. Capitol in North America, Odeon in France, Electrolia in Germany, etc. Also included in this set is a book explaining the cutting technique used and showing the equipment, as well as full-sized colour re-prints of

the original sleeves. A stylus-alignment turntable mat was also included.
Sgt. Pepper . . . Mobile Fidelity UHQR pressing MFQR 1 100. 1982. Taking things to a ridiculous extreme Mobile Fidelity did a run of 5,000 pressed on quarter-inch thick vinyl.

Other Japanese sets

The ten British mono albums were also re-released in Japan in 1982, but pressed in glowing red vinyl.

There is also an alternate British album boxed set pressed in Japan which includes four album-sized photo mirrors. 1982.

There are many, many items I've neglected to mention, but as you can doubtless understand they're worth a book to themselves.

Be Bop Deluxe

British singles

Teenage Archangel/Jets At Dawn Smile LAFS-001. 1973. A very rare independent release.
Between Two Worlds/Lights Harvest HAR-5091. 1975. Withdrawn.

British album

BBC *In Concert* Radio Series. BBC Transcription Service 140017. 1976.

American singles

Live In The Air Age EP Harvest white vinyl twelve-inch promo, number unknown. 1977. Also given away with the *Live In The Air Age* album.
Live Kicks EP. Harvest twelve-inch promo, number unknown. 1977.
Be Bop's Biggest EP. Harvest twelve-inch promo, number unknown. 1978. Made to promote *The Best And The Rest Of Be Bop Deluxe* compilation.

American albums

BE BOP DELUXE/TOM PETTY *Rock Around The World* Radio Series. 1978. Both live in Boston.
Modern Music Radio Series. 1978. Music and chat from Boston.

Jeff Beck

British single

Plinth/Water Down The Drain Columbia, number unknown. 1968. Withdrawn, but promo copies exist.

British album

Rough And Ready   Quad mix.   Epic Q-64619.   1974.

American albums

The Jeff Beck Group   Quad mix.   Epic EQ-31331.   1974.
Everything You Ever Wanted To Hear   Epic promo AS-151.   1974.   A compilation.
JEFF BECK/THE YARDBIRDS   *Rock Around The World*   Radio Series, number 117. (Dated 1 November 1976).
Musical Montage   Epic promo AS-796.   1978.   Another promo compilation.
Then And Now   Epic promo, number unknown.   1979.   A compilation made to promote the *There And Back*.
Innerview   Radio Series.   Series 16, programme 3.   1981.
Beck, Bogert and Appice live.   *Retrorock*   Radio Series   (Dated October 1981).

Odds and sods

BECK BOGERT AND APPICE   *Live In Japan*   Japan CBS-Sony EPGJ-1112.   1973.
Secret Policeman's Ball. The Music   UK Springtime HAHA-6004.   1981.   This has both Beck and Clapton playing together live.

Capt. Beefheart

American singles

Diddy Wah Diddy/Who Do You Think You're Fooling   A & M 794.   1966.
Moonchild/Frying Pan   A & M 818.   1966.

Both the above are extremely rare, but promos may be easier to find.

Click Clack/Glider   Reprise promo PRO-514.   1972.
Low Yo Yo Stuff/Too Much Time   Reprise promo PRO-547.   1973.

American albums

Beefheart recorded one album for A & M in 1966, but it was never released.
Shiny Beast (Bat Chain Puller)   Warner test pressing, number unknown.   1978.

This test pressing contained tracks which didn't appear on the finished version.

British singles

Captain Beefheart EP.   A & M AME-600.   1971.   This was a collection of the four A & M tracks on the one disc, complete with picture sleeve. Needless to say, it didn't sell and was deleted very quickly.
Sampler EP   Virgin picture disc SIXPACK-1.   1978.   Made for export purposes, but some were re-imported into Britain.
Ice Cream For Crow   Virgin one-sided promo, number unknown.   1982.

British albums

So far there have been seven different UK issues of *Safe As Milk*. The first was on Pye International NPL-28110. 1967. Mono only.

Safe As Milk Marble Arch MAL-1117. 1968. Mono only.

Safe As Milk Buddah 623 171. 1969. Hereafter all were in stereo.

Dropout Boogie Buddah 99 series 2349 002. 1970. This was *Safe As Milk* re-titled. This retailed at 99p.

Safe As Milk Buddah BDLP-4014. 1974.

The File Buddah FILD-008. 1977. This double album contains the entire *Safe As Milk* album.

Safe As Milk PRT NCP-1004. 1982. This was the last full issue.

Music In Sea Minor PRT ten-inch DOW-15. 1983. This mini-album has six tracks from *Safe As Milk*.

Odds and sods

DIR Broadcasting Interview album. USA. (Dated 18.12.78). This has a Beefheart interview.

Blue Collar UK/USA MCA. 1978. This soundtrack album had some new material by the Captain, including his brilliant *Hard Working Man*.

Shiny Beast (Bat Chain Puller) One minute radio spots. USA Warner open reel promo PRO-515. 1979.

The Bee Gees

British singles

Boogie Child/B side unknown. RSO, number unknown. 1977. Withdrawn, but promos do exist.

Night Fever RSO one-sided promo SNF-1. 1978.

Night Fever/Down The Road RSO twelve-inch promo PPSP-1. 1978.

Saturday Night Fever Sampler EP. RSO twelve-inch promo PPSP-12. 1978.

British album

Short Cuts RSO promo BGLP-1. 1979. A compilation of hits.

American singles

Don't Forget To Remember To Forget Long and short versions. Atco promo 6702. 1969.

Rare, Precious And Beautiful Atco juke box EP SD37-264. 1968.

Odessa EP. Atco EP-4535. 1968. This came with a picture sleeve.

You Should Be Dancing/Boogie Child/Subway/You Stepped Into My Life RSO twelve-inch promo PRO-013. 1976. An early twelve-inch issue.

Nights On Broadway 2:52 radio edit in mono and stereo. RSO promo RS-515. 1976.

BEE GEES/WET WILLIE *What's It All About?* Radio Series 420. c.1977.
Rest Your Love On Me Mono and stereo. RSO promo RS-913. 1978. This promo was given to country stations only.
Tragedy/Inside And Out/Search Find RSO twelve-inch promo RPO-1008. 1979.
The Bee Gees Greatest Sampler. RSO promo EP-200. 1980.

American albums

Rare Precious And Beautiful/RAY CHARLES   *The Other Ray Charles* sampler. Atlantic-Atco promo, number unknown. 1969. One side each.
Odessa One-album sampler. Atco promo TL-142. 1969.
Rock Around The World Radio Series, number 192. 1978.
Robert W. Morgan Radio Series. (Dated 2.12.78).
Robert W. Morgan Radio Series. (Dated 3.3.79).
Words And Music Of The Bee Gees RSO promo SMP-1. 1979. A publisher's sampler.
Unichappel Publisher's Sampler RSO promo PUB-1000. c.1980. Another publisher's sampler.

Odds and sods

All This And World War Two UK Riva/USA 20th Century Fox. 1976. The Bee Gees appear on this soundtrack.
Sgt. Pepper's Lonely Hearts Club Band UK A & M/USA RSO. 1978. This, to my mind, dreadful soundtrack album again had The Bee Gees.
Spirits Having Flown Japan Nautilus audiophile, number unknown. 1981.

Pat Benetar

American single

Day Gig/Last Saturday Trace Records 5293. 1976. This small label was based in Richmond, Virginia.

Pete Best

British single

I'm Gonna Knock On Your Door/Why Did I Fall In Love With You Decca F-11929. 1964. Decca must have signed Best as an attempt to play down the fact that they had turned down the Beatles. (To be fair to Dick Rowe and Decca, on hearing the Beatles audition tape, would *you* have signed them?)

American singles

Boys/Kansas City Cameo C-391. 1964. It's thought that the Cameo label turned down their option on taking the Beatles at one time. *Boys,* was, of course, a song which Ringo sang.

I Wanna Be There/Anyway Original Beatles' Drummer Records 800. 1964. The sound of Pete Best banging his own drum.

I Can't Do Without You Now/Keys To My Heart Mr Maestro 711. c.1965. Some copies were pressed on blue vinyl.

Casting My Spell/I'm Blue Mr Maestro 712. 1965.

If You Can't Get Her/The Way I Feel About You Happening HA-1117. c.1966.

I Want You/Carosel Of Love Capitol 2092. 1967.

American albums

Best Of The Beatles Savage BM-711. 1964. The misleading title fooled a lot of people into thinking that this was previously unreleased Fab Four product.

The Beatle That Time Forgot Audio Fidelity, number unknown. 1982. This was the interview album from the *Like Dreamers Do* package. (More like the Beatle That's Best Forgot!).

The B 52's

American singles

Rock Lobster/52 Girls Boo Fant Records DR-52. 1978. An independent US release from Athens, Georgia.

Rock Lobster/Planet Claire/Mess Around Warner twelve-inch promo PROA-836. 1978.

Private Idaho/Party Out Of Bounds Warner twelve-inch promo PROA-890. 1979.

Strobe Light/Give Me Back My Man Warner twelve-inch promo PROA-927. 1979.

Mesopotamia/Deep Sleep/Cake Warner twelve-inch promo PROA-1016. 1981.

British singles

Rock Lobster/52 Girls Island PSR-438. 1979. This single was given away with initial copies of their first album.

Future Generation/Instrumental version Island ISD-107. 1983. Initial copies came with a free single, *Planet Claire/There's A Moon.*

Big Star

American single

Oh My Soul 5:37 and 2:47 versions. Ardent promo ARA-2909. 1972.

American album

Big Star Third Album PVC 7903. 1978. This has thirteen tracks including *Downs* and *Whole Lotta Shakin'.*

British albums

Big Star Third Album Aura AUL-703. 1978. This UK version does not include the two above-mentioned tracks, but does include *For You* which isn't on the American version.

Big Star/ISAAC HAYES Sampler. Stax promo, number unknown. 1978. This features tracks from their two Ardent albums and the *Shaft* soundtrack.

Black Sabbath

British singles

Evil Woman/B side unknown. Fontana TF-1067. 1970. This was their only release on Fontana and was very quickly re-issued on Vertigo V-2.

Children Of The Grave/STATUS QUO *Roundhouse Blues* Phonogram promo DJ-005. c.1974.

British albums

The first four Black Sabbath albums were originally released on Vertigo from 1970 to 1974. The rights then transferred to WWA Records until 1976, when the NEMS label gave them their latest resting place.

American albums

BLACK SABBATH/BLUE OYSTER CULT King Biscuit Radio Series. (Dated Sept. 1980).
BLACK SABBATH/THE SCORPIONS King Biscuit Radio Series. (Dated 30.8.82).

Blancmange

British singles

Irene And Mavis EP. Blahh! Records, number unknown. 1979. Their first release was this hilarious EP.

Living On The Ceiling London one-sided promo BLANCDJ-3. 1982. This has altered lyrics. Instead of *Up The Bloody Tree* it was *Up The Cuckoo Tree*.

Living On The Ceiling/THE PASSAGE Track. Melody Maker flexi. 1983.

Stephen Luscumbe can also be heard on various Portsmouth Symphonia albums.

Blondie

American singles

Prototypes EP. No label. 1976. This was an independently made EP of demos. *The songs were Thin Line, Out In The Streets, Platinum Blonde* and *Puerto Rico.* Only 200 were made, but it has been counterfeited.

*X Offender/*B side unknown. Private Stock PS-45097. 1977. It seems that all copies that have turned up so far are mono and stereo promos.

In The Flesh/X Offender Private Stock PS-45141. 1977. This was the official single from the first album.

One Way Or Another/Just Go Away Chrysalis twelve-inch promo CDJ-10. 1979.

Dreaming/Living In The Real World Chrysalis twelve-inch promo CDJ-14. 1979.

What's It All About? Radio Series, number 497/8. 1979. This had Henry Mancini on side two.

*Call Me/*GIORGIO MORODER *Night Drive* Polydor twelve-inch promo PRO-124. 1980.

*Call Me/*Instrumental version. Chrysalis CHS-2414. 1980. There are two different sleeves for this: the first used a still from the *American Gigolo* movie, while the second was a garish pink and purple photo cover.

What's It All About? Radio Series, number 603. 1981.

Call Me Sung in Spanish/Instrumental version. Salsoul twelve-inch SG-341. 1980. Not a promo, but an odd track leased to the Latino disco based label.

Rapture 6:33 and 4:50 versions. Chrysalis twelve-inch promo 25-PDJ. 1981.

Warchild Same on both sides. Chrysalis twelve-inch promo 39-PDJ. 1982.

Island Of Lost Souls Same on both sides. Chrysalis twelve-inch promo 40-PDJ. 1982.

American albums

BLONDIE/THE TUBES *Rock Around The World* Radio Series, number 194. (Dated April 1978).

Live In London ABC-Supergroups *In Concert* Radio Series SGC-105. 1979.

Parallel Lines Chrysalis CHR-1192. 1979. Original copies had a 3:54 version of *Heart Of Glass.*

At Home With Debbie Harry And Chris Stein Chrysalis promo 24-PDJ. 1980. An interview album.

Robert R. Klein Radio Series, number 13. 1980.

Innerview Radio Series. Series 10, programme 4. c.1981.

Retrorock Radio Series (Dated March 1981). A live show from the *Parallel Lines* tour of 1979.

British singles

In The Flesh/X Offender Private Stock PVT-105. 1977. Their only Private Stock single in Britain.

Picture This/Fade Away And Radiate Chrysalis CHS-2242. 1978. Pressed in a very limited yellow vinyl edition.

Fan Club Flexi Flexi Records FLX-146. 1980.

Rapture Long and short versions. Chrysalis promo BLODJ-1. 1981.

Rapture Edited. Chrysalis one-sided promo BLO-1-DJ. 1981.

The Tide Is HIgh Chrysalis one-sided twelve-inch promo DH-201. 1981.

BLONDIE AND SAM FIVE FREDDIE B LOVE *Yuletown Throwdown/*Two other acts.

Flexipop 015 Lyntone LYN-10840. 1982. The main cut on this flexi was a new rap version of *Rapture.*

Odds and sods

Roadie Film soundtrack. UK/USA Warner. 1980. This had a new track by Blondie, a live version of *Ring Of Fire*.

THE NEW YORK BLONDES Featuring MADAM X *Little GTO*/RODNEY AND THE BRUNETTES *Holocaust On Sunset Boulevard* UK London-Bomp HLZ-10574. 1981. This escaped in 1981 and was quickly withdrawn at the insistence of Chrysalis. Debbie Harry had recorded a guide vocal track for Rodney Bingenheimer, a DJ at KROQ Radio in Pasadena, to follow when making his first record. However, Bomp released the Debbie Harry version much to her annoyance as she claimed that she had a cold when making it. The proper version with Bingenheimer on vocals was eventually released in America, but not in Britain. In addition, London Records in Germany released a special dual groove twelve-inch pressing, limited to fifty copies.
Parallel Lines Japan Mobile Fidelity audiophile MFSL-1-064. 1981.

Blue Oyster Cult

American singles

THE STALK FOREST GROUP *What Is Quicksand/Arthur's Comics* Elektra EK-45693. 1969. Only a few hundred promo copies of this rarity were made. This was basically the first line up of BOC. The counterfeits that are on the market use an alternate label design.
The Live Bootleg Columbia ten-inch promo AS-40. 1973. An early live outing. As always, counterfeits exist.
Godzilla Live and studio versions. Columbia promo AC7-1156. 1977.
Godzilla Same on both sides. Columbia twelve-inch promo AS-447. 1977.
Roadhouse Blues Long and short versions/*Veterans Of Psychic Wars* Columbia twelve-inch promo AS-1441. 1982.

American albums

BLUE OYSTER CULT/THE BABY'S King Biscuit Radio Series (Dated 16.3.80).
BLUE OYSTER CULT/BLACK SABBATH King Biscuit Radio Series (Dated Sept. 80).
BOC Live in Nassau/LOVERBOY Westwood One Radio Series, number 81-3. 1981.
Westwood One Radio Series, number 81-14. 1981.
In Concert Radio Series, number 82-11. 1982.
Westwood One Radio Series, number 82-83. (Dated 7.6.82).

Marc Bolan and T. Rex

British singles

MARC BOLAN *The Wizard/Beyond The Rising Sun* Decca F-12288. 1965.
MARC BOLAN *The Third Degree/San Francisco Poet* Decca F-12413. 1965.
MARC BOLAN *Hippy Gumbo/The Misfit* Parlophone R-5539. 1966.

Although these three singles were given a full release, promos may be easier to find than the regular copies.

TYRANNOSAURUS REX *King Of The Rumbling Spires/Do You Remember* Regal-Zonophone RZ-3022.   1968.   The promo copies came with a picture sleeve showing an old man sitting on a chair smoking a pipe.

TYRANNOSAURUS REX *By The Light Of The Magical Moon/Find A Little Wood* Regal-Zonophone RZ-3025.   1969.   The promo copies may have come with a picture sleeve.

T. REX *Ride A White Swan/Jewell* Octopus OCTO-1. 1970. Withdrawn. It was eventually released on Fly Records. Test pressings of the Octopus version exist.

Electric Warrior Preview single including *Jeepster*. Fly promo GRUB-1. 1971.

Christmas In A T. Rex World Fan club flexi. 1972.

*Solid Gold Easy Action/*Fifth Dimension tracks. EMI mispress. 1973.

MARC BOLAN Interviewed by Steve Dixon. Cube promo BINT-1. c.1974.

T. REX *Sailors Of The Highway* Fan club flexi, number and date unknown.

T. REX *Solid Gold Easy Action/*THE PARTRIDGE FAMILY *Breaking Up Is Hard To Do* EMI mis-press. 1973.

T. REX *The T. Rex Christmas Box EP* EMI MARC-12. 1974. Withdrawn. Although labels were printed the record was never actually pressed. The tracks were *Christmas Bop, Telegram Sam* and *Metal Guru*.

T. REX *Life's A Gas/Blessed Wild Apple Girl* Cube ANTS-001. 1975. Given away by the fan club.

British albums

MARC BOLAN *Hard On Love* Track 2406 101. 1972. Withdrawn and replaced by *The Beginning Of Doves* album of demos.

MARC BOLAN AND T. REX *Zinc Alloy . . .* EMI BLNA-7751. 1975. The sleeve that came with the first few thousand was a poster fold-out, individually numbered.

T. REX *T. Rex In Concert* Marc On Wax ABOLAN-1. 1982. A limited edition white-label version was pressed in a re-mixed form without audience noise.

T. REX *T. Rex In Concert* Marc On Wax picture disc ABOLAN-1-P. There are two different back designs for this.

American singles

TYRANNOSAURUS REX *Ride A White Swan/Is It Love* Blue Thumb SP-6115/6. 1970. This was given away with the re-issued *Unicorn* album.

John Peel interviews Marc Bolan. Blue Thumb promo, number unknown. c.1970.

What's It All About? Radio Series, number and date unknown.

American albums

An Interview With Marc Bolan Reprise promo PRO-511. c.1972. Marc was interviewed by Michael Cuscuna.

Ride A White Swan MFP export issue MFP-5274. 1972. Made by Capitol for the UK market.

Where's The Champagne Rainbow black vinyl test pressing. 1982. Made for Rhino records as a test pressing for their picture disc album.
The Interview LP, Chicago '69 What Records, number unknown. 1982. Another interview album.

Odds and sods

Glastonbury Fayre UK Revelation REV-1. 1973. Marc Bolan contributes to this infamous album.
I Love To Boogie Re-mix/*Baby Boomerang* French EMI-Pathe twelve-inch 2C 052 98232. 1977. This twelve-inch mix has not appeared in Britain.

The Boomtown Rats

British singles

Rat Trap Ensign one-sided promo ENY-16-DJ. 1978. This version has altered lyrics. The line 'Scab encrusted sores' was replaced by another line (which I can't quite make out) rather than mixing out or bleeping the line. The story doesn't end there though; some store copies have this DJ version, pressed by mistake.
The Rat Pack Ensign, number unknown. 1978. A plastic wallet of their first six singles in their original sleeves.
Don Laoghaire Flexipop 003. 1980. A one-sided freebie. As with all flexipops, hard vinyl copies were given to radio stations.
Charmed Lives/No Hiding Place Mercury MER-106. 1982. The first few thousand came with a free single *Nothing Happened Today/Storm Breaks*.

British album

Mondo Bongo Edited highlights. Mercury one-sided promo, number unknown. 1981.
BBC *In Concert* Radio Series. BBC Transcription Service CN-4008/S. 1982.
Art Rock Phonogram white label promo, number unknown. c.1982.

American album

THE BOOMTOWN RATS/A FLOCK OF SEAGULLS Westwood One Radio Series. 1983.

American singles

Rat Trap/Joey's On The Street Columbia twelve-inch promo AS-544. 1979.
Someone's Looking At You/I Don't Like Monday's Live version. Columbia 1-11248. 1980. The B side track has not yet appeared in Britain.
I Don't Like Monday's (live)/*Someone's Looking At You/Do The Rat* Columbia twelve-inch promo AS-746. 1980.
Banana Republic/Up All Night/Mood Mambo Columbia twelve-inch promo AS-920. 1981.

Odds and sods

Secret Policeman's Ball. The Music UK Springtime HAHA-6004. 1981. This has an excellent live acoustic version of *I Don't Like Monday's*.

David Bowie

British single

Everybody by now should be aware of Bowie's '60s recordings for labels Vocailion, Coral, Pye, Parlophone, Deram, Philips and Mercury. Awareness of these singles is now common knowledge, even to non-collectors, so I won't delve into their history too much.

DAVID JONES AND THE KING BEES *Liza Jane/Louie Louie Go Home* Vocalion VN-9221. 1964. Beware of counterfeits without the optional centre!

DAVID JONES AND THE KING BEES *You're Holding Me Down/I've Gotta* Coral Q-62492. 1964.

THE MANNISH BOYS *Take My Tip/Pity The Fool* Parlophone R-5250. 1965. This was a band that featured Bowie.

THE LOWER THIRD *You've Got A Habit Of Leaving/Baby Loves That Way* Parlophone R-5315. 1965. Another Bowie band.

At this time there were many other artists with similar names which put Bowie collectors into fits of confusion. The following have not been, nor ever will be, David Bowie: Davy Jones on Philips, Pye, Colpix and Bell; David John and The Mood on Vocalion; The King Pins on Oriole.

DAVID BOWIE AND THE LOWER THIRD *Can't Help Thinking About Me/And I Say To Myself* Pye 7N-17020. 1966.

DAVID BOWIE *Do Anything You Say/Good Morning Girl* Pye 7N-17079. 1966.

I Dig Everything/I'm Not Losing Sleep Pye 7N-17157. 1966.

DAVID BOWIE AND THE LOWER THIRD *Love You Till Tuesday/Over The Wall We Go* EMI-Disc acetate. 1966. The A side version is slower than the later album cut. Both of these have yet to be given a fully legal release; Possibly they're just demos.

DAVID BOWIE *Rubber Band/London Boy* Deram DM-107. 1966.

The Laughing Gnome/Gospel According To Tony Day Deram DM-123. 1967.

Love You Till Tuesday/Did You Ever Have A Dream Deram DM-137. 1967.

Space Oditty/The Wild Eyed Boy From Freecloud Philips BF-1801. 1969. This single was available in both mono and stereo versions, the stereo being the rarer of the two. It's possible that the stereo mix is different.

The Prettiest Star/Conversation Piece Mercury MF-1135. 1970. This also came with a ludicrously rare picture sleeve. Marc Bolan plays guitar making this equally rare to both Bowie and Bolan fans.

Memory Of A Free Festival Parts 1 and 2 Mercury 6025 026. 1970. As with all

49

the Mercury singles, the bootleggers haven't been idle.

Holy Holy/Black Country Rock   Mercury 6025 049.   1971.

Bombers/London Bye Ta Ta/All The Young Dudes   RCA metal acetate.   1972. It's not known whether these tracks were meant to be released in this format.

John I'm Only Dancing/Hang On To Yourself   RCA 2263.   1973.   The original 1973 pressing features a mainly acoustic version of the song, while more recent pressings feature the more funky version recorded in 1975.

BOWIE   *Hits Sampler*   'Record Mirror' flexi Lyntone LYN-2929.   1974.   This also has some commentary, but not by Bowie.

Young Americans   5:06 and 3:11 versions.   RCA promo RCA-2523-DJ.   1975.

1984/You Didn't Hear It From Me/Holy Holy/Man In The Middle   Fan club single.   c.1976.   This apparently is not a flexi. I don't know if this features any alternate versions, etc.

DJ/Repetition   RCA BOW-3.   1978.   Five hundred copies were pressed in green vinyl. RCA have always claimed that it was a mistake. Straight up!

BOWIE AND BING CROSBY   *Peace On Earth* and *Little Drummer Boy* Medley.   Long and short versions.   RCA promo PROBOW-12.   1982.   My regular copy has the short version with this promo number on the run-off groove. (Are all regular copies like this?) The twelve-inch contained the full version with the chat at the beginning. RCA BOWT-12.

Let's Dance   Long version/Cat People   Long version.   EMI-America cassette single TC-EA-152.   1983.   Although Bowie had a few cassette singles released by RCA, this was the only tape that featured any alternate versions. In this case the full-length *Cat People*.

Modern Love   Long studio version/Live version.   EMI-America twelve-inch 12EAS-158.   1983.   Some early copies came with a large poster.

China Girl   Single version.   EMI-America twelve-inch promo, number unknown. 1983.   This may not have a B side. The seven-inch version was circulated on this twelve-inch as a pre-release.

Rebel Rebel/Song For Bob Dylan   RCA BOW-514.   1983.   This is a mispress single from the *Bowie Lifetimes* set of twenty re-issue singles.

British albums

Love You Till Tuesday   Deram DML-1007 mono. SML-1007 stereo.   1967.   In spite of Bowie's later superstar status, I wonder who bought this when it was first released?

David Bowie   Philips SBL-7912.   1969.   As far as I know this was never released in mono. Although this was re-leased as the *Space Oddity* album by RCA in 1973, the original gatefold sleeve is much better. I'm unaware of any counterfeit.

The Man Who Sold The World   Mercury 6388 041.   1971.   This has the by now famous 'drag cover' which is infinitely better than the RCA re-issue. It has, however, been counterfeited, but is imperfect: the spine has the credits the wrong way around, as well as using a dull, flat sleeve instead of the original textured cover.

The World Of David Bowie   Decca PA-58 mono. SPA-58 stereo.   c.1970.   This cash-in album has so far turned up in at least three different sleeves. The first has a

Space Oddity era photo, the second has a *Ziggy Stardust* period shot while the third version has a 1974 photo.

Diamond Dogs   RCA APL 1-0578.   1974.   The first 1,000 copies show the dogs' genitalia on the back cover. This detail was later air-brushed out.

Changesonebowie   RCA-1055.   1976.   The initial 1,000 copies contained an alternate version of *John I'm Only Dancing* which was the version which was eventually released as a single in 1979. The proof cover which came with some test pressings is in colour instead of the black and white finished copy.

Stage   RCA PL-02913.   1978.   This live double album was available in both green and yellow vinyl for a short period.

Rare Bowie   RCA PL-45406.   1982.   A limited edition hand stamped edition was made.

Changestwobowie   RCA Double Fun series DF-1.   1983.   This package had the album and cassette together in a cardboard holder for a limited period for the normal album price.

Bowie Lifetimes   RCA promo LIFETIMES-1.   1983.   A rare promo album sampler to promote the *Lifetimes* set of album re-issues at £2.99 each.

American singles

DAVID BOWIE AND THE LOWER THIRD   *Can't Help Thinking About Me/And I Say To Myself*   Warner 5818.   1966.   His first, and rarest, American release. Promos are easier to find than regular copies.

DAVID BOWIE   *The Laughing Gnome/Gospel According To Tony Day*   Deram DER-20079.   1967.

This Is A Happy Land/Rubber Band   Deram DER-85009.   1967.   *Rubber Band* is re-mixed, making it even more sought after.

Love You Till Tuesday/Did You Ever Have A Dream   Deram DER-85016.   1967. As in Britain, Bowie had no success with these Deram releases in the USA.

Space Oddity/Wild Eyed Boy From Freecloud   Mercury 72949.   1969.   A remarkably different mix of the A side makes this a must for Bowiephiles. A full intro is used instead of a fade-in, as well as a badly re-mixed ending. The promo version with *Space Oddity* on both sides, Mercury promo MDJ-133, has been counterfeited.

Memory From A Free Festival Parts 1 and 2   Mercury 73075.   1970.   This did nothing in the USA either.

All The Madmen Parts 1 and 2   Mercury 73173.   1971.   As this was not released as a single in Britain, this could be re-mixed. The promo version has part one in both mono and stereo. Mercury promo MDJ-311 may have been counterfeited.

Space Oddity   5:05 and 3:39 versions.   RCA promo 74-0876.   1973.

Time   5:08 and 3:38 versions.   RCA promo DJBO-0001.   1974.

Rock 'n' Roll Suicide/Quicksand   RCA export issue LPBO-5021.   1974.   This was made for Britain and was not given a release in the USA.

Rebel Rebel/Lady Grinning Soul   RCA APBO-0287.   1974.   The A side is completely different to the British single version.

Space Oddity/Moonage Daydream/Life On Mars/It Ain't Easy   RCA promo EP45-103.   1974.

Rock 'n' Roll With Me   4:17 and 3:28 versions.   RCA promo JB-10105.   1975.
Young Americans   5:06 and 3:11 versions.   RCA promo JB-10152.   1975.
Fame   4:12 and 3:30 versions.   RCA promo JB-10320.   1975.
Heroes   6:07 and 3:29 versions.   RCA twelve-inch promo JD-11151.   1977.
BOWIE/FRANK ZAPPA *Whats It All About?* Radio Series 547/8. 1977.
Beauty And The Beast/Fame   RCA twelve-inch promo JD-11204.   1978.
Star/What In The World/Breaking Glass   RCA twelve-inch promo white vinyl DJL 1-3255.   1978.
John I'm Only Dancing/Golden Years RCA twelve-inch promo JD-11886. 1979.
Ashes To Ashes   Long and short versions/*Space Oddity*   1980 version.   RCA twelve-inch promo DJL 1-3795.   1980.
BOWIE/BOB DYLAN *What's It All About?* Radio Series MA-1791. 1980.
Fashion   4:45 and 3:23 versions.   RCA twelve-inch promo JD-12140.   1980.
The Elephant Man   Radio Spots.   Label details unknown.   Promo.   1980.   Made to promote the Broadway production featuring Bowie in the lead role as the famous Victorian freak. A one-sided white label single.
Cat People   Possibly the same on both sides.   MCA-Backstreet promo picture disc, number unknown.   1982.   His most sought-after rare record of recent years.
Cat People   6:41 and 4:08 versions.   MCA-Backstreet twelve-inch promo L33-1759.   1982.
Let's Dance   Long and short versions/*Cat People*   EMI-America twelve-inch promo SPRO-9904/5.   1983.
China Girl   Long version/*Shake It*   Long version.   EMI-America twelve-inch promo SPRO-9951/2.   1983.

American albums

David Bowie   Deram DE-16003 mono. DES-18003 stereo.   1967.   Essentially the *Love You Till Tuesday* album. The mono version was promo only.
Man Of Words, Man Of Music   Mercury SR-61246.   1969.   This was the American version of the Philips album *David Bowie,* although they did edit the track *Unwashed And Somewhat Slightly Dazed.*
The Man Who Sold The World   Mercury SR-61325.   1971.   The most obvious difference between this and the British version is that this doesn't have the drag cover. It was replaced by a cartoon cover similar to the sleeve of the American *Images* album on London. As always, counterfeits exist.
David Bowie Now!   RCA promo DJL 1-2697.   1977.   A sampler album.
Superstars Radio Network Present An Evening With David Bowie   RCA promo DJL 1-3036.   1977.   An interview album to promote *Stage* and includes four songs from the album and of which counterfeits do exist.
1980 All Clear   RCA promo DJL 1-3545.   1980.   Another compilation.
The David Bowie Radio Special. Volume One   RCA promo DJL 1-3829.   1980. An interview album with music.
RCA Radio Special Series   RCA promo DJL 1-3840.   1980.   Yet another interview album.

Retrorock Radio Series (Dated 6.9.82).
Rolling Stone Continuous History Of Rock 'n' Roll Radio Series. 1982.
A three-album set with three sides of Bowie and three sides of The Stones.
Let's Talk EMI-America promo SPRO-9960/1. 1983. An open-ended interview
album, with script, as well as five songs from the *Let's Dance* album.
Ziggy Live RCA QPL 2-4862. 1983. A very rare clear vinyl pressing was made.
ABC Rock Radio Network presents David Bowie live in Montreal 1983. 1983.

Odds and sods
Singles

Ragazza Sola, Ragazza Solo/Wild Eyed Boy From Freecloud Italian Philips
BW-704208. 1969. The A side has the tune of *Space Oddity,* but new lyrics written
by someone called Mogul. The title translates as *Lonely Boy, Lonely Girl.* White
label juke box copies have been counterfeited. There is apparently a Japanese
version as well.
Heros (Heroes sung in French)/*V 2 Schneider* French RCA PB-9167. 1978.
Helden (Heroes in German)/*V 2 Schneider* German RCA PB-9168. 1978.
Heroes (Sung in English/Sung in French/Sung in German)/*V 2 Schneider*
Australian RCA 20629. 1978. A seven-inch EP.
Boys Keep Swinging/Fantastic Voyage Spanish RCA promo picture disc, number
unknown. 1978.
Amsterdam/Ragazza Sola, Ragazza Solo Spanish RCA promo, number and date
unknown.
Peter And The Wolf Sampler. USA RCA green vinyl twelve-inch promo
JD-11306. 1978. A one-sided disc. This has narration by Bowie.

Odds and sods
Albums

The Man Who Sold The World Dutch Mercury, number unknown. 1971. This
Dutch version is even rarer than the British. It has a square sleeve which folds out
into a circular poster with Bowie's face inside of a smashed watch on one side and
Bowie with an eagle's body on the other.
Glastonbury Fayre UK Revelation REV-1. 1973. This includes Bowie's *The
Supermen.* This track is also available as a bootleg single picture disc.
Heroes German RCA PL-12522. 1978. This has a half-German, half-English
version of the title track.
Peter And The Wolf USA RCA-Red Seal ARL 1-2743. 1978. Bowie contributed
narration to this version played by the Philadelphia Orchestra conducted by
Eugene Ormandy. Some copies were also pressed in green vinyl.
The Rise And Fall Of Ziggy Stardust Japan Mobile Fidelity audiophile MFSL
1-064. 1982.
Let's Talk Scandinavian EMI-America, number unknown. 1983. An interview
picture disc, not a promo.

Bow Wow Wow

British singles

Louis Quatorze EMI-one-sided promo WOW-1. 1980. Made to promote *Your Cassette Pet.*

*Mile High Club/*B side unknown. Tour D'Eiffel Records, number unknown. 1981. Possibly a concert freebie. Recorded for EMI but not released until 1982 on the *I Want Candy* compilation.

Elimination Dancing/King Kong Flexipop 018 (Lyntone LYN-11358). 1982.

I Want Candy/See Jungle/Go Wild In The Country/Chihuahua RCA cassette single RCXK-004. 1983.

British album

See Jungle, See Jungle . . . RCA cassette LPK-3000. 1981. This contains one extra song *The Joy Of Eating Raw Flesh.*

American singles

Prince Of Darkness/Chihuahua RCA twelve-inch promo JD-12323. 1981.

I Want Candy Mono and stereo versions. RCA twelve-inch promo JD-13231. 1982.

Baby Oh No Long and short versions. RCA twelve-inch promo JD-13306. 1982.

Love Peace And Harmony Long and short versions. RCA twelve-inch promo, number unknown. 1983.

American album

RCA Radio Special, Volume 15 RCA promo DJL 1-4193. 1982. An interview LP.

The Box Tops

American singles

The Letter/Happy Times Sound Sphere 77001. c.1967. This was the original independent release.

Cry Like A Baby/Fields Of Clover Sound Sphere, number unknown. 1967. Details as above.

The Letter/Happy Times Philco-Ford Hip Pocket records HP-27. c.1968. A mini-disc.

Odds and sods

Mi Sento Felice (Cry Like A Baby sung in Italian)/B side unknown. Spanish, label unknown SIR-20072. c.1967.

Jackson Browne

American singles

Before The Deluge/BRUCE SPRINGSTEEN track.   Asylum twelve-inch promo AS-11442.   1978.   From the *No Nukes* soundtrack.
The Load Out-Stay/Stay   Asylum twelve-inch promo AS-11389.   1978.
Hold On Hold Out   Same on both sides.   Asylum twelve-inch promo AS-11477. 1980.
Somebody's Baby/Crow On The Cradle   Asylum twelve-inch promo 67989.   1982.

American albums

Interview album.   (Talks about his first two albums).   Navy Radio Service 7427. c.1974.
Late For The Sky   Quad mix.   Asylum EQ-1017.   1974.
Rock Around The World   Radio Series, number 167.   (Dated 16.10.77).

British album

Late For The Sky   Quad mix.   Asylum K2-43007.   1974.

Odds and sods

No Nukes   Soundtrack.   UK/USA Asylum.   1978.   This contains live tracks.
No Nukes MUSE Views   USA Asylum promo, number unknown.   1978.   An interview to accompany the above. Sponsored by the Musicians Union for Safe Energy.
Bread And Roses   UK/USA Fantasy.   1978.   Live material recorded at a folk festival in Berkley, California in 1977.
King Biscuit presents MUSE live   (Dated 25.11.79).   This American triple-album set features Browne live among others.

Buffalo Springfield

American albums

Buffalo Springfield   Atco 33-200 mono, SD33-200 stereo.   1966.   The first pressings included the track *Baby Don't Scold Me*. The album was re-issued when *For What It's Worth* became a hit in America; the running order of the album was changed and *Baby Don't Scold Me* was excluded. There is also in existence a Gold Star acetate of alternate takes of tracks from the first album.
LAST TIME AROUND AND KING CURTIS   *Sweet Soul*   Sampler.   Atco promo, number unknown.   1968.
Retrospective and IRON BUTTERFLY   *Ball*   Sampler.   Atco promo TLST-140.   1969.

British album

Buffalo Springfield   Atlantic 587 070 mono, 588 070.   1966.   This first UK pressing befell a fate similar to its American counterpart.

Buggles

British single

Living In The Plastic Age 5:10 and 3:47 versions. Island promo WIT-6540. 1980.

British album

Age Of Plastic Island one-sided promo RSS-18. 1980. This four-track sampler contains an alternate *Video Killed The Radio Star.*

American singles

Clean Clean/Living In The Plastic Age Island twelve-inch promo PROA-859. 1980.
Fade Away/On TV Carerre flexi, number 5. 1982. Given away with subscription copies of *Trouser Press* magazine.

Kate Bush

British singles

Never For Ever Sampler EMI promo flexi SFI-562. 1980. This has excerpts from three songs, *Delius, Blow Away* and *Egypt.*
Kate Bush On Stage EP. EMI MIEP-2991. 1980. This was initially available in a gatefold sleeve, but then reduced to a single sleeve. The promo version was a double single.
Them Heavy People/Don't Push Your Foot On The Heartbreak EMI PSR-442. This was also used for the juke box copies.
L'Amour Looks Something Like You/James And The Cold Gun EMI PSR-443. These two may have come with the gatefold sleeve mentioned earlier.

British album

The Kick Inside EMI picture disc. EMCP-3223. 1979. This was one of the rarer items to come from the spate of coloured vinyl releases in the late 1970s.

American single

The Dreaming Sampler EP EMI-America twelve-inch promo SPRO-9847-8. 1982.

American albums

The Kick Inside Harvest SW-11751. 1978. This Harvest label version features the original American sleeve for the album. It showed Kate brushing her hair back with her hands. Because this sleeve was so popular with her fans in Britain, EMI imported a batch of sleeves from America and put them on UK copies for a while. The second version of the American album, on EMI-America SW-17003 and released in 1979, had the more familiar British cover.

Self Portrait, The Kate Bush Radio Special   EMI-America promo SSA-3020. 1979.   This includes an interview as well as music.

Foreign single
Ne T'en Fui Pas/Un Basir D'Enfant French EMI-Pathe PM-102.   1983.   These songs were an attempt to break into the French language charts. The A side appeared as the B side of *There Goes A Tenner* in Britain, where the B side, a French version of *The Infant Kiss* has yet to appear here.

The Buzzcocks

British singles
Spiral Scratch EP New Hormones Records ORG-1.   1977.   Original copies came with a plastic label, whereas the 1979 re-issues had paper labels. The real difference is that the re-issue includes the words 'with Howard Devoto' on the front cover.
Whatever Happened To United Artists one-sided promo UP-36316-DJ.   1978. This was sent to radio stations to cover up the fact that the A side to this was called *Orgasm Addict* – a daytime radio favourite!
What Do I Get United Artists one-sided promo UP-36348-DJ.   1978.   A similar story to the one above, but this time covering up the B side *Oh Shit*. Some copies of The Strangler's single *Peaches* has *Oh Shit* on the B side by mistake.
Moving Away From The Pulsebeat United Artists one-sided twelve-inch promo UALP-15.   1978.

British album
Singles Going Steady United Artists UAK-30279.   1981.   Withdrawn in March. This was to be released in Britain to counter the flood of American imports on IRS SP-001. White label test pressings exist of this United Artists version which was released on Liberty later in the year.

American single
Parts 1, 2 and 3 IRS red vinyl twelve-inch promo SP-70955.   1981.   A compilation of their last three singles.

American album
Lest We Forget ROIR tapes, number unknown.   1983.   A live show.

Odds and sods
Short Circuit. Live At The Electric Circus UK Virgin ten-inch blue vinyl album VCL-5003.   1979.   The Buzzcocks play live.
The Roxy, London WC2 UK Harvest SHSP-4069.   1979.   Two live tracks here.
C 81 UK NME-Rough Trade tape COPY-001.   1981.   This has a new studio track *I Look Along*.

The Byrds

American singles

THE BEEFEATERS *Please Let Me Love You/Don't Be Long* Elektra EK-45013. 1964. A pre-CBS release using their original name.

THE BYRDS *Mr Tambourine Man* Same on both sides. Columbia red vinyl promo 4-43271. 1965.

All I Really Want To Do Same on both sides. Columbia red vinyl promo 4-43332. 1965.

Feel A Whole Lot Better Same on both sides. Columbia red vinyl promo 4-43332. 1965. The two above promos were actually a double-sided single, therefore two promos were sent to radio stations.

Turn Turn Turn Same both sides. Columbia red vinyl promo 4-43424. 1966.

Some were available in the early 1970s from the CBS record club for $1 each!

Fifth Dimension Interview single. Columbia promo JZSP-116003. 1966.

He Was A Friend Of Mine One-sided Columbia promo JZSP-116476. 1967.

The Byrds EP. Columbia promo CV-10287. c.1967. This includes *Never Goin' Back, Chimes Of Freedom, Rock 'n' Roll Star* and *Lover Of The Bayou*.

American albums

Twenty Golden Hits TV Products. Number and date unknown. This label also released one Beatles compilation.

Retrorock Radio Series (Dated 28.9.81).

Rolling Stone Continuous History Of Rock And Roll Radio Series, No. 41. 1981.

British singles

THE BEEFEATERS *Please Let Me Love You/Don't Be Long* Pye international 7N-25277. 1964. This was re-issued in 1971 on Elektra 2101 007.

The Byrds also appeared on several soundtracks. *Candy* on ABC, *Easy Rider* on Dunhill and *Banjoman* on Sire.

J. J. Cale

THE LEATHER COATED MINDS *Trip Down Sunset Strip* Album on American Vibra 6003 and UK Fontana STL-5412. Released in 1966. This was the recording debut of J. J. Cale in a hippie group.

American singles

It's A Go Go Place/Dick Tracy Liberty 55840. c.1966.

Outside Looking In/In Our Time Liberty 55881. c.1966.

After Midnight/Slow Motion Liberty 55931. 1967. This was recorded seven years before his more famous version on Shelter records.

British Singles

Outside Looking In/In Our Time Liberty LIB-55881. c.1966.
Katy Cool Lady/Juan and Maria Juarez Blues Shelter JJ-1. 1979. Given away with some copies of the *Five* album.
Mama Don't Edited. Shelter one-sided promo WIP-6697-DJ. 1981. This edits out drug references.

British album

J. J. Cale Shelter promo ISADJ-1. c.1976. A compilation album.

John Cale

American singles

Dirty Ass Rock 'n' Roll Island one-sided promo IXP-3. 1977.
Disco Clone Label details unknown. 1978. A twelve-inch one-sided disc, limited to 1,500.
Dead or Alive/Honi Soit A & M twelve-inch promo SP-17154. 1981.

American Albums

Hear Fear Island promo IXP-2. 1976. An interview album to promote the *Fear* album.
Sabotage Spy-IRS records SP-004. 1980. This superb live album has yet to be released in Britain.

Odds and sods

Troublemakers USA Warner PROA-867. 1982. This compilation features an out-take from the *Academy In Peril* album, *Temper*.

The Cars

American singles

My Best Friend's Girl/Dontcha Stop Elektra twelve-inch promo, number unknown. 1978.
Good Times Roll/All Mixed Up Elektra twelve-inch promo AS-11405. 1979.
Let's Go/That's It Elektra twelve-inch promo AS-11421. 1979.
Candy O/Double Life Elektra twelve-inch promo, number unknown. 1979.

American albums

Rock Around The World Radio Series, number 218. 1978.
Robert W. Morgan Radio Series. 1979.
New Horizons In Music Radio Series. (Dated 15.10.79).

ABC *Supergroups in Concert*   Radio Series SGC-104.   1980.

THE CARS/PAT BENETAR   King Biscuit Radio Series.   (Dated 8.6.80).

BBC *Rock Hour*   Radio Series, number 147.   (Dated 23.11.80).

THE CARS/EDDIE MONEY   King Biscuit Radio Series.   (Dated 16.2.81).

THE CARS/APRIL WINE   King Biscuit Radio Series   *The Best Of Biscuit.* (Dated 7.6.81).

Innerview   Radio Series. Series 16, programme 1.   1981.

Westwood One Radio Series, number 82-4.   1982.

NBC *Source*   Radio Series   (Dated April 82).

Retrorock   Radio Series   (Dated 3.5.82). Taken from the *Candy O* tour.

Retrorock   Radio Series   (Dated 4.10.82).

NBC *Source*   Radio Series   (Dated 19.12.82).

British singles

Just What I Needed/I'm In Touch   Elektra K-12301.   1978.   Withdrawn.

Good Times Roll/All Mixed Up   Elektra K-12352.   1979.   A limited edition came with a free badge.

Double Life/Got A Lot On My Head   Elektra picture disc K-12385-P.   1979. Their rarest picture disc single, limited to 1,000.

Shake It Up/Cruiser   Elektra picture disc K-12583-P.   1982.   There are two different picture discs for this. The first was grey and pink, while the second was black and pink.

British album

Candy O   Elektra K-52148.   1979.   The first 2000 copies omitted the title on the front cover, so WEA put a title sticker on the shrink wrap, as well as a hand written note, e.g. *No. 0001 of 2,000.*

Odds and sods

Both *The Cars* and *Candy O* have been pressed in audiophile format by Nautilus Records in 1981.

Carlene Carter

American single

Never Together   Same on both sides. Warner twelve-inch promo PROA-724. 1978.

British album

Blue Nun F Beat XXLP-12.   1981.   This was deleted very quickly and replaced by a new version with three extra tracks.

Harry Chapin

American singles

THE CHAPINS *Old Time Music/The Swinging Group* Rockland records 664. c.1968. A rare independent release.

THE CHAPINS *Working' On My Life/*B side unknown. Epic 5-10761. c.1969. Most copies that have turned up so far are double-A-sided promos.

HARRY CHAPIN *A Better Place To Be* Same on both sides. Elektra twelve inch promo AS-45327. 1977.

HARRY CHAPIN/MELANIE *What's It All About?* Radio Series 156. Date unknown.

HARRY CHAPIN/PAUL DAVIS *What's It All About?* Radio Series 252. Date unknown.

American albums

THE CHAPINS *Chapin Music* Rockland Records 66. c.1969. The Chapins were Harry and his brother Tom.

Sounds Like The Navy Radio Series. Label details and date unknown. Hosted by Sam Riddle, this has Harry introducing his songs. He also helped to compile a double album of PSA's to promote a Social Security programme. This consists of five-minute spots of Harry singing, etc.

Robert W. Morgan Radio Series. (Dated 25.11.78).

Cheap Trick

The roots of Cheap Trick can be found in two groups. The first was a band called THE GRIM REAPERS which released one single in America, HOUND DOG on Smack records 15-5. c.1968. The other was FUSE which cut one self-titled album on USA Epic BN-26502 in 1968. A single was also released *Hound Dog/Cruisin* Epic 5-10514.

American singles

I Want You To Want Me Appeared on a yellow vinyl promo EP with other artists. Epic promo AE7-1129. 1976.

Dream Police Long and short versions. Epic promo 9-50774. 1979.

Voices/The House Is Rockin' Epic twelve-inch promo AS-722. 1980.

From Tokyo To You EP twelve-inch promo AS-518. 1979. This was a seven-track mini album taken from the *Cheap Trick At Budokan* album which at the time was only a Japanese import. The response to this promo EP persuaded CBS to release the album in the States.

Everything Works If You Let It Long and short versions. Epic promo ten inch AS-790. 1980.

Everything Works If You Let It Same both sides. Epic AE7-1206. 1980.

Although it states 'demonstration only' on the label it is in fact a free single which came with the *Found All The Parts* ten inch EP. When this ten inch was expanded to a twelve inch in 1983 the free single had disappeared.

Day Tripper Same both sides. Epic promo AE7-1211. 1980. This is a promo to promote the ten inch *Found All The Parts*.

CHEAP TRICK/ROGER McGUINN *What's It All About?* Radio Series MA-1787 (533-4). 1979.

American albums

Robert W. Morgan *Profiles In Rock* Radio Series. Date unknown.

Retrorock Radio Series (Dated 19.7.82).

Westwood One Radio Series (Dated Aug. 1982).

Westwood One Radio Series (Dated Oct. 1982).

In Concert Radio Series, number 8217. (Dated Aug. 1982).

British singles

So Good To See You/You're All Talk Epic EPC-6199. 1978. This was withdrawn, but promos may exist.

I Want You To Want Me Studio and live versions. Epic promo EPC-7258-DJ. 1979. Made to promote *Cheap Trick At Budokan*.

Dream Police Sampler EP Epic promo, number unknown. 1980.

Foreign single

Cheap Trick Talk Japanese Ongakasha flexi E-4275. 1979.

Oh Boy Japanese cardboard picture disc single. Label details unknown. c.1978.

Eric Clapton

British singles

*I Am Yours/*B side unknown. Polydor 2001 096. 1970. Withdrawn.

*Little Wing/*B side unknown. Polydor 2058 305. 1972. Withdrawn.

Wonderful Tonight/Further Up The Road RSO twelve-inch promo JONX-001. 1979. This was a numbered promo limited to 500 to promote the *Just Another Night* live double-album set.

British albums

Clapton RSO 2479 702. 1976. A withdrawn compilation album.

Time Pieces RSO RSDX-3. 1982. Another withdrawn compilation, this time a double set. This was shelved in favour of a single album version.

Money And Cigarettes Duck cassette 92-3722-4. 1983. This cassette version contains an interview which takes up the whole of side two.

Backless, 461 Ocean Boulevard and *Slowhand* RSO boxed set, BOX-3. 1983. This comes in a white box package.

American singles

Knocking On Heaven's Door   4:21 and 3:40 versions. RSO promo RS-513.   1975.
Slowhand On White   RSO twelve-inch promo in white vinyl PRO-035.   1977.
This is a sampler EP to promote the *Slowhand* album.
Promises/Watch Out For Lucy   RSO twelve-inch promo RPO-1005.   1977.
Backless   Sampler EP.   RSO twelve-inch promo   RPO-1009.   1978.
ERIC CLAPTON/ORLEANS   *What's It All About?*   Radio Series single 561/562.   c.1978.

American albums

There's One In Every Crowd   Quad mix RSO QD-4806.   1974.
461 Ocean Boulevard   Quad mix RSO QD-4801.   1974.
King Biscuit Radio Series   (Dated 17.5.81).
BBC *Rock Hour*   Radio Series   (Dated June 1981).
ERIC CLAPTON/FRANKIE LYMON   *Sounds Of Solid Gold*   Radio Series, number 4.
1982.

Odds and sods

Clapton has appeared on many other peoples albums over the years, too many to
mention here!
RSO Prime Cuts   UK RSO ten inch album SINGL-1.   1974.   This has one new
Clapton track *Smile.*
Secret Policeman's Ball. The Music   UK Spingtime HAHA-6004. 1982. This live
album has both Clapton and Beck playing together live in London.
Slowhand   Japan Mobile Fidelity audiophile MFSL 1-030.   1980.
Just One Night   Japan Nauilus audiophile, number unknown.   1981.

Clapton's contributions for other people have taken him from The Beatles *White
Album* and George Harrison's *Concert For Bangla Desh* to Ringo's *Rotogravure*
albums, among others.

The Dave Clark Five

British singles

Chaquita/In Your Heart   Ember EMBS-156.   1962.
I Knew It All The Time/That's What I Said   Piccadilly 7N-35050.   1963.
I Walk The Line/First Love   Piccadilly 7N-35088.   1963.

These three were rare pre-Columbia recordings.

Mulberry Bush/Chaquita   Columbia DB-7011.   1963.   Their first Columbia
release was a failure.

British EP

Teen Scene '64   Ember EMBEP-4540.   1964.   Although this was a various artists
EP, it did include the two DC5 Ember tracks.

British album

The Dave Clark Five And The Washington DC's Ember FA-2003. 1964. This is in reality a compilation, with the DC 5's two Ember tracks given leading priority.

American singles

First Love/I Walk The Line Laurie LR-3188. 1963. Pre-British invasion.
Chaquita/In Your Heart Jubilee 45-5476. 1964. This was the first of many versions of this single in America.
I Walk The Line/First Love Rust 5078. 1964.
Chaquita/In Your Heart Crown CSI-473. 1965.
That's What I Said/I Knew It All The Time Congress CG-212. 1965.
Chaquita/In Your Heart Crown CSI-644. 1965.
Catch Us If You Can/Everybody Knows Auravison one-sided cardboard disc, given away with Pond's Cold Cream in 1965.
Do You Love Me/CHAD AND JEREMY track. Nabisco Shreddies flexi givaway. 1965.
Everybody Knows/LULU *The Best Of Both Worlds* Epic promo. 1968.

American EP's

Greatest Hits Epic juke box issue ST5-26185. 1966.
More Greatest Hits Epic juke box issue ST5-26221. 1967.

American albums

Glad All Over Epic LN-24093. 1964. There are two different covers for this. The cover without the instruments is the rarer of the two.
Chaquita, In Your Heart Cortleigh 1073. 1964. This is a various artists compilation.
The Dave Clark Five And The Playbacks Crown 5400. 1964. Another cash in.
Beat Battle Of The World Groovemaster BR-140. 1965. Doubtless the same old Ember and Piccadilly tracks regurgitated, along with other acts.
Having A Wild Weekend 8 radio spots. Warner promo SP-3248. 1965.
The Dave Clark Five Interviews Epic promo one-sided album XEM-27238. c.1965.

The Clash

British singles

Remote Control/London's Burning CBS twelve-inch promo 12-5293. 1978.
Capital Radio/Interview with Tony Parsons/Listen CBS CL-1. 1977. This was sent to people who returned the red token which came with the initial pressings of the first album, along with a coupon from the NME. About 10,000 were made.
I Fought The Law/Gates Of The West CBS promo 7324-DJ. 1979. This was a two-track sampler from the *Cost Of Living* EP.
Take A Gamble/Wave Bye Bye To The Boss CBS twelve-inch promo, number unknown. 1980.

Should I Stay Or Should I Go/Straight To Hell CBS A-2646. 1983. Some copies have a laser design etched on one side of the disc.

British album

Give 'Em Enough Rope CBS 82431. 1978. Promo copies came with a poster highlighting all the countries that were at war with each other in 1978.

American singles

Groovy Times/Gates Of The West Epic AE7-1178. 1979. This was given as a freebie with *The Clash* album.
I Fought The Law/Gates Of The West/Groovy Times Epic twelve-inch promo AS-617. 1979.
London Calling/Clampdown/Lost In The Supermarket/Card Cheat Epic twelve-inch promo AS-723. 1979.
Train In Vain Same both sides. Epic ten-inch promo AS-749. 1979.
Clampdown/New Cadillac/Spanish Bombs Epic ten-inch promo AS-788. 1979.
The Magnificent Seven/Lightning Strikes/One More Time/One More Club Epic twelve-inch promo AS-905. 1980.
Should I Stay Or Should I Go Was released as a single five times in America from 1982 to 1983. The reason is unknown.

American albums

Sandinista Now! Epic promo AS-913. 1980. This was a twelve-track compilation, taken from the three-album set. I am bound to say that in my opinion this ought to have been released instead of the inferior six sides we were given.
If Music Could Talk Epic promo AS-952. 1981. An interview album to promote *Sandinista*.
Combat Rock Epic FE-37689. 1982. The first batch of this album have the track *Inoculated City* in its original form. The lyrics mention *Two Thousand Flushes* which is the name of a toilet cleaner made by a company called FlushCo. FlushCo threatened to sue unless they altered the offending line. Not wishing to confront FlushCo, The Clash had the line changed. So the first 150,000 copies have the *two thousand flushes* version. I don't know if this was changed in Britain.
Combat Rock Epic picture disc promo AS-99-1592. 1982.
Combat Rock Epic promo camouflage vinyl FE-37689. 1982.
The World According To The Clash Epic promo AS-1574. 1982. Not the thoughts of 'Chairman Strummer', but a compilation.

Odds and sods

The Clash Japan Epic 5P-103. 1980. An eight single set with picture sleeves in a boxed set.
JANIE JONES AND THE LASH *House Of The Ju Ju Queen/Sex Machine* UK Big Beat NS-91. 1983. What's left of the Clash played on this.
Concerts For Kampuchea UK/USA Atlantic. 1981. This live album features The Clash among others.

Eddie Cochran

American singles

THE KELLY FOUR *Strollin' Guitar*/B side unknown. Silver 4001. c.1955. Probably his first recording.

THE COCHRAN BROTHERS *Tired And Sleepy/Fool's Paradise* Ekko 3001. 1956.

THE COCHRAN BROTHERS *Two Blue Swingin' Stars/Mr Fiddle* Ekko 1003. 1956.

THE COCHRAN BROTHERS *Guilty Conscience/Your Tomorrow's Never Come* Ekko 1005. c.1956.

EDDIE COCHRAN *Skinny Jim/Half Loved* Crest 1026. 1957. His first solo release.

Teenage Heaven/I Remember Liberty 55177. 1959. Early pressings have the words *Teen Age* instead of *Teenage*.

British singles

Pretty Baby/Think Of Me United Artists FREE-12. 1978. A free single given away with *The Singles Album*.

The Singles Album Sampler. United Artists promo FREE-16. 1978. This may have been one sided, but an acetate recently came to light from Pye studios. It was a ten-inch disc with the track *Don't Wake The Kids* and the same number FREE-16.

Joe Cocker

British singles

I'll Cry Instead/Precious Words Decca F-11974. 1964. His first, obscure, single. However it appears on the *Hard Up Heroes* Decca double album sampler.

I've Been Trying/Saved Action ACT-002. 1967. A hard vinyl single given away with Sheffield student rag magazine *Twikker*.

Ruby Lee/Talking Back To The Night Island export issue WIP-6818. 1982. Export singles are still being made.

With JENNIFER WARNES *Up Where We Belong* Flexi disc. 1983. More details are unknown.

American singles

I'll Cry Instead/Precious Words Philips 40255. 1964.

VANCE ARNOLD *I'll Cry Instead/Precious Words* Press, number unknown. 1964. Released under the pseudonym of Vance Arnold. As Press had the rights to the record through London records deal with British Decca, why they released a version under an alias is not clear.

I'll Cry Instead and *Precious Words*/THE YOUNGBLOODS Two tracks. Mercury promo EP-97. c.1964.

With A Little Help From My Friends/Something's Going On A & M 991. 1968.

With A Little Help From My Friends/Bye Bye Blackbird A & M 991. 1968. This had two different B sides.

With A Little Help From My Friends 3:25 version mono and stereo. A & M promo 991. 1968. The AM radio version.
With A Little Help From My Friends 4:55 version mono and stereo. A & M promo 991. 1968. The FM radio version.
Ruby Lee/Seven Days Island twelve-inch promo PR-349. 1982.

American albums
Luxury You Can Afford Asylum picture disc promo DP-400. 1978.
JOE COCKER/MARSHALL CRENSHAW King Biscuit Radio Series (Dated 22.8.82).

Odds and sods
Woodstock. Volume One UK Atlantic /USA Cotillion. 1970. Cocker live!

Phil Collins

Before Phil Collins joined Genesis he was in a band called FLAMING YOUTH. They released two singles *Guide Me Orion/Man, Woman And Child* UK Fontana TF-1057. 1969. *From Now On/Space Child* UK Fontana 6001 003. 1970. They also released one album *Ark 2* UK Fontana STL-5533/USA UNI 73075. 1970.

British singles
In The Air Tonight/The Roof Is Leaking Virgin VSK-102. 1981. A very limited edition was issued in a gatefold sleeve with a black and white cartoon book drawn by Phil's brother Clive.
In The Air Tonight Edited version. Virgin one-sided promo VSDJ-102. 1981.
You Can't Hurry Love/I Cannot Believe It's True Virgin picture disc VSY-531. 1983. A very limited release.

American singles
You Can't Hurry Love Same on both sides. Atlantic twelve-inch promo PR-470. 1983.
I Cannot Believe It's True Long and short versions. Atlantic promo 7-89869. 1983.
I Cannot Believe It's True Studio and live versions. Atlantic twelve-inch promo PR-496. 1983.
Like China Same on both sides. Atlantic twelve-inch promo, number unknown. 1983.

American albums
Hot News Radio Series (Dated March 1981).
BBC *Rock Hour* Radio Series, Number 349. 1981.
BBC *Rock Hour* Radio Series, Number 213. (Dated March 1981).
ABC *Superstars in Concert* Radio Series. 1982.

Odds and sods

Secret Policeman's Ball. The Music UK Springtime HAHA-6004. 1982. This has a brilliant acoustic version of *In The Air Tonight*.

FRIDA *I Know There's Something Going On* Album. UK. Epic/USA Atlantic. This album features a Frida and Phil duet *Here We Are*.

Ry Cooder

British singles

Money Honey/Billy The Kid Reprise promo PRO-514. 1973.
Chicken Skin Music EP. Reprise promo PRO-644. 1977.
Crazy 'Bout An Automobile/The Very Thing/Look At Granny Run/If Walls Could Walk Warner twelve-inch promo PROA-943. 1980.

American albums

The Ry Cooder Radio Show Reprise promo PRO-558. 1976.
RY COODER/MANFRED MANN King Biscuit Radio Series (Dated 12.4.81).
Borderlive Warner promo, number unknown. 1981. A live show.

British single

Gypsy Woman/Alimony Warner K-17952-F. 1982. Initial copies came with a free single *Teardrops Will Fall/It's All Over Now* SAM-149.

Sam Cooke

American singles

Win Your Love For Me Same on both sides. Keen blue vinyl stereo promo 2006. 1958.

DALE COOKE *Loveable/Forever* Speciality 596. 1956. For some reason he used an alias for his first solo single.

Just For You/B side unknown. SAR 122. c.1960. His only release on his own label.

You Understand Me/I Belong To Your Heart RCA 61-7730. 1961. A rare stereo single release.

A Change Is Gonna Come RCA one-sided promo SP45-173. 1964. This was made for radio stations shortly after his death.

American EP's

All the following are juke box EP's:
Sam Cooke Sings RCA LPC-126. 1960. This was made for Specialty records.

Twistin' The Night Away RCA VP2-2555. 1961.
The Twist RCA VP3-2555. 1961.
That's Why I'm Moving Out RCA VP5-2555. 1961.
The Best Of Sam Cooke RCA VLP-2625. 1962.
Sam Cooke At The Copa RCA VL-2970. 1963.
The Best Of Sam Cooke Volume Two RCA VL-3373. 1964.

British single
*That's Heaven To Me/*B side unknown. Immediate. 1966. Withdrawn.

Alice Cooper

Alice's first recording to be released was thought to be with THE SPIDERS *Why Don't You Love Me/*B side unknown. USA Mascot records 112. c.1966. He was also in a band called The Nazz, but this was not the Todd Rundgren group.

American singles
Reflected/Living Straight 101. 1969. His first, rare, single.
Shoe Salesman Straight promo 7398. 1970. This may have been promo only.
Nobody Likes Me A cardboard disc, origin and date unknown.
Billion Dollar Babies Warner juke box EP LLP-208. 1973.
Hello Hurray 4:16 and 3:01 versions. Warner promo WB-7673. 1973.
Teenage Lament '74/Hard Hearted Alice Warner export issue K-16345. 1974. This was made for Britain.
Muscle Of Love Warner juke box EP LLP-235. 1974.
School's Out 3:26 and 2:19 versions. Warner promo WBS-8607. 1976.
Clones Same both sides. Warner twelve-inch promo PROA-864. 1979.
Who Do You Think We Are Same both sides. Warner twelve-inch promo PROA-971. 1980.
I Like Girls Same on both sides. Warner twelve-inch promo PROA-1059. 1981.

American albums
Billion Dollar Babies Quad mix. Warner BS4-2685. 1974.
Muscle Of Love Quad mix. Warner BS4-2748. 1974.
Greatest Hits Quad mix. Warner W4-2803. 1974.
Rock Around The World Radio Series, number 155. (Dated July 1977).
The Alice Cooper Radio Show Warner promo PROA-789. 1978.
Rock Around The World Radio Series (Dated April 1978).
Rock Around The World Radio Series (Dated Jan. 1979).
Innerview Radio Series. Series 13, programme 4. c.1980.
ABC *Superstars In Concert* Radio Series SGC-108. c.1980.
Earth News Radio Series. c.1981.

British singles

Slick Black Limosine/Billion Dollar Babies   Sampler.   Warner/NME flexi (Lyntone) LYN-2585/6.   An *NME* freebie.

I'm Flash/ELKIE BROOKS   *Trapped* Chrysalis promo CHS-2069.   1974.   Taken from the *Flash Fearless* album.

No More Love At Your Convenience/B side unknown.   Warner K-17914.   1982. This was dropped in favour of *Seven And Seven Is*.

Odds and sods

THE SPIDERS   *Don't Blow Your Mind*/B side unknown.   USA SC records 003. 1967.

Flash Fearless vs. The Zorg Women. Parts 5 and 6   UK Chrysalis CHR-1081. 1975.   A cartoon fantasy set to music with a supergroup line up including Alice Cooper.

Sgt. Pepper . . .   UK A & M/USA RSO.   1978.   More Cooper soundtrack involvement.

Roadie UK/USA Warner.   1980.   Another movie soundtrack which includes two excellent tracks by Alice *Pain* and *Road Rats*.   These would have made a good single.

Elvis Costello

British singles

DAY COSTELLO   *The Long And Winding Road*/B side unknown.   Spark SRL-1042. 1970.   His first single was (rightly?) totally ignored.

ELVIS COSTELLO   *Red Shoes*/MAX WALL *Dream Tobacco* Stiff BUY-15.   1977.   A mispressing, *Miracle Man* should have been the B side.

Watching The Detectives Long and short versions.   Stiff promo BUY-20-DJ. 1977.

Stranger In The House/Neat Neat Neat Radar SAM-83.   1978.   This freebie was given with the *This Year's Model* album.

Radio Radio/Tiny Steps Radar twelve-inch promo ADA-24.   1978.

Wednesday Week/Talking In The Dark Radar RG-1.   1978.   A concert freebie given away at his Christmas concerts at The Dominion in London. The sleeve is similar to that of the *Hollywood High* EP, but in red.

Live At Hollywood High EP Radar SAM-90.   1978.   Given as a freebie with the *Armed Forces* album.

Accidents will Happen/Talking In The Dark/Wednesday Week Radar ADA-35. 1979.   This came in two different sleeves. The first was blank white with a colour graphic design (taken from the video) on the inside of the sleeve, giving the impression that the thing is inside out! The second sleeve had a photo of the band posing outside a fish factory – this time on the outside.

I Can't Stand Up For Falling Down/Girl's Talk Two Tone CHS-TT-7.   1980. Withdrawn before it reached the shops, although it was sent to reviewers, radio stations, etc. Most copies that were pressed by Chrysalis were thought to have been destroyed. Later in 1980 some more copies were pressed, this time by WEA as a concert freebie. These copies had the familiar black and white Two Tone label and had the number XX-1 on the run-off groove.

New Amsterdam EP F Beat XX-5-EP. 1980. The picture disc edition has turned up with several coloured rims. Blue, clear, white and black were used.

Ten Bloody Mary's And Ten How's Your Fathers EP F Beat promo EL-1. 1980. This is a vinyl sampler of the cassette compilation of B sides, etc.

Trust EP F Beat twelve-inch promo EL-2. 1981.

Almost Blue Sampler. F Beat promo EC-1. 1981.

Good Year For The Roses/Your Angel Steps Out Of Heaven F Beat XX-17. 1981. The picture sleeve was thought to have been withdrawn, but a few, as always, crept into the shops.

Sweet Dreams Same on both sides. F Beat XX-19. 1981. A mis-press.

Big Sister F Beat one-sided promo, number unknown. 1982.

Imperial Bedroom Sampler. F Beat promo EC-2. 1982.

Man Out Of Time edited/Interview/*Man Out Of Time* full version. F Beat promo XX-28-DJ. 1982.

Party Party/BANANARAMA *No Feelings* A & M promo PARTY-5. 1982.

Punch The Clock Promo pack. F Beat promo, number unknown. 1983. This consists of two singles and a green-label EP in a special plastic wallet. The chance of getting hold of any of these promo EP's is limited; as most of them had a run of only about twenty copies.

British albums

Armed Forces Radar cassette RAC-14. 1978. This included one extra track *Accidents Will Happen* taken from the free, live EP.

Get Happy F Beat promo XXPROMO-1. 1980. This has the whole album spread over two twelve-inch singles.

Ten Bloody Mary's And Ten How's Your Fathers F Beat cassette XXC-9. 1980. A collection of B sides, etc. came initially in a gold case, later replaced by a black box.

Almost Blue Introductions by Elvis. F Beat promo ECCHAT-1. 1981. A double album limited to 2,000, with 1,000 copies specially numbered and autographed by the band. The album includes Elvis talking about the making of the album and the songs, etc.

A Conversation With Elvis Costello F Beat promo ECCHAT-2. 1982. A similar set to the above. This time for the *Imperial Bedroom* album.

American singles

Alison/Miracle Man Columbia 3-10641. 1977. Elvis' first USA single featured a completely re-mixed version of the A side, which as yet, has not been released in Britain.

Alison/Watching The Detectives Columbia 3-10705. 1977. The same re-mix of *Alison*, this time with a new B side, released only a few months after the one above.

Radio Radio/NICK LOWE *Cruel To Be Kind*/MINK DEVILLE *Soul Twist* Columbia-

Capitol twelve-inch promo AS-443. 1978. This orange vinyl rarity was made to promote a tour featuring these three acts.

Live A Hollywood High EP Columbia AE7-1171. 1979. This seven-inch disc was given away with the *Armed Forces* album. A twelve-inch promo pressing was also made AS-529.

My Funny Valentine/Peace, Love And Understanding Columbia red vinyl promo single made for St. Valentine's day in 1979. AE7-1172.

Taking Liberties EP Columbia twelve-inch promo AS-847. 1980. This came with the white *Costello* label design.

Tom Snyder interview. Columbia twelve-inch promo AS-958. 1980. This also includes *Watch Your Step.*

Man Out Of Time/Beyond Belief/Tears Before Bedtime (This last track isn't credited on the label). Columbia twelve-inch promo AS-1510. 1982.

American albums

My Aim Is True Columbia JC-35037. 1977. This American version includes *Watching The Detectives* which isn't on the UK edition.

This Year's Model Columbia JC-35331. 1978. This American version includes *Radio Radio* which at the time had not been released in Britain.

My Aim Is True/This Year's Model Sampler. Columbia promo picture disc, no number. 1978. A much sought after item which to my knowledge has not yet been counterfeited.

Rock Around The World Radio Series, number 180. (Dated Jan. 1978). This also has Robert Gordon on side two.

Rock Around The World Radio Series, number 204. (Dated July 1978). NICK LOWE is on side two.

Armed Forces Columbia JC-35709. 1979. This American version included the track *Peace Love And Understanding* which didn't appear on the UK version.

Almost Blue Introductions by Elvis. Columbia promo AS-1318. 1981. Similar to the British.

ELVIS COSTELLO/DEVO. King Biscuit Radio Series. 1981.

Odds and sods
Singles

NICK LOWE AND HIS SOUND *Peace Love And Understanding* UK Radar ADA-26. 1978. This was the B side to Nick Lowe's single *American Squirm* – the same version that appeared on the American *Armed Forces* album.

Armed Forces Canada CBS JC-35709. 1979. A yellow vinyl pressing was made, limited to 1,500 copies.

GEORGE JONES *Stranger In The House* UK Epic EPC-8560. 1979. Taken from the George Jones album *My Very Special Guests.* A promo EP issued by CBS in Britain also featured this track. This single was re-issued in a picture sleeve in 1981 to cash in on the success of Costello's *Good Year For The Roses.*

Save The Children PSA's. USA promo single DWP-611. c.1981. Other artists also appear.

MADNESS *Tomorrow's Just Another Day* EP UK Stiff twelve-inch BUYIT-169. 1983. Costello performs a great version on side two.

Albums

Jem Import Collection Series   USA Jem promo, number 4.   (Dated Sept. 1977).   This includes Elvis' *I'm Not Angry* recorded live in London 1977.
Live At The El Macambo Canadian CBS promo CDN-10. 1978. Limited to 500 only, this live album has been counterfeited in the USA. It was recorded for CHUM-FM in Toronto.
Live Stiffs Live UK/USA Stiff. 1978. This includes some live Costello from the first Stiff package tour in 1977. When Music For Pleasure re-issued the album in 1981 they faded the track of *I Just Don't Know What To Do With Myself* earlier.
Americathon UK/USA CBS-Lorimar. 1980.   This film soundtrack included Elvis' track *Crawling To The USA*.
Concerts For Kampuchea UK/USA Atlantic. 1981. More live tracks.
Fundametal Frolics UK BBC REB-435. 1981. A live version of *The Psycho Song* is included here.

Cream

American singles

Wheels Of Fire EP. Atco EP-4525. 1967. A regular release, not a promo.
Crossroads Long and short versions. Atco promo 6646. 1969.

American albums

Wheels Of Fire/THE NEW YORK ROCK 'n' ROLL ENSEMBLE with the same. Sampler. Atco promo TLST-119/120. 1967.
Goodbye/VANILLA FUDGE *Near Beginning* Atco promo TLST-141. 1969. Again, one side each.
'Rolling Stone' magazine. Continuous History Of Rock 'n' Roll Radio Series, number 28. 1981.

Creedence Clearwater Revival

The band had recorded many tracks before they became known as CCR.
All originate in the USA unless noted.
TOMMY FOGERTY AND THE BLUE VELVETS   *Have You Ever Been Lonely/Bonita* Orchestra records 1010. c.1961.

The following singles were credited to THE GOLLIWOGS:
Don't Tell No Lies/Little Girl Does Your Mother Know Fantasy 590. 1964.
You Came Walking/Where You Been Fantasy 597. 1965.
You Got Nothing On Me/You Can't Be True Fantasy 599. 1965.
Brown Eyed Girl/You Better Be Careful Scorpio 404 and UK Vocalion VF-9226. 1965.

Fight Fire/Fragile Child   Scorpio 405 and UK Vocalion VF-9283.   1966.
Walking On The Water/You Better Get It   Scorpio 408.   1967.
Porterville/They Call It Pretending   Scorpio 412.   1967.   This was later re-issued under the CCR name, with the same label and number, in 1968.

THE GOLLIWOGS tracks were compiled on an album *The Golliwogs, Pre Creedence* Fantasy F-9474.   1975.

American singles

45 Revolutions Per Minute   Fantasy promo 2832.   1968.   An interview record.
Interview.   Fantasy promo 2838.   1969.
I Heard It Through The Grapevine/JOHN FOGERTY   *Rockin' All Over The World* Fantasy twelve-inch promo F-759-DLP.   1976.   The A side is the full-length version.

American albums

Retrorock Radio Series, number 8228.   (Dated July 1982).   A live concert from 4 July, 1971.
Live At The Royal Albert Hall   Fantasy MPF-4501.   1982.   In 1981 Fantasy proudly announced that they had found a CCR concert recorded at the famous London venue in 1970. However, it appears that someone goofed! The album was actually recorded at the Oakland Colosseum in California. All original American sleeves showed the Albert Hall, while the new copies feature the Oakland details on the sleeve.
Cosmo's Factory   Mobile Fidelity audiophile pressing MFSL-1-037.   1981.   This was pressed in Japan, but available in the USA.

Odds and sods

The Spirit Orgazmus Of Jeronimo And Creedence Clearwater Revival   German Bellaphon BI-1527.   c.1969.   This album had a limited run in pink vinyl.
In the mid-seventies the Chinese Holy Hawk label issued an eight album boxed set by CCR.

Marshall Crenshaw

American singles

Something's Gonna Happen/She Can't Dance   Shake SHK-104.   1981.   An independent twelve-inch release.
Cynical Girl/Rave On/Somebody Like You   Warner twelve-inch promo PROA-2003.   1983.
Whenever You're On My Mind   Same track on both sides.   Warner twelve-inch promo PROA-2036.   1983.

American album

MARSHALL CRENSHAW, A FLOCK OF SEAGULLS AND HAIRCUT 100.   In Concert Radio Series,

number 82-15.   (Dated March 1982).
BBC *Rock Hour* Radio Series, number 435.   (Dated 28.8.83).

British singles
Something's Gonna Happen/She Can't Dance   Albion seven-inch ION-1029 and twelve-inch 12ION-1029.   1982.   This is the British version of his first release in a different sleeve.
Whenever You're On My Mind/Jungle Rock/Somebody Like You   Warner twelve-inch W-9630-T.   1983.   This was withdrawn, although the seven-inch was released.
Superman 3   Film soundtrack album Warner 92-3879-1.   1983.   Crenshaw performs *Rock On*.

The Crickets

American single
THE CAMPS   *The Ballad Of Batman/Batmobile*   Parkway P-974.   1966.   This recording is thought to be The Crickets using an alias.

American albums
The Crickets   Liberty LRP-3351 mono, LST-7351. Stereo.   1964.   This album was given another two releases in the same year. The first re-package was titled *California Sun* to exploit the surf craze (Liberty also had Jan and Dean at the time). The second version *The Liverpool Sound Of The Crickets* – was obviously to cash in on you know who!

Jim Croce

American singles
Life And Times   ABC juke box EP LLP-232.   1972.   Also used for promo purposes PRO-769.
I Got A Name   Quad mix ABC juke box EP LLP-QD-258.   1973.
JIM CROCE/GARY WRIGHT   *What's It All About?*   Radio Series. Date and number unknown.

American albums
JIM AND INGRID CROCE   *Jim And Ingrid Croce*   Capital SMAS-315.   1969.   This was ignored until Capitol re-released it to cash in on his early '70s success.
Life And Times   Quad mix ABC-Command CQ-40007.   1974.
I Got A Name   Quad mix ABC-Command CQ-40008.   1974.

Crosby Stills and Nash

American singles

Wasted On The Way   Same track on both sides.   Atlantic twelve-inch promo PR-445. 1982.
Southern Cross/Too Much Love To Hide   Atlantic twelve-inch promo PR-457. 1982.

American albums

NBC *Source*   Radio Series, number 383. 1982.
Retrorock   Radio Series, number 8212. 1982.
CSN   (Boat cover)   Nautilus audiophile pressing, number unknown. 1982.
Woodstock   CSN appeared on *both* volumes of this festival compilation.
King Biscuit presents MUSE live. (Dated 25.11.79). This American triple album radio show features CS&N live with others.

Crosby Stills Nash and Young

American single

Deja Vu   Atlantic juke box EP LLP-7200.   1972.

American albums

A Rap With Crosby Stills Nash And Young   Atlantic promo 18102.   1973.   An interview album.
Celebration Copy, CSNY Month   Atlantic promo PR-165.   1973.   This compilation album was officially released in Germany, Atlantic ATL-40273.
Deja Vu   Mobile Fidelity audiophile pressing. 1982.

The Dakotas

British singles

The Cruel Sea/The Millionaire   Parlophone R-5044. 1963.
Humdinger/Magic Carpet   Parlophone R-5064. 1963.
Oyeh/My Girl Josephine   Parlophone R-5203. 1964.

British EP

Meet The Dakotas   Parlophone GEP-8888. 1963. This is their first two singles back-to-back.

American single

The Cruel Sea/The Millionaire Liberty 55618. 1963. This was pre-British invasion.

Roger Daltrey

British singles

Say It Ain't So/Satin And Lace Polydor 2058 948. 1976. Withdrawn in favour of *Say It Ain't So/The Prisoner* Polydor 2058 986.
Love's Dream/Orpheus Song A & M AMS-7206. 1976. This single also featured Rick Wakeman and was taken from the *Lisztomania* soundtrack album.
Wagner's Dream/Love's Dream/RICK WAKEMAN *Count Your Blessings* A & M Lyntone LYN-3176/7. 1976. This flexi was given away with *19* magazine.
Polydor twelve-inch promo, number unknown. 1980. Dialogue and interview to promote the *McVicar* soundtrack album.
Without Your Love/Say It Ain't So Joe Polydor POSP-181. 1981. This was very quickly re-issued with an extra track *Free Me*.
Without Your Love Polydor one-sided promo McVICAR-3. 1981.

British albums

Ride A Rock Horse Polydor Record Club ACB-199. 1976.
McVicar Soundtrack Polydor POLD-5034. 1980. A very limited edition was pressed in clear vinyl.
McVicar Soundtrack Polydor cassette POLDC-5034. 1980. The original cassette edition had a *Best Of Roger Daltrey* compilation on side two.

American singles

Love's Dream/Orpheus Song A & M 1779. 1976. Daltrey and Rick Wakeman together.
One Of The Boys/STEVE GIBBONS *Don't Say Goodbye* MCA twelve-inch promo L33-1962. 1976.
Say It Ain't So 4:08 and 3:15 versions MCA promo 40765. 1977.
Avenging Annie 4:31 and 3:11 versions MCA promo 40800. 1977.
Martyrs And Madmen Long and short versions MCA promo 52051. 1982.

American albums

McVicar On Record Polydor promo SA-038. 1980. An interview album. Rock Around The World, number 156. 1980.
Lisztomania Soundtrack album UK A & M AMLK-64563. 1975. This is the only soundtrack album, other than The Who, that he appears on. It was also released in the USA SP-4563.

The Damned

British singles

Morning Bird Young Blood International YB-1067. 1974. Many people have made the mistake of thinking that this is Sensible, Scabies and Co. when it's actually nothing to do with them and merely 'same name, different band.'

Stretcher Case Baby/Sick Of Being Sick Stiff promo DAMNED-1. 1977. Some copies were also given away at an NME staff party.

Love Song/Buglar Dodgy Demo records, number unknown. 1978. This white-label single was made to fill the gap between leaving Stiff and joining Chiswick. They later re-recorded the tracks for Chiswick.

White Rabbit/Rabid Over You/Seagull Chiswick CHIS-130. 1980. Withdrawn in Britain, but released in Germany. Chiswick 0037 074.

There Ain't No Sanity Clause/Hit or Miss Chiswick promo CHIS-139-DJ. 1980. A two-track sampler from an EP.

The Damned Stiff Singles Collection Stiff GRAB-2. 1981. The four Stiff singles with their original sleeves in a plastic wallet.

Lovely Money Edited/*I Think I'm Wonderful* (with *Go Get 'Em Floyd* ending)/*Lovely Money* disco version. Bronze promo BRODJ-149. 1982. The regular shop copies feature a full-length A side, as well as an alternate ending to *Wonderful* which had to be changed for copyright reasons.

Dozen Girls Edited/*Take That/Mine's A Large One Landlord/Torture Me* Bronze promo BRODJ-156. 1982.

British albums

Damned, Damned, Damned Stiff SEEZ-1. 1977. Some early copies had a photo of Eddie And The Hot Rods on the back cover, apparently there by mistake.

The Black Album Chiswick CWK-3015. 1979. This EMI pressed version had the original gravestone cover, whereas the more recent 1983 re-issue has a plain black cover (which is a pastiche of The Beatles' *White Album*).

American album

The Black Album IRS SP-70012. 1979. Shortened to single album length from the original British double.

Odds and sods

Each one of the group has appeared on other people's records, or have made solo records.

The Moonlight Tapes UK Danceville records DANCE-1. 1980. This compilation has the group playing *Teenage Dream* under the name of THE SCHOOL BULLIES.

Lovely Money EP Dutch Bronze 2101 248. 1982. The B side of this Dutch version plays at 33rpm, instead of 45rpm on the British version.

Dave Davies

Dave Davies recorded enough material for a solo album on Pye in 1967, but it was never released. The untitled album was announced in the music press. The completed tracks were *Love Me Till The Sun Shines, Funny Face, Suzannah's Still Alive, Lincoln County, There's No Life Without Love, Hold My Hand, Creeping Jean, Crying, Do You Wish To Be A Man, Mr. Reporter, The Shoemaker's Daughter* and *Are You Ready Girl*. Five of these twelve songs have not yet appeared, although a tape is in circulation.

American single
Doing The Best For You/Nothing More To Lose   RCA twelve-inch promo JD-12148.   1979.

The Spencer Davis Group

British EP
The Hits Of The Spencer Davis Group   Philips cassette MCF-5003.   1968.   A short-lived series of tape EP's.

American single
Gimmie Some Lovin/Blues In F   United Artists 50108.   1966.   There is an alternate version of the A side.

Odds and sods
Faces And Places   New Zealand Direction Records, number unknown.   1964. Includes live material by the SPENCER DAVIS RHYTHM AND BLUES QUARTET.
Rock Generation. Volume Five   French BYG records 529 705.   1972.   This record also includes RHYTHM AND BLUES QUARTET tracks recorded live in Birmingham in 1964.
Twenty Years Of British Rock   USA NBC-Source Radio Series.   1983.   This ten-album set is narrated by Spencer Davis.
The History Of British Blues   USA Sire SAS-3701.   1973.   A Decca demo track. *Mean Old Frisco* turns up here, recorded in 1964.
Here We Go 'Round The Mulberry Bush   Film soundtrack British United Artists SULP-1186.   1967.   They contribute to the soundtrack as well as Traffic.

Deep Purple

Pre-Purple singles
These are British unless noted:
RITCHIE BLACKMORE   *Little Brown Jug/Getaway*   Oriole CB-314.   1964.
EPISODE SIX (Ian Gillan and Roger Glover)

Put Yourself In My Place   Pye 7N-17018.   1967.
I Hear Trumpets Blow/True Love Is Funny   Pye 7N-17110.   1967.
Here There And Everywhere   Pye 7N-17147.   1967.
Love Hate And Revenge   Pye 7N-17244.   1968.   Also on USA Elektra EK-45617.
I Can See Through You   Pye 7N-17376.   1968.
Morning Dew   Pye 7N-17330.   1968.   Also on USA Congress CG-7007.
Lucky Sunday   Chapter One CH-103.   1969.
Mozart vs. The Rest   Chapter One CH-104.   1969.
MAZE (Ian Paice and Roger Evans)
Catari, Catari   MGM.   c.1967.
M15 (Ian Paice and Roger Evans)
You'll Never Stop Me Loving You   Parlophone R-5486.   1965.

Most of these singles are pretty obscure, so I apologise for missing B sides, etc.

British singles

Hush/One More Rainy Day   Parlophone R-5708.   1968.   Promo copies came with
a picture sleeve.
Hallelujah/April Part One   Harvest HAR-5006.   1970.   Again, the promo issue
was in a picture sleeve.
Concerto For Group And Orchestra   Edited highlights.   EMI promo PSR-325.
1970.

British albums

Shades Of Deep Purple and *The Book Of Taliesyn*   EMI-Executive cassette only
double play issue TC2EXE-1017.   1972.
Machine Head   Quad mix Harvest Q4SHVL-7504.   1974.
The Singles Album Mark 2   Purple TPS-3514.   1977.   All British copies were
pressed in purple vinyl. As the album was only a limited edition, all the master
plates were smashed afterwards.

American singles

Smoke On The Water   4:34 and 3:48 versions Warner promo WBS-7710.   1973.
Woman From Tokyo   5:50 and 2:56 versions Warner promo WBS-7737.   1973.
Made In Japan   Warner juke box EP, number unknown.   1973.
Just Might Take Your Life   4:46 and 3:35 versions Warner promo WBS-7784.
1974.
Burn   3:42 and 3:36 versions Warner promo WBS-7809.   1974.
Burn   Warner juke box EP LLP-250.   1974.

American albums

Concerto For Group And Orchestra   Tetragrammiton T-131.   1970.   This was
quickly deleted and re-issued on Warner WS-1860.
Stormbringer   Quad mix Warner-Purple PR4-2832.   1975.
BBC *Rock Hour,* number 48.   Date unknown.
Retrorock   Radio Series   (Dated 16.8.82).

Derek and the Domino's

British single

Tell The Truth/Roll It Over Polydor 2058 057. 1971. Withdrawn. Both sides were produced by Phil Spector.

American singles

Tell The Truth/Roll It Over Atco 6780. 1971. Withdrawn.
Layla 2:43 AM radio version Atco promo 6809. 1971.
Layla 7:10 FM radio version Atco promo 6809. 1971.

Some promos of *Layla* were pressed in red vinyl. Beware of counterfeits!

Devo

American singles

Jocko Homo/Mongloid Booji Boy Records 7033-114. 1977. Their first release on their own independent label.
Satisfaction/Sloppy Booji Boy Records, number unknown. 1978.
Strange Pursuit Warner promo PRO-813. 1978.
Gates Of Steel/Whip It/Mr B's Ballroom Warner twelve inch promo PROA-881. 1979.
Be Stiff/Gates Of Steel/Freedom Of Choice/Whip It Warner twelve-inch promo PROA-928. 1979.
Working In A Coal Mine Same both sides Asylum twelve-inch promo AS-11523. 1981.
Working In A Coal Mine/B side unknown. Warner BSK-3595-EP. 1981. Given away with the *New Traditionalists* album.
Jerkin' Back 'n' Forth/Through Being Cool, plus one other track. Warner twelve-inch promo PROA-993. 1981.
That's Good Warner twelve-inch promo picture disc PROA-2006. 1982. This probably has the same track on both sides.
Doctor Detroit Same both sides MCA-Backstage twelve-inch promo L33-1106. 1983.

American albums

Devo Live Warner promo WBMS-115. 1980. Later released due to public demand.
Jim Ladd Interview Radio Show. Series 19, programme 3. 1980.
DEVO/ELVIS COSTELLO King Biscuit. 1980.
BBC *Rock Hour,* number 245. (Dated Nov. 1981).
DEVO/U2 King Biscuit. (Dated 31.1.82).

Jocko Homo/Mongolid   Booji Boy DEV-1.   1978.   This came in two different sleeves: the first was a fold-out gatefold sleeve, while the second was a normal single sleeve.
Satisfaction/Sloppy   Booji Boy DEV-2.   1978.   Withdrawn with this number. Eventually issued with the number BOY-1. The picture sleeve is different from the American version.
Be Stiff/Social Fools   Stiff BOY-2.   1978.   The black vinyl copies came with picture sleeves, while the clear vinyl copies came with normal Stiff bags.
Come Back Jonee/Social Fools   Virgin VS-223.   1979.   The grey vinyl copies came with a sticker on the cover hiding a statue's face. A flexi disc came with their first British album *Are We Not Men*   Virgin VDJ-27.   1978.
Urghh A Music War!   UK A & M AMLX-64692.   1981.   This film soundtrack featured Devo playing live.

Dexy's Midnight Runners

British singles

Dance Stance/I'm Just Looking   Parlophone R-6028-DJ.   1979.   The promo version has a different vocal mix on the A side.
The Celtic Soul Brothers   Edited Mercury one sided promo DEXYSDJ-8.   1981.
Come On Eileen   Edited Mercury one-sided promo DEXYSDJ-9.   1982.
Jackie Wilson Said/Howard's Not At Home   Mercury DEXYS-10.   1982. Withdrawn.   Some copies were pressed with the *Howard* label on the B side, but the track is actually *Let's Make This Precious*. These mispressed records, with orange plastic labels, were used as juke box copies.

American album

DEXY'S/CULTURE CLUB   BBC College Concert Radio Series.   (Dated 17.4.83).

Neil Diamond

American singles

NEIL AND JACK   *What Will I Do?/You Are My Love At Last*   Duel 508.   An obviously rare release from around 1962.
NEIL AND JACK   *I'm Afraid/Till You've Tried Love*   Duel 517.   c.1962.
At Night/Clowntown/I've Never Been The Same   Acetate, label details unknown. c.1963.   The last song has never been released.
I'm A Believer/Someday Baby   Bang B-586.   1968.   Some copies were pressed in stereo.
Clowntown/At Night   Columbia 4-42809.   1964.   His first solo release.

Cherry Cherry/Girl You'll Be A Woman Soon   Ford-Philco Hip Pocket HP-5. 1968.
Solitary Man/You Got To Me   Hip Pocket HP-17.   1968.
Two Bit Manchild   Same both sides UNI promo red vinyl 55075.   1968.
Touching You, Touching Me   Radio Spots.   UNI promo 73071.   1970.
What's It All About?   Radio Series, number 209.   c.1976.
Song Sung Blue   Same both sides, Columbia promo AE7-1115.   c.1977.
Beautiful Noise   3:14 and 3:05 versions, Columbia promo 3-10452.   1977.
September Morn   Edited.   Same on both sides.   Columbia promo AE7-1193. 1980.
What's It All About?   Radio Series, number 582.   c.1980.
Heartlight   Columbia one-sided twelve-inch promo picture disc AS-99-1586. 1982.

American juke box EP's

Stones   UNI 34871.   1971.
Gold   UNI LLP-127.   c.1972.
His Twelve Greatest Hits   MCA 34989/LLP-275.   1973.
Serenade   Columbia 7-32299.   1973.

American albums

Open ended interview.   UNI promo LP-1913.   c.1968.
Neil Diamond   UNI promo ND-11.   c.1970.
It's Happening   MCA Special Products 734727.   c.1971.   This was a cut-price album with THE SUPREMES featured on side two.
Gold   Decca-CBS Record Club 245012.   c.1971.
Chartbusters   Harmony H-30023.   1971.   This compilation with various artists features *Clowntown* and *I've Never Been In Love* by Diamond.
Serenade Quad mix Columbia PCQ-32919.   1974.
Jonathan Livingston Seagull   Columbia – Masterworks half-speed andiophile pressing HC-42550.   1981.
NEIL DIAMOND/OLIVIA NEWTON JOHN   *Sounds Of Solid Gold*   Radio Series, number 11.   1982.
NEIL DIAMOND/BRENDA LEE   *Sounds Of Solid Gold*   Radio Series number 34.   1982.

British single

Twenty Golden Greats   Sampler EP MCA promo PSR-434.   1978.   Includes four songs as well as some sales talk.

British albums

Serenade   Quad mix CBS Q-69067.   1974.
Beautiful Noise   Quad mix CBS Q-86004.   1976.
Beautiful Noise   CBS 8-track cartridge 80-86004.   1976.   As the four channels didn't run for the same length of time a short reprise of the title track was included on the end of channel four.

Odds and sods

JAN TANZY *New Boy In Town* USA Columbia 4-43219. c.1963. An early Neil Diamond composition which he never recorded himself.

THE BAND *The Last Waltz* Soundtrack album on Warner. Diamond appears on this triple live set.

Hot August Night Mobile Fidelity audiophile pressing MFSL-2-024. 1980.

Neil Diamond Chinese Lyong Fang 2451/60. Date unknown. A ten-album boxed set.

Dion

American singles

DION AND THE TAMBERLANES *The Chosen Few/Out In Colorado* Mohawk 45-105. 1957. Later taken up for national distribution on Jubilee 5294.

THE BELMONTS *Teenage Clementine/Santa Margarita* Mohawk 106. 1957.

THE BELMONTS *Tag Along/We Went Away* Mohawk 107. 1957. Dion is featured on both of these.

DION AND THE BELMONTS *Be Careful Of The Stones You Throw* Same on both sides. Columbia blue vinyl promo 4-42810. 1963.

Doctor Rock 'n' Roll 4:04 and 2:26 versions Warner promo WB-7704. 1972.

New York City Song 3:45 and 3:35 versions Warner promo WB-7793. 1973.

Seagull/Soft Parade Warner promo PRO-537. 1973.

What's It All About? Radio Series, MA-1538. Date unknown.

The Wanderer Warner one-sided promo PROS-814. 1982. Made to promote the excellent movie *The Wanderers*.

American albums

Runaround Sue Laurie LLP-1009 mono, LLP-2009 stereo. 1961. This was issued in a very limited green vinyl run.

Runaround Sue Laurie-Capitol Record Club DT-91027. c.1964.

Abraham Martin And John Laurie-Capitol Record Club DT-91577. c.1968.

American EP's

Teenager In Love Laurie juke box issue ST7-609. 1960.

I've Cried Before Laurie juke box issue ST7-610. 1960.

British single

Born To Be With You/Good Lovin' Man PSI promo DJ-100. 1977.

Odds and sods

*Donna La Prima Donna/*B side unknown. Italian CBS 121-053. c.1963. The A side is sung in Italian.

Bitter End Years USA Roxbury RX3-300. 1976. This triple-album compilation features Dion from his singer-songwriter days.

Dire Straits

British singles

Romeo And Juliet   Edited Vertigo one-sided promo MOVIEDJ-1.   1981.
Skateaway   Edited Vertigo one-sided promo MOVIEDJ-2.   1981.
Sultans Of Swing   Long and short versions Vertigo promo.   1982.
Telegraph Road/Private Investigation   Vertigo twelve-inch promo.   1982.
Twistin' By The Pool/If I Had You   Vertigo promo and juke box issue DSDJ-2.   1983.

British albums

Dire Straits   Vertigo half-speed cut edition HS-9102 021.   1982.
Makin' Movies   Vertigo half-speed cut edition HS-6359 034.   1982.

American singles

Sultans Of Swing   5:49 and 4:44 versions Warner promo WBS-8736.   1978.
Sultans Of Swing   Long version/*Eastbound Train/Sultans Of Swing*   Short version Warner twelve-inch promo PROA-783.   1978.
Once Upon A Time In The West   5:24 and 3:00 versions Warner promo WBS-49082.   1979.
Skateaway/Tunnel Of Love   Warner twelve-inch promo PROA-926.   1981.
Romeo And Juliet   Long and short versions, Warner promo WBS-49688.   1981.

American albums

Robert R. Klein   Radio Series, number 17.   1979.
DIRE STRAITS/GRAHAM PARKER   BBC *Rock Hour,* number 138.   (Dated Sept. 1980). This was later re-issued number 321.
Dire Straits Live   Warner Brothers Music Show promo WBMS-109.   1980.
Retrorock   Radio Series.   (Dated 12.4.82).   Recorded c.1979.
DIRE STRAITS/LOVERBOY   King Biscuit Radio Series.   (Dated 5.7.81).
DIRE STRAITS/DIONNE WARWICK   *Sounds Of Solid Gold*   Radio Series, number 28. 1981.
BBC *Rock Hour*   Number 345.   1981.
Interview with Mark Knopfler   Warner Brothers Music Show promo cassette WBMS-125.   1983.

Odds and sods

The Hope And Anchor Front Row Festival   UK Warner-Albion K-66077.   1978. This excellent compilation features live Dire Straits.
The Honky Tonk Demos   UK Oval OVLM-5003.   1979.   This features a demo version of *Sultans Of Swing* recorded in 1977.

Mark Knopfler has also appeared on albums by Bob Dylan, Kate and Anna McGarrigle, Phil Lynott and others.

Donovan

British single

With the JEFF BECK GROUP *Barabajagal/Bed With Me* Pye 7N-17778. 1969. The B side was later re-titled *Trudi*.

British album

Donovan Rising Epic, number unknown. 1976. Withdrawn.
Sunshine Superman Same on both sides. Epic promo red vinyl 5-10045. 1966.

American album

Innerview Radio Series. c.1980.

Odds and sods

Jennifer Juniper Sung in Italian. Italian Epic, number unknown. 1967.
Brother Sun, Sister Moon Soundtrack album. German HMV 3C 064 93393. 1970. Donovan contributes to this soundtrack.
Donovan Live In Japan, Spring Tour 1973 Album. Japan Epic ECPM-25. 1973.
Neutronica Album. German RCA, number unknown. 1982. His first 1980's album hasn't as yet been released in Britain or America.
Secret Policeman's Ball, The Music Soundtrack album. UK Springtime HAHA-6004. 1982. Donovan plays live here.
Love Is Only Feeling Album. German RCA, number unknown. 1983. Another German only album.

The Doors

American singles

Break On Through/Light My Fire Ford-Philco Hip Pocket records HP-9. 1968. A rare mini-disc.
The Doors Hit Kit Elektra promo boxed set of four singles. Number and date unknown.
What's It All About? Radio Series, number 122. c.1973. A post-Morrison interview featuring *Ships with Sails*.

American albums

A six-track white label album of demos made for CBS in 1966 is in existence.
The Best Of The Doors Quad mix Elektra EQ-5035. 1974. This album was released in quad only in America.
An American Prayer Specially banded for radio play. Elektra promo 5E-502. 1978.
THE DOORS/JEFFERSON STARSHIP *Rock Around The World* Radio Series, number 231. (Dated Jan. 1979).

Robert W. Morgan *Profiles* Radio Series. Number and date unknown.
Innerview Radio Show. Series 14, programmes 7 to 10. c.1980. A four-album set.
Rock 'n' Roll Never Forgets (Dated 12.7.82). A five-album set.
Three Hours For Magic BBC *Rock Hour* Number unknown. 1982.
Three Hours For Magic Radio spots album. BBC *Rock Hour*. 1982. A one-sided album.
NBC Source Number 23. 1982. A three album set.
THE DOORS/OLIVIA NEWTON JOHN *Sounds Of Solid Gold* Radio Series, number 32. 1982.

British single

Ghost Song/Roadhouse Blues Elektra SAM-94. 1978. Given as a freebie with the 1978 re-issue of *Hello I Love You* Elektra K-12215. It also came with a nice gatefold sleeve with lyrics.

British album

The Best Of The Doors Quad mix Elektra K2-42143. 1974. This was also available in stereo.

Odds and sods

JIM MORRISON *Ace In The Hole* USA Curly Q records 001-2. Date unknown. This is not a solo single by The Doors' singer.
The Doors Mobile Fidelity audiophile pressing from Japan MFSL-1-051. 1981.

Dr. Hook

American singles

The Dr Hook Bonus Disc Columbia AE7-1076. c.1972. An album givaway.
Bankrupt, Free Stimu Capitol promo SPRO-8220. 1976. Sampler EP for their *Bankrupt* album.
When You're In Love With A Beautiful Woman Disco mix. Capitol twelve inch promo SPRO-9119. 1978.
What Do You Want For Christmas? Capitol promo SPRO-9273. 1978. This is a thank you disc for DJ's who played their records.
Sexy Eyes Capitol twelve-inch promo SPRO-9342. 1979. Probably the same track on both sides.
Girls Can Get It Casablanca twelve-inch promo NBD-20231. 1981.

British singles

Interview single. CBS promo. c.1973.
DR HOOK AND FRIENDS *Cover Of The Radio Times* CBS one-sided promo 1037. 1973. This was Dr Hook's answer to the BBC's ban on their single *Cover Of The Rolling Stone* because it constituted advertising.

For You From Dr Hook   Capitol twelve-inch promo PSLP-314.   1978.   This three-track EP featured as the main track *When You're In Love With A Beautiful Woman.*

Odds and sods

Who Is Harry Kellerman And Why Is He Trying To Kill Me?   Soundtrack album. USA Columbia C-30791.   1972.   Dr Hook appeared in this Dustin Hoffman movie.

Duran Duran

British singles

Planet Earth   EMI twelve-inch promo one-sided PSLP-331.   1981.
Duran Duran Sampler.   EMI twelve-inch promo PSLP-344.   1981.   A four-track sampler from their first album.
My Own Way   Three versions.   EMI twelve-inch promo, number unknown.   1982.
Hungry Like The Wolf   EMI twelve-inch promo, number unknown.   1982.
Rio   Edited EMI   one sided promo EMI-5346.   1982.

American singles

Planet Earth/To The Shore   Harvest twelve-inch promo SPRO-9636.   1981.
Careless Memories   Both sides Harvest twelve-inch promo SPRO-9663.   1981.
Girls On Film   Club version/single version.   Harvest twelve-inch promo SPRO-9680.   1982.
Hungry Like The Wolf/Rio   Plus one other.   Harvest twelve-inch promo SPRO-9786.   1982.
Hungry Like The Wolf/Time/Lonely Nightmare   Harvest twelve-inch promo, number unknown.   1982.
Rio and two THOMAS DOLBY tracks.   Harvest twelve-inch promo SPRO-9862.   1982.

American albums

Duran Duran   Harvest ST-12158.   1981.   This was re-issued on Capitol records in 1983 with an extra track *Is There Something I Should Know.*
BBC *Rock Hour*   Number 328.   (Dated 11.7.82).   Recorded live at the Hammersmith Odeon.
NBC Source concert Radio Series, number unknown.   1982.

Odds and sods

The New British Invasion!   Canadian Capitol.   1982.   This four-track sampler EP featured Duran Duran, Thomas Dolby and others. It sold in stores for 39 cents.
Nite Romantics   EP Japan EMI-Toshiba twelve-inch.   1981.   The title track has yet to be released in Britain.
Union Of The Snake/Secret Oktober   Dutch EMI.   1983.   This came with a free flexi disc, more details as yet unknown.

Ian Dury

Dury was once a member of KILBURN AND THE HIGH ROADS who released one album for Dawn records in 1973 – *Handsome*.

British singles

Sex And Drugs And Rock 'n' Roll/England's Glory/Two Steep Hills   Stiff FREEBIE-1.   1978.   Awarded as a prize in an NME competition.
What A Waste/Wake Up Make Love With Me   Stiff twelve-inch promo BUY-2712.   1978.
Hit Me With Your Rhythm Stick/There Ain't Half Been Some Clever Bastards Stiff BUY-38.   1978.   A special re-mix was issued when the record reached Number One in early 1979. They made sure it was a limited edition, by pressing only one copy!
Reasons To Be Cheerful Part Three/Common As Muck   Stiff twelve-inch promo R12BUY-50.   1979.   The A side is the seven-inch mix.
·*I Want To Be Straight/That's Not All*   Stiff BUY-90.   1980.   There were two different picture sleeves for this. The first had a school badge on the front, while the second had a group photo.
Spasticus Autisticus   Disco mix.   Polydor promo twelve-inch DURYX-1. 1982.

British albums

New Boots And Panties Stiff SEEZG-4.   1979.   Re-issue.   This gold vinyl issue included *Sex And Drugs And Rock And Roll* which wasn't on the original copies.
Do It Yourself Stiff SEEZ-14.   1979.   Original promo copies came with a note explaining that the only track that radio stations could play before the album was released was *This Is What We Find*.
4000 Weeks Holiday Polydor white label cassette, no number.   1983.   This preview copy tape had some songs and mixes which didn't appear on the finished version released in early 1984.

American singles

Wake Up Make Love With Me/Billaricay Dickie Stiff twelve-inch promo SP-19. 1978.   The A side was originally specially re-mixed for America, but it did appear in Britain as the B side to *What A Waste*.
Hit Me With Your Rhythm Stick/There Ain't Half Been Some Clever Bastards Epic-Stiff twelve-inch promo AS-619.   1979.
. . . Rhythm Stick/. . . Clever Bastards Epic-Stiff AE7-1179.   1979.   Given away with the *Do It Yourself* album.

American albums

New Boots And Panties Stiff STF-002.   1978.   *Sex And Drugs . . .* was included on this American version and was heavily imported into the UK.
IAN DURY/ELO.   Modern Music Radio Series, number unknown.   1978.
BBC *Rock Hour* Radio Series, number 215.   (Dated April 1981).

Odds and sods

Live Stiffs Live   UK Stiff GET-1.   1979.   Has some live tracks.
Do It Yourself   Stiff records worldwide.   1979.   Issued in 27 different sleeves worldwide, including ten in Britain alone. This featured Crown wallpaper designs.
C 81   NME-Rough Trade cassette COPY-001.   1981.   This has the previously unreleased track *Close To Home*. British only release.
Concerts For Kampuchea   UK Atlantic K-60153.   1981.   More live tracks.
NME Dancing Master   UK NME cassette NME-001.   1981.   This has *The Inbetweenies* live.
Fundemental Frolics   UK BBC REB-435.   1981.   More live music.

Bob Dylan

American singles

As It Is Before/Time And Again
Death By Fire/To Care At All
Celebration For A Passage Of Time   One sided.
When You Were Full Of Wonder/Mad Lydia's Waltz
These four acetates were cut for demo purposes by Elektra records in 1961. All were red label seven-inch discs. Apparently Dylan sounds totally unlike his CBS recordings of a year later.
Other acetates from his CBS days exist with alternate takes, mixes and songs, etc.
Corrina Corrina/Mixed Up Confusion   Columbia 4-42656.   1963.   This was thought to have been withdrawn.
Blowing In The Wind   2:47 version/*Don't Think Twice*   Columbia promo JZSP-75606/7.   1964.
Subterranean Homesick Blues   Same both sides.   Columbia red vinyl promo 4-43242.   1965.   The promo also came with an extremely rare picture sleeve.
Like A Rolling Stone   Parts 1 and 2.   Columbia promo JZSP-110939.   1965.
Like A Rolling Stone   Same both sides.   Columbia red vinyl 4-43346.   1965.   This was also pressed up on blue vinyl promo.
Positively Fourth Street   Same both sides.   Columbia red vinyl promo 4-43389.   1966.
Can You Please Crawl Out Your Window   Columbia 4-43389.   1966.   Possibly a mispress as the same number was used on *Positively Fourth Street*.   B side unknown.
One Of Us Must Know   Long and short versions.   Columbia promo JZSP-11347.   1966.
Rainy Day Women Numbers 12 And 35   Same both sides.   Columbia red vinyl promo 4-43592.   1966.
I Want You   Same both sides.   Columbia red vinyl promo 4-43683.   1967.
Just Like A woman   Same both sides.   Columbia red vinyl promo 4-43792.   1967.
If Not For You/Tomorrow Is A Long Time   Columbia promo AE7-1039.   1971.
Tangled Up In Blue   Long and short versions.   Columbia promo 3-10106.   1975.

All The Tired Horses   Columbia promo AE-25.   1975.   This may have the same track on both sides.

Hurricane   Full version, mono and stereo versions.   Columbia promo 3-10245. 1975.

Hurricane   Mono and stereo versions.   Columbia promo 3-10245.   1975.   This single version 'part one' has a bleep in the appropriate place.

Baby Stop Crying   5:17 and 4:17 versions.   Columbia promo 3-10805.   1978.

Changing Of The Guards   6:36 and 3:39 versions.   Columbia promo 3-10851. 1978.

Four Songs From Renaldo And Clara   EP Columbia twelve-inch promo AS-422. 1978.   This has four live songs in their complete form, as opposed to edited versions in the film. Out of four-and-a-quarter hours of film, about eighty minutes is actually music. The rest consists of boring scenarios with the singers, players and roadies acting out a tedious story with no recognisable plot. There are still people who think Dylan is a genius – they have not seen this film.

You Gotta Serve Somebody   5:22 and 3:57 versions.   Columbia promo 1-11072. 1979.

Saved/Are You Ready/What Can I Do For You   Columbia twelve-inch promo AS-798.   1980.

Heart Of Mine/Shot Of Love/Trouble/Every Grain   Columbia twelve-inch promo AS-1263.   1981.

BOB DYLAN/CHER   *What's It All About?*   Radio Series number 3052.   c.1981.

BOB DYLAN/DAVID BOWIE   *What's It All About?*   Radio Series MA-1791.   1981.

Sweetheart Like You/Man Of Peace/I And I/Neighbourhood Bully   Columbia twelve-inch promo AS-1770.   1983.

American EP

Bringing It All Back Home   Columbia juke box issue 7-9128.   1965.

American albums

Nine-song publisher's sampler.   Warner Brothers 7-Arts publishing promo XTD-221567.   1963.   This is a one-sided album pressed by Columbia which featured demo versions of the following songs: *John Brown, Long Ago Far Away, Only A Hobo, Long Time Gone, Ain't Gonna Grieve, Death Of Emmett Till, I'll Keep It With Mine, I'd Hate To Be You On That Fateful Day* and *I Shall Be Free.*

The Freewheelin' Bob Dylan   Columbia mono CL-1986 and stereo CS-8786. 1963.

There are two extremely rare versions of this album in existence. The first was pressed by Columbia in California and included the songs *Rocks And Gravel, Let Me Die In My Footsteps, Gamblin' Willie's Dead Man's Hand* and *Talkin' John Birch Society Blues.*   300 copies were pressed and given to radio stations.

The East Coast pressing had the title *Solid Gravel* instead of *Rocks And Gravel. Talkin' John Birch Society Blues* was removed from the album by Columbia, fearing a lawsuit. Dylan himself deleted the other songs mentioned above.

Highway 61 Revisited   Columbia mono CL-2398.   1964.   This mono mix contained a shorter version of *It Takes A Lot To Laugh*. Plus an alternate version *From A Buick 6*.

Blonde On Blonde Columbia mono C2L-41. 1966. This mono mix is radically different to the stereo mix.

Bob Dylan vs. A. J. Webberman, The Historic Confrontation Folkways FB-5322. c.1971. This album featured an interview cum argument conducted over the phone. Dylan quickly had the album withdrawn.

The Story Of Bob Dylan BBC/London Wavelength open reel radio show from 1973.

Planet Waves Ashes And Sands Records 7E-501. 1973. This was to be his own label, but the album eventually turned up on the label's distributors Asylum Records.

With THE BAND *Before The Flood* Island IDBD-1. 1974. An export issue made for Britain.

Planet Waves Quad mix Asylum EQ-1001. 1974.

Nashville Skyline Quad mix Columbia CQ-32872. 1974. This is supposed to be very different to the original stereo mix.

Blood On The Tracks Columbia PC-33235. 1975. There are three different back covers. The first had liner notes by Pete Hamill, with incorrect personnel credits. This was then replaced by a drawing which filled up the entire back cover. By now, however, Hamill had won a Grammy for best liner notes of 1975, so the first version of the sleeve was re-instated, but this time with white lettering instead of black.

Desire Quad mix Columbia PCQ-33892. 1976.

Bob Dylan And The Rolling Thunder Revue. Rock Around The World Radio Series, number 91. (Dated 2.5.76).

A Musical Biography. Rock And Religion Radio Series. 1979. A two-album set. Side one: *Protest Years 1961-1964*. Side two: *Prophet 1964-1973*. Side three: *Karmic Dylan*. Side four: *The New Bob Dylan 1979*. Twenty-five songs plus interviews, etc.

The London Interview, July 1981 Columbia promo AS-1259. 1981. Recorded for WNEW-FM in New York.

Electric Lunch Columbia promo AS-1471. 1982. This is an eight-track promotion sampler for *Planet Waves* and *Before The Flood* to which Columbia had acquired the rights from Asylum in 1982.

BOB DYLAN/GRATEFUL DEAD *Royalty Of Rock* Radio Series made by TM Special Products.

British singles

Leopard Skin Pillbox Hat/Most Likely CBS 202700. 1966. A very rare picture sleeve came with the first few copies. Picture sleeves are thought to exist with some of his other '60s singles: *Can You Please Crawl Out Of Your Window, One Of Us Must Know, Rainy Day Women* and *I Want You*.

Hurricane Edited and bleeped CBS promo 3878-DJ. 1975.

Changing Of The Guard 6:36 and 3:39 versions. CBS promo 6895-DJ. 1978.

Forever Young 5:27 and 4:25 versions. CBS promo 7473-DJ. 1980.
Jokerman Long and short versions. CBS promo A-4055-DJ. 1983.

British albums

Blonde On Blonde Mono mix CBS DDP-66012. 1966. This is the same mono mix as the American. It also has a different photo spread in the middle to the stereo.
Desire Quad mix CBS Q-86003. 1976.

Odds and sods

Broadside USA Folkways FR-5315. 1963. This has two tracks by Dylan using the alias Blind Boy Grunt.
Broadside Ballads USA Folkways BR-5301. 1963. Two more by Blind Boy Grunt.
Washington Rights March USA Broadside BR-592. 1963. Two live tracks by Dylan using his own name.
Hurricane/Knocking On Heavens Door/Main Theme/Blowing In The Wind/Interview. Austrian CBS flexi, number unknown. Date unknown.
Zenith Salutes The Teen Sound Album USA Columbia Special Products SP-223. c.1966. This has an alternate mix of *Pledging My Time*.
The World Of Folk Music USA Warner promo album, number unknown. c.1964. This has a Dylan interview as well as *North Country Girl* and *Only A Hobo*.
Newport Broadside UK Fontana TL-6038. 1965. Live tracks.
Newport Folk Festival Evening Concert, Volume One UK Fontana TL-6041. 1965. Live tracks.
Concert For Bangla Desh Album UK Apple STCX-3385. 1971. More live material.
Bob Dylan In Concerto A twelve-inch disc given away with the Italian magazine *Gong*, number 5A/6B, in 1976. It features poorly-recorded live versions of *Just Like A Woman, Simple Twist Of Fate, Knocking On Heaven's Door* and others recorded in 1975.
The Last Waltz UK Warner K-66016. 1978.

The Eagles

American singles

Lyin' Eyes Long and short versions. Asylum promo E-45279. 1975.
THE EAGLES/LYNN ANDERSON *What's It All About!* Radio Series 186. c.1976.
Please Come Home For Christmas/Funky New Year Asylum twelve-inch promo AS-11402. 1977.
THE EAGLES/KOOL AND THE GANG *What's It All About?* Radio Series 256. c.1978.

7-inch Promo-only items
Top (left to right) ROLLING STONES *Let It Rock;* PINK FLOYD *Comfortably Numb.* Middle (left to right) GENESIS *Turn It On Again;* TOM PETTY *Straight Into Darkness.* Bottom (left to right) PAUL McCARTNEY *Band On The Run;* NEIL YOUNG *Time Fades Away* EP.

THE EAGLES/KRIS KRISTOFFERSON *What's It All About?* Radio Series MA-1505. c.1979.

American albums

On The Border Quad mix. Asylum EQ-1004. 1975.
One Of These Nights Quad mix. Asylum EQ-1039. 1975.
A Conversation With The Eagles. King Biscuit Radio Series. Number unknown. c.1980. A five-album set.
Greatest Hits Volume Two Asylum. 1981. It was announced in Billboard that this album would feature two previously unreleased songs. By the time the album was eventually released in 1982 it only had one new song, *After The Thrill Is Gone*.
Innerview Radio Series. Series 18, programmes 8 & 9. Date unknown.

British album

Desparado Asylum K-53003. 1982. This is a special audiophile pressing made by Nimbus and distributed by mail order through *Hi-Fi Today* magazine.

Echo and The Bunnymen

British singles

Pictures On My Wall/Read It In Books Zoo CAGE-004. 1979. Their first single which as yet has not been re-released.
Do It Clean Karova twelve-inch promo, number unknown. 1981.
Do It Clean/Read It In Books Karova SAM-128. 1980. This was given away with later copies of the *Crocodiles* album. Those who didn't get it the first time could get theirs by sending 20p to WEA to cover postage.
Crocodiles Long and short versions. Karova promo ECHO-1. 1981. Taken from the *Shine So Hard* EP.
JOHN PEEL *Session* 1979. Karova cassette, number unknown. 1982. This came with *The Cutter* single bought at chart return shops.

Odds and sods

Urghh A Music War UK A & M AMLX-64692. 1981. Live tracks.

Duane Eddy

American albums

Lonesome Road/I Almost Lost My Mind Jamie juke box issue JLP-71.
Loving You/Anything Jamie juke box issue JLP-72.
Peter Gunn/All Along The Navajo Trail Jamie juke box JLP-73.
Hard Times/Along Came Linda Jamie juke box JLP-74.

The Battle/You Are My Sunshine Jamie juke box JLP-75.

These were all stereo 33 rpm juke box singles made in the early '60s.

SANFORD CLARK AND DUANE EDDY *Sing 'Em Some Blues* Jamie J-1107. c.1962.
Eddy only appears on one side of this single.

American EP's
Twangin' The Golden Hits RCA juke box issue VLP-2993. 1963.
Guitar Man RCA-Wurlitzer juke box issue WLP-1100. 1963.

American albums
Songs From Our Heritage Jamie JLP-703011. 1961. Initial copies came in red
vinyl with a gatefold sleeve and a poster.
Duane Eddy In Person Jamie-Capitol Record Club ST-90663. c.1964.
The Twang's The Thang Jamie-Capitol Record Club ST-91301. c.1965.

Dave Edmunds

Dave Edmunds appeared in at least three recording bands before going solo: THE
IMAGE, THE HUMAN BEINGS, and most famous, LOVE SCULPTURE.

THE IMAGE *Come To The Party/Never Let Me Go* Parlophone R-5281. 1965.
THE IMAGE *Home Is Anywhere/I Hear Your Voice Again* Parlophone R-5352.
1965.
THE IMAGE *Let's Make The Scene/I Can't Stop Myself* Parlophone R-5442. 1966.
THE HUMAN BEINGS *Morning Dew/It's A Wonder* Columbia DB-8230. 1967.

Love Sculpture
Singles
These were UK singles unless specified.

River To Another Day/Brand New Woman Parlophone R-5664. 1967.
Wang Dang Doodle/The Stumble Parlophone R-5731. 1968.
Sabre Dance/Think Of Love Parlophone R-5744. 1968. Also released in the
USA on Parrot PAR-335.
Seagull/Farandole Parlophone R-5807. 1968.
In The Land Of The Few/Farandole Parlophone R-5831. 1969. Also on USA
Parrot PAR-342.

Albums
These were UK albums unless specified.
Blues Helping Parlophone PMC-7059 mono, PCS-7059 stereo. 1968. American
Rare Earth RS-505 in 1969.
Forms And Feelings Parlophone PCS-7090 stereo only. 1969. Also USA Parrot
PAS-71035.

Recordings under Dave Edmund's own name and with Rockpile are as below.

British singles

Live At The Venue EP Arista JUKE-1. 1982. Given with the *DE 7th* album.
*Run Run Rudolph/*STING *Tutti Frutti* A & M promo PARTY-2. 1982. Taken from the *Party Party* six pack soundtrack.

American singles

*Run Rudolph Run/*CHAS & DAVE *Auld Lang Syne* A & M twelve-inch promo, number unknown. 1982. Taken from the *Party Party* soundtrack.
Information Columbia one-sided promo, twelve-inch picture disc AS-99-1725. 1983.

British album

Rockpile Collection Regal-Zonophone SRZA-8503. 1971. Withdrawn. Replaced by *Dave Edmunds' Rockpile* SRLZ-1026. The first version may have come in a gatefold sleeve. It's possible that the track listing is the same.

American albums

College Radio Network Presents Dave Edmunds Swansong promo PR-320. 1978. Includes an interview as well as live version of *I Hear You Knocking*. Beware of counterfeits.
DAVE EDMUNDS/DWIGHT TWILLEY BAND King Biscuit Radio Series (Dated 27.6.82). BBC *Rock Hour* Number 347. 1982.
Information Columbia promo picture disc, number unknown. 1983.
BBC *Rock Hour* Number unknown. 1983. Recorded at Uncle Sam's, somewhere in Massachusetts.

Odds and sods

JILL READ *Maybe/Wang Dang Doodle* UK Parlophone, number unknown. 1969. Possibly Edmunds using an alias. *Maybe* turned up in stereo on *Bunch Of Stiffs* compilation album. The single was given a full re-release by Dutch Stiff in 1978.
Christmas At The Patti UK United Artists UDX-205/6. 1973. A double ten inch compilation recorded live in Swansea 1972. It features *Run Run Rudolph* live.
Stardust UK Ronco/US Arista. 1975. This double album features Dave Edmunds and the film's fictional band The Stray Cats as well as The Electricians (also known as Brinsley Schwarz).
A Bunch Of Stiffs UK Stiff SEEZ-2. 1978. Not only featuring the Jill Read track, but a solo version of *Jo Jo Gunne* from 1968.
Pebbles, Volume 4 Australian BFD Records. 1979. This is a surfing anthology which has an excellent Edmunds' track, *London's A Lonely Town,* featuring Jan Berry and Brian Wilson, recorded at Rockfield in 1976. This has not appeared anywhere else. The Beach Boys managed to get this album withdrawn from sale in 1981 because they were included without their permission.
CARLENE CARTER AND DAVE EDMUNDS *Baby Ride Easy* UK F Beat single XX-8. 1980. Edmunds is only on the A side.

Party Party Soundtrack album. UK A & M AMLH-68551. 1983. This has a studio version of *Run Run Rudolph*.

Theme From Saturday Superstore UK BBC single. 1983. Has Edmunds on vocals, and is seen on the sleeve.

Electric Light Orchestra

British singles

Livin' Thing/Fire On High United Artists UP-36184. 1976. A very limited edition in blue vinyl.

Showroom/Roll Over Beethoven Harvest twelve-inch promo PSLP-213. 1977. This was later given a full release in 1978 as Harvest 12HAR-5179.

Can't Get It Out Of My Head/Evil Woman Jet juke box issue ELO-1JB. 1977.

Strange Magic/Ma Ma Ma Belle Jet juke box single ELO-2JB. 1977. The two singles above were taken from a four-track seven-inch EP.

British albums

The Lost Planet Harvest. 1973. This album was announced, but actually turned up as *ELO II*.

On The Third Day Warner K-56021. 1974. This issue had a gatefold sleeve with a square cut out in the middle of the front cover revealing a photo of Jeff Lynne. When it was re-issued by Jet Records in 1977 it came in the white American cover.

Electric Light Orchestra Quad mix Harvest Q4SHVL-797. 1974.

Ole Elo Jet JETLP-19. 1976. It's probable that this version of the album was withdrawn; American copies brought over as imports were replaced by Dutch copies carrying the JETLP-19 number.

Out Of The Blue Jet UAR-100. 1977. There are two different blue vinyl pressings of this: one is light, clear blue while the other is a heavier, darker blue.

Secret Messages Jet cassette JETCX-527. 1983. This tape version has a sticker on the case claiming to have an extra track, but it doesn't actually say what it is.

In addition, there have been two album boxed sets:

Three Light Years Jet JETBX-1. 1978. This contains the albums *On The Third Day, Eldorado* and *Face The Music*.

Four Light Years Jet JETBX-2. 1980. A four-album box with *New World Record, Out Of The Blue* (double album) and *Discovery*. Also included was a seven-inch single of Jeff Lynne's *Doin' That Crazy Thing*.

American singles

Living Thing Jet one-sided twelve-inch promo blue vinyl SP-137. 1976.

Mr Blue Sky Jet twelve-inch promo AS-474. 1978.

It's Over Long and short versions. Jet promo ZS8-5052. 1978.

Hold On Tight/Time Medley. Jet twelve-inch promo AS-1252. 1981.

Twilight Same both sides. Jet twelve-inch promo AS-1319. 1981.

Secret Messages/B side unknown.   Jet twelve-inch promo AS-1736. 1983.

American albums

No Answer United Artists UAS-5573. 1972. The American version of the first album.
Ole ELO Jet-United Artists gold vinyl promo SP-123. 1976.
A Box Of Their Best Jet BZ-35531. 1980. The same as the UK *Four Light Years*, including the Jeff Lynne single as a twelve-inch.
Both Sides Of ELO American Forces Radio and Television Service P-17179. Date unknown.
ELO/IAN DURY *Modern Music* Radio Series. 1978.
ELO/MOODY BLUES *Sounds Of Solid Gold* Number 35. 1982.
ABC *Spotlight Special* Radio Series. Date unknown.

Odds and sods

Nightbird & Co.   Radio Series, number 297/300.   Date unknown.   This double album set had one side of ELO music and chat.
The Night The Light Went Out In Long Beach Germany Warner WBK-56058. A live set from 1974.
Eldorado USA CBS Masterworks audiophile. 1981.
Discovery USA CBS Masterworks audiophile HZ-45769. 1981.
Greatest Hits USA CBS Masterworks audiophile HZ-46310. 1981.
Time Japan CBS audiophile 30AP-2263. 1981.

Emerson Lake and Palmer – ELP

British single

Brain Salad Surgery/Excerpts from the *Brain Salad Surgery* album.   NME Manticore LYN-2762, pressed by Lyntone. A flexi given with the *NME* in 1974.

British album

Works, Volume One Atlantic promo, number unknown. 1976. Contains re-mixes and edited highlights.

American singles

Take A Pebble/Lucky Man Cotillion promo PR-176. 1971.
Lucky Man Long and short versions in mono. Cotillion promo 44106. 1971.
Lucky Man Long and short versions in stereo. Cotillion promo 44106. 1971.
Brain Salad Surgery/Still You Turn Me On Manticore promo 2003PR. 1974.
Tiger In A Spotlight Long and short versions. Atlantic promo 3641. 1976.

American albums

Trilogy Cotillion-Capitol Record Club issue SMAS-94773. c.1973.

Works Edited highlights.   Atlantic promo PR-271.   1977.

Superstars Radio Network Present ELP On Tour Atlantic promo PR-281.   1977.

Rock Around The World Radio Series, number 163.   (Dated 3.10.77).

Retrorock Radio Series (Dated Aug. 1981).

ELP/YES *Retrorock* Radio Series (Dated 13.9.82).

Odds and sods

Mar Y Sol Soundtrack album.   USA Atco SD2-705.   1972.   This features ELP playing live at the Puerto Rico pop festival.

Pictures At An Exhibition   Japan Mobile Fidelity audiophile pressing MFSL-1-031.   1980.

Works Sampler.   German Ariola double promo EP, number unknown.   1977.

John Entwistle

British singles

I Wonder/Made In Japan Track 2094 107.   1973.   This may have been withdrawn and replaced by *Made In Japan/Hound Dog* Track 2094 107.

British album

The Ox Track 2404 014 (Backtrack 14).   1970.   Not actually credited to Entwistle, this is a collection of his songs with The Who.

American single

Too Late The Hero/Dancin' Master Atco twelve-inch promo PR-398.   1981.

American albums

Who's Ox MCA promo LL-1926.   c.1974.   A compilation sampler.

Hot News Radio Series (Dated July 1981).

John Entwistle and Roger Glover Guest DJ's on Rolling Stone magazine Radio Series.   1981.   A three-album set.

Odds and sods

Flash Fearless . . . UK Chrysalis CHR-1081.   1975.   Entwistle plays on this album.

The Everly Brothers

American singles

The Sun Keeps Shining/Keep A Loving Me Columbia 21496.   c.1956.   Their first single is also their rarest.

Walk Right Back/Ebony Eyes Warner yellow vinyl promo 5199.   1961.   This also came with a rare picture sleeve.

Pass The Chicken And Listen Interview single RCA promo SP45-409.   1971.

American EP's

Rockin' With The Everly Brothers   Cadence juke box EP LLP-3.   c.1960.
Dream With The Everly Brothers   Cadence juke box issue LLP-4.   c.1960.
The Everly Brothers Golden Hits   Warner juke box issue EB-1471.   1962.
Souvenir sampler.   Warner promo PRO-135.   c.1968.   This has excerpts from ten songs plus an interview.
The Everly Brothers show   Warner juke box issue LLP-120/EB-1858.   1970.

American albums

A Date With The Everly Brothers   Warner WS-1395.   1961.   The original packaging has a gatefold sleeve with photo inserts.
Both Sides Of An Evening   Sampler.   Warner ten-inch promo PRO-134.   1962.
The Very Best Of The Everly Brothers   Warner-Capitol Record Club ST-91343.   c.1965.
The Everly Brothers Show   Warner-Capitol Record Club STBO-93286.   c.1970.

British singles

Lighting Express/I'm Here To Get My Baby Out Of Jail   London.   1962.   This was withdrawn, although test pressings may exist.
Cathy's Clown/Always It's You   Warner WB-1.   1960.   This was the only Warner Brothers 78 rpm single in Britain, albeit in a very limited run.
You're Just The Lady I Was Looking For/Whatever Happened to Judy?   Lightning BONUS-1.   1980.   This was the freebie single which came with the *Everly Brothers Single Set*   SET-1, which featured fifteen singles in new picture sleeves complete with a book and discography.

Odds and sods

The Everly's singing a Coca Cola jingle was featured on a German EP made for that company and included other artists.   c.1963.
The Bitter End Years   US Roxbury RX3-300.   1977.   A triple-album collection of artists who made live appearances at this New York coffee house over the years.
November 9th 1955   Dutch CBS Special Products, made for Bear Family Records, twelve-inch BFE-15075.   1981.   An EP with the four songs they recorded for Columbia *Keep A Lovin' Me/The Sun Keeps A Shinin/If Her Love Isn't True/That's The Life I Lead.*
PHIL EVERLY   *Ich Bin Dein (I Am Yours* sung in German)*/Don't Feel Like Dancing*   German Elektra ELK-12381.   1977.

The Faces

British singles

Dishevelment Blues/Ooh La La   Sampler.   Warner-Sound For Industry SFI-139. 1973.   A flexi given with the *NME* in April 1973.
*Borstal Boys/*B side unknown.   Warner K-16281.   1973.   Withdrawn.

British album

Coast To Coast   Disc version Mercury 9100 001.   Cassette version Warner K4-56027.   1974.   Separate label deals for The Faces and Rod Stewart led this confusing release.

American singles

The Faces' first two American singles were credited to THE SMALL FACES.
Around The Plynth/Wicked Messenger   Warner 7393.   1969.
Had Me A Real Good Time/Rear Wheel Skid   Warner 7442.   1970.
Had Me A Real Good Time   3:59 and 2:50 versions.   Warner promo 7442.   1970.

American album

Coast To Coast   Disc version Mercury SRM 1-697.   Cassette version Warner 2752.   1974.

Odds and sods

Reading Festival '73   UK GM records GML-1008.   1973.   This featured a live version of *I Wish It Would Rain*.

Georgie Fame

British singles

THE BLUE FLAMES   *J. A. Blues/Orange Street*   R & B Records JB-114.   1964.
THE BLUE FLAMES   *Stop Right Here/Rik's Tune*   R & B Records JB-126.   1964.
These two are rarer than rare, being London area independent pressings.
Getaway   One-sided promo of the original Esso petrol commercial made in 1964 for pirate radio and 208-Luxembourg.
Daylight   Island one-sided twelve-inch promo IDJ-25.   1976.

American EP

The Ballad Of Bonnie And Clyde   Epic juke box issue ST5-26368.   1968.

The Georgie Fame who recorded for Chancellor Records in America in the early '60s is nothing to do with Clive Powell's alias.

Brian Ferry

Before Ferry joined Roxy Music he was in a band called THE BANSHEES who released three singles for Columbia in the UK:
Don't Say Goodnight/I Got A Woman   Columbia DB-7361.   1964.
Big Building/Mockingbird   Columbia DB-7530.   1965.
Yes Indeed/I'm Gonna Keep On Loving You   Columbia DB-7752.   1965.

British singles

A Hard Rain's Gonna Fall Edited Island one-sided promo WIP-6170-DJ. 1973.
These Foolish Things Sampler EP Island promo, number unknown. 1973.
The Price Of Love Island one-sided promo IEP-1-DJ. 1976.
The Price Of Love/Shame Shame Shame Island promo, number unknown.
1976. Also used for juke boxes.
Hold On I'm Coming/Take Me To The River Polydor twelve-inch promo
PPSP-10. 1978.

Ferry appears on one soundtrack album:
All This And World War Two UK Riva/USA 20th Century Fox. 1976.

Flamin' Groovies

American albums

Sneakers Snazz Records R-2371. 1968. This ten-inch album was limited to 2,000
only. It has been counterfeited.
The Flamin' Groovies Now! Sire SRK-6059. 1977. This version has *Blue Turns
To Grey* and *Paint It Black* which aren't on the British version.
Jumpin' In The Night Sire SRK-6067. 1978. Again, more non-UK tracks,
Werewolves Of London and *It Won't Be Wrong*.

British albums

The Flamin' Groovies Now! Sire 9103 333. 1977. This is the original Phonogram
pressing. The WEA pressed re-issue of 1978 not only added two tracks *Blue Turns
To Grey* and *When I Heard Your Name,* but gave the album a new sleeve.

Odds and sods

ROGER RUSKIN SPEAR *Electric Shocks* UK United Artists UAG-29381. c.1973.
This album features The Groovies on several tracks.
River Deep Mountain High/So Much In Love French Underdog-Carrere 49-785.
1981. This is probably their only legal release that hasn't appeared in Britain or
America. There are also three singles on Skydog Records from France, but due to
their inclusion in the *Bootleg Bible* their legality is doubtful.

Fleetwood Mac

British album

Then Play On Reprise RSLP-9001. 1970. Originally intended for release on
Apple Records. When the album was finally released, it came with a gatefold cover
with a drawing of a centaur taking up most of the front gatefold. The album titles
were relegated to half the back cover. When the album was re-issued by WEA it was

reduced to a single sleeve with white titles on a black background.

American singles

Albatross/THE GUN   *Race With The Devil*   Epic promo JZSP-139213/JZSP-139609.   1968.   Possibly on red vinyl.

For Your Love 3:44 and 3:10 versions.   Reprise promo RPS-1188.   1973.

Go Your Own Way/Silver Springs Warner twelve-inch promo PROA-652. 1977.

Tusk/Never Make Me Cry Mono and stereo versions of both.   Warner twelve-inch promo PROA-831.   1979.

Sara Edited mono and stereo versions.   Warner twelve-inch promo PROA-845. 1979.

FLEETWOOD MAC/THE OUTLAWS   *What's It All About?*   Radio Series MA-1176. c.1980.

Think About Me Same both sides.   Warner twelve-inch promo PROA-853. 1980.

Fireflies   Re-mix.   4:05 and 3:32 versions.   Warner twelve-inch promo PROA-932. 1980.

Sisters Of The Moon 4:40 and 4:14 versions.   Warner promo WBS-49500. 1981.

Hold Me Same both sides.   Warner twelve-inch promo PROA-1040.   1982.

American albums

Then Play On Reprise RS-6368. 1970. The album was re-issued shortly after with *Oh Well* replacing two tracks.

Tusk Re-mix sampler.   Warner promo PROA-866.   1979.

Robert W. Morgan Radio Series. Part one with fifteen songs.   Part two with twenty-two songs. 1979.

Innerview Radio Series.   More details are unknown.

FLEETWOOD MAC/NICK MASON   BBC *Rock Hour* Radio Series number 230.   1980.

Westwood One Radio Series (Dated 30.8.82 and Sept. 1982).

FLEETWOOD MAC/PAUL ANKA *Sounds Of Solid Gold* Radio Series, No. 19. 1982.

Westwood One Radio Series.   1983.   A three album live set recorded in Los Angeles in 1982.

Odds and sods

OTIS SPANN & FLEETWOOD MAC   *Walkin'/Temperature Is Risin' 98.8*   UK Blue Horizon 57-3155.   1969.

Rumours Nautilus audiophile pressing.   1981.   Pressed in America.

Fleetwood Mac Japan Mobile Fidelity audiophile pressing MFSL-1-012.   1981.

They have also appeared on many other artists' records including John Mayall, Eddie Boyd and Clifford Davis (their manager), among others.

Flo and Eddie

American singles

The Fluorescent Leech And Eddie Radio sports EP.   Reprise promo PRO-333. 1972.

Feel Older Now   Same both sides.   Reprise promo RPS-112.   1972.   This only appeared as a promo, and then only in the Detroit area.
Flo And Eddie Meet The Wolfman/Carlos The Bull   Reprise promo PRO-564. 1975.
Let Me Make Love To You/Come To My Rescue   Columbia 3-10028.   1976.   This was re-issued on Columbia 3-10204.

American albums
Flo And Eddie Interview Barry Mann   RCA promo DJL 1-1162.   c.1973.   This was made to promote Mann's *Survivor* album.

Flo and Eddie also take up one side of a US Navy Broadcasting Service double album along with *The Movies, New Riders Of The Purple Sage,* and one other. c.1976.

Foreigner

American singles
Blue Morning, Blue Day   Mono and stereo versions.   Atlantic blue vinyl promo 3543.   1979.
Urgent   Same both sides.   Atlantic twelve-inch promo PR-393.   1979.
Waiting For A Girl Like You   Same both sides.   Atlantic twelve-inch promo PR-406.   1981.
Head Games   Same both sides.   Atlantic twelve-inch promo PR-440.   1981.
Break It Up   4:13 and 3:14 versions.   Atlantic promo 4044.   1981.

American albums
Rock Around The World   Radio series, number 160.   (Dated 12.9.77).
King Biscuit Radio series   (Dated 30.3.80).
Innerview   Radio Series. Series 9, programme 12.   c.1980.
Robert W. Morgan   *Profiles In Rock*   Radio Series   (Dated 28.6.80).
The Best of Biscuit   Radio Series   (Dated 4.1.81).
NBC *Source*   (Dated June 1981).
Westwood One Radio Series.   1982.
NBC *Source*   Radio Series   (Dated April 1982).
FOREIGNER/UFO   King Biscuit   (Dated 15.8.82).

Odds and sods
Double Vision   Japan Mobile Fidelity audiophile pressing MFSL 1-152.   1982.

The Four Seasons

This group made many recordings under other names before becoming The Four Seasons. American only noted.

The Four Lovers

You're The Apple Of My Eye/The Girl In My Dreams   RCA 47-6518.   c.1956.
Honey Love/Please Don't Leave Me   RCA 47-6519.   1956.
Jumbalaya/Be Lovey Dovey   RCA 47-6646.   1956.
Happy Am I/Never Never   RCA 47-6768.   1957.
The Stranger/Night Train   RCA 47-6819.   1957.
My Life For Your Love/Pucker Up   Epic 5-9255.   1957.

The following three are among the rarest rock 'n' roll records ever made. So few copies were made it's a wonder why they were released in the first place.

THE VILLAGE VOICES   *Redlips/Too Young To Start*   Topix 45-6000-V.
BILLY DIXON AND THE TOPICS   *I Am All Alone*   More details are unknown.
THE TOPICS   *The Girl In My Dream*   More details are unknown.

American singles
The Four Seasons

Bermuda/Spanish Lace   Gone 45-5122.   1960.
I'm Still In Love With You/That's The Way The Ball Bounces   Alanna 555.   1960.
Love Knows No Season/Hot Water Bottle   Alanna 558.   1960.
Don't Sweat It Baby/That's The Way   JB Records 464.   c.1961.

All the above are pre-Vee-Jay singles and are, to say the least, rare.

Things Go Better With Coke   McCain-Erikson advertising agency.
The Jingle Single   Magic Carpet EP-502.
Joey Reynolds Theme   Wibbage WXYZ-121003.
Some Of The Best Music Makers   and Coke advert.   Music Maker.
Paflik Shoe Advert   BBD & O advertising agency.
All the above were radio station ad's made in the mid-1960s.

The Wonder Who

Peanuts/My Sugar   Vee Jay 717.   1964.
Don't Think Twice/Sassy   Philips 40324.   1966.
Good Ship Lollipop/You're Nobody   Philips 40380.   1966.
Lonesome Road/Seasons Around   Philips 40471.   1966.

These singles were made under a pseudonym and feature Frankie Valli singing in a style similar to The Newbeats' *Bread And Butter*.

American EP's
The Four Lovers

The Four Seasons   RCA EPA-869.   1957.

Joyride RCA EPA-871. 1957.
Shake A Hand and *Stranger/*TEDDY KING Two songs. RCA promo DJ-64. 1957.

The Four Seasons

Genuine Imitation Life Gazette Philips juke box PL-2704. 1966.
Edizione D'Oro Philips juke box PL-2705. 1967.
Golden Vault Of Hits Philips juke box PL-810. 1968.

American albums

THE FOUR LOVERS *Joyride* RCA LPM-1317. 1957. In 1984, a £150 item!
THE FOUR SEASONS *Folknanny* Vee Jay LP-1082. 1963. This was later re-titled
Stay And Other Great Hits.
Who Loves You? Excerpts/CAT STEVENS *Numbers* Excerpts. American Forces
Radio & TV Services P-15690. 1975.
Who Loves You? Warner-Curb Records BS-2900. 1975. The original sleeve
showed a girl dancing on somebody's hand. Since nobody liked that one, they
changed it to a black sleeve with graphics.

British singles

*Stay/*B side unknown. Stateside export issue, number unknown. 1963.
Bye Bye Baby/Searching Wind Philips BF-1395. 1966. Due to an error while
mastering, a backwards tape noise appears in the middle of the A side. (This is not
The Four Seasons experimenting with psychedelia).
Whatever You Say/Sleeping Man Warner K-16107. 1971. Legend has it only
400 copies were made, although I don't know if this includes the promos.

British EP's

Hits Of The Four Seasons Philips cassette MCP-1000. 1968.
The Four Seasons Story Sampler. Private Stock EP PVT-50-DJ. 1976.

Odds and sods

WADE FLEMMONS *When It Rains It Pours* USA Vee Jay 578. 1964.
THE KOKOMOS *No Lies* USA Josie 906. c.1964.
THE FOUR SEASONS Sing backing vocals on both of these. They probably did plenty
of others.

Free

British singles

Broad Daylight/The Worm Island WIP-6054. 1969.
I'll Be Creeping/Sugar For Mr Morrison Island WIP-6062. 1969. Their first
two singles didn't sell so are now much sought after. *I'll Be Creeping* came with a
picture bag, making it even more sought after.
All Right Now/Mouthful Of Grass Island WIP-6082. This has three different
label designs. The first issue in 1970 has the pink label with a white 'I' on the left.

The 1974 re-issue has the white label with a pink rim and the word 'Island', in the form of an island, at the bottom. The third 1978 re-issue has an orange and blue label.

All Right Now/B side unknown.   Island juke box issue IEPJB-6.   1978.
All Right Now   (4:15 version)   Island one-sided promo IEP-6-DJ.   1978.

British album

The Free Story   Island ISLD-7.   1974.   A limited run of 5,000 numbered copies complete with a four-page leaflet. The cassette version is still on catalogue.

American singles

The Stealer/Broad Daylight   A & M 1230.   1971.
The Stealer/Lying In The Sunshine   A & M 1230.   1971.
Two different B sides for the same single:
All Right Now   (3:30 version)/*The Stealer*   (3:13 version)   A & M 1720.   1975.
All Right Now   (4:14 version)/*The Stealer*   (2:30 version)   A & M-Forget Me Nots 8550.   c.1975.   Yet more edits.

Billy Fury

British singles

Hippy Hippy Shake/Glad All Over   Decca export issue F-40719.   1964.
Silly Boy Blue/One Minute Woman   Parlophone R-5681.   1968.   The A side is a rare David Bowie composition.
Devil Or Angel   Polydor POSP-528.   1982.   This single is the original mix with orchestra.
The single was re-released shortly after his death with a new mix, without the strings, which Billy didn't like in the first place.
Devil Or Angel   Polydor-Fury flexi BF-001.   1983.   Mix unknown.
Two-track sampler   From the *We Want Billy* album (tracks unknown).   Decca twelve-inch promo, number unknown.   1983.

British album

The Sound Of Fury   Decca ten-inch album LF-1329.   1959.   His first album which is still in demand over twenty years after it's first release. Decca re-issued the album with its original packaging in 1981. This time they changed the number to LFT-1329.
Echoes Radio Show Interview With Stuart Colman   Polydor ten-inch promo, number unknown.   1982.

Odds and sods

Discs A Go Go   UK Decca DFE-8520.   1963.   This compilation EP features one previously unreleased Fury track *Don't Walk Away*.

Fourteen New Recordings   UK Decca LK-4695.   1964.   Includes one new Fury track *This Diamond Ring.*
That'll Be The Day   UK Ronco MR-2002/3.   1973.   This soundtrack double album features his version of Pete Townshend's *Long Live Rock.*
Heroes And Villains   UK Dakota OTA-1001.   1983.   This charity album has some live songs.

Peter Gabriel

British singles

Solsbury Hill   Same both sides.   Charisma CB-301.   1977.   It's unusual to find a British promo in this form.
Modern Love/Slowburn   Charisma CB-302.   1977.   Promo copies came with a photo label showing a naked woman. Regular copies came with normal silver plastic labels.
Solsbury Hill   Charisma one-sided flexi SFI-381.   1978.   This live version, recorded in New York, was a concert freebie.
Biko   Edited/*Shosholoza*   Charisma promo and juke box issue CBDJ-370.   1979.
Games Without Frontiers   (single version)/*Family Snapshot*   (sung in German). Charisma white label twelve-inch GAB-112.   1983.   This was given away with some copies of the *I Don't Remember* twelve-inch.
Peter Gabriel Plays Live   Sampler EP.   Charisma twelve-inch promo RAD-10.   1983.

British album

Peter Gabriel Plays Live   and TONY BANKS   *The Fugitive*   Sampler album. Charisma promo white label REP-1.   1983.

American singles

D.I.Y.   Same both sides.   Atlantic twelve-inch promo PR-310.   1978.
I Don't Remember/And Through The Wire   Mercury twelve-inch promo MK-157.   1979.
Shock The Monkey/I Have The Touch/Kiss Of Life   Geffen twelve-inch promo PROA-1062.   1983.

American albums

Security   Geffen promo Quiex II pure vinyl pressing GHS-2011.   1982.   Interview and music from *Security* Geffen promo cassette WBMS-124.   1982.
Peter Gabriel Plays Live   Geffen promo Quiex II pure vinyl pressing, number unknown.   1983.

German singles

Speil Ohne Grenzen (Games Without Frontiers) Edited/The Start/I Don't Remember   (in English).   Charisma 6000 448.   1979.

Rare Picture Sleeves
Top PHIL COLLINS *In The Air Tonight* (fold-out).   Middle (left to right) SEX PISTOLS
Credit Card; TODD RUNDGREN *Band The Drum All Day*.   Bottom (left to right) SQUEEZE
Packet of Three; GODLEY & CREME *Under Your Thumb*.

Schock Den Affen (Shock The Monkey)/Soft Dog   Charisma 6000 876.   1982.
Both are short versions.

German albums

Peter Gabriel, Ein Deutsches Album (Third album).   Charisma 6302 035.   1979.
The entire third album is in German with some re-mixes.
Peter Gabriel, Ein Deutsches Album (Fourth album).   Charisma 6302 221.   1982.
The entire fourth album is sung in German with some re-mixes.

Odds and sods

CHARLIE DRAKE   *You'll Never Know/I'm Big Enough For Me*   Charisma UK
CB-270.   1976.   Gabriel co-wrote and co-produced this monstrosity.
JIMMY PURSEY   *Animals Have More Fun/Sus*   UK Epic EPC-1336.   1981.   Co-
written and co-produced by Gabriel.

Peter Gabriel has also worked on the following: TRB *Bully For You,* TOM ROBINSON
Atmospherics, KATE BUSH *Never For Ever* album, among others.

All This And World War Two   US 20th Century Fox 2T-540.   1976.   He sings
Strawberry Fields on this double-album soundtrack.
ROBERT FRIPP   *Exposure*   UK EG EGLP-101.   1979.   Gabriel does vocals on this
album.
Bristol Recorder Volume Two   UK Bristol Recorder BR-002.   1980.   This has three
excellent live tracks *Humdrum, Not One Of Us* and *Ain't That Peculiar.*
Music And Rhythm   UK WEA K-68045.   1982.   A double album compilation to
raise money for the WOMAD festival. It has the album debut of *Across The
Water.*

Art Garfunkel

American singles

ARTIE GARR   *Private World/Forgive Me*   Octavia 8002.   c.1982.
ARTIE GARR   *Beat Love/*B side unknown.   Warwick 515.   c.1961.
ART GARFUNKEL   *All I Know/Mary Was An Only Child*   Columbia promo
quadraphonic mix 4-45926.   1973.

American albums

Angel Clair   Quad mix.   Columbia CQ-31474.   1974.
Watermark   Columbia test pressing AL/BL-34975.   1978.   This test pressing has a
track which never appeared on the final release.

British album

Angel Clair   Quad mix.   CBS Q-69021.   1974.

J. Geils Band

American singles

Bloodshot   Atlantic juke box EP LLP-219/SD7-7260.   1974.

One Last Kiss   Long and short versions.   EMI-America twelve-inch promo SPRO-8967.   1978.

Just Can't Stop Me/I Could Hurt You/Wild Man   EMI-America twelve-inch promo SPRO-9133/4.   1979.

*Comeback/*B side unknown.   EMI-America twelve-inch promo SPRO-9301/2.   1979.

Love Stinks   Studio version/JUKE JOINT JIMMY AND THE HOUSE ROCKERS   *Love Stinks* Live version.   EMI-America twelve-inch promo SPRO-9395.   1980.   The B side of the above is the J. Geils Band using an alias.

Flamethrower   EMI-America twelve-inch promo SPRO-9725.   1982.

Freeze Frame   Long and short versions.   EMI-America promo, number unknown. 1982.

I Do/Sanctuary   EMI-America twelve-inch promo SPRO-9863.   1983.

American albums

Bloodshot   Atlantic red vinyl promo SD-7260.   1974.

Rock Around The World   Number 158.   c.1978.

Robert W. Morgan   *Profiles*   Radio Series.   1979.

Three Into One   BBC *Rock Hour*   Radio Series.   1982.

Odds and sods

Mar Y Sol   USA Atco SD2-705.   1972.   Live music from the 1972 Puerto Rico pop festival.

Love Stinks   USA Nautilus audiophile NR-25.   1981.

Generation X

British singles

Wild Youth/No No No   Chrysalis CHS-2189.   1978.   A pressing error. The B side should have been *Wild Dub*.

Dancing With Myself/Untouchables   Chrysalis promo GENDX-1.   1980.

American single

Dancing With Myself/Happy People   Chrysalis twelve-inch promo.   1980.

Genesis

British singles

Silent Sun/That's Me Decca F-12735. 1967. Their first release.
A Winter's Tale/One Eyed Hound Decca F-12775. 1968.
Sour Turns To Sweet/In Hiding Decca F-12949. 1968.

Most Genesis fans would already know about these, but none of them would have bought them!

Happy The Man/Seven Stones Charisma CB-181. 1972. Easily their rarest UK release. It escaped in a picture sleeve with mediaeval lettering at the top. The A side is a non-album track, although a re-mixed version appeared on the *One More Chance* compilation album on British Charisma CLASS-3 in 1974. This version excluded the opening harmony vocals. The original single version was used on the *As Through Emerald City* bootleg, but a poor copy was used.
Looking For Someone/Visions Of Angels Charisma promo GS-1/2. 1973. Made to promote the *Tresspass* album, it was never scheduled for release.
Watcher Of The Skies Charisma. 1973. Withdrawn. This was probably the American mix. Acetates are thought to exist of this ultra-rarity.
Twilight Alehouse Genesis fan club flexi. No number. 1975. This track originally appeared a year earlier as the B side of *I Know What I Like*.
Counting Out Time/Riding The Scree Charisma CB-238. 1974. The A side has a new intro.
The Carpet Crawlers/The Waiting Room (Evil Jam) Charisma CB-251. 1975. The B side is another non-album rarity, taken from a concert recorded for radio in Los Angeles in 1974. The concert became the basis for the bootleg *As Through Emerald City*.

All the Charisma singles up to, and including, *The Carpet Crawlers* were issued as double A sided promos, i.e. the A side is on both sides. There are many other Genesis non-album B sides released since 1975, but they should still be fairly easy to get.

A Trick Of The Tail/Ripples Charisma CB-277. 1976. While regular shop copies have silver labels, the juke box issues have purple plastic labels.
Abacab/Another Record Charisma CB-388. 1981. There are three different label designs for release. The first has a coloured paper label design which was actually made in West Germany. The second has a design similar to the *Turn It On Again* label with the *Duke* logo at the top. The third is a special juke box issue with the Genesis logo at the top.
Paperlate/You Might Recall Charisma juke box issue JBGEN-1. 1982. Two label designs for this. The first has a silver plastic label, while the second has a green plastic label; both have the same lettering and design.
The Lady Lies Flexipop 021 (Lyntone LYN-11806). Given with *Flexipop* in 1982. This track is taken from a BBC Radio One broadcast recorded in 1980 at the Lyceum Ballroom in London.

Firth Of Forth Genesis Information flexi GI-01. 1983. A live recording, but edited. The full version later turned up on the *That's All* twelve inch later in the year.

British albums

From Genesis To Revelation Decca LK-4990 mono and SKL-4990 stereo. 1968. The only Genesis album to be released in mono, although I don't know if it contains a different mix. Both versions came with a lyric sheet.

Genesis, In The Beginning Decca SKL-4990. 1973. A stereo-only re-release of the Decca album, this time with a new sleeve featuring a serpent wrapped around a globe.

The Genesis Collection, Volume One Charisma CGS-102. 1975. A double album re-package of *Trespass* and *Nursery Chryme* to fill the gap between Peter Gabriel's departure and new Genesis product.

The Genesis Collection, Volume Two Charisma CGS-103. 1975. Released the same time as volume one, this one featured *Foxtrot* and *Selling England By The Pound*. These two double sets were only around for a very short while and are now extremely rare to find in mint condition.

Abacab Charisma CBR-102. 1981. This came in three different sleeve colour co-ordinations.

American singles

Silent Sun/That's Me Parrot PAR-3018. 1969. All the copies of their American debut that have turned up so far seem to be white label promos. It's possible that it was withdrawn from release, making regular copies gold-dust.

There were many bands in America at the time called Genesis. One, on Mercury, even released an album *In The Beginning* in the late 1960s, completely throwing the collectors of the real McCoy. Other bands called Genesis released singles on Scepter, Buddah and Rare Bird Records. For a while London Records, who distributed Parrot, considered re-naming them Revelation for the American market. (From Genesis to Revelation, eh?)

Nursery Chryme EP Charisma promo, number unknown. 1972. A sampler to promote an early tour.

Watcher Of The Skies/Willow Farm Charisma CAA-103. 1973. The A side features a mix which, as yet, has not appeared in Britain. In the late 1970s Fontana in Germany released the *Rock Theatre* album which contained this rare mix.

Entangled/Ripples Atco 7050. 1976. These are edited versions from the *Trick Of The Tail* album, but the promo version of the single contained the full versions.

Follow You Follow Me/Inside And Out Atlantic 3474. 1978. This has an alternate mix of the A side.

Go West Young Man/Scenes From A Night's Dream Atlantic 3511. 1978. The A side is the track *Deep In The Motherlode* edited and re-titled.

Go West Young Man Same both sides Atlantic twelve-inch promo PR-311. 1978.

Turn It On Again/Evidence Of Autumn Atlantic 3751. 1980. The A side features a new mix which, again, hasn't appeared in Britain. It has a brighter drum mix and omits the false start and count-in.

Turn It On Again Studio version/live version. Atlantic twelve-inch promo PR-369. 1980. This has the single mix on side one as well as an unreleased live recording, made at The Theatre Royal in London's Drury Lane on side two. Yet again, this hasn't appeared in Britain.

No Reply At All 4:37 and 4:00 versions. Atlantic promo 3858. 1980.

Man On The Corner Same on both sides. Atlantic twelve-inch promo, number unknown. 1981.

Abacab Same on both sides. Atlantic twelve-inch promo, number unknown. 1981.

No Reply At All Same on both sides. Atlantic twelve-inch promo PR-404. 1980.

Paperlate (Studio version)/*Turn It On Again* (Live version). Atlantic seven-inch promo PR-453, and twelve-inch promo PR-442. 1982.

Mama Same on both sides. Atlantic twelve-inch promo PR-535. 1983.

American albums

Trespass ABC-Impulse ASD-9205. 1971. How this 'rock album' came to be released on a 'jazz label' is a mystery. The album was later re-released on ABC Records ABCX-816.

From Genesis To Revelation London XPS-643. 1974. This made it's debut in America five years after the UK issue. It was issued in the same sleeve as the British original.

Three Sides Live Atlantic SD2-2000. 1982. This differs substantially from the British release. The fourth side on the UK issue has the band live in 1977, whereas the American fourth side has five studio tracks. These are *Paperlate, You Might Recall, Me And Virgil, Evidence Of Autumn* and *Open Door* all of which have appeared on singles in Britain.

There are also many radio station shows which have been transcribed onto disc and sold as syndicated shows throughout America.

Rock Around The World Number 120. (Dated 21.11.76).

Innerview Number 3. (Dated July 1978).

BBC *Rock Hour* Number unknown. Recorded at Knebworth, England. 1978.

NBC *Source* (Dated Nov. 1980).

NBC *Source* (Dated 24.4.81).

BBC *Rock Hour* Number 243. 1981. Interviews and music from *Abacab*.

Mellow Yellow Radio Series (Dated 10.4.82).

BBC *Rock Hour* Radio Series (Dated 24.4.82). Recorded in London in 1977.

King Biscuit Radio Series (Dated 20.6.82).

Westwood One *Off The Record* Radio Series (Dated 19.9.82).

Retrorock Radio Series Number 47/8. 1982.

Odds and sods

I Know What I Like/After The Ordeal French Charisma, number unknown. 1974. Withdrawn, although picture sleeved copies do exist.

Genesis Canada Atlantic, no number. 1981. A superb boxed set with these

albums. *Selling England By The Pound, The Lamb Lies Down On Broadway, A Trick Of The Tail, Wind And Wuthering, Seconds Out, Duke, Abacab, Spot The Pigeon* EP and the book *I Know What I Like.* Limited to 2,000 only.
Man On The Corner/Submarine   German Vertigo, number unknown.   1981. Special re-mix of the A side.
Man On The Corner/Submarine   Spanish Vertigo, number unknown.   1981. Another special re-mix.
A Trick Of The Tail   Japan Mobile Fidelity audiophile MFSL 1-064.   1982.

Gerry and The Pacemakers

British singles
Ferry 'Cross The Mersey/Don't Let The Sun Catch You Crying   EMI 2814. 1978.   The picture sleeve for this was withdrawn, but promo copies exist.
*Ferry 'Cross The Mersey/You'll Never Walk Alone/*THE DRIFTERS *Saturday Night At The Movies*   Creole Blast From The Past 17.   1980.   An odd release.

American albums
Greatest Hits   Capitol Record Club issue T-90384.   c.1965.
Don't Let The Sun Catch You Crying   Laurie-Capitol Record Club DT-90555. c.1966.
Ferry 'Cross The Mersey   Soundtrack.   United Artists-Capitol Record Club T-90812.   c.1966.

Gary Glitter

British singles
Paul Raven

*Too Proud/*B side unknown.   Decca F-11202.   c.1960.
Walk On By/All Grown Up   Parlophone R-4812.   1962.
Tower Of Strength/Living The Blues   Parlophone R-4847.   1962.
*Soul Thing/*B side unknown.   MCA MU-1035.   1968.   The B side may be *Musical Man.*
Stand/Soul Thing   MCA MKS-5053.   1970.
The four Parlophone tracks were re-issued in 1978 by EMI.
Paul Raven   EP EMI NUT-2855.   1978.

PAUL MONDAY   *Here Comes The Sun/*B side unknown.   MCA, number unknown. c.1970.

(Before anyone complains, I apologise for being rather vague in detail about some of these singles. They are, in my opinion, some of the worst records ever made. As they didn't sell, hard details are difficult to trace).

American singles

PAUL RAVEN *Goodbye Seattle/Wait For Me* Decca 32714. c.1969. Doubtful if ever released in Britain.

GARY GLITTER/B. J. THOMAS *What's It All About?* Radio Series 137/138. c.1975.

Odds and sods

RUBBER BUCKET *We're All Living In One Place/*B side unknown. UK MCA, number unknown. c.1970. This time an obnoxious lyric, a would-be *Give Peace A Chance,* sung to the tune of *Amazing Grace.*

Jesus Christ Superstar Soundtrack album. UK MCA MKPS-2011/2. 1971. Glitter was featured on this, the original version of the Rice and Lloyd-Webber musical.

Saturday Scene UK Philips, number unknown. 1974. This album features an interview with Gary.

The Rocky Horror Show Australian Stetson Records SRLP-6. c.1978. The Aussie soundtrack album version found our hero playing Frank N. Furter.

The British Electrical Foundation's Music Of Quality And Distinction UK Virgin-BEF V-2219. 1982. This album features Gary's excellent version of Elvis' *Suspicious Minds.*

Godley and Creme

GODLEY AND CREME had worked on other peoples records before making their own. Kevin Godley had been a member of The Mockingbirds, as well as Hotlegs, with Lol Creme and Eric Stewart.

LOL *Naughty Lola/*B side unknown. UK Columbia single. c.1967. Some people are convinced that this is Lol Creme. Details are needed.

DAVE BERRY *Chaplin House* UK Decca F-13080. 1970. One of the few singles that both Godley and Creme were both involved with as far as writing and production chores at the time.

FRABJOY AND RUNCIBLE SPOON *I'm Beside Myself/Animal Song* UK Marmalade 598 019. 1969. This is thought to be the first real Godley and Creme track to be released. An album was recorded, but not released as the Marmalade label folded.

Marmalade 100% Proof UK Marmalade 643 314. 1969. A cheapo compilation which featured the beautiful *Too Fly Away* by Kevin Godley, although it was in fact Frabjoy and Runcible Spoon. This track was re-released in 1976 on the *Rare Tracks* compilation on UK Polydor 2482 274. Again, it was credited to Kevin Godley.

British singles

Concequences Edited highlights. Mercury double single promo SAMP-017. 1977.

Under Your Thumb/Power Behind The Throne Polydor POSP-322. 1981. Polydor weren't anticipating big sales for this single so they only printed 2,000 picture sleeves. This picture-sleeved copy also featured a shorter version of the song *Under Your Thumb*. All these copies came with paper labels. When sales picked up, a longer version with plastic labels was released.

Snack Attack   Long and short versions.   Polydor promo PODJ-412.   1982.

British albums

Concequences   Edited highlights.   Mercury promo LKP-1001.   1977.   A white label album with about fifty minutes of the triple-album set.

Ismism   Polydor POLD-5043.   1981.   The initial copies came with a white cover with die-cut holes making up the title. After the first batch of the album was sold, Polydor reverted to a black cover with red printed holes.

The Go Go's

American singles

Our Lips Are Sealed/We Got The Beat/Tonight   IRS twelve-inch promo SP-70956.   1981.

We Got The Beat/How Much More   IRS twelve-inch promo SP-70959.   1981.

Vacation/Beatnik Beach   IRS twelve-inch promo SP-70961.   1982.

American albums

Westwood One Radio Series, number 81-12.   1981.   Live at The Metro, Boston.

THE GO GO'S/THE BLASTERS   Westwood One   *In Concert*   Series, number 82-13. (Dated July 1982).

THE GO GO'S/THE BEAT   NBC *Source*   Radio Series   1982.   The Beat are The English Beat.

British single

We Got The Beat/How Much More   Stiff BUY-78.   1980.   They did this one-off single for Stiff while they supported Madness on a UK tour. It escaped most people's attention.

Odds and sods

Urgh, A Music War!   UK A & M AMLX-64692.   1981.   This has live music.

Brimstone And Treacle   Soundtrack.   UK A & M AMLH-64915.   1982.   This may have previously released tracks.

Grateful Dead

American singles

Stealin/Don't Ease Me In   Scorpio 003-201.   1966.   A rare independent release. It has been counterfeited.

Working Man's Dead   Radio Spots.   Warner promo PRO-414.   1968.
American Beauty   Radio Spots.   Warner promo PRO-438.   1969.
American Beauty   Warner juke box EP LLP-226.   c.1970.
Shakedown Street   Radio Spots.   Arista promo.   (Dated 23.10.77).

American albums

For Dead Heads Only   Grateful Dead RD-102/SP-114.   1976.   A free album given
with *Steal Your Face*.
Terrapin Station   Banded for radio play.   Arista promo AL-7001.   1976.
The Tenth Anniversary Album   Warner promo PROA-289.   1977.
Recently Dead   Arista promo SP-35.   1977.
Rock Around The World   Radio Series, number 101.   c.1977.
Innerview   Radio Series.   c.1978.
King Biscuit   (Dated 26.10.80).   A retrospective.
Earth News   Radio Series   (Dated 10.11.80).
NBC *Source*   Radio Series   (Dated Feb. 1981).
Westwood One Radio Series   (Dated 3.8.81).
GRATEFUL DEAD/BOB DYLAN   *Royalty Of Rock*   Radio Series.   TM Special Products.
c.1982.

British single

Dark Star   Edited.   Warner promo SAM-79.   1977.   This was made to promote
the *What A Long Strange Trip It's Been* anthology.

British album

For Dead Heads Only   Grateful Dead FREE-2.   1976.   A free album given away
with *Steal Your Face*.

Odds and sods

KEN KESEY   *The Acid Trip*   USA Sound City Productions EX2-7690.   c.1967.   The
Dead play as Kesey reads excerpts from his book.
The Fillmore. The Last Days   USA Fillmore, number unknown.   c.1971.

The Grateful Dead were one of the last bands to play at this famous San Francisco
venue. This triple album has some live material.

Glastonbury Fayre   UK Revelation Records REV-1.   1972.   This triple album
has some Dead live tracks. These tracks have been bootlegged on an American
twelve-inch.
American Beauty   Japan Mobile Fidelity audiophile pressing MFSL-1-014.   1980.

Steve Hackett

Before joining Genesis he was a member of QUIET WORLD who released one single on
Pye's progressive label, Dawn, in 1970.   *Love Is Walking/Children Of The World*
Dawn DNS-1005.

British singles

Narnia/Please Don't Touch Charisma promo SH-001. 1978.
Clocks/Acoustic Set/Tigermoth Charisma twelve-inch CELL-13. 1983. This white label, twelve-inch came with initial copies of the *Cell 151* twelve-inch.
Walking Through Walls Charisma. 1983. Withdrawn. Acetates of this unreleased re-mix are in existence.

American single

Star Of Sirius Chrysalis promo PRO-633. 1976. This may have the same track on both sides.

American album

STEVE HACKETT/BILLY SQUIRE BBC *Rock Hour* Number 249. (Dated Feb. 1981). Recorded at the Reading Festival in 1981.

Haircut 100

British singles

Fantastic Day (Live version)/*Ski Club Of Great Britain* Arista picture disc CLIPD-3. 1982. The live version of the A side only appeared on this picture disc.
Pelican Dance King Size EP Arista twelve-inch promo TERRY-1. 1982. This is a four-track sampler from their first album.
Whistle Down The Wind Arista CLIP-5. 1983. Withdrawn in February 1983. It later turned up as Nick Heyward's first solo single.
Prime Time/Two Up Two Down Polydor HC-1. 1983. Initial copies came with a plastic bag sleeve.

British album

Blue Hat For A Blue Day Arista HCC-101. 1982. Withdrawn December 1982. Test pressings were probably made for this album, as a sleeve does exist. This depicts 1920s and 1930s models and film stars around a blue border, with a photo in colour of the band in the middle. The graphics have the band's name in their usual lettering style at the top above the photo, and the album title below the photo in black.

American single

Fantastic Day/Ski Club Of Great Britain/Love's Got Me In Triangles/Calling Captain Autumn Arista twelve-inch promo SP-139. 1982.

American album

HAIRCUT 100, MARSHALL CRENSHAW AND A FLOCK OF SEAGULLS BBC *In Concert* Radio Series, number 82-15. (Dated March 1982).

Hall and Oates

Before teaming up as a duo, Daryl Hall had made a few records in different bands.

CELLAR DOOR *Princess And The Soldier* USA Bell 45-049. c.1969. B side unknown.

GULLIVER *Everyday's A Lonely Day/Angelina* USA Elektra EK-45689. 1970.

GULLIVER *Everyday's A Lonely Day/A Truly Good Song* USA Elektra EK-45698. 1970.

GULLIVER *The ReasonWhy*/B side unknown. USA Chelsea CH-3063. c.1976. This was probably re-released to cash in on Hall and Oates.

GULLIVER *Gulliver* Album. USA Elektra EKS-74070. 1970. Their only album. This band also featured Tim Moore.

American singles

WHOLE OATES *Goodnight*/B side unknown. Atlantic 2922. 1972.

WHOLE OATES *I'm Sorry*/B side unknown. Atlantic 2939. 1972. Their first duet singles were released using this strange name. It's probable that only mono and stereo promos of these singles have come to light.

She's Gone 5:15 and 3:24 versions. Atlantic promo 2993. 1973.

She's Gone Atlantic promo PR-265. 1974. Possibly an EP.

She's Gone 5:15 and 3:24 versions. Atlantic promo 3332. 1976.

Back Together Again/STEPHEN DEES *Kerry* RCA twelve-inch promo JD-11022. 1977. Hall and Oates produced Stephen Dees' RCA album *Hipshot*.

Do What You Want, Be What You Are Long and short versions. RCA twelve-inch promo JD-11302. 1977.

I Don't Want To Lose You Same both sides. RCA twelve-inch promo JD-11431. 1978.

Post Static EP. RCA twelve-inch promo DJL 1-3512. 1979.

Running From Paradise Same both sides. RCA twelve-inch promo JD-11770. 1980.

How Does It Feel Same both sides. RCA twelve-inch promo JD-12053. 1981.

I Can't Go For That Long and short versions. RCA promo, number unknown. 1982.

Did It In A Minute Same both sides. RCA twelve-inch promo JD-13080. 1982.

One On One Same both sides. RCA twelve-inch promo JD-13428. 1983.

Maneater/Family Man RCA twelve-inch promo JD-13363. 1983.

British single

Your Imagination Mono and stereo versions. RCA promo 239. 1982. An unusual British promo.

American albums

Along The Red Ledge RCA red vinyl promo DJL 1-2804. 1977.

RCA Radio Special Interview Series. RCA promo DJL 1-3832. 1980.

RCA Radio Special Interview Series, number 13.   RCA promo DJL 1-4179.   1981.
NBC *Source*   (Dated Feb. 1981).
Voices Around The World   Radio Series.   1981.
HALL AND OATES/GEORGE THOROGOOD   *Direct News*   Radio Series DN-64.   1981.
NBC *Source*   (Dated Aug. 1981).
Retrorock   Radio Series   (Dated Nov. 1981).

British albums

Private Eyes   Album and cassette pack.   RCA Double Fun Series, number
unknown.   1983.   Quickly deleted.
Rock 'n' Soul Part One   RCA PL-84858.   1983.   Available in several different
coloured covers.

Odds and sods

DARYL HALL   *A Lonely Girl/Vicky*   USA Parallax 404.   Date unknown.   His first
solo release.

Roy Harper

British singles

Take Me In Your Eyes/Pretty Baby   Strike JH-304.   1966.   An obscure
independent release. Both tracks are non-album.
Sail Away/Cherishing The Lonesome   Harvest HAR-5140.   1977.   This single,
credited to Roy Harper's Black Sheep, was taken from the withdrawn *Commercial
Break* album. It's possible that this single was withdrawn as well.
Sail Away   Long and short versions.   Harvest promo HAR-5140-DJ.   1977.
Refferendum Another Day/Tom Tiddler's   Harvest PSR-407.   1977.   A free
single given away with the *Bullinamingvase* album.
Mrs Space   Harvest promo PSR-408.   1977.   I don't know if there's a B side for
this.

British albums

Sophisticated Beggar   Strike Records, number unknown.   1966.   This was the first
issue of this album, and the rarest. It was re-issued in 1970 on Youngblood SYB-8
and then on Big Ben Records BBX-502 in 1975.
ROY HARPER'S BLACK SHEEP   *Commercial Break*   Harvest SHSP-4077.   Withdrawn
from release by EMI in December 1977.
Bullinamingvase   Harvest SHSP-4060.   1979 re-issue.   This new version was
released by EMI after protest from 'The Black Boar', a famous feeding hole for
lorry drivers and bands on the run. They objected to the 'slanderous reference' to
the establishment in Harper's song *Watford Gap*. The track was later replaced by
Breakfast With You.

American albums

ROY HARPER/LOU RAWLS Sampler album with one side each. Capitol promo, number unknown but dated Feb. 1970.
Introducing Roy Harper Chrysalis promo PRO-620. c.1977. A great compilation of the man's work including contributions from fans such as Paul McCartney, Ian Anderson as well as Led Zeppelin's *Hat's Off To Harper*.

George Harrison

British albums

Wonderwall Music Apple TAP-1 mono, STAP-1 stereo. 1968. These were the original catalogue numbers. They were later changed to APCOR-1 mono and SAPCOR-1 stereo. This was the only Harrison album released in mono.
All Things Must Pass Apple STCH-639. 1970. When the test copies were being pressed a box with a cloth hinge was originally chosen to hold the package together. This proved to be too expensive, so the idea was ditched. Some copies with the cloth hinge are still around somewhere.
Somewhere In England Dark Horse K-56870. 1980. Originally withdrawn. The first track listing contains the songs *Sat Singing, Flying Hour, Tears Of The World* and *Lay His Head*. These songs were later taken off when the album finally turned up in the middle of 1981. The reason was George's reaction to John's death. When he decided to write some songs based on his feelings at the time, the previously mentioned songs had to be scrapped. Some American copies of the first version are in existence, but it's debatable whether British copies were pressed. The easy way to tell the first version from the second is that the second version has *All Those Years Ago,* obviously written after Lennon's death. Apparently the first sleeve has George's face over a map of Britain.
Gone Troppo Dark Horse K-57025. 1982. The album eventually appeared with the number 92-3734-1.

American singles

Don't Let Me Wait Too Long/B side unknown. Apple 1866. 1974. This was withdrawn.
This Song Mono and stereo versions. Dark Horse promo DRC-8294. 1976. The promo comes with a special sleeve telling the story of the *My Sweet Lord, He's So Fine* courtcase.
All Those Years Ago Same on both sides. Dark Horse twelve-inch promo PROA-949. 1981.
Wake Up My Love Same on both sides. Dark Horse twelve-inch promo PROA-1075. 1982.

American albums

The Dark Horse Radio Special Dark Horse promo SP-22002. 1974. This was made by A & M to promote Harrison's new label and contains an interview with the man himself.

Thirty Three And A Third Dialogue album. Dark Horse promo PRO-649. 1976. An interview album with script. Counterfeits exist.
George Harrison Radio Spots. Dark Horse promo, open reel DH-007. 1978.
My Sweet George Rock Around the World Radio Series, number 61. 1978.
Gone Troppo Dark Horse promo, Quiex II pure vinyl pressing 92-3734-1. 1982.

Odds and sods

LOUISE CALDWELL HARRISON *All About The Beatles* USA Recar Records 2012. c.1965. His sister gets the limelight on this interview album.
All Things Must Pass Columbian Apple 10057/8. 1970. This is a double album version in a gatefold sleeve.
Concert For Bangladesh Radio Spots. USA Apple/20th Century Fox promo, number unknown. 1971. This was made to promote the movie.
Concerts For Bangladesh UK Apple STCX-3385. 1971. Has live music. There is also a flexi disc from *Bravo* magazine in Germany featuring an interview with George.

Justin Hayward

British singles

London Is Behind Me/Days Must Come Pye 7N-17014. 1966. His first single.
I Can't Face The World Without You/I'll Be Here Tomorrow Parlophone R-5496. 1966. His second single, equally as obscure.

British album

JUSTIN HAYWARD AND JOHN LODGE *Blue Jays* Threshold cassette KTHC-12. 1975. For some reason the tape version has a longer version of *I Dreamed Last Night*.

American albums

JUSTIN HAYWARD & JOHN LODGE *The Making Of Blue Jays* Threshold promo THSX-101. 1975.
JUSTIN HAYWARD/CAPTAIN BEEFHEART DIR Broadcasting Radio Series (Dated 18.12.78).

Odds and sods

War Of The Worlds UK CBS 96000. 1978. He appears on this superstars concept album.

Jimi Hendrix

British singles

JIMI HENDRIX AND CURTIS KNIGHT *How Would You Feel/You Don't Want Me* Track 604 009. 1968. The only Track single with Curtis Knight.

Gloria   One-sided.   Polydor JIMI-1.   1978.   A free single given away with *The Essential Jimi Hendrix* album.
The Jimi Hendrix Single Pack   Polydor 2608 001.   1980.   This was a set of six singles in a wrap-around cardboard cover. All the singles were pressed in France. The singles were . . .
Hey Joe/Stone Free   Polydor 2141 275.
Purple Haze/Fifty First Anniversary   Polydor 2141 276.
The Wind Cries Mary/Highway Child   Polydor 2141 277.
The Burning Of The Midnight Lamp/The Stars That Play With Laughing Sam's Dice   Polydor 2141 278.
All Along The Watchtower/Long Hot Summer Night   Polydor 2141 279.
Voodoo Chile/Gloria   Polydor 2141 280.

British albums

Are You Experienced   Track 612 001 mono, 613 001 stereo.   1967.
Axis   Bold As Love   Track 612 003 mono, 613 003 stereo.   1968.
Smash Hits   Track 612 004 mono, 613 004 stereo.   1968.

The first three Hendrix Track albums were also available in mono, but I don't know if they're different mixes.

Smash Hits   Polydor Record Club ACB-00219.   Early 1970s.

American singles

Dolly Dagger   4:45 and 3:35 versions.   Reprise promo RPS-1044.   1971.
Red House/Spanish Castle Magic   Rolling Stone magazine flexi.   c.1973.
Gloria   One-sided.   Reprise MS-2293-EP.   1979.   Given with *The Essential Jimi Hendrix, Volume Two*.
Gloria   Same both sides.   Reprise promo MS-2293-EP.   1979.
Little Drummer Boy/Silent Night/Auld Lang Syne   Reprise promo PRO-595. c.1975.   There have been picture disc copies of this that have turned up in the last few years, but they're all bootlegs.
Little Drummer Boy/Silent Night/Auld Lang Syne   Reprise twelve-inch promo PROA-840.   1979.

American albums

The Band Of Gypsies   Capitol Record Club R-104148.   Date unknown.
The Jimi Hendrix Experience   Reprise-Capitol Record Club SW-93371.   c.1974.
Midnight Landing   Excerpts/RUFUS unknown tracks.   American Forces Radio and Television Service P-15693.   1975.
The Hendrix Conversation   Rock Around The World   Radio Series.   1978.
BBC *Rock Hour*   Number 248.   c.1981.   Music and interviews.
Rock 'n' Roll Never Forgets   Radio Series, made by Westwood One.   Dated 6.6.82.   A ten-album set.
The Interview   Rainbow RNDF-254.   1982.   This was a black vinyl test pressing for the Rhino label picture disc only release.

Odds and sods

Woodstock Volumes one and two. UK Atlantic/USA Cotillion. 1970. Includes live music.

A flexi was given away with the German magazine *Poster Press* in the mid-1970s. This one-sided disc featured *Hey Joe* as well as an interview with Hendrix's girlfriend, Monika Dannerman.

The Hollies

British albums
The Vintage Hollies World Record Club ST-979. c.1967.
Stay With The Hollies World Record Club STP-1035. c.1968.
The Hollies Regal SREG-2024. c.1967. An obscure, cheapo album.

American singles
Stay/Now Is The Time Liberty 55674. 1963. Their first American release. Issued before any hint of a British invasion. This is rare.
*Carrie Anne/*TREMELOES *Silence Is Golden* Epic red vinyl promo 5-10180/5-10184. 1967.
*Stop In The Name Of Love/*B side unknown. Atlantic twelve-inch promo PR-502. 1983.

American albums
The Hollies, Volume One CBS-Realm 8026. Date unknown.
The Hollies, Volume Two CBS-Realm 8027. Date unknown. These two may have been record club issues.
Everything You Wanted To Hear Epic promo AS-138. 1972. A compilation.

Odds and sods

THE HOLLIES AND PETER SELLERS *After The Fox/Foxtrot* UK United Artists UP-1152/USA United Artists 56079. 1966. Theme from a Peter Sellers movie about a man who gets people to rob a bank thinking that they're making a movie about a bank job. Confused? The B side is a Burt Bacharach instrumental. A soundtrack album was also released, USA United Artists UA-LA 286-G.
Non Prego Per Me/Devi Avere Fiducia Inme Both songs sung in Italian. Italian Dischi Parlophon (not Parlophone) QMSP-16402. 1967. This was made for the San Remo song festival.
The Air That I Breathe Appears on a compilation EP *Music For 5AM* made by Mercury for Yardley's perfume. Mercury YARD-002. British. 1978.

Buddy Holly

American singles

Blue Days, Black Nights/Love Me   Decca 29854.   1956.
Modern Don Juan/You Are My One Desire   Decca 9-30166.   1956.

His first two singles are his rarest.

BUDDY HOLLY/KENNY ROGERS   *What's It All About?*   Radio Series 585/6.   c.1981.   I don't know if this included an interview.

American EP

That'll Be The Day   Decca ED-2575.   1957.   This features *That'll Be The Day, You Are My One Desire, Blue Days Black Nights* and *Ting A Ling.* Issued in a picture sleeve, this is another prime rarity. He had other EP's released on Brunswick and Coral.

American albums

That'll Be The Day   Decca DL-8707.   1957.   A £200 item. Beware of counterfeits which don't have the blue inner sleeve.
BUDDY HOLLY/ROLLING STONES   *Sounds Of Solid Gold*   Radio Show, number 6. 1982.
BUDDY HOLLY/BARRY MANILOW   *Sounds Of Solid Gold*   Radio Series, number 31. 1982.

British singles

Blue Days, Black Nights/Love Me   Brunswick 05581.   1957.   His first British release which was taken from American Decca. This single did nothing when released. His second single *Peggy Sue,* on Coral, was the one to take off.
Peggy Sue/Everyday   Vogue-Coral Q-72293 (45 rpm), Coral Q-72293 (78 rpm). 1957.   Why these two labels issued the same single isn't known.

British EP

Listen To Me   Coral FEP-2002.   1957.   The initial pressings came with a brown tinted sleeve.

British albums

Holly In The Hills   Coral LVA-9227.   1965.   Decca, who pressed the album, credited the track *Wishing* as being on the album, but it in fact turns out to be *Reminiscing,* which shouldn't have been on the album. *Wishing* was included from the second pressing onwards.
The Buddy Holly Story   World Record Club SM-301/5.   1975.   A five-album set with a book.
The Complete Buddy Holly   MCA-Coral CDMSP-807.   1978.   The best boxed set with six albums and a book. It features the following:
Lubbock, Texas. Western And Bop   CDLM-8071.

Nashville, Tennessee. Changing All Those Changes CDLM-8072.
Clovis, New Mexico. Buddy Holly And The Crickets CDLM-8073.
Clovis, New Mexico And On To New York CDLM-8074.
New York, N.Y. Planning For The Future CDLM-8075.
The Collector's Buddy Holly This included interviews as well as tracks he produced for other people.

Odds and sods

Buddy Holly Countywise Dutch Coral LPC-96101. 1958. An extremely rare eight-track ten-inch album.
NORMAN PETTY TRIO *Moondreams*/B side unknown. USA Columbia 4-41039. c.1958. Supposedly has Holly on guitar.
That'll Be The Day Seven Up flexi PBF-0005. A one-sided flexi of unknown origin.
The Legend Of Buddy Holly Dutch Charly 399-021/2. c.1978. This was withdrawn just after it hit the racks. It included rare TV material as well as interviews, etc.
EDDIE COCHRAN *Words And Music* UK Rock Star RSRLP-1005. 1981. This album contains a Buddy Holly interview from American radio in 1957. So why is it on an Eddie Cochran album?

Human League

British single

OMD *Souvenir*/HUMAN LEAGUE *Hard Times* Virgin. 1982. A mispress. Forty were made and thirty-five were recalled to the factory. The A side should have been *Love Action*.

American singles

Don't You Want Me A & M-Virgin twelve-inch promo SP-17184. 1982. This is probably the fifteen minute version.
Don't You Want Me/Love Action A & M Virgin twelve-inch promo SP-12045. 1982.
Love Action Edited, probably on both sides. A & M-Virgin AM-2425. 1982.
Hard Times/Love Action/Love Action Instrumental. A & M-Virgin twelve-inch promo SP-12049. 1982.
Fascination Long mix/dub mix. A & M-Virgin twelve-inch promo, number unknown. 1983.

Odds and sods

THE MEN *Don't Depend On You/Crawl* UK Virgin VS-269 and twelve-inch VS-26912. 1979. The League under an alias.
Methods Of Dance Compilation. UK Virgin OVED-5. 1981. This has the previously unavailable track *Do Or Die Dub*.

Flexi Discs
Top (left to right) DAVID BOWIE *Record Mirror* free disc; SQUEEZE *Wrong Way*. Middle (left to right) JAM *Move On Up;* KATE BUSH *Never Forever*. Bottom (left to right) MADNESS *Patches* magazine giveaway; SPIRIT *Dark Star* magazine giveaway.

129

Iron Maiden

British singles

The Soundhouse Tapes Rock Hard Records ROK-1. 1979. Their own label. An independent release.
Women In Uniform/Invasion EMI 5105. 1980. The original sleeve showing Margaret Thatcher in combat gear.

Odds and sods

Metal For Muthas UK EMI EMC-3318. 1979. This compilation first attracted EMI to the band.

Joe Jackson

Before joining A & M for a solo career he was with a band called ARMS AND LEGS who released three singles in Britain.
She'll Surprise You/Janice MAM 140. 1976.
Heat Of The Night/Good Times MAM 147. 1976.
*Is There Any More Wine/*B side unknown. MAM 156. 1977.

British singles

Is She Really Going Out With Him/Do The Instant Mash A & M AMS-7392. 1978. This is the first version of this single. It came with a picture sleeve showing Joe in front of a black-and-white striped wall. This design was also used for the Dutch single. When the single was re-released in 1979 *You Got The Fever* was on the B side.
Steppin' Out/Another World A & M AMS-8262. 1982. For some reason, this has two different sleeves. The first has a picture with the titles on the right, while the second is just a graphic cover with titles taking up the whole sleeve.

British album

Look Sharp A & M AMLH-64743. 1979. A & M pressed a very limited edition in white vinyl after the *Is She Really Going Out With Him?* single had been a hit.

American single

Steppin' Out Long and short versions. A & M twelve-inch promo SP-17201. 1982.

American albums

Look Sharp A & M SP-3666. 1979. This was a double album ten-inch set with poster. It was this package that persuaded A & M to press *One More Time* as a ten-inch white vinyl single in the UK, complete with badge.

I'm The Man A & M SP-18000. 1980. A truly ridiculous piece of packaging consisting of a five-single set, with picture sleeves, and a poster in a boxed set, which makes up the album.
NBC *Source* Radio Series (Dated 2.6.80).
King Biscuit Radio Show (Dated 4.5.80).
BBC *Rock Hour* Number 202. (Dated Jan. 1981).

Odds and sods
Real Men EP. Dutch A & M twelve-inch, number unknown. 1982. The track *Un Ulto Mundo* appears on this twelve-inch which hasn't appeared in either Britain or America.

The Jam

British singles
In The City/Takin' My Love Polydor 2058 866. 1977. Their first single was issued in a very limited picture sleeve. Although all their early picture sleeves were re-released in 1980, they were slightly different. In the case of *In The City* the original sleeve had a curved edge on the sleeve opening, where as the re-issue had a straight edge.
Going Underground/Dreams Of Children Polydor double single version POSPJ-113. 1980. The first 100,000 had a free single *Away From The Numbers/This Is The Modern World/Tube Station* Polydor 2816 024.
*Start/*VILLAGE PEOPLE *You Can't Stop The Music* Polydor 2059 266. 1980. A mispress, although I don't know how many were done.
Absolute Beginners/Tales From The Riverbank Polydor POSP-350. 1981. The initial 100,000 came with a lyric sheet.
Precious Polydor one-sided promo PODJ-400. 1982. I assume that this is the short mix.
That's Entertainment/Tube Station Polydor POSP-482. 1982. This was finally given a full British release about a year after it had got into the UK charts as a German import on Metronome 0030 364. The B side was a live version.
Beat Surrender/Shopping Polydor double single version POSPJ-540. 1982. The free single this time being *Move On Up/Stoned Out Of My Mind/War* Polydor JAM-1.
Beat Surrender Radio version. Polydor one-sided promo PODJ-540. 1982. This replaces the 'bullshit' line with an inaudible one. Some of these promos came as double singles with the free single mentioned above.
Just Who Is The Five O'Clock Hero/The Great Depression Polydor 2029 504. 1982. Released in Britain after only being available on import from Germany. (Same label and number). British Polydor didn't bother pressing the twelve-inch version which was also imported.
Interview with Paul Weller and Bruce Foxton. Picture disc single. 1983. Limited to 1200 only.

When The Jam singles were re-issued at the end of 1982, just after the announcement of their break up, some came as sets with a paper strip holding the singles together.

Snap Medley. Polydor white-label promo LEE-1. 1983. An excellent medley of eleven hits edited to promote the *Snap* album.

Jam Live At Wembley EP. Polydor SNAP-45. 1983. A free EP given away with the initial pressings of the *Snap* album. This live recording was made at their last official gig in November 1982.

Smithers Jones On both sides. Polydor POSP-69. Date of pressing unknown, but it originally came out in 1979. The A side should have been *When You're Young*.

There have also been a series of great flexi discs from various sources over the years.

Pop Art Poem/Boy About Town Flexipop 002 (Lyntone LYN-9048). 1981. Available in both yellow and blue vinyl. Hard vinyl, white label, copies were sent to radio stations. The track later turned up on the Flexipop album in a re-mixed form.

Move On Up Polydor PAULO-100. 1982. Given away in the Christmas edition of *Melody Maker*. This live recording was apparently made in the Far East.

When You're Young, *Funeral Pyre* and *Tales From The Riverbank* have all been given away with the fan club.

British albums

In The City and *This Is The Modern World* Polydor 2683 074. 1980. This double album set wasn't obtainable for long. It was also made available in 1983 as a double cassette, along with a few others.

Snap Polydor SNAP-1. 1983. The initial copies came with a free live EP mentioned earlier. These tracks were also included on the cassette edition SNAPMC-1.

American singles

In The City/Takin' My Love Polydor PD-14442. 1977. Their first American release escaped everybody's attention, partly due to the fact that not many copies actually made it to the shops. Most of the copies in existence are promos, although they do come in picture sleeves. It's possible that the single may even have been withdrawn.

Mr Clean/English Rose/To Be Someone Polydor twelve-inch promo PRO-078. 1979. This has a censored version of *Mr Clean*.

The Butterfly Collector/Strange Town Polydor PD-14553. 1979. A reversal of sides for their third American single. Promo copies were pressed in yellow vinyl.

Mr Clean/Tube Station Polydor PD—14566. 1979. The full version of *Tube Station*, with sound effects at the end, was used here.

Going Underground/The Dreams Of Children Polydor PRO-145. 1980. This white label single was given away with the *Setting Sons* album.

Sound Effects Sampler EP. Polydor twelve-inch promo PRO-149. 1980.

A Town Called Malice Same on both sides. Polydor twelve-inch promo PRO-180. 1982.

Beat Surrender   Censored version, same on both sides.   Polydor promo, number unknown.   1982.

American albums
This Is The Modern World   Polydor PD 1-6129.   1978.   This American version adds *All Around The World*. Promo copies came with a sticker on the front cover warning DJ's about bad language on some tracks.
Setting Sons   Polydor PD 1-6249.   1980.   This added *Strange Town*.
BBC Rock Hour   Radio Series, number 223.   (Dated June 1981).
BBC *College Concert*   Radio Series   (Dated 5.12.82).   Recorded in Newcastle.

Odds and sods
Start/ORIGINAL MIRRORS   *Boys Cry*   Dutch Polydor 2059 266.   1980.   A mispress.
NME Dance Master   NME cassette 001.   1981.   This has *When You're Young* recorded live.

The James Gang

American singles
Ladies Man/Everybody Knows   Ascot AS-2168.   c.1966.
Right String But The Wrong Yo Yo/B side unknown.   Ascot AS-2205.   c.1966.
I wonder if these two singles are by Joe Walsh's band?

American album
Miami   Quad mix.   Atco QD36-102.   c.1974.

British single
Stop/Take A Look Around   Stateside SS-2173.   1969.   Withdrawn, although promo copies may exist.

Jan and Dean

Jan Berry used to be in a duo with Arnie Ginsberg called – surprise, surprise – JAN AND ARNIE. They cut several singles.

Jan and Arnie
Jennie Lee/Gotta Get A Date   Arwin 108.   1957.
Gas Money/Bonnie Lou   Arwin 111.   1957.
I Love Linda/The Beat That Can't Be Beat   Arwin 113.   1958.
Gotta Get A Date   Dot 45-16116.   1958.   This re-issue probably has *Jennie Lee* on the A side.
Gas Money/Bonnie Lou   Dot, number unknown.   c.1958.

Summertime Summertime/California Lullaby Jan and Dean 401. 1966. This was later taken up by Johnny Burnette's label Magic Lamp 401 in 1966. (The same label released a Karen Carpenter single in 1967).
In The Still Of The Night/Girl You're Blowing My Mind Warner 7240. 1967. Withdrawn, but promos exist. This is actually a Dean Torrence solo as Jan Berry was still ill.

American EP's

JAN AND ARNIE *Jan And Arnie* Dot EP-1093. c.1958.
JAN AND DEAN WITH THE BEL AIRE BANDITS *The Legend Of Batman* Last Ride Records 7801. Date unknown. Possibly a bootleg. The official *Jan And Dean Meet Batman* EP on Liberty also has the same number.

American albums

Jan And Dean Dore Records 101. c.1961. Their first, and extremely rare, album.
Take Linda Surfin' Liberty LRP-3294. 1964. Early copies have the full title *Mr Boss Man Takes Linda Surfin'* on the spine of the cover.
Dead Man's Curve Liberty LRP-3361. 1964. This has two different front cover designs. The first is a black and purple negative type design, while the second has a red background and a photo.
Save For A Rainy Day Jan and Dean Records JDS-101. 1968. Mixed in mono only, this was given a very limited independent release. It was really a Dean Torrence solo to help pay for Jan's hospital bills.
Save For A Rainy Day Columbia CS-9461. 1968. Withdrawn. Not only was it re-mixed for stereo, but it included an extra track *Lullaby In The Rain*. Columbia backed out at the last minute. Copies may exist.
Jan And Dean With The Soul Surfers Jan and Dean Records LJ-101. c.1968. The only other independent release from their own label.

The following is a list of their weird compilations. Dates are unknown.

Jan And Dean With The Satellites Design DLP-181.
The Heart And Soul Of Jan And Dean International Artists 250.
Shindig Design DLP-190.
The Jan And Dean Story. Greatest Hits Ruby RR-34022.
The Jan And Dean Story Ruby RR-34080.
All of these probably feature pre-Liberty material.

JAN AND DEAN/CHER *Sounds Of Solid Gold* Radio Series, number 5. 1981.

Odds and sods

JAN BERRY *Tomorrow's Teardrops/My Midsummer Night's Dream* USA Ripple 6101. c.1961. A rare early solo release.
JAN AND DEAN, JOHNNY BURNETTE and others *Christmas From Liberty* USA Liberty promo F-4513. 1963. This has Christmas messages from Liberty artists.
THE RALLY PACKS *Move Out Little Mustang/Bucket Seats* USA Imperial 66036. 1964. Jan and Dean using an alias.

Odds and sods

JAN AND DEAN and others *Let's Swing For Coke* EP. USA Coca-Cola. c.1964.
OUR GANG *Summertime Summertime/Theme From Leon's Garage* USA Brer Bird
Records 001. 1966. A Dean Torrence solo.
THE LAUGHING GARVEY *Vegetables/Snowflakes* USA White Whale WW-261.
1967. This time Brian Wilson helped out Dean Torrence on this one. The name
came from an old Laurel and Hardy movie *Laughing Gravy.*
THE LEGENDARY MASKED SURFERS *Summertime Summertime/Gonna Hustle You*
USA United Artists 50958. 1973.
THE LEGENDARY MASKED SURFERS *Summer Means Fun/Gonna Hustle You* USA
United Artists UA-XW 270-X. 1973. This band consisted of Dean Torrence,
Terry Melcher and Bruce Johnston.
JAN BERRY *Don't You Just Know It/Blue Moon Shuffle* USA Ode 66034. 1973.
Withdrawn.
JAN BERRY *That's The Way It Is/Little Queenie* USA Ode 66154. 1977.
Withdrawn.

This list doesn't take into account different mixes and productions for others on
which they've appeared. As you can see, Jan and Dean have probably had more
hardcore rarities than the average artists. This has resulted in some pretty devoted
fans, willing to shell out $100+ for many of their rarities, time and time again.
(This book is dedicated to people like them!)

Japan

British singles

Gentlemen Take Polaroids/The Experience Of Swimming Virgin VS-379. 1980.
A limited edition came with a free single *The Width Of A Room/Burning Bridges.*
Cantonese Boy/Burning Bridges Virgin VS-502. 1982. A limited edition came
with a free single *Gentlemen Take Polaroids/The Experience Of Swimming.*
Nightporter Edited. Virgin one-sided promo VSDJ-552. 1982.

British album

Assemblage Ariola-Hansa cassette ZCHAN-001. 1982. This cassette re-issue
contains previously unreleased live and re-mixed music on side two.

American singles

Sometimes I Feel So Low Same both sides. Ariola-America twelve-inch promo
7727. 1979.
Canton Same both sides. Epic-Virgin twelve-inch promo, number unknown.
1981.
Life Without Buildings Epic-Virgin flexi given away with *Trouser Press* magazine,
number 3. 1982.

American album

Interview album   Ariola-America promo, number unknown.   1979.

Odds and sods

Adolescent Sex Sung in Japanese, plus others.   Japan Victor thick red vinyl flexi, number unknown.   c.1979.

Jefferson Airplane

American singles

Stereo Review EP. RCA SP33-564. c.1969.   This free EP featured *Somebody To Love/White Rabbit/Volunteers/The Ballad Of You Me And Pooniel*.
White Rabbit/Somebody To Love Grunt white vinyl promo FB-10988.   1977.

American album

Bless It's Pointed Little Head Interview album. RCA promo, number unknown. 1969.

British album

Surrealistic Pillow   RCA SF-7889.   1967.   For some reason the UK edition excludes *White Rabbit*.

Odds and sods

Woodstock, Volumes One And Two   UK Atlantic/USA Cotillion.   1971.   This has live music.

Jefferson Starship

American singles

Runaway/Hot Water   Grunt twelve-inch promo JD-11303.   1977.
Light The Sky/Hyperdrive   Grunt twelve-inch promo JD-11426.   1978.
Find Your Way Back/Modern Times Grunt twelve-inch promo JT-12213.   1980.
Save Your Love/Wild Eyes Grunt twelve-inch promo JD-12333.   1981.
Stairway To Cleveland Grunt one-sided twelve-inch promo JD-13016.   1982.
Be My Lady   Grunt twelve-inch promo JD-13349.   1982.   Probably same both sides.
Black Widow   Same both sides.   Grunt twelve-inch promo JD-13409.   1983.

American albums

Gold   Grunt promo picture disc DJL 1-3363.   1978.
RCA Radio Special, number 19.   Grunt promo DJL 1-4569.   1982.   Interview album to promote *Modern Times*.

Rock Around The World Radio Series, number 209. (Dated 14.8.78).
JEFFERSON STARSHIP/THE DOORS *Rock Around The World* Radio Series, number 231. (Dated Jan. 1979).
Robert W. Morgan *Profiles* Radio Series. c.1979.
King Biscuit Radio Series (Dated 19.7.81).
Robert R. Klein Radio Series, number 52. (Dated 1981).
Innerview Radio Series, Series 17, programme 5. c.1981.
King Biscuit Radio Series (Dated 3.1.82).
Earth News Radio Weekend Special c.1982.
Royalty Of Rock Radio Series. c.1983.

Jethro Tull

British singles

JETHRO TOE *Sunshine Day/Aeroplane* MGM 1384. 1967. This had the old familiar yellow label that graced many Connie Francis singles of the fifties. EMI, who pressed the single, screwed up the band's name. Both of these tracks appeared on the Polydor compilation album *Rare Tracks* 2482 274 in 1976. Beware of counterfeits of this single. They come from America and don't have the original push out centre holes, opting for the large juke box sized hole as used in the USA. The label copying is, unfortunately, perfect.
A Stitch In Time/Sweet Dream Chrysalis white vinyl CHS-2260. 1979. Some early copies have the full 4:20 version, while more common later pressings have an edited version.

American singles

Stand Up Radio Spots EP. Reprise promo PRO-353. 1969.
Ring Out Solstice Bells/Christmas Song/March The Mad Scientist/Fan Dance Chrysalis twelve-inch promo 3-PDJ. 1976.
Dark Ages/North Sea Oil Chrysalis twelve-inch promo 18-PDJ. 1979.
JETHRO TULL/ROBERT PALMER *What's It All About?* Radio Series MA-1785. c.1979.

American albums

Thick As A Brick Edited and banded for radio. Reprise promo MS-2072. 1972.
A Passion Play Edited for radio. Chrysalis promo CHR-1040. 1973.
War Child Quad mix. Chrysalis CHR4-1067. 1974.
The Jethro Tull Radio Show Chrysalis promo PRO-622. c.1976.
1982 Tour Sampler Chrysalis promo 47-PDJ. 1982. A compilation album.
Robert W. Morgan *Profiles* Radio Series. c.1982.
Innerview Radio Series, Series 13, programme 10. c.1982.
King Biscuit Radio Series (Dated 6.12.81).
NBC *Source* Radio Series, number 21. (Dated 14.2.82).

Odds and sods

Living In The Past/APHRODITE'S CHILD   *I Want To Live*   French flexi given away with Le Metier magazine.   Date unknown.
Broadsword And The Beast   Japan Mobile Fidelity audiophile MFSL 1-092.   1982.

Joan Jett

American singles

Little Drummer Boy   Same on both sides.   Boardwalk twelve-inch promo NBS-007.   1980.
Summertime Blues   One-sided. Boardwalk, number unknown.   1981.   Given as a freebie with the *Bad Reputation* re-issue.
Crimson And Clover   Same on both sides.   Boardwalk twelve-inch promo NBS-012.   1982.
Crimson And Clover/Oh Woe Is Me   Boardwalk twelve-inch promo NPS-616. 1982.
Do You Wanna Touch/Summertime Blues   Boardwalk twelve-inch promo NBS-019.   1983.
Fake Friends   Same on both sides.   MCA-Blackheart twelve-inch promo, number unknown.   1983.

American albums

Bad Reputation   Blackheart Records JJ-707.   1980.   An independent pressing of 5,000. These sold out in a week which eventually led to a deal with the late Neil Bogart's Broadwalk label.
JOAN JETT/THE ROMANTICS   King Biscuit Radio Series   (Dated 14.2.82).
JOAN JETT/MARSHALL TUCKER/DAN ACKROYD   Robert R. Klein Radio Series, number 13.   c.1982.
ABC Supergroups *In Concert*   Radio Series   (Dated 21.8.82).

British albums

Bad Reputation   Ariola ARL-5058.   1980.   The Ariola version has the track *Hanky Panky* which was replaced by *Wooly Bully* and *Do You Wanna Touch* on the Epic EPC-25045 re-issue in 1982.
I Love Rock 'n' Roll   Epic EPC-85686, and picture disc EPC-11-85686.   1982. The UK version has *Oh Woe Is Me* instead of *Little Drummer Boy* which appears on the American version.

Odds and sods

Urgh A Music War   UK A & M ALMX-64692.   1981.   Has live music.

Billy Joel

Billy Joel had already been in two recording bands before he went solo. His first official recordings were made with a band called THE HASSLES, although he had done session work before that.

The Hassles' Singles (American unless noted)
You Got Me Hummin'/I'm Thinking United Artists 50215. 1967. Also released in Britain on United Artists UP-1199.
Every Step I Take/I Hear Voices United Artists 50258. 1967.
Four O'Clock In The Morning/Let Me Take You To The Sunshine United Artists 50450. 1968.
Night After Day/Country Boy United Artists 50513. 1968.

The Hassles' Albums (American unless noted)
The Hassles United Artists UAS-6631. 1967.
Hour Of The Wolf United Artists UAS-6699. 1968.
THE HASSLES/TOMMY LEONETTI Veteran's Administration Radio Series 70768. c.1967. Hosted by Joel.

A Hassles' album has also been released in Australia.
The Hassles Australian EMI. Number and date unknown. The cover includes various press clippings about the band.

The second band Joel was a part of was in fact a duet called ATILLA.
Atilla USA Epic E-30030. 1970. Their only album, which, by the way has been counterfeited.

The following are released under Billy Joel's Name.

American singles
Everybody Loves You Now/She's Got A Way Family Productions FPA-0900. 1972. His first solo single released on Family Productions, distributed by Paramount.
Tomorrow Is Today/Everybody Loves You Now Family Productions FPA-0906. 1972.
My Life Long and short versions. Columbia promo 3-10853. 1979.
Big Shot Long and short versions. Columbia promo 3-10913. 1979.
Honesty Same on both sides. Columbia twelve-inch promo AS-592. 1979.
You May Be Right With and without intro sound effects. Columbia promo 1-11231. 1980.
Sometimes A Fantasy/All For Layna Columbia twelve-inch promo AS-865. 1980.
Sometimes A Fantasy 4:19 and 3:39 versions. Columbia promo 1-11379. 1980.
Pressure Long and short versions. Columbia twelve-inch promo AS-1550. 1982.

Say Goodbye To Hollywood/Miami 2017   Columbia twelve-inch promo
AS-1298. 1981.
An Innocent Man   Sampler EP.   Columbia twelve-inch promo AS-1718.
1983.

American albums

Cold Spring Harbor Family Productions FP-2700. 1972. This first album was a
humiliation to Joel, not because of the songs, but because of the way the album
turned out. While the album was being recorded the multi-track tape machine was
running a slower speed than it should have been, so when the album was being
mixed they transferred the multi-track tape to another machine which was running
at the correct speed. The album was released to the annoyance of Joel whose voice
sounded as if he'd been inhaling pure helium. The album was finally re-released
in 1983 on Columbia, this time not only at the right speed, but with a new mix.
The Spring Harbor Is Cold Family Productions promo FP-2707. 1972. This
exists as an acetate only. A radio show concert, at the right speed, made to promote
his first album. It appeared as an album and a single, and features some songs that
were later to appear on the *Piano Man* album.
Cold Spring Harbor Excerpts/JAKE HOLMES American Forces Radio And
Television Service 392. 1972.
Piano Man Quad mix. Columbia PCQ-32544. 1974.
Souvenir Columbia one-sided promo AS-326. c.1974. A live album.
Interchords Columbia promo AS-402. 1976. An interview album.
Now Playing Columbia promo AS-453. 1978. A 'greatest hits' compilation.
Rock Around The World Radio Series, number 186. (Dated 20.3.78).
Billy Joel Columbia April-Blackwood Publishers promo ABS-1. 1978. A boxed
set of five albums.
Robert W. Morgan Radio Series. 1979.
Songs From The Attic Sampler and interview album. Columbia promo AS-1343.
1981.
Retrorock Radio Series (Dated 10.1.83).
Many of his albums have been pressed in audiophile format by CBS-Masterworks.
These include *The Stranger, 52nd Street* and *Glass Houses*.

British singles

She's Got A Way/Tomorrow Is Today Philips 6078 001. 1972. The British single
from the *Cold Spring Harbour* album.
The Entertainer/B side unknown. Philips, number unknown. 1973. This single
appeared on Philips even though the album it came from was released on CBS. It's
possible that this single was withdrawn after CBS intervention.
Ballad Of Billy The Kid/If I Only Had The Words Philips 6078 018. 1973.
Again, from the CBS album *Piano Man*. May have been withdrawn.
Tell Her About It/Easy Money CBS A-3665. 1983. The original sleeve for this
was similar to the *Innocent Man* album cover. When the single was re-released in
December 1983 it appeared in a new sleeve.

140

British albums
Cold Spring Harbour   Philips 6369 150.   1972.   The British version was also too fast like the American.
Piano Man   Philips 6369 160.   1973.   Withdrawn and released on CBS 80719.
Now Playing   CBS promo BJ-1.   1978.

Odds and sods
In Harmony, Volume Two   UK CBS/USA Columbia.   1982.   A charity Christmas album which has a new Joel track.

Elton John

Elton John made many recordings before becoming famous. His first recordings were made with the band BLUESOLOGY:
Come Back Baby/Time's Are Getting Tougher   UK Fontana TF-594.   1966.
Mr Frantic/Everyday I Have The Blues   UK Fontana TF-668.   1967.
Since I Found You Baby/Just A Little Bit   UK Polydor 56195.   1967.

He then did a stint with THE BREAD AND BEER BAND who released one single:

The Dick Barton Theme/Breakdown Blues   UK Decca F-12891.   1969.   This was then re-issued on UK Decca F-13354 in 1973.

During this time he was making money doing vocals for budget labels like Music For Pleasure and Avenue. These were made available for stores like Tesco's, Woolworth's, etc. Several of Elton's cover versions of current hits (of the late 1960s, early 1970s), appear through a series of six-track EP's from Avenue records. There include *Cottonfields, Signed Sealed Delivered I'm Yours* and *Natural Sinner*. He also cut *My Baby Loves Loving* for MFP's *Top Hits* album series in 1969.

These are in existence some acetates of unreleased songs from this time. All are British.
In The Morning   EMI-Disc.
Sarah's Coming Back   DJM Publishing.
I Can't Go On Living Without You   DJM Publishing TEM-1687/8.   1969.   This was a demo for his Eurovision song contest entry. He was beaten by *Boom Bang A Bang*.

There are probably many more from around this period as he was writing for other acts.

British singles
I've Been Loving You/Here's To The Next Time   Philips BF-1643.   1968.
Lady Samantha/All Across The Heavens   Philips BF-1739.   1969.
His first two solo singles were both released in mono.

It's Me That You Need/Just Like Strange Rain DJM DJS-205. 1969. Issued in a very rare picture bag.

Friends Mono and stereo versions. DJM promo DJS-244. 1972. It's very unusual to find a British promo issued in this American form.

Rocket Man/Goodbye/Holiday Inn DJX-501. 1972. Issued in a gatefold sleeve for the initial first few thousand.

Bite Your Lip Rocket one-sided twelve-inch promo PSLP-206 (GUAD-1). 1977. This is the long disco mix.

The Elton John Singles Collection DJM EJBOX-12. 1979. A twelve-single boxed set. The singles, complete with new picture sleeves, were also available separately.

*Goaldiggers Song/*Various messages from celebrities. Rocket GOALD-1. c.1977. Made to promote the Goaldigger's charity which helped raise money to provide football pitches for kids throughout Britain. Five hundred copies were made and sold by mail order for £5 each.

Mama Can't Buy You Love/Strangers Rocket XPRES-20. 1979. Withdrawn. The *Victim Of Love/Strangers* single on Rocket XPRES-21 replaced it.

Dear God/Tactics Rocket XPRES-45. 1981. Issued as a limited edition double single with *Steal Away Child/Love So Cold* Rocket ELTON-1.

Empty Garden 5:09 and 3:59 versions. Rocket promo XPRESDJ-77. 1982.

Jump Up Sampler EP. Rocket twelve-inch promo, number unknown. 1982.

All Quiet On The Western Front/Where Have All The Good Times Gone Rocket XPRPO-88. 1982. A very limited edition poster sleeve.

I Guess That's Why They Call It The Blues/Lord Choc Ice Goes Mental Rocket XPRES-91. 1983. This came with a very limited edition 'lumpy' sleeve with a raised musical note figure on the front.

Kiss The Bride/Dreamboat Rocket EJS-2. 1983. A limited edition came with a free single *Song For Guy/Ego* Rocket EJS-2/2.

Cold As Christmas/Crystal Rocket EJS-3. 1983. Another double single. This time the cover had changed. Instead of the colour drawing, the new sleeve was white with graphics in the centre, with a message on the front stating that the free single was a Christmas present from Elton. The single was *Don't Go Breaking My Heart/Snow Queen* with Kiki Dee. Rocket EJS-3/2.

British albums

Empty Sky DJM mono DJMLP-403. 1969. His only album to be released in both mono and stereo.

17-11-70 DJM DJLPH-414. 1971. The British and American versions have different mixes. The British version was mixed at DJM studios, while the American mix was done at Trident studios in London.

Honky Chateau DJM DJLPH-423. 1972. The press were treated to a free bottle of wine grown at the studios vinyard whilst trying to review the album. The required effect was get the reviewers bottled out of their skulls so as to give the album a glowing review.

Captain Fantastic And The Brown Dirt Cowboy DJM DJLPX-1. 1975. 2,000 copies were pressed in brown vinyl as well as some autographed sleeves.

Candle In The Wind St Michael 2094 0102. c.1978. A cheapo album made for Marks and Spencers.
Elton John DJM 14512. c.1978. A limited edition boxed set of five albums.
Too Low For Zero Rocket HISPD-24. 1983. Initial pressings came with a die cut front cover revealing coloured shapes. After this became too expensive to carry on Phonogram used a more regular sleeve on which the coloured shapes were printed.
The Superior Sound Of Elton John DJM compact disc 810062-2. 1983. This features his hits specially re-mixed for CD.

American singles

Lady Samantha/B side unknown. DJM 70008. 1969. His first American single. This is his rarest American release.
ELTON JOHNS *From Denver To L.A.*/THE BARBARA MOORE SINGERS *Warm Summer Rain* Viking Records 1010. 1969. Taken from the soundtrack of the movie *The Games*. The movie starred Michael Crawford as a Briton hoping to gain gold for running at The Olympics. *(Chariots Of Fire* came twelve years later). *The Games* also starred Ryan O'Neil, Charles Aznavour and a few Australians. Elton's contribution can be heard wafting out of a bedside tranny.
Lady Samantha/It's Me That You Need Congress CG-6017. 1969. A re-issue of the DJM single, and it still went un-noticed.
Border Song/Bad Side Of The Moon Congress CG-6022. 1970.

The two above were issued on a UNI subsidiary. *Border Song* was very quickly re-issued on UNI-55246.

Tiny Dancer 6:12 and 3:45 versions. UNI promo 55318. 1972.
Tumbleweed Connection UNI juke box EP LLP-143/L33-1903. 1972. This was also used for promo purposes.
Crocodile Rock MCA promo S45-1024. 1973. This may be edited.
Love Song 5:32 and 4:40 versions. MCA promo S45-1938. c.1973.
Don't Shoot Me I'm Only The Piano Player MCA juke box EP LLP-207/34961. 1973.
Rocking In The Cradle Of Liberty MCA Special Products 40364. 1974. This has the same number as *Philadelphia Freedom*. Clues anyone?
Pinball Wizard/TINA TURNER *Acid Queen* Polydor promo PRO-002. 1974. Taken from the *Tommy* soundtrack album.
Bite Your Lip Rocket one-sided twelve-inch promo L33-1172. 1976.
Blue Moves Sampler EP. Rocket blue vinyl twelve-inch promo L33-1953. 1976.
Ego/Flintstone Boy MCA twelve-inch promo L33-1979. 1978.
Victim Of Love/Strangers MCA twelve-inch promo L33-1850. 1979.
Johnny B. Goode/Thunder MCA twelve-inch promo L33-1854. 1979.
ELTON JOHN/BOBBY VINTON *What's It All About?* Radio Series. c.1980.
Nobody Wins/Je Veux D'La Tendresse Geffen twelve-inch promo PROA-948. 1980.
Chloe/Fanfare Geffen promo GEF-49788. 1981.
Empty Garden 5:09 and 3:59 versions. Geffen promo GEF-50049. 1982.

Empty Garden   5:09 and 3:59 versions.   Geffen twelve-inch promo PROA-1018. 1982.

ELTON JOHN/ANNE MURRAY   *What's It All About?*   Radio Series 333.   Date unknown.

I'm Still Standing   Same on both sides.   Geffen twelve-inch promo PROA-2025. 1983.

Kiss The Bride   Long and short versions.   Geffen twelve-inch promo PROA-2066. 1983.

American albums

ELTON JOHN/ATLANTA RHYTHM SECTION   *Rock Around The World*   Radio Series, number 222. (Dated 15.11.78).

ELTON JOHN/LINDA RONSTADT   Playboy Silver Anniversary Radio Series, number 5. (Dated Nov. 1978).

Victim Of Love   MCA promo boxed set of four twelve-inch singles 4L33-1848. 1979.

A Single Man   MCA picture disc MCAP-14591.   1979.   Apparently this is a different mix to the regular black vinyl version.

The Best Of Elton John. Volume One   Columbia Special Products P-16196.

The Best Of Elton John. Volume Two   Columbia Special Products P-16197.

Dates are unknown on these two limited edition compilations.

ELTON JOHN/CHER   *Billboard Yearbook '79*   Radio Series   (Dated 11.12.79).

BBC *Rock Hour*   Radio Series, numbers 61 & 62.   1980.

Dick Clark interviews Elton John   Mutual Broadcasting   (Dated 4.7.81).

BBC *Rock Hour*   Radio Series, number 152.   c.1982.

NBC *Source*   Radio Series   (Dated 7.7.82).

Direct News Radio Series DN-52.   1982.

Westwood One Radio Series   (Dated 30.8.82).

Goodbye Yellow Brick Road   Superdisk audiophile SD-216614.   1982.

NBC *Source*   Radio Series   (Dated 23.12.82).

Odds and sods

JOHN BALDRY   *Iko Iko*   UK/USA Warner.   1972.   This single features both Elton and Rod Stewart on vocals.

Friends   Soundtrack album.   UK/USA Paramount.   1972.   This album features Elton's musical score for this inferior *Love Story*-type movie.

NEIL SEDAKA   *Bad Blood*   UK Polydor 2058 532.   1974.   Elton sings co-lead vocal on this single.

JOHN LENNON   *Whatever Gets You Through The Night*   UK/USA Apple.   1974.

Another uncredited co-lead vocal on this single from John's *Walls And Bridges* album.

Tommy   Soundtrack album.   UK/USA Polydor.   1975.   His version of *Pinball Wizard* on this album is different to the DJM single version.

Gli Opera/Sorry Seems To Be The Hardest Word   Italian Rocket single, number unknown.   c.1977.   The A side, whatever it is, is sung in Italian.

Je Veux D'La Tendresse (The original French *Nobody Wins)/Fools In Fashion* French Rocket 6000 675. 1980.
ELTON JOHN AND FRANCE GALL *Les Areuse/Donner Pour Donner* French single, label and number unknown. 1981. Available in both seven and twelve inch formats. A cassette single was also made.
ELTON JOHN AND KIKI DEE *Loving You* UK Ariola ARO-269. 1982. Elton sings on the A side only.
Greatest Hits, Volume One Japan Nautilus audiophile pressing, number unknown. c.1981.
The Superior Sound Of Elton John 1983. This British compact disc compilation has now been released in Germany on vinyl.

Southside Johnny

American albums
Live At The Bottom Line Epic promo AS-275. 1976. A promo only live album.
SOUTHSIDE JOHNNY AND THE ASBURY JUKES/ROBIN LANE AND THE CHARTBUSTERS King Biscuit Radio Series (Dated Aug. 1980).

British single
Little Girl So Fine/I Ain't Got The Fever Epic EPC-5230. Withdrawn in 1977.

Bruce Johnston

American singles
Bruce and Terry (Melcher)
Custom Machine Columbia 4-42956. c.1962.
Summer Means Fun/Yeah Columbia 4-43055. 1963.
I Love You Model T/Carmen Columbia 4-43238. 1963.
Four Strong Winds/Raining In My Heart Columbia 4-43378. 1964.
Thank You Baby/Come Love Columbia 4-43479. 1964.
Don't Run Away/Girl It's Alright Columbia 4-43582. 1964.

The Rogues
Who'll Be The One/B side unknown. Beckingham 1085. c.1982.
Everyday/Roger's Reef Columbia 4-43190. c.1963.

Bruce Johnston
Do The Surfer Stomp Parts 1 & 2 Ronda 1003. 1963.
Do The Surfer Stomp Parts 1 & 2 Donna 1354. 1963. This was a national re-issue.
Soupy Shuffle Stomp/Moon Shot Donna 1364. 1964.
The Original Surfer Stomp/Pyjama Party Del-Fi 4202. Date unknown.

American albums

BRUCE JOHNSTON'S SURFING BAND   *Surfing Pyjama Party*   Del-Fi DFST-1288.   Date unknown.

BRUCE JOHNSTON   *Surfin' 'Round The World*   Columbia CL-2057 mono, CS-8857 stereo.

Jon and Vangelis

Jon Anderson and Vangelis first came together on the track *So Long Ago So Clear* on the Vangelis album *Heaven And Hell*.   UK RCA RS-1025.   1976.

British single

Friends Of Mr Cairo   Long version/*Beside*   Polydor twelve-inch promo POSPX-258.   1981.   Polydor thought it a spiffing idea to package this radio station freebie in a round blue film can. One wonders how much this cost Polydor. Guess who pays for it in the end.

British album

The Friends Of Mr Cairo   Polydor POLD-5039.   1981.   This comes in three different sleeves. The first is white with black graphics and raised figures on the left. This was quickly changed to similar raised figures in the middle. The third version is a brown cover with a colour photo of Jon and Vangelis in the middle.

American singles

I Hear You Now   4:12 and 3:37 versions.   Polydor promo PD-2098.   1980.
The Friends Of Mr Cairo   Long and short versions.   Polydor promo PD-2181. 1981.
State Of Independence/Friends Of Mr Cairo   Polydor twelve-inch promo PRO-163.   1981.
I'll Find My Way Home   Same on both sides.   Polydor twelve-inch promo PRO-181.   1982.

Joy Division

British singles

An Ideal For Living   EP.   Enigma PSS-139.   1978.   The number of people who bought this when it was released could be counted on one hand.
An Ideal For Living   EP.   Anonymous Records twelve-inch ANON-1.   1979. A re-issue of the above. Again, not many people south of Manchester were able to find it.

Odds and sods

Atmosphere/Dead Souls   French Sordide Sentimental SS-33002.   1979.   About 1,000 copies of this were made.

Atmosphere/She's Lost Control   USA Factory twelve-inch FACTUS-2.   1979.
A Factory Sampler   EP.   UK Factory FAC-2.   1979.   This contains *Digital* and
Glass.
Earcom 2   UK Fast FAST-9.   1979.   This mini album features *Auto Suggestion*
and *From Safety To Where*.
Electric Circuit, Live At The Electric Circus   UK Virgin blue vinyl ten-inch album
VCL-5003.   1979.   This has a live version of *At A Later Date*.

Most of the rare odds and sods were given a full release on the *Still* album in 1982.
You'll have to scout around bootlegs for any more un-exhumed material.

Kansas

American singles
Man The Storm Cellars, Kansas Is Koming   Kirshner promo ASZ-74.   1973.   This
is a radio spots EP for their first album.
Play The Game (alternate version)/Pre-release montage from *Vinyl Confessions*
Kirshner twelve-inch promo AS-1451.   1981.

American albums
The Kansas Mini Concert   Kirshner promo AS-555.   1978.   This has four cuts
from their *Two For The Show* album segued together on one side and banded
together on the other side.
Leftover Radio Show   Burns Media Radio Series.   c.1977.
Innerview   Radio Series.   Series 9, programme 6.   c.1978.
Robert W. Morgan *Profiles In Rock*   Radio Series.   c.1979.
Innerview   Radio Series.   Series 11, programme 8.   c.1979.
Retrorock   Radio Series.   (Dated 2.82).   Live in New York in 1976.
Westwood One Radio Series.   (Dated 26.7.82).

Kid Creole and The Coconuts

American singles
Before forming Kid Creole and The Coconuts, August Darnell had masterminded
Doctor Buzzard's Original Savannah Band which had made two albums for RCA
and one for Elektra in the mid- to late seventies.

American singles
Going Places   Same on both sides.   Sire-Ze twelve-inch promo PROA-969.   1981.
I'm A Wonderful Thing   Same on both sides.   Sire-Ze twelve-inch promo
PROA-1026.   1981.
Stool Pigeon   Plus two others.   Sire-Ze twelve-inch promo PROA-1064.   1982.

Odd Shapes and Diameters
Top SQUEEZE *Pulling Mussels From The Shell* six-inch single.   Middle KINKS *Misfits* square promo.   Bottom NEIL YOUNG *Re-ac-tor* orange vinyl triangle disc.

148

British single

Me No Pop I Edited. Ze promo WIP-6711-DJ. 1981. This is a one-sided promo which edits out the line about a VD clinic.
Stool Pigeon/In The Jungle Ze double single UWIP-6793. 1982. The free single was *He's Not Such A Bad Guy/There But For The Grace Of God Go I.*

Odds and sods

The Ze Christmas Record UK/USA Ze. 1981. Re-issued in a different form in 1982.
Dancin' Master UK NME cassette 001. 1981. This includes a live *There But For The Grace Of God Go I.*

Greg Kihn Band

American singles

Remember/Satisfied Beserkley twelve-inch promo B-12001. 1977.
Roadrunner AM & FM mixes. Beserkley twelve-inch promo AS-11427. 1979.
Can't Stop Hurting Myself Same on both sides. Beserkley twelve-inch promo AS-11471. 1980.
Breakup Song (live version)/*The Girl Most Likely* Beserkley twelve-inch promo AS-11506. 1982.

There is also in existence a Greg Kihn Band and The Rubinoos six-track live twelve-inch promo. c.1981.

American albums

Westwood One Radio Series. 1980.
GREG KIHN BAND/WILLIE NILE King Biscuit Radio Series. (Dated 10.5.81).
GREG KIHN BAND/PHILIP NORMAN (Author of *The Beatles Shout*). Robert R. Klein Radio Series. (Dated 17.5.81).
RKO Capitol live show. Ten-inch open reel. 1981.
BBC *Rock Hour* Radio Series. (Dated 11.4.82).
King Biscuit Radio Series. (Dated 16.5.82).
GREG KIHN BAND/POINT BLANK *In Concert* Radio Series, number 82-12. (Dated 6.82).
NBC Source Radio Series. (Dated 11.6.82).
Westwood One Radio Series. (Dated 21.6.82).

Odds and sods

Bserk Times German Beserkley double album 6.28457 DP. 1978. This has some live tracks recorded at the *Rockpalast* in 1977.

Carole King

Oh Neil/A Very Special Boy   Alpine 75.   1959.   Her reply to Neil Sedaka's *Oh Carol* allegedly written about Carole King.
Goin' Wild/Right Girl   ABC-Paramount 45-9921.   c.1959.
Baby Sittin/Under The Stars   ABC—Paramount 45-9986.   c.1960.
Short Mort/Queen Of The Beach   RCA 47-7560.   c.1960.
It Might As Well Rain Until September/Nobody's Perfect   Companion 2000.   1962.   This was the original issue before changing to Dimension 2000.

The other singles mentioned above are extremely obscure early Brill Building tracks and have probably never been re-issued anywhere.

A Road To Nowhere/Some Of Your Lovin   Tomorrow 7502.   1967.   The B side featured her own version of the Dusty Springfield classic.
Music   Ode 70 Records juke box EP LLP-77013.   1972.
Tapestry   Ode 70 Records juke box EP LLP-77009.   1972.
Main Street Saturday Night/Disco Tech   Capitol twelve-inch promo SPRO-8864.   1977.
Touch The Sky   Sampler.   Capitol twelve-inch promo SPRO-9103/4.   1977.
Morning Sun/Sunbird   Capitol twelve-inch promo SPRO-8957.   1977.
Move Lightly   Long and short versions. Capitol promo P-4718.   1977.
One To One   Same on both sides.   Atlantic twelve-inch promo PR-427.   1982.

American Odds and sods

During the sixties Carole King was a member of THE PALISADES and THE CITY.
THE PALISADES   *Make The Night A Little Longer/Heaven Is Being With You*   Chairman 45-4401.   c.1966.
THE CITY   *Paradise Alley/Snow Queen*   Ode ZS7-113.   1968.
THE CITY   *Why Are You Leaving/That Sweet Old Roll*   Ode ZS7-119.   1968.
THE CITY   *Now That Everything's Been Said*   Ode album Z12-44012.   1969.   This album was counterfeited in the early 1970s to cash in on King's success with *Tapestry*.
The theory has come forward recently that Carole King was in fact Little Eva (of *Locomotion* fame). Carole King hasn't yet said anything on the matter.

King Crimson

British singles

Catfood/Groon   Island WIP-6080.   1970.   A much sought after non-album A side, along with a cute picture sleeve, makes this a must.
Thela Hun Ginjeet/Elephant Talk/Indiscipline   EG twelve-inch promo KCX-001.   1981.

American singles

The Court Of The Crimson King 3:22 & 2:18 versions. Atlantic promo 2703. 1970.

Larks Tongues In Aspic Sampler EP. Atlantic promo PR-190. 1974. This features *Easy Money/Exiles/Larks Tongues Part Two*.

Elephant Talk/Thela Hun Ginjeet/Mette Kudasai Warner-EG twelve-inch promo PROA-1005. 1981.

Heartbeat/Neal, Jack And Me/Saturday In Tanzier Warner-EG twelve-inch promo PROA-1045. 1982.

American albums

KING CRIMSON/JEAN LUC PONTY *Rock Around The World* Radio Series, number 127. 1976.

The Return Of King Crimson Warner-EG promo, number unknown. 1981. An interview album to promote *Discipline*.

BBC *Rock Hour*. 1981. Live in Amsterdam.

Odds and sods

King Crimson Japan Mobile Fidelity audiophile, no number. 1983. A boxed set of all their albums pressed in audiophile format.

The Kinks

British singles

You Still Want Me/You Do Something To Me Pye 7N-15636. 1964. Their second, and still rarest single. According to legend it only sold 127 copies. Their next single *You Really Got Me* sold even more. There is in existence an EMI-Disc acetate of alternate versions of these two songs. Query. Being EMI-Disc, does this imply that it was meant for an EMI label? (Columbia for example).

Well Respected Man/Milk Cow Blues Pye export issue 7N-17100. 1966.

Mr Pleasant/This Is Where I Belong Pye export issue 7N-17314. 1966.

These two had the familiar red and black Pye labels and eventually turned up in Greece and Turkey amongst other countries. Some may have been re-imported into Britain.

At this time Pye were in the habit of making black and white picture sleeves for their singles, so it's possible that there may be some Kinks' picture sleeves for their Pye releases.

Celluloid Heroes RCA one-sided promo RCA-2299-DJ. 1973. This may have been edited.

Holiday Romance Mono and stereo versions. RCA promo RCA-2478-DJ. 1974. It's very unusual to get UK promos in this format.

Rock 'n' Roll Fantasy Long and short versions. Arista promo 189-DJ. 1977.

Better Things/Massive Reductions Arista 415. 1982. Initial copies came with a free single *Lola/David Watts* both recorded live. Arista KINKS-1. As everybody bought the double single, the regular single on its own is harder to find.

Give The People What They Want Sampler EP. Konk twelve-inch promo STORE-4. 1981.

Don't Forget To Dance Edited. Arista one-sided promo ARISTDJ-524. 1983.

British EP's

Percy Pye 7NX-8001. 1971. Not all copies came with the black and white picture bag.

The Kinks Pye Yesteryear series, export issue AMEP-1001. c.1975. This little beauty never made it back into Britain. It consisted of The Kinks first two singles back to back, so it includes *You Do Something To Me,* their rarest track to date. Not only did it come in a colour photo sleeve, but it was also pressed in both red and blue vinyl.

British albums

The Kinks Are The Village Green Preservation Society Pye NSPL-18233. 1967. The original pressings have a twelve-track line up including *Days* and *She's Got Everything.* For some reason Ray Davies decided that he didn't like this one and made Pye change it. Pye replaced it, about a week later, with a new fifteen-track version which now included *Animal Farm, Big Sky, All Of My Friends Were There, Last Of The Steam Powered Trains* and *Down By The Riverside.* Apparently an alternate *People Take Pictures* was used on the first version. People wishing to change their old copy for the new version could do so at record shops. It's probable that Pye destroyed all the twelve-track copies that were returned, making existing copies real gems.

All The Good Times Pye IIPP-100. 1973. A four-album boxed set, available only for a short period.

The Kinks File Pye FILD-001. 1976. This has two different sleeves. The first has a red cover with a cut away top revealing the inner sleeves. The second version, issued about three years later, had a different tinted cover and details of contents, etc. on the front. Altogether, I think, a ghastly design from all angles.

Give The People What They Want Arista-Konk SPART-1171. 1981. The original mix of this album appeared in America in September 1981, and was scheduled for release in Britain shortly after. Ad's appeared in the music press for the album, but a couple of weeks later another advert appeared with the word 'cancelled' across the middle. Ray Davies was in fact re-mixing the album especially for the British market, and it was this version which appeared in early 1982. It's probable that British test pressings exist of the original American mix.

State Of Confusion Arista 205 275. 1983. The track *To Catch A Thief* may have been scheduled to appear on this album, but it never turned up.

State Of Confusion Arista 405 275. 1983. This tape edition contains two extra songs, *Noise* and *Long Division. There are also two slightly different covers for the* tape. The first version has a green cover while the second version is red with 'Super S' at the top. This is a reference to the type of tape used.

Greatest Hits. Dead End Street PRT KINK-1. 1983. The hits album was a cash-in on the success of *Come Dancing*. All copies came with a free ten-inch *Dead End Street* which had some rare and previously un-released tracks. In early 1984 the whole package was re-issued with a new ten inch with different tracks and a different cover. PRT KINK-2. The tracks included on the new ten inch were more common album cuts.

American singles

Long Tall Sally/I Took My Baby Home   Cameo C-308.   1964.   Cameo didn't release any other Kinks' singles until they had taken off with *You Really Got Me* on Reprise.
Long Tall Sally/I Took My Baby Home   Cameo C-345.   1964.
You Still Want Me/You Do Something To Me   Cameo C-348.   1964.

Beware of two EP's on Cameo. One features the above four tracks on blue vinyl with a promo white label, while the other features live tracks from '60s TV, taken from the *One For The Road* video. They're both very clever bootlegs.

Arthur   Radio Spots single.   Reprise promo PRO-352.   1969.
Celluloid Heroes   6:17 and 4:39 versions.   RCA promo 74-0852.   1973.
Money Talks   3:44 and 3:26 versions.   RCA promo DJBO-0275.   1974.
Preservation   Long and short versions.   RCA promo JH-10121.   1979.
Sleepwalker/THE HOLLYWOOD STARS   *All The Kids*   Arista promo SP-5.   1976. Pressed on yellow vinyl.
Misfits   Sampler EP.   Arista square-shaped promo SP-22.   1978.   This 9" × 9" square disc was housed in an octagonally shaped cardboard sleeve, taking the misfits gag to an extreme.
The Kinks' Holiday Classic   *Father Christmas/Rock 'n' Roll Fantasy*   Arista twelve-inch promo SP-34.   1977.
Superman re-mix/*Low Budget*   Arista twelve-inch CP-700.   1978.   This re-mix hasn't appeared in Britain.
Superman   Long and short versions.   Arista twelve-inch promo SP-45.   1978.
Low Budget   Radio spots single.   Arista promo.   (Dated 10.7.79).
Catch Me Now I'm Falling   Long and short versions.   Arista promo AS-0458. 1979.
A Fistful Of Kinks   EP.   Arista twelve-inch promo SP-85.   1980.   A four-track sampler from the *One For The Road* live set, plus a colour poster.
THE KINKS/MARILYN McCOO   *What's It All About?*   Radio Series 445.   1980.
Father Christmas/Superman   Arista-Flashback FL-80106.   1980.   Some copies were given to the first 200 through the gates of their New Year's Eve 1980 concert in New York. These came in special commemorative covers.
THE KINKS/REX SMITH   *What's It All About?*   Radio Series 493/4.   1981.
THE KINKS/GLEN CAMPBELL   *What's It All About?*   Radio Series 559/560.   1981.
Come Dancing/Noise   Arista twelve-inch promo CP-152.   1983.

American EP

Kinda Kinks   Reprise playtape, number unknown.   c.1967.   This may have been the only Kinks title in this series.

American albums

Greatest Hits Reprise-RCA Record Service RS-6217. c.1966.

Now Then And Inbetween Reprise promo PRO-328. c.1971. This compilation is probably more famous for its packaging. It comes as a boxed set with grass (from the village green, of course) a puzzle, a sticker, a postcard, a consumer's guide to The Kinks, a letter and the album. The album is previously released songs in complete and medley form. Apparently there are at least two different versions with different dates on the letter which also comes with the set as well as different photos on the crossword.

Arthur . . . Reprise-Capitol Record Club SMAS-93034. c.1971.

The Kinks Kommemorative Set Produced by the Kinks Appreciation Society of Ann Arbor, Michigan in 1974. It includes a booklet, two photos as well as a one-sided disc. A demo version of *This Strange Effect* recorded c.1965. (This was eventually recorded by Dave Berry. The single appeared on Risti records.)

Modern Music Radio Series. (Dated 13.8.78).

The Low Budget Interview Arista promo SP-69. 1979. Ray Davies interviewed by Ed Sciaky.

ABC Supergroups *In Concert* Radio Series, number unknown. c.1980.

BBC *Rock Hour* Radio Series, number 244. (Dated 1.11.81). Recorded in 1978.

NBC *Source* Radio Series, number 82-66. (Dated 19.2.82).

Westwood One Radio Series, number 82.6. 1982.

Retrorock Radio Series. (Dated 23.8.82). Recorded live in 1966 and 1971.

State Of Confusion Arista cassette, number unknown. 1983. Like the British version the American cassette has *Noise* and *Long Division*.

Odds and sods

SHEL NAYLOR *One Fine Day/It's Gonna Happen* UK Decca F-11856. 1964. Although credited to Shel Naylor this is actually Shel Talmy. The Kinks back him up on both sides of this single. The A side is a Ray Davies song that The Kinks never released. I'm not sure if The Kinks played on the follow-up single *How Deep Is The Ocean/La Bamba* UK Decca F-11776.

THE LARRY PAGE ORCHESTRA *Kinky Music* UK Decca LK-4692. 1966. This is an odd, and very obscure, album of orchestral versions of Kinks' songs arranged by Ray Davies himself. It also featured *One Fine Day* the song mentioned above. This album was re-issued by Rhino Records in America, RNLP-058, in 1983.

THE JOHN SCHROEDER ORCHESTRA *The Virgin Soldiers March/*B side unknown. UK Pye 7N-17862. 1969. A Ray Davies instrumental from the soundtrack to the *Virgin Soldiers* movie.

THE KINKS *Apeman/Rats* Denmark Pye, number unknown. 1970. The A side is a different take of the song which only appeared here.

The Knickerbockers

Before re-naming themselves The Knickerbockers, they had cut two singles for

Atlantic using the name THE CASTLE KINGS. Both were released in America only:
You Can Get Him/Frankenstein   Atlantic 2107.   c.1973.
Jeanette/Caissons Go Rolling   Atlantic, number unknown.   c.1963.

THE KNICKERBOCKERS   *Lies*/B side unknown.   USA Lana 156.   1965.   This was possibly the original local independent label release, which was later taken up for national distribution by the Challenge label.

Kraftwerk

British single
Pocket Calculator   English version/German version. EMI promo, number unknown.   1981.

British album
Technopop   EMI EMC-3407.   1983.   Withdrawn.

American singles
Autobahn   Same on both sides.   Vertigo promo VEDJ-9.   1975.
Kraftwerk's Disco Best   EP.   Capitol twelve-inch promo, number unknown. 1978.   This includes *Robots/Neon Lights/Trans Europe Express*.
Showroom Dummies/Les Mannequinnes   Capitol twelve-inch promo SPRO-8502.   1978.
Pocket Calculator/Dentaku   Warner twelve-inch promo PROA-951.   1981.
Numbers/Computer World/Computer Love   Warner twelve-inch promo PROA-973.   1981.

Odds and sods
Radioactivity   Album.   German Kling Klang, number unknown.   1975.
Man Machine   Album.   German Kling Klang, number unknown.   1977.
Computer Welt   Album.   German Kling Klang, number unknown.   1981.
The three above albums have German vocals throughout.
Die Roboter/B side unknown.   German Kling Klang.   1978.   This German language single appeared on red vinyl.
Computer World   French EMI album.   1981.   This has *Mini Calculator* sung in French.
Trschen En Reder/Dentaku   German Kling Klang.   1981.   Both sung in German.
Das Model/The Model   German Kling Klang.   1981.   The A side is sung in German.
Computer Welt/Nummerer/Computer   German Kling Klang seven and twelve-inch.   1981.

Billy J. Kramer and The Dakotas

The Dakotas solo recordings are listed under their own entry earlier in the book.

British singles
Billie J. Kramer

Chinese Girl/Town Of Tuxley Toymakers   Reaction 591 014.   1967.
1941/His Love Is Just A Lie   NEMS 56-3396.   1968.   NEMS was, of course, Brian Epstein's company, but this label was formed after he died.
Colour My Love/B side unknown.   MGM 1474.   1969.
Stayin' Power/Blue Jean Queen   BASF BA-1006.   1974.
Fool Like You/B side unknown.   Decca F-13426.   1975.
Darlin' Come To Me/B side unknown.   Decca F-13442.   1975.
San Diego/B side unknown.   EMI 2661.   1976.
Ships That Pass In The Night/B side unknown.   EMI 2740.   1977.
Blue Christmas/B side unknown.   Hobo 010.   1978.   Pressed on blue vinyl.
Silver Dream/Lonely Lady   JM records, number unknown.   1981.
Rockit/Dum Dum   Runaway BJK-1.   1982.
Can't Live On Memories/Stood Up   RAK 359.   1983.
Apologies for being a little, more than a little, vague about the B sides of these. As yet, Billy J. Kramer has not released a solo album.

American single

1941/His Love Is Just A Lie   Epic 5-10331.   1968.

American singles
Billy J. Kramer and The Dakotas

Do You Want To Know A Secret/I'll Be On My Way   Liberty 55586.   1963.
I'll Keep You Satisfied/I Know   Liberty 55643.   1963,
Bad To Me/Do You Want To Know A Secret   Liberty 55667.   1964.
All of these were released pre-British invasion.

Denny Laine

I'll just mention his post-Moody Blues and pre-Wings material here. Balls was his first band after The Moody Blues. It also featured Trevor Burton, ex-member of The Move.
BALLS   *Fight For My Country/Janie Slow Down*   Wizard WIZ-101.   1971. Released in Britain. This was re-issued shortly after under the name of Trevor Burton on UK Wizard WIZ-103, and USA Epic 5-10851.

British singles

Say You Don't Mind/Ask The People   Deram DM-122.   1967.
Too Much In Love/Catherine's Wheel   Deram DM-171.   1968.
Say You Don't Mind/Ask The People   Deram DM-227.   1971.   This was re-released to cash in on Colin Bluntstone's 1971 cover version.
Find A Way Somehow/Move Me   Wizard WIZ-104.   1971.
Caroline/The Blues   Paladin PAL-5014.   c.1973.

British album

Ah Laine!   Wizard SWZ-2001.   1971.

American single

Say You Don't Mind/Ask The People   Deram DER-7509.   1967.

American album

Ah Laine!   Reprise MS-2190.   1971.

Led Zeppelin

British singles

Communication Breakdown/Good Times Bad Times   Atlantic 584 269.   1969. Withdrawn.
Whole Lotta Love/Livin' Lovin' Maid   Atlantic 584 309.   1970.   Withdrawn.
Immigrant Song/Hey, Hey What Can I Do?   Atlantic 2091 043.   1970. Withdrawn.
D'Ya Maker/Grunge   Atlantic K-10296.   1972.   Withdrawn.

Promos exist of all these withdrawn singles. It must have been Jimmy Page's idea not to release singles in Britain as Robert Plant did when he left Led Zeppelin.

Trampled Underfoot/Black Country Woman   Swansong DC-1.   1975.   This was given to record shops if they ordered twenty or more copies of the *Physical Graffitti* album. The single came in a black and white Swansong sleeve with special limited edition on the back.

British albums

Led Zeppelin   Atlantic 588 171.   1969.   The initial pressings had the name *Led Zeppelin* in blue on the front cover. This was quickly changed to orange. As far as I know this album was released in stereo only.
In Through The Out Door   Swansong SSK-59410.   1979.   This was issued in six different sleeves depicting different angles of a bar-room scene, as seen through the eyes of the six people in the bar. The sleeves are catalogued A to F on the bottom of the spine. To make things more interesting the album came wrapped in a brown paper bag which was then shrink wrapped, so you had no chance of seeing what sleeve you were getting.

American singles

Whole Lotta Love   Long and short versions. Atlantic promo 2690.   1970.
LED ZEPPELIN   *Whole Lotta Love*/KING CURTIS   *Whole Lotta Love*   Atlantic 2690/Atco 6779. A peculiar promo.   1970.
Gallows Pole   Mono and stereo versions.   Atlantic promo PR-157.   1971.
Dazed And Confused/I'm Gonna Leave You   Atlantic promo EP-1019.   c.1971.
Stairway To Heaven   Stereo on both sides.   Atlantic promo PR-175.   1972.
Stairway To Heaven   Mono and stereo versions.   Atlantic promo PR-269.   1972.
Led Zeppelin IV   Atlantic juke box EP LLP-171.   1972.
Houses Of The Holy   Atlantic juke box EP LLP-213.   1973.
D'ya Maker   Long and short versions.   Atlantic promo 2986.   1973.
Trampled Underfoot   3:38 edited version.   Mono and stereo versions.   Swansong promo SS-70102.   1975.   Probably made for AM radio.
Fool In The Rain   6:08 & 3:20 versions.   Swansong promo SS-71003.   1979.

Some copies of one of the *Stairway To Heaven* promos have turned up on blue vinyl in the last few years. They are, as always, counterfeits. The single was never pressed on blue vinyl in America.

American albums

Climb Aboard Led Zeppelin/DUSTY SPRINGFIELD   *Dusty In Memphis*   Sampler with one side each.   Atlantic promo TLST-135.   1969.
Led Zeppelin III   Mono mix.   Atlantic promo SD-7201.   1971.   Pressed, presumably for AM radio. I don't know if the mix is different to the stereo.
Physical Graffitti   Sampler.   American Forces Radio and Television Service, number unknown.   1975.
BBC *Rock Hour*   Radio Series, number 143.   1981.   This was recorded at the Royal Albert Hall in 1971.
Innerview   Radio Series.   Series 4, programme 12.   c.1981.   Sponsored by Toyota.
NBC Source Radio Series, number 29.   (Dated Aug. 1982).   A six-album set.
BBC *Rock Hour*   Radio Series, number 242.   c.1982.
LED ZEPPELIN/THE DRIFTERS.   *Sounds Of Solid Gold*   Radio Series, number 28.   1982.

Odds and sods

Save The Children Fund PSA's.   USA single including Led Zeppelin and others.   1978.
Two Originals Of Led Zeppelin   German Atlantic, number unknown.   c.1974.
This withdrawn album was compiled without Led Zeppelin's permission. It was simply the first two albums back to back.
LED ZEPPELIN/SUPERTRAMP   USA.   *What's It All About?*   Radio Series single 613/4.   c.1981.
Led Zeppelin II   Japan Mobile Fidelity audiophile pressing, number unknown.   1981.
Friends/Celebration/Since I've Been Loving You   Brazillian Rock Espectacular magazine freebie single, number 3.   Date unknown.

Arthur Lee

Before joining LOVE Arthur Lee was in several recording bands.
THE AMERICAN FOUR   *Luci Baines/Soul Food*   USA Salma 2001.   c.1964.
ARTHUR LEE AND THE LAG'S   *The Ninth Wave/Rumble Still Skins*   USA Capitol 4980.
c.1964.
ARTHUR LEE   *Do The Markin/*B side, label, number, etc. unknown.   c.1964.

British single
I Do Wonder/Just Us/Do You Know/Happy   Da Capo records CAP-1001.   1978.
An independent release. These tracks later turned up on his Rhino label album.

John Lennon

British singles
PLASTIC ONO BAND   *Give Peace A Chance/Remember Love*   Apple 13.   1969.   Some
copies also carry a Parlophone number R-5795.
PLASTIC ONO BAND   *You Know My Name/What's The News Mary Jane?*   Apple
1002.   1970.   Withdrawn, although acetates exist.
JOHN   *Power To The People/*YOKO   *Open Your Box*   Apple R-5892.   1971.   Some
copies have the halved Apple label on side one.
JOHN AND YOKO   *Woman Is The Nigger Of The World/Sisters O Sisters*   Apple
R-5973.   1972.   Withdrawn.   Promo copies may exist.
JOHN LENNON   *Whatever Gets You Through The Night/*John Lennon interviewed
by Bob Mercer, plus sales talk.   EMI promo PSR-369.   1974.
Number Nine Dream   Long and short versions.   Apple promo R-6003-DJ.   1974.

British albums
JOHN AND YOKO   *Unfinished Music One. Two Virgins*   Apple-Track SAPCOR-2.
1968.   Track Records, through Polydor, took distribution chores on this album as
EMI refused to touch it because of the sleeve. These copies have the Track logo at
the bottom of the label which later copies don't have. It's possible that mono copies
exist.
Unfinished Music Two. Life With The Lennons and *Wedding Album*   It goes
without saying that these are rare in their original form with complete inserts,
innersleeves, etc.
PLASTIC ONO BAND   *Live Peace In Toronto*   Apple CORE-2001.   1970.   Original
copies came with a calender.
Imagine   Apple PAS-10004.   1971.   Again, original copies came with an inner
sleeve, poster and a photo.
Imagine   Quad mix.   Apple Q4PAS-10004.   c.1974.   This quad mix came
complete with freebies mentioned above.

American singles

The Luck Of The Irish/Attica State Apple 1846. 1972. Withdrawn.

Slippin' And Slidin'/Ain't That A Shame Apple 1883. 1975. Another withdrawn single, although mono and stereo promos exist for both sides. *Slippin' And Slidin'* Mono and stereo versions. Apple promo PRO-8148.

*Just Like Starting Over/*YOKO *Kiss Kiss* Geffen twelve-inch promo PROA-919. 1980.

JOHN LENNON/PAUL McCARTNEY *What's It All About?* Radio Series, number and date unknown.

JOHN LENNON *What's It All About?* Radio Series 635/6. c.1981. This has Lennon on both sides.

Happy Christmas/Beautiful Boy Geffen twelve-inch promo PROA-1079. 1982.

American albums

JOHN AND YOKO *Unfinished Music One. Two Virgins* Apple-Tetragrammaton T-5001. 1968. This company, whose name is almost unpronounceable, released their debut album in the USA because Capitol didn't like the sleeve, although they eventually gave in and released it on Apple ST-3351. Beware of pirate eight-track cartridges on Orbit ORB-7023. The originals were Tetragrammaton F5-5001.

KYA Peace Talk Capitol pressed promo album. 1969. John and Yoko interviewed by Tom Campbell.

John Lennon and Ringo Starr interviewed by Billy Pearl. Army Radio Service. (Dated Feb. 1974).

Imagine (excerpts)/CHI-LITES tracks. American Forces Radio and Television Service, number unknown. c.1972.

Roots. John Lennon Sings The Great Rock 'n' Roll Hits Adam VIII 8018. 1974. The great Lennon mystery! The recording of the *Rock 'n' Roll* album was brought to an abrupt halt when Phil Spector, the producer, was involved in a near fatal car crash, so the album was finished off much later without him. Morris Levy, who owned Adam VIII label, claimed that Lennon had assigned the album to him in a contractual commitment. The release of the album went ahead on Adam VIII with full TV advertising. Obviously Lennon was displeased that his new album had to be released on a TV mail-order label, so he sued, and won. The finished album was released on Apple records as *Rock 'n' Roll* in 1975. The original Adam VIII album is a real peach as it has two songs, *Angel Baby* and *Be My Baby,* which never appeared on the Apple version. Also, to cap it all, the mix is different. In the meantime, the two unreleased songs have since appeared on an excellent bootleg single, while the whole album has been bootlegged on King Kong Records.

NBC Source Radio Series. 1981.

BBC *Rock Hour* Radio Series. 1981. A five-album set of the Andy Peebles interview in New York, December 1980.

Dick Clark Memorial Special. 1981. A three-album boxed set.

The John Lennon Collection Geffen promo Quiex II pure vinyl pressing LS-2023. 1982.

Odds and sods

MUSKATEER GRIPEWEED   *How I Won The War*   UK United Artists single UP-1196. 1966.   John Lennon is to be heard in the background of this, the theme from the Dick Lester film 'How I Won The War'. The track was re-issued in 1983 on the compilation *Liverpool 1983-1968* on the UK See For Miles CM-118.

THE ELASTIC OZ BAND   *Do The Oz/God Save Oz*   UK/USA Apple. 1972.   John can be heard on the A side.

The Long Rap/The Short Rap   USA Cotillion promo PR-104/5.   1972.   This has John talking about Ronnie Hawkins and promoting his first Cotillion album *Ronnie Hawkins*. Blue vinyl counterfeits exist.

Happy First Birthday Capital Radio   UK Warner promo SAM-20.   1974.   This single has a message from John in New York.

ELTON JOHN AND JOHN LENNON   *I Saw Her Standing There*   UK DJM/USA MCA. 1975.   The B side to *Philadelphia Freedom* featured this live track recorded at Madison Square Gardens, New York in November 1974.

ELTON JOHN AND JOHN LENNON   28 November 1974.   UK DJM seven-inch DJS-10965 and German DJM twelve-inch 0934 006.   1981.   This EP consisted of the three songs they recorded live that night, all in the wrong order! *I Saw Her Standing There, Lucy In The Sky With Diamonds* which was Elton's single at the time, and *Whatever Gets You Through The Night*. The German twelve-inch sleeve boasts that this was Lennon's last public performance. It wasn't. He did a Lew Grade benefit show in 1975.

The Final Interview   Brazillian flexi, given away with *Somtres* magazine in 1981. This was his final radio interview.

JOHN AND YOKO   *Double Fantasy*   Japan Nautilus NR-47.   1982.   This also includes a beautiful poster.

Jackie Lomax

Before signing with Apple in 1968, Lomax had been a member of a Liverpool band called THE UNDERTAKERS which made several singles:
Everybody Loves A Loser/Mashed Potatoes   UK Pye 7N-15543.   1964.
Money/What About Us   UK Pye 7N-15562.   1965.
Just A Little Bit/Stupidity   Pye 7N-15607.   1965.
THE TAKERS   *Think/If You Don't Come Back*   UK Pye 7N-15690, and USA Interphon IN-7709.   1966.

American singles

One Minute Woman/Genuine Imitation Life Gazette   Epic 5-10270.   c.1967.
Lavender Dream   4:08 and 2:44 versions.   Warner promo WB-7564.   c.1972.
Lavender Dream/Let The Play Begin   Warner promo PRO-574.   1972.

American album

An Interview With Jackie Lomax   Warner promo PRO-520.   1972.

Love

American singles
Stephanie Knows Who/Orange Skies Elektra EK-45608. 1967. Withdrawn.
I Love You Capitol 2078. c.1967. As far as I know, this has no connection with Arthur Lee's band of the same name, although Lee was with Capitol in the early 1960s

There is also a single by Love on LSD records. Details anyone?

Odds and sods
Dr Rhino And Mr Hyde UK Beggars' Banquet BEGA-35. 1981. This compilation features a previously unreleased live track *Time Is Like A River*. It was recorded at their re-union concert in 1978 and didn't appear on the *Love Live* album on USA Rhino.

Nick Lowe

Before Brinsley Schwarz, Lowe was in a band called KIPPINGTON LODGE. They released five unsuccessful singles for EMI in the late '60s:
Shy Boy/Lady On A Bicycle UK Parlophone R-5645, and USA Capitol 2236. 1967.
Rumours/And She Cried UK Parlophone R-5677. 1967.
Tell Me A Story/Understand UK Parlophone R-5717. 1968.
Tomorrow Today/Turn Out The Light UK Parlophone R-5750. 1968.
In My Life/I Can See Her Face UK Parlophone R-5776. 1968.
Rumours/Lady On A Bicycle/And She Cried/Shy Boy UK EMI Nut series 2894. 1979. An EP in a picture sleeve to cash in on Lowe's late '70s success.

British singles
Bowi EP. Stiff twelve-inch promo LAST12-1. 1977.
My Heart Hurts/Pet You And Hold You F Beat XX-23-F. 1982. This came with a free single *Cracking Up/Peace Love And Understanding* SAM-147.
Nick The Knife EP. F Beat promo NL-1. 1982.

American singles
NICK LOWE *Cruel To Be Kind*/ELVIS COSTELLO *Radio Radio*/MINK DEVILLE
Soul Twist Columbia-Capitol twelve-inch promo orange vinyl AS-443. 1978.
Ragin' Eyes Same on both sides. Columbia twelve-inch promo AS-1628. 1983.

American albums
Pure Pop For Now People Columbia JC-35329. 1978. Although this has a

162

similar cover to the British *Jesus Of Cool* album, it is almost entirely different in content.

NICK LOWE/ELVIS COSTELLO   *Rock Around The World*   Radio Series, number 204. (Dated July 1978).

Labour Of Lust   Columbia JC-36087.   1979.   This American version includes *American Squirm,* but excludes *Endless Grey Ribbon* which is on the British album.

NBC Source Radio Series.   c.1981.

The Interrogation Of Nick Lowe   Columbia promo AS-1400.   1982.   This is a history of Nick Lowe with an interview and solo music featuring some tracks that hadn't, as yet, appeared on official albums. This album was made to promote *Nick The Knife.*

BBC *Rock Hour*   Radio Series, number 36.   (Dated 27.6.82).

Odds and sods

TARTAN HORDE   *Bay City Rollers We Love You/Rollers Theme*   UK United Artists UP-35891, and Japan Liberty LLR-20114. 1975.

DISCO BROTHERS   *Let's Go To The Disco/Everybody Dance*   UK United Artists UP-36057.   1976.

TARTAN HORDE   *Roller Show/A La Rolla, Part One*   Japan United Artists CM-66. c.1978.

NICK LOWE   *Keep It Out Of Sight/Truth Drug*   Dutch Dynamite DYR-45007.   1976. This also appeared on the compilation album *Light Up The Dynamite*   UK Magnum Force MFLP-006.   1982.

NICK LOWE   *Live At The El Macambo*   EP.   Canada CBS promo, number unknown.   1978.   Apparently, only 50 copies of this EP were made to accompany Elvis Costello's live promo album.

A Bunch Of Stiffs   UK Stiff SEEZ-2.   1977.   This superb compilation album has an old United Artists' recorded track *I Love My Label.*

Stiff Live Stiffs   UK Stiff GET-1.   1978.   Nick Lowe's LAST CHICKEN IN THE SHOP perform *I Knew The Bride* and *Let's Eat.*

Lynyrd Skynyrd

American singles

I've Been Your Fool/Gotta Go   Label details unknown.   c.1971.

Need All My Friends/Michelle   Shade Tree 101.   c.1971.

Gimmie Back My Bullets   Same both sides.   MCA. promo S45-1966.   1975.

One More From The Road   Sampler EP.   MCA twelve-inch promo L33-1946. 1976.

Down South Junkin'/What's That Smell?/Lend A Helpin' Hand/Call Me The Breeze   MCA twelve-inch promo L33-1988.   1977.

American albums

Foxtrot Rock Around The World Radio Series, number 110. c.1976. A whole live album.

Street Survivors MCA-3029. 1977. The original sleeve for this, their last album, showed members of the band in flames. This was later withdrawn for a plainer white sleeve after half the members of the band were killed in a plane accident. The *flame sleeve* is still available in Britain.

Madness

British singles

The Prince/Madness Two Tone TT-3. 1979. The pressing came with the black and white paper label, with Walt Szazbo, the Two Tone mascot, on the left.

Night Boat To Cairo/Deceives The Eye Stiff juke box issue BUYJB-71. 1980. A two-track sampler from their *Work Rest And Play* EP. This was also used as a promo.

Swan Lake/Don't Quote Me On That Stiff twelve-inch promo MAD-1. 1979.

The Return Of The Los Palmos Seven/That's The Way To Do It Stiff BUY-108. 1981. This was released in two different sleeves. The first was of cartoon characters of Madness, while the second had a colour photo sleeve.

The Madness Pack Stiff GRAB-1. 1982. A limited edition set of the first six Stiff singles in picture sleeves, housed in a clear plastic wallet. The cartoon sleeve of *Los Palmos Seven* was used.

Never Ask Twice Stiff one-sided promo, number unknown. 1982.

House Of Fun Stiff. 1982. Now here's a funny thing! Some promos may not have the fairground sound effects at the end. When the single was first played on the radio these sound effects were missing because the song had a natural fade after the last chorus, but lo! sometime later, fairground noises started appearing. Am I imagining things, or what?

Our House Edited re-mix. Stiff one-sided promo BUYJB-163. 1982. This is a special radio play version of the twelve-inch warp mix. It proved so popular that Stiff pressed up a limited edition of 5,000 for public consumption.

Wings Of A Dove/Behind The Eight Ball Stiff BUY-181. 1983. Again, this came in two different sleeves. The first is white with a dove and raised lettering, while the second is a colour version with a similar design.

There have been some fascinating flexis as well.

Patches Brings You A Few Minutes Of Madness Stiff (Lyntone) LYN-8680. 1981. Given away with the teenage girls' magazine *Patches*. It includes sundry silly messages as well as their touching rendition of *Release Me*. Also included is an incomplete version of a song from the *Absolutely* album. This is their best flexi yet, showing excellent use of this medium.

Take It Or Leave It Dialogue excerpts. Lyntone LYN-10208. 1982. Given away with Event magazine in London. Hardly any music or funnies on this one.

164

Odd Shapes

Top THE POLICE *Message In A Bottle* Star-shape with wallet sleeve.　Lower left PSYCHEDELIC FURS playable picture sleeve.　Lower right GENESIS *That's All*.

My Girl Flexipop 019 (Lyntone LYN-11546). 1982. This is a much slower version of one of their best.

American singles

One Step Beyond/My Girl/Madness Sire twelve-inch promo PROA-852. 1980. *Our House* Stretch mix/*Madhouse* (dub mix) Geffen twelve-inch, number unknown. 1983. This B side mix hasn't appeared in Britain.

American albums

BBC *Rock Hour* Radio Series. 1983. Recorded at the Hammersmith Odeon in London.
Madness Geffen GHS-4003. 1983. This should have really have been called *Meet The Maddies* as it's a collection of single and album cuts that America had ignored for too long.

Odds and sods

The band called Madness that recorded for Epic records in Britain in the late 70's are not the nutty boys.
Uno Paso Adalante (*One Step Beyond* sung in Spanish)/*Mistakes* Spanish Stiff, number unknown. 1980.
Dance Craze UK Two Tone TT-5004. 1981. This is the soundtrack to the Two Tone movie, filmed live in 1981 with The Specials, Selecter, etc.
The M.I.S. Players Present Thirty Minutes Of Culture UK MIS cassette. 1982. This is a tape available only through the Madness Information Service. It is the Maddies taking off time from recording *House Of Fun* to make a spoof radio show. A tale of murder, mystery and intrigue in Radio Playhouse, as well as 'live' music from The Pyramid Club.
Racket Packet UK NME cassette 006. 1983. This features *Grey Day* recorded live at a charity show in London.
A Wonderful Time Up Here UK Stiff promo FREEB-3. 1982. A Christmas message from The Maddies is included here.

Mama's and Papa's

American singles

Interview single. Dunhill promo SPD-13. Date unknown.
If You Can Believe Your Eyes And Ears Dunhill juke box EP 50010. 1966.
Papa's And Mama's Dunhill juke box EP 50031. 1967.
People Like Us Dunhill juke box EP 50106. 1971.

American album

Live At The Monterey International Pop Festival Dunhill DSX-50100. 1970. This was a posthumous release. Recorded in 1967 at the first real hippie festival, it wasn't publicised and sold very few copies.

British album

If You Can Still Believe Your Eyes And Ears This album was announced by EMI in 1971, but never turned up. It may have been the working title for *People Like Us.*

Manfred Mann

British singles

Ski, The Full Of Fitness Food/Sweet Baby Jane Ski 01. 1971. This single was given away by Ski yoghurt as it was used as an advertising jingle on TV.
Michelin Theme Acetate only MIC-1. c.1971. Another advert jingle. They also used to supply music for a Mannekin cigar ad' in the late '60s. This was eventually released as *A B Side,* the B side to Ragamuffin Man.

British EP's

The Hits Of Manfred Mann Philips cassette-only issue MCF-5002. 1968.
The Hits Of Manfred Mann And DDDBM&T Philips cassette-only issue MCF-5005. 1968.

American singles

54321/Without You Prestige P-312; 1964. This was issued on the famous jazz label, in an attempt to cash in on the British invasion, and is their rarest USA release.
Do Wah Diddy Diddy/Bring It To Jerome Plus two others. United Artists promo EP 10030. c.1966.
Quinn The Eskimo/By Request Edwin Garvey Mercury 72770. 1968. Early copies were printed with this A side title instead of *The Mighty Quinn.*
Spirits In The Night 3:20 and 2:56 versions. Warner promo WBS-8355. 1977.
MANFRED MANN/GARY 'FLIP' PAXTON *What's It All About?* Radio Series MA-1084. c.1977.

American albums

MANFRED MANN/ANDREW GOLD *Rock Around The World* Radio Series. (Dated 4.4.75).
A Tale Of Manfred Mann Rock Around The World Radio Series, number 138. (Dated 4.3.77).
Rock Around The World Radio Series, number 137. (Dated March 1977).
Rock Around The World Radio Series, number 148. (Dated 29.5.77).
BBC *Rock Hour* Radio Series, number 59. c.1979.
MANFRED MANN/RY COODER King Biscuit Radio Series. (Dated 12.4.81).

Odds and sods

What's New Pussycat? Soundtrack album. USA United Artists UAM-4128 mono. 1964. This may also be in stereo.

Come Tomorrow (Sung in German)/B side unknown. German HMV, number unknown. 1965.
Charge Of The Light Brigade Soundtrack album. USA United Artists UAS-5177. 1965.

Marillion

British single
Garden Party/Charting The Single/Margaret EMI twelve-inch 12EMIS-5393. 1983. The EMIS precis denotes that this came with a very limited edition poster.

American single
He Knows You Know edited/*Chelsea Morning* edited. Capital twelve-inch promo SPRO-9930. 1983.

Odds and sods
Reading Rock '82 UK England-Mean MNLP-82. 1983. This has a couple of live tracks. One of the tracks, *He Knows You Know,* also appeared on *The Marquee Collection 1958-1983, Volume Three* UK England MAR-3. 1983.

George Martin

As most of George Martin's recorded work has included many Beatles songs, I think it only fair to list a complete discography. Most, if not all, of Martin's Beatles recordings are orchestral.

British singles
All My Loving/I Saw Her Standing There Parlophone R-5135. 1964.
Ringo's Theme/And I Love Her Parlophone R-5166. 1964.
All Quiet On The Mersey Front/Out Of The Picture Parlophone R-5222. 1965.
I Feel Fine/Niagra Theme Parlophone R-5256. 1965.
Yesterday/Another Girl Parlophone R-5375. 1966.
The Family Way Theme/Love In The Open Air United Artists UP-1165. 1966. These are two Paul McCartney compositions.
Pulp/B side unknown. United Artists, number unknown. c.1972.

British EP
Music From 'A Hard Day's Night' Parlophone GEP-8930. 1964.

British albums
Off The Beatles Track Parlophone PMC-1227 mono, PCS-3057 stereo. 1964.

George Martin Plays Help!   Columbia SX-1775 mono.   Columbia-Studio Two TWO-102 stereo.   1965.
George Martin Instrumentally Salutes The Beatles Girls   United Artists ULP-1157 mono, SULP-1157 stereo.   1966.
And I Love Her   Columbia-Studio Two TWO-141.   1966.   Stereo only issue.
The Family Way   Film soundtrack.   Decca LK-4847 mono, SKL-4847 stereo. 1966.
By George   Sunset SLS-50182.   1973.
Live And Let Die   Film soundtrack.   United Artists UAS-29475.   1973.
Beatles To Bond And Bach   Polydor 2383 304.   1975.
Off The Beatle Track   Charly-See For Miles CM101.   1982.
Beatles To Bond And Bach   IMP 105.   1983.   A cheapo album made for Marks and Spencers.

American singles
Ringo's Theme/And I Love Her   United Artists 745.   1964.
*A Hard Day's Night/*B side unknown.   United Artists 750.   1964.
All Quiet On The Mersey Front/Out Of The Picture   United Artists 831.   1965.

American albums
Off The Beatle Track   United Artists UAM-3377 mono, UAS-6377 stereo.   1964.
A Hard Day's Night   United Artists UAM-3383 mono, UAS-6383 stereo.   1964.
George Martin Plays Help!   United Artists UAM-3448 mono, UAS-6448 stereo. mono, UAS-6420 stereo.   1965.
George Martin Plays Help   United Artists UAM-3448 mono, UAS-6448 stereo. 1965.
George Martin Instrumentally Salutes The Beatle Girls   United Artists UAS-6539 stereo.   1966.   There may be a mono for this.
The Family Way   Film soundtrack.   London M-76007 mono, MS-82007 stereo. 1966.
London By George   United Artists UAS-6647.   1967.
Live And Let Die   Film soundtrack.   United Artists UA-LA 100-G.   1973.

Odds and sods
Ferry 'Cross The Mersey   Film soundtrack.   UK Columbia/USA United Artists. 1964.   Martin was musical director for this excellent movie.
A Hard Day's Night   Film soundtrack.   USA United Artists UAM-3366 mono/UAS-6366.   1964.   He was again musical director as well as supplying some incidental music, as he did with *Ferry 'Cross The Mersey*.
Yellow Submarine   Film soundtrack.   UK/USA Apple.   1969.   George Martin's soundtrack music takes up the whole of the second side.

There is also in existence an acetate of George's music for *Magical Mystery Tour* in 1967.   EMI-Disc acetate.

Paul McCartney

British singles

WINGS *Love Is Strange/I Am Your Singer* Apple R-5932. 1972. Withdrawn. Promos may exist.

PAUL McCARTNEY AND WINGS *Band On The Run* 5:09 and 3:50 versions. EMI promo R-5997-DJ. 1974. This was a white EMI label.

Junior's Farm 4:20 and 3:03 versions. Apple promo R-5999-DJ. 1974. This has the regular whole and halved Apple label.

Sally G/Junior's Farm Apple R-5999. 1975. Their rarest official UK release. The A and B sides were swopped in early 1975 as DJ's, probably bored with the A side (I hated it), flipped the disc to find the marginally better *Sally G.*

WINGS *Silly Love Songs* Long and short versions. Parlophone promo R-6014-DJ. 1976.

Let 'Em In 5:08 and 3:43 versions. Parlophone promo R-6015-DJ. 1976.

Mull Of Kintyre/Girl's School Parlophone R-6018. 1977. White label test pressings were made on blue vinyl. It's possible that blue vinyl copies, in their regular form, made their way into shops.

Mull Of Kintyre Long and short versions. Parlophone promo R-6018-DJ. 1977.

With A Little Luck Long and short versions. Parlophone promo R-6019-DJ. 1978.

Goodnight Tonight Long version/*Daytime Nightime Suffering* Parlophone twelve-inch 12YR-6023. 1979. There are two different sleeves for this. The first has a glossy colour photo cover with a Parlophone inner sleeve. As this was very expensive to make EMI later changed the cover to a hard cardboard version of the Parlophone inner sleeve design.

Waterfalls 4:41 and 3:22 versions. Parlophone promo R-6037DJ. 1980.

Temporary Secretary Parlophone one-sided promo R-6039-DJ. A special seven-inch edited version. The regular shop copies were twelve-inch only.

PAUL McCARTNEY AND MICHAEL JACKSON *Say Say Say* UK re-mix. Parlophone one-sided twelve-inch promo, number unknown. 1983. This was a special Britain only re-mix.

British albums

McCartney Apple PCS-7102. 1970. Original promo copies came with a self interview by McCartney (with help from Peter Brown) on a sheet of paper.

WINGS *Back To The Egg* Parlophone promo box set edition, probably no number. 1979. Some promo copies were also pressed as picture discs. This is probably the rarest McCartney item of all, and if you want one don't expect any change out of £200.

PAUL McCARTNEY *The McCartney Interview* Parlophone CHAT-1. 1980. This was deleted on the day of issue.

American singles

Mary Had A Little Lamb/Little Woman Love Apple 1851. 1972. There are two variations to the picture sleeve for this. One had both A and B side titles on the front, while the other had just the A side title.

PAUL McCARTNEY AND WINGS *Jet/Mamunia* Apple 1871. 1974. Withdrawn.

Jet Long and short versions. Apple promo, number unknown. 1974.

Band On The Run 5:09 and 3:50 versions. Apple promo PRO-6825. 1974.

Junior's Farm 4:20 and 3:03 versions. Apple promo PRO-6999. 1974.

WINGS *Let 'Em In* 5:08 and 3:43 versions. Capitol promo SPRO-8424. 1976.

Maybe I'm Amazed Long and short versions. Capitol twelve-inch promo SPRO-8574. 1977.

Goodnight Tonight 7:25 and 4:18 versions. Columbia twelve-inch promo 23-10940. 1979.

Waterfalls/Check My Machine Columbia 1-11335. 1980. The picture sleeve for this was withdrawn after a few days.

Coming Up Studio and live versions. Columbia twelve-inch promo AS-775. 1980. This may be McCartney's rarest US issue.

Coming Up Live version. Columbia one sided disc AE7-1204. 1980. This white label single was given with the initial copies of the *McCartney II*.

Waterfalls 4:41 and 3:22 versions. Columbia promo 1-11335. 1980.

Ebony And Ivory (with STEVIE WONDER)/*Ballroom Dancing/The Pound Is Sinking* Columbia twelve-inch promo white vinyl AS-1444. 1982.

Take It Away Special 3:50 edit. Same on both sides. Columbia promo 38-03018. 1982.

Say Say Say (with MICHAEL JACKSON) Same on both sides. Columbia twelve-inch promo AS-1758. 1983.

American albums

Brung To You By Ram Apple one-sided promo SPRO-6210. 1971. This is an interview album with radio spots.

PAUL McCARTNEY AND WINGS *Band On The Run Interview Album* Apple promo SPRO-2955/6. 1974.

PAUL McCARTNEY AND WINGS *Band On The Run* Apple SO-3415. 1974. The USA edition has *Helen Wheels* which isn't on the UK version.

WINGS *Wings Over America* Capitol promo SWCO-11593. 1977. Promo copies came on red, white and blue vinyl.

The McCartney Interview Columbia promo A2S-821. 1980. This is a beautifully packaged double-album set. Album one is the interview on its own, while album two has interview excerpts with music from the *McCartney II* album. It also came with a hundred page black and white photo book and a transcription of the interview. Counterfeits were made, but these don't include the book.

PAUL McCARTNEY AND WINGS *Band On The Run* CBS Masterworks audiophile pressing HC-46482. 1982.

BBC *Rock Hour* Radio Series. (Dated April 1982). This is the Desert Island Discs radio special with Roy Plomley.

BBC *Rock Hour* (Dated 6.6.82). This is an hour long interview with Andy Peebles, with music from *Tug Of War*. This was first broadcast on UK Radio One. There is also another *Tug Of War* interview from the BBC, this time on a ten-inch open reel. This interview also has contributions from Stuart Grundy and Alexis Korner.

NBC Source (Dated June 1982). This was titled *Paul McCartney Today*.

Paul McCartney And Bob Harris Talk About Buddy Holly MCA promo BH-1. 1983. Made to promote *For The First Time Anywhere* album.

Odds and sods
Singles

THE GEORGE MARTIN ORCHESTRA *Love In The Open Air/Theme From The Family Way* UK United Artists UP-1165. 1966. Paul McCartney wrote the main theme and incidental music for this Haley Mills and Hywel Bennett movie. There are other versions by The Tudor Minstrels on USA London LON-1012, Sounds Sensational on UK HMV POP-1584, USA Capitol 5957, and The Casino Royals on UK London HL-10122. All of these were from 1966.

PAUL AND LINDA McCARTNEY *Eat At Home/Smile Away* Spanish Odeon 04864 and Japan Apple AR-2879. 1972. This single was never intended for official release anywhere, but these countries went ahead anyway.

THE COUNTRY HAMS Walking In The Park With Eloise/Bridge Over The River Suite UK EMI 2220 and USA EMI 3977. 1973. This was one of the results of McCartney's trip to Nashville. Also playing on this are Chet Atkins and Floyd Cramer. The A side was written by Paul's dad. The single was re-issued in 1982 with a new label design. Bootleg picture discs are in existence.

PERCY 'THRILLS' THRILLINGTON *Uncle Albert, Admiral Halsey/Eat At Home* UK Regal Zonophone EMI-2594. 1975. Two tracks from Thrillington's album.

WINGS *Let 'Em In/Beware My Love* Re-mix. French Pathe twelve-inch 980627. 1977. This French twelve-inch has a unique mix of the B side.

SUZIE AND THE RED STRIPES *Seaside Woman/B Side To Sea Side* USA Epic 8-50403 and twelve-inch promo AS-361. 1977. Beware of bogus twelve-inch copies on red vinyl. The record was released under this name as people would not buy it if they knew Linda McCartney was singing. It was eventually given a full release in Britain in 1979, first using the Suzy And The Red Stripes name. This version is A&M AMS-7461. All copies were on yellow vinyl, but some came in a special limited edition boxed set, complete with ten miniature saucy postcards and a button badge. The single was re-released a year later under Linda McCartney's name (a very brave thing to do, if you ask me). This time a new sleeve was used, and a twelve inch was made, AMSP-7461.

WINGS *Mull Of Kintyre/Girl's School* Israel Capitol R-6018. 1977. This was pressed on clear yellow vinyl as well as a black sleeve with the usual British design.

WINGS *Everyday/*THE WHO *Sister Disco/*ROCKPILE AND ROBERT PLANT *Little Sister* USA Atlantic twelve-inch promo, number unknown. 1981. Taken from the *Concerts For Kampuchea* album.

MICHAEL JACKSON AND PAUL McCARTNEY *The Girl Is Mine/*MICHAEL JACKSON *Can't Get Outta The Rain* USA Epic 39-03288. 1982. Also released on a cheapo low fidelity one-sided disc ENR-03372. The British copy was Epic EPCA-2729. In addition, there was a very limited edition picture disc, EPCA-11-2729. The record was also released as a twelve-inch in Holland EPC12-2729. After a while CBS in America noticed that DJ's were fading the record before it got to the embarrasing chat piece at the end. So CBS issued a new promo without the chat: Epic promo 39-03288. There have been two red vinyl issues of this single so far – the first from Israel in 1982, and the second from the pack of nine Jackson singles release by UK CBS at Christmas 1983.

JOHN WILLIAMS *Paul McCartney's Theme From The Honourable Consul*/Other artist on B side. UK Island Visual Arts IS-155. 1983.

Tapes

Paul McCartney Radio Special USA Rolling Stone Magazine News Service five-inch open reel lasting 13:50 mins. Date unknown.

Tug Of War Interview. USA BBC-London Wavelength, ten-inch open reel. 1982. This also features Stuart Grundy and Alexis Korner.

SFX magazine numbers 11 and 12. This was a short-lived British news and interviews magazine on a C60 cassette. These two editions from July 1982 feature a McCartney interview.

Paul McCartney's Bedside Manner UK open-reel radio show made for hospital radio. 1983. This hour long show was inspired by his work for Radio GOSH (Great Ormand Street Hospital). This tape features songs *Get Well Soon, Do What The Nurse Tells You,* as well as jingles and stories.

Albums

THE GEORGE MARTIN ORCHESTRA *The Family Way* Film soundtrack. UK Decca and USA London (full details see George Martin). 1966.

WINGS *Wildlife* USA Rot Records RR-218. c.1974. This was made by R.O.R. Music Promotions, supposedly a record club paying royalties.

PERCY 'THRILLS' THRILLINGTON *Percy 'Thrills' Thrillington* UK Regal-Zonophone EMC-3175 and USA Capitol ST-11642. 1975. An instrumental arrangement of the *Ram* album. Percy is really Paul of course. Some British promos came with different sleeves to the released version.

Columbia's Twenty One Top Twenty USA Columbia promo A2S-700. 1978. This has the only album appearance of *Goodnight Tonight.*

Concerts For Kampuchea UK/USA Atlantic. 1981. This has a whole side of Wings and Rockestra live in London in 1979. This turned out to be McCartney's last live appearance.

WINGS *Venus And Mars* Uruguay Apple SAPL-30535. 1975. This Apple issue was only issued in Uruguay making this the last new Apple release anywhere in the world.

MIKE McGEAR *McGear* UK Centre Labs, no number. Date unknown. This was a special six-track only re-issue of his 1974 Warner Brothers album which featured Paul heavily. This version was in a limited edition of 500 numbered and autographed copies. It may have been mail order only. Recently an eighteen-track hits compilation made by EMI in Japan appeared in promo form only.

M.C.5.

American singles

Kick Out The Jams/Motor City Is Burning Elektra promo MC5-1. 1968. The regular copy had the number EK-45648.

Looking At You/Borderline A2 records 333. Date unknown. Is this a bootleg? It was also given a release by the Skydog label in France, M-001, in the mid-'70s.

One Of The Guys/I Can Only Give You Everything AMG records 1001. Date and more details are unknown.

I Just Don't Know/I Can Only Give You Everything Grease, number unknown. Date and more details are unknown.

American albums

Kick Out The Jams Elektra EK-74042. 1968. Original copies have liner notes which were later withdrawn and altered. The offending line was the now famous 'Kick out the jams, kick off the motherfuckers!'

Babes In Arms ROIR tapes, number unknown. 1983. A collection of out-takes live tracks etc., made available on this cassette.

Solos, odds and sods

Gold Soundtrack album. UK Mother MO-4001. 1971. This has two new M.C.5 tracks.

UP (The John Sinclair Freedom Rally) *Free John Now/Prayer For John* USA Rainbow 22191. c.1972. Sinclair was the perpetrator behind the White Panther Party, and subsequently went to jail shortly after leaving the M.C.5. Among the clique of Sinclair supporters was John Lennon who wrote a song for Sinclair which appeared on the awful *Some Time In New York City* album in 1972.

THE WORD *The Nazz/Cast Your Bread* USA Charisma CA-3502 and UK Charisma CB-345. 1979. This tribute to Lord Buckley's jive talking version of the New Testament was nearly a hit when first released. Charisma tried again in 1982, this time releasing the record under Sinclair's own name.

WAYNE KRAMER *Ramblin' Rose/Get Some* UK Chis-Stiff or Stiff-Wick DEASUK-1. 1978. A joint co-operation between Stiff and Chiswick records. This record aimed to raise £10,000 to get Kramer out of jail, where he was serving five years for cocaine trafficking.

WAYNE KRAMER *The Harder They Come/East Side Girl* UK Radar ADA-41. 1979. This single was made for Radar shortly after his release from jail.

ROBIN TYNER AND THE RODS *Till The Night Is Gone/Flipside Rock* UK Island WIP-6418. 1977. Tyner came to England in the summer of '77 to survey the punk scene. His observations were included in a brilliant piece in the NME. While in England he MC'd (geddit?) the Chelmsford punk festival, met up with Eddie And The Hot Rods, and promptly made this one-off single with them.

Meatloaf

American singles

STONEY AND MEATLOAF *The Way You Do The Things You Do/What You See Is What You Get* Rare Earth R-5033-F. 1973.

Presence Of The Lord/More Than You Deserve RSO RS-407. 1974. His first solo outing and his only RSO release.

Two Out Of Three Ain't Bad Long and short versions. Epic promo 8-50513. 1977.

You Took The Words Right Out Of My Mouth/Bat Out Of Hell Epic twelve-inch promo AS-382. 1977.

Bat Out Of Hell/You Took The Words Right Out Of My Mouth/Paradise By The Dashboard Lights Epic twelve-inch promo AS-415. 1978.

Paradise By The Dashboard Lights Epic promo AE7-1157, and twelve-inch promo AS-477. 1978. These two probably have the same track on both sides.

Peel Out/I'm Gonna Love Her For Both Of Us Epic twelve-inch promo AS-1277. 1981.

American albums

STONEY AND MEATLOAF *Stoney And Meatloaf* Rare Earth RS-528. 1973. This was re-released in 1978 to cash in on his solo success. This version with a new sleeve was on Prodigal P7-10029R1.

Live At Father's Place Epic promo AS-409. 1978. This is, more or less, *Bat Out Of Hell* live. Beware of counterfeits on red vinyl, the original is on black vinyl only.

Rock Around The World Radio Series. 1980. Live music, plus other artists.

BBC *Rock Hour*. 1978. Live at The Hammersmith Odeon in 1978.

NBC *Source* (Dated 20.9.81).

British singles

STONEY AND MEATLOAF *The Way You Do The Things You Do/What You See Is What You Get* Rare Earth RES-103. 1973. This was re-issued on Prodigal PROD-10 in 1978.

You Took The Words Right Out Of My Mouth Long and short versions. Epic promo EPC-5980-DJ. 1978.

Bat Out Of Hell Long and short versions. Epic promo EPC-7018-DJ. 1978.

Deadringer Sampler EP. Epic promo, number unknown. 1981.

Midnight At The Lost And Found/Fallen Angel Epic DA-3748. 1983. Initial copies came with a free single *Bat Out Of Hell* live/*Deadringer* live.

British albums

STONEY AND MEATLOAF *Stoney And Meatloaf* Rare Earth SRE-3005. 1973. This was re-issued on Prodigal PDL-2010 in 1978.

Odds and sods

The Rocky Horror Picture Show   UK Ode SP-77026.   1974.   Meatloaf sings *Whatever Happened To Saturday Night* and *Eddie Teddy*.
Intergalactic Touring Band   UK Charisma CDS-4009 and USA Passport PB-9823. 1978.   Meatloaf does some guest vocals.
Live At The El Macambo   Canada CBS promo CDN-9.   1978.   Recorded for CHUM-FM in Toronto.
Bat Out Of Hell   German Epic half-speed copy EPCM-82419.   1981.

Steve Miller

The Steve Miller Band first appeared on the Chuck Berry album *Live At The Fillmore Auditorium* on USA Mercury SR-61138.   1967.

American singles

Living In The USA   4:03 and 3:10 versions.   Capitol promo PRO-4705.   1973.
True Fine Love/Dance Dance Dance   Capitol twelve-inch promo SPRO-9008. 1976.
Macho City   Long and short versions.   Capitol twelve-inch promo SPRO-9734. 1981.
Abracadabra   Same on both sides.   Capitol twelve-inch promo SPRO-9797.   1982.

American albums

Anthology   Capitol Record Club issue R-223186.   1973.
Innerview   Radio Series, number 525.   c.1978.

British single

Macho City   Full version.   Same on both sides.   Mercury twelve-inch promo STEVE-12.   1981.

Odds and sods

Fly Like An Eagle   Japan Mobile Fidelity audiophile MFSL-1-021.   1980.
Greatest Hits 1974-1978   UK Mercury audiophile HS-9919 916.   1982.
Revolution   Soundtrack album.   USA United Artists UAS-5785.   Date unknown. This has a new version of *Mercury Blues*.

Joni Mitchell

American singles

Clouds   Radio Spots.   Reprise promo PRO-333.   1968.
Chelsea Morning/B side unknown.   Reprise promo PRO-337.   1968.

Baby You're So Square, plus others.   Geffen twelve-inch promo PROA-1081. 1982.

American albums
Court And Spark   Quad mix.   Asylum EQ-1001.   1974.
Innerview   Radio Series.   Series 14, programmes 12 and 13.   c.1980.
Wild Things Run Fast   Geffen Quiex II pure vinyl pressing promo GHS-2019. 1982.

British single
Chinese Cafe/Ladies Man   Geffen DA-3122.   1983.   Initial copies came with a free interview single.

British album
Original Pye records pressing of her first album used the title *My City Was Fair* on the label. The album is also known as *Joni Mitchell* and *Songs To A Seagull*. How many titles are there for this album?

Odds and sods
Alice's Restaurant   Film soundtrack.   USA United Artists UAS-5195.   1969.   She contributes to the soundtrack of this hippie 'Carry On' type movie.
Court And Spark   Japan Nautilus audiophile pressing, number unknown.   1982.
The Hissing Of Summer Lawns   UK Asylum K-53018.   1982.   Pressed by Nimbus records in audiophile format and sold through a hi-fi mag.

Moby Grape

Before changing their name to Moby Grape they had cut one single as The Misfits.
Little Piggy/Lost Love   USA Imperial 66054.   c.1965.

American singles
Fall On You/Changes   Columbia 4-44170.
Sitting By The Window/Indifference   Columbia 4-44171.
8:05/Mister Blues   Columbia 4-44172.
Omaha/8:05   Columbia 4-44173.
Hey Grandma/Come In The Morning   Columbia 4-44174.
These tracks were taken from the first album *Moby Grape* and were all released in the same week.   1967.
Omaha/8:05   Columbia promo JZSP-118976.   1967.   A special promo to plug the first album.

American albums
Moby Grape   Columbia CL-2698 mono, CS-9498 stereo.   1967.   The initial copies with a sleeve showed band member Don Stevenson making a one-fingered 'up

yours' sign while holding a washboard. This was later air-brushed over by CBS giving the impression that his finger had been severed.

Wow Columbia CXS-3. 1968. Initial copies came with a free album, *Grape Jam* Columbia MGS-1.

Moby Grape, Wow and *Grape Jam* were all re-issued by San Fransisco Sound Records in audiophile versions in 1981.

The Monkees

American singles

A Little Bit Me/She Hangs Out Colgems 66-1003. 1966. The B side was quickly changed to *A Girl I Knew Somewhere* on Colgems 66-1004.

The Monkees Colgems juke box EP LLP-101. 1966.

More Of The Monkees Colgems juke box EP LLP-102. 1967.

Teardrop City/A Man Without A Dream Colgems SP45-191. 1968.

American albums

The Monkees Present Colgems COS-117. 1969.

Changes Colgems COS-119. 1969.

A Barrel Full Of Monkees Colgems SCOS-1001. c.1970.

These three albums were all released when the Monkees had ceased to be cute. The result was that they didn't sell and were quickly deleted when Colgems sold out to Bell Records.

Golden Hits Colgems PRS-329. A post break-up Colgems release. c.1970.

The Monkees Laurie House LH-8009 (RCA Special Products DPL2-0188). c.1974. A TV advertised album.

She Hangs Out Koala 14654. c.1978. Probably a pirate album.

THE MONKEES/BRENDA LEE *Sounds Of Solid Gold* Radio Series, number 20. 1982.

British album

The Monkees Reader's Digest, number unknown. 1983. This was a free album given with a boxed set of '60s hits, etc.

Odds and sods

Valleri/Tema Dei Monkees RCA-Italiana 1546. 1967. The B side was sung in Italian.

There was also a set of cardboard discs, probably given away with breakfast cereals in the late '60s. All are American.

I'm A Believer Number 1.

Papa Gene's Blues Number 2.

Forget That Girl Number 3.

Mary Mary/The Day We Fell In Love Number 4.

The Monkees' Song Book USA Epic BN-24248. c.1967. Anonymous artists play The Monkees' hits, a typical album of the time.

Monty Python

British singles

Flying Sheep/Man With Three Buttocks BBC, number unknown. 1970. a rare release.
Monty Python's Tiny Black Round Thing NME-Charisma flexi SFI-1259. 1974. There was another flexi at the same time from Zig Zag magazine featuring Monty Python.
Python On Song EP Charisma double single MP-001. 1975. Made to promote the 'Monty Python And The Holy Grail' movie. It consisted of *The Lumberjack Song/The Spam Song* CBS-268, and *Bruce's Song/Eric The Half A Bee* PY-2. *Brian/Always Look On The Bright Side Of Life* Bleeped version. Warner promo K-17495-PRO. 1980.

British albums

The Monty Python Instant Record Collection Charisma CAS-1134. 1979. This originally came with a cover, folding out into a box with phony album titles along one side, to give the impression of a collection of albums, with such titles as *Frank Sinatra: My Way, Or Else.*
Contractual Obligations Album Charisma CAS-1152. 1981. The initial pressings came with the track *Farewell To John Denver* which includes a part of one of his recordings, apparently used without permission. This was later withdrawn.

American singles

The Least Bizarre EP Buddah promo CMP-EP. c.1974.
Contractual Obligation Album Sampler. Arista twelve-inch promo SP-101. 1981.

American albums

Live At The City Center, April 1976 Arista AL-4073. 1976. This was not released in Britain.
Matching Tie And Handkerchief Banded for radio play. Arista promo AL-4039. 1976.

Odds and sods

A Poke In The Eye With A Sharp Stick UK Transatlantic TRA-331. 1977. This is a brilliant compilation of British comedy, featuring not only The Pythons, but The Goodies, Peter Cook, John Bird's version of the painting of the last supper (complete with kangaroos), Eleanor Bron and many others.

The Moody Blues

British singles

Life Not Life/B side unknown.   Decca.   1967.   Withdrawn.
Gemini Dream   Same on both sides.   Threshold twelve-inch promo BLUE-1.
1981.

American singles

Go Now/Lose Your Money   London LON-9726.   1965.   When first released in
1965 it had a purple and silver label, this was then quickly changed to the blue and
black 'swirl' label.
Gemini Dream   Same on both sides. Threshold twelve-inch promo MK-174.   1981.
Sitting At The Wheel   Same on both sides.   Threshold twelve-inch promo
MK-241.   1983.
Blue World   Same on both sides.   Threshold twelve-inch promo MK-237.
1983.

American albums

In The Beginning   Deram DES-18051.   1971.   This is a re-release of their first
American album *The Moody Blues Number One, Go Now* and was deleted very
quickly.
A Question Of Balance   Threshold-Capitol Record Club SMAS-93329.   c.1973.
Interview album.   Threshold promo THSX-100.   c.1973.
Robert W. Morgan.   Radio Series.   (Dated 18.11.78)..
THE MOODY BLUES/ROD STEWART   *Rock Around The World*   Radio Series.   1978.
ABC *Supergroups In Concert*   Radio Series, SGC-101.   1981.   A three-album set.
King Biscuit Radio Series.   (Dated 21.2.81).
Westwood One Radio Series, number 81-27/8.   1981.
King Biscuit Radio Series.   (Dated 10.10.81).
THE MOODY BLUES/THE SEARCHERS   *Sounds Of Solid Gold*   Radio Series, number 26.
1982.
THE MOODY BLUES/ELO   *Sounds Of Solid Gold*   Radio Series, number 35.   1982.

Odds and sods

The Days Of Future Past   Japan Mobile Fidelity audiophile pressing MFSL-1-042.
1980.
On A Threshold Of A Dream   Japan Nautilus audiophile pressing NR-21.   1981.

Van Morrison

American singles

Brown Eyed Girl/Midnight Special   Philco-Ford Hip Pocket HP-16.   1968.

Wavelength   6:07 and 3:57 versions.   Warner promo WBS-8661, and twelve-inch promo PROA-755.   1977.
Summertime In England/Hymns Of Ancient Peace   Warner twelve-inch promo PROA-911.   1981.

American album
Live At The Roxy   Warner Brothers Music Show promo WBMS-102.   1978.
Retrorock   Radio Series.   (Dated 9.11.81).

Odds and sods
The Bitter End Years   USA Roxbury RX3-300.   1976.   Live tracks from the '60s are included here.
The Last Waltz   UK/USA Warner.   1978.   Sings on this live set.
Moondance   USA Superdisc audiophile pressing SD-110.   c.1981.

Motorhead

Before forming Hawkwind and Motorhead, Lemmy had been in at least two recording bands. The first was Reverend Black and The Rockin' Vicars, which cut one single for Irish Decca, *Zing Went The Strings Of My Heart,* in 1963. They then shortened the name to THE ROCKIN' VICARS and released singles in Britain:
I Go Ape/Someone Like You   Decca F-11993.   1964.
It's Alright/Stay By Me   CBS 202051.   1965.
Dandy/I Don't Need Your Kind   CBS 202241, and USA Columbia 4-43818.   1965.
GROUP X   *Rohi*   UK Fontana.   1968.   B side and number unknown. This was a one-off single for this band which later changed their name to Hawkwind.

British singles
Leavin' Here/Born To Lose   Stiff BUY-9.   1977.   Withdrawn.   It was eventually released as part of a boxed set of singles in 1978.
Beerdrinkers EP.   Big Beat seven-inch promo NS-61.   1980.   The regular shop copies were twelve-inch only.
Motorhead/City Kids   Big Beat NSP-13.   1980.   A white vinyl pressing limited to ten copies only.
The Train Kept A Rollin'   Flexipop 007.   1981.   A one-sided flexi disc.

Mott the Hoople

British singles
Honaloochie Boogie   Apple Custom one-sided acetate.   1973.
Roll Away The Stone   CBS one-sided promo 1895-DJ.   1973.

British album

MOTT/LONE STAR   BBC Transcription Service 139949.   1976.   Side one has Mott without Ian Hunter.

The Move

British singles

Cherry Blossom Clinic/Vote For Me   Regal-Zonophone, number unknown. 1968.   Withdrawn.
Something Else From The Move   Two-track sampler.   EMI one-sided promo PSRS-315.   1968.   This came with a picture sleeve.

American singles

Brontosaurus   3:10 (AM radio version) Mono and stereo versions.   A & M promo 1197.   1970.
Brontosaurus   4:25 (FM radio version) Mono and stereo versions.   A & M promo 1197.   1970.
Chinatown/Down On The Bay   MGM K-14322.   1971.   Withdrawn.   This should not have been released by MGM in the first place and was withdrawn one day after release. White label promos have been counterfeited. The single was eventually given a full release on United Artists 50876 with an edited A side.
Tonight/Don't Mess Me Up   Capitol 3126.   1972.   Another quickly deleted single.
Tonight/My Marge   United Artists UA-XW 202-W.   1972.   This was the version that took its place.

American albums

The Best Of The Move   A & M SP-3625.   1975.   Promo copies were re-titled *First Move.*

Odds and sods

Something Else From The Move   German Cube twelve-inch, number unknown. 1981.   An excellent re-release of this classic. It was also made available on the French album *Something Else From The Move*   Cube 2326 045.   1980.

Nazz

There is some confusion as to what was, and what wasn't issued by The Nazz. So here is a complete discography.

American singles

Hello It's Me/Open My Eyes   SGC 001.   1968.   This has been counterfeited in a hard cardboard cover and red vinyl.

Hello It's Me   4:00 and 2:50 versions.   SGC promo 001.   1968.
Not Wrong Long/Under The Ice   SGC 006.   1969.
Open My Eyes/Hello It's Me   SGC 001.   1969.   A re-issue of the first single with sides flipped.
Some People/Magic Me   SGC 009.   1969.
Kicks/Magic Me   SGC 009.   1969.   A pronto re-release with a new A side.

American albums

Nazz   SGC SD-5001.   1968.
Nazz Nazz   SGC SD-5002.   This was also pressed in red vinyl.   1969.
Nazz III   SGC SD-5004.   1970.   Also pressed on green vinyl.

White label counterfeits exist of these.

Nazz III   SGC SD-5004.   1970.   This was pirated as a picture disc in the early '80s.
BBC *Play Music*   Radio Series.   Date unknown.   Made to promote the *Nazz III* album.
Nazz   Rhino RNLP-109.   1983.
Nazz Nazz   Rhino RNLP-110.   1983.   Pressed in red vinyl.
Nazz III   Rhino RNLP-111.   1983.   Not pressed in green like the original.

British singles

Open My Eyes/Hello It's Me   Atlantic 584 224.   1968.   Withdrawn.
Open My Eyes/Hello It's Me   SGC 219 001.   1968.   *Open My Eyes* is a different mix to the USA version.
Hello It's Me/Crowded   SGC 219 002.   1969.
Not Wrong Long/Under The Ice   Atco, number unknown.   1969.   Possibly withdrawn.

British album

Nazz   SGC 221 001.   1968.   This is one of the rarest British album releases of the late '60s.

Odds and sods

The Todd Rundgren Radio Show   Bearsville promo PRO-524.   1972.   This promo features a previously unreleased Nazz re-mix *Christopher Columbus* and an alternate take of *Open My Eyes*.

Michael Nesmith

Before joining The Monkees Nesmith had cut a few tracks using a different name.
MICHAEL BLESSING   *A New Recruit/A Journey With*   USA Colpix CP-787.   1964.
MICHAEL BLESSING   *What Seems To Be/Until It's Time For You To Go*   USA Colpix CP-792.   c.1964.

American singles

Just A Little Love/Curson Terrace   Edan 1001.   c.1965.
Texas Morning/Tumbling Tumbleweeds   RCA promo SP45-263.   1974.
Rio/Casablanca Moonlight   Pacific Arts PA-104.   1976.
Rio/Life, The Unsuspecting Captive   Island IS-088.   1976.   This took the place of
the previous version when *Rio* had become a hit in Britain.
Cruisin/Horserace   Pacific Arts twelve-inch promo, number unknown.   1978.

American album

The Mike Nesmith Radio Special   Pacific Arts promo PAC7-1300.   1976.

Odds and sods

MIKE, JOHN AND BILL   *How Can You Kiss Me/Just A Little Love*   USA Omnibus 239.
1963.   His first release.
Mike Nesmith Presents The Witchita Train Whistle Sings   USA Dot DLP-25851,
and UK Dot SLDP-516.   1968.   Mike Nesmith arranged this album of
instrumental versions of his mid '60s songs.
WITCHITA TRAIN WHISTLE   *Tapioca Tundra/Don't Cry Now*   USA Dot D-17152.
1967.   This was the single from the album.
WITCHITA TRAIN WHISTLE/GEORGE VAN EPPS   American Forces Radio and Television
Service P-10893.   1968.
THE FIRST NATIONAL BAND   *Trip Down/When It Was Good*   USA Monument
MON-1031.   c.1969.   There may have been a Nesmith connection here.

Randy Newman

American singles

Golden Grideon Boy/Country Boy   Dot 45-16411.   c.1962.   An extremely rare
release.
Bee Hive State/B side unknown.   Reprise 0284.   c.1964.   Another rarity. Even
more odd is a ten-inch promo 78 rpm pressing which was made.
Until You Hear From Me   One-sided.   Schroeder Music Publishing.   c.1965.
Made as a demo for publishing purposes.
Gone Dead Train/B side unknown.   Reprise 0945.   1969.   Taken from the
Performance soundtrack.
Spies/Political Spies   Warner twelve-inch promo PROA-860.   1979.
The Blues   (with Paul Simon) radio version, mono and stereo mixes.   Warner
promo WBS-7-29803.   1983.   This alters the line 'selling his ass' to 'selling himself'.

American albums

Randy Newman   Reprise RS-6286.   1967.   This is the first version of this album.
The cover has a side shot of Newman's face and the title in brown.

Randy Newman Creates Something New Under The Sun   Reprise RS-6286.   Date unknown.   This is the same as the previous album, but with a different sleeve. This version has a sky-blue cover with Newman standing on clouds, the album title at his feet.   The back covers of the two albums are the same, i.e. lyrics.
Randy Newman Live   Reprise promo PRO-484.   1971.   Originally intended as a promo-only live album, but due to public reaction it was given a full release on Reprise RS-6459.   The cover of the original promo is white, with the titles in black, whereas the finished released version added a black and white photo.
Good Old Boys   Quad mix.   Reprise MS4-2193.   1974.
The Songs Of Randy Newman   IMG Records 1000.   Date unknown.   A twenty-eight song compilation.   These were possibly cover versions and '60s tracks that Newman had written for others. Gene Pitney had hits with two of his songs *Just One Smile* and *Nobody Needs Your Love More Than I Do*. Alan Price had recorded *Simon Smith* as well as *Tickle Me*. Cilla Black, The Fleetwoods and Frankie Laine were also given Randy Newman songs in the '60s.
Rock Around The World   Radio Series.   c.1978.

British single

The Blues   (with Paul Simon).   Possibly one sided.   Warner promo W-9803. 1983.   This is the same altered lyric as on the American version.

Odds and sods

THE BEAU BRUMMELS   *Triangle*   US Warner WS-1692.   1967.   Newman was the arranger on this album.
PEGGY LEE   *Is That All There Is*   US Capitol STAO-382.   1969.   Another arrangement task on this superb album of Leiber and Stoller songs.
Performance   Soundtrack.   UK/USA Warner.   1969.   Newman contributes to the soundtrack of this Mick Jagger and Edward Fox movie.

The Nice

British single

The Thoughts Of Emerlist Davjack   Sampler and interview by John Peel. Immediate promo AS-2.   1967.

British albums

The Nice, Volume One   Charly export issue CR-30019.   c.1976.
The Nice, Volume Two   Charly export issue CR-30014.   c.1976.
The Thoughts Of Emerlist Davjack   Charly export issue CR-30021.   c.1976.

These were all made for France and re-imported into Britain.

Harry Nilsson

American singles

JOHNNY NILES *Donna*/B side unknown.   Mercury, number unknown.   c.1963. Any more details about this, or any other Johnny Niles releases would be gratefully received.

Sixteen Tons/I'm Gonna Lose   Tower 103.   c.1964.

You Can't Take Your Love/B side unknown.   Tower 195.   1965.

Growing Up/She's Yours   Tower 244.   1965.

Good Times/Growing Up   Tower 518.   c.1968.   This may have been a cash-in release.

Everybody's Talkin/One   RCA-Victor 74-0161.   1969.   The single version of the A side is re-mixed with a single-track vocal, whereas the *Aerial Ballet* album version has a double, or triple, tracked vocal.

The Point   Sampler.   RCA promo SP45-248.   1972.

Nilsson Schmilsson   Single set.   RCA promo, number unknown.   1972.   This is a five-single set which makes up the album.

A Little Touch Of Schmilsson In The Night   RCA juke box EP DFTO-2005. 1973.

American albums

Spotlight On Harry Nilsson   Tower ST-5095.   c.1968.   Possibly released to cash in on his late '60s success.

The Point   RCA LPSX-1004.   1972.   This is the gatefold cover with a cartoon book telling the whole story in words and pictures. The album was then re-released without the book on RCA LSP-4417.

Aerial Pandemonium Ballet   RCA, number unknown.   1972.   This album of re-mixes from the first two albums was ignored when released.

The Scatalogue   RCA promo SP33-567.   1974.   This is a promo only compilation. Beware! There is also another album called *The Scatalogue* which is a bootleg of un-released studio cuts.

Schmilsson   Solo Music 165.   Date unknown.   A cash-in compilation of sixties demo's, etc.

Nilsson Schmilsson   Quad mix.   RCA APD 1-0319.   1974.

Du It On Mon Dei   Quad mix.   RCA APD 1-0817.   1974.

Sandman   Quad mix.   RCA APD 1-1031.   1975.

Rock 'N' Roll   Pickwick SPC-3321.   c.1977.   A wierd compilation.

Innerview   Radio Series.   c.1980.

British single

Without You/Other artist.   RCA-Record Year LB-2.   c.1979.   A strange issue. It probably originated from a company like the Reader's Digest.

British albums

The Point   With book.   RCA LPSX-1004.   1972.

The Point   Without book.   RCA SF-8166.   c.1973.

Aerial Pandemonium Ballet RCA SF-8326. 1972. Again, this was ignored in Britain.

Odds and sods

BUCK EARL *I Guess The Lord Must be In New York City*/B side unknown. USA RCA 74-0755. c.1970. One magazine article hinted that this may be Nilsson himself.
Midnight Cowboy EP. United Artists promo from America 70043. c.1969. By the way, the version used in the movie is different.
Skidoo Film soundtrack. USA RCA, number unknown. 1969. This movie was one of the last made by Groucho Marx.
Son Of Dracula Film soundtrack. UK/USA Rapple. 1973. Nilsson starred alongside Ringo Starr in this horror movie spoof.
Jump Into The Fire One-sided. RCA promo single, number unknown. 1973. This was made to promote the *Son Of Dracula* movie. I don't know if this single is UK or USA.
The World's Greatest Lover Film soundtrack. USA RCA ABL 1-2709. 1977. Nilsson contributed to the score of this Gene Wilder movie.
Popeye Film soundtrack. UK Epic/USA Boardwalk. 1980. Another Nilsson soundtrack, this time to the Robin Williams and Shelly Duvall movie.

The Nitty Gritty Dirt Band

American singles

Mr Bojangles Long and short versions. Liberty 56197. 1968.
Mr Bojangles/Uncle Charlie interview. Liberty ten-inch promo 78 rpm disc, number unknown. 1968.
Radio interview United Artists promo SP-37. c.1971.
Two-record set including a one-sided interview single. United Artists promo SP-69. c.1973.

American albums

1975 interview album United Artists promo SP-117. 1975.
THE DIRT BAND *Dreams* Sampler. United Artists promo SP-469. 1979.

Gary Numan

TUBEWAY ARMY *That's Too Bad/Oh Didn't I Say* UK Beggars' Banquet BEG-5. 1977.
TUBEWAY ARMY *Bombers/Blue Eyes/O.D. Receiver* UK Beggars' Banquet BEG-8. 1978.
TUBEWAY ARMY *Down In The Park/Do You Need Service* UK Beggars' Banquet

BEG-17. 1978. A twelve-inch version also featured a Gary Numan solo track *I Nearly Married A Human* BEG-17-T.

All these pre-*Are Friends Electric* singles are still much sought-after.

British singles

Remember I Was Vapour/On Broadway Beggars' Banquet SAM-126. 1980. This was given away with the *Telekon* album. There is also a special fan club EP with unreleased music from 1981.

British albums

TUBEWAY ARMY *Tubeway Army* Beggars' Banquet BEGA-4. 1978. The first album came in a rare blue vinyl pressing.

GARY NUMAN *The Pleasure Principal* Beggars' Banquet BEGA-10. 1979. The promo slick cover has a blue background instead of a brown one.

Telekon Beggars' Banquet cassette BEGA-19. 1980. The proof sleeve had the garish red stripes blacked out.

Telekon Beggars' Banquet cassette BEGA4-19. 1980. This tape version has two extra tracks *We Are Glass* and *I Die, You Die.*

Living Ornaments Beggars' Banquet BOX-1. 1981. This double album boxed set consisted of two live albums. *Living Ornaments '79* BEGA-24, and *Living Ornaments '80* BEGA-25. It was deleted three months after release.

American singles

Are Friends Electric Same both sides. Atco twelve-inch promo DSKO-235. 1979.

Are Friends Electric/You Are My Vision Atco promo picture disc, number unknown. 1979.

White Boys And Heroes Same on both sides. Atco twelve-inch promo, number unknown. 1982.

Odds and sods

Photograph German Beggars' Banquet, number unknown. 1981. This compilation album was withdrawn after a few weeks of release at the insistence of Numan. Quite a few copies made it to Britain.

Urgh, A Music War UK/USA A & M. 1981. This has live music.

Phil Ochs

American single

Outside A Small Circle Of Friends Censored version/full version. A & M promo 891. c.1968.

American album

Interviews with Phil Ochs Folkways FB-5321. Date unknown on this obscurity.

Freebies and Limited Editions
Top (left to right) THE POLICE *Man In A Suitcase;* SEX PISTOLS *Submission.* Middle (left to right) HIGH NUMBERS *I'm The Face;* GRAHAM PARKER *Silly Thing.* Bottom (left to right) TALKING HEADS *Psycho Killer;* T REX *Ride A White Swan.*

Odds and sods

Newport Folk Festival '64 (Evening Concerts) USA Vanguard VSD-79184. 1964. This has live music.
Gunfight At Carnegie Hall Canada A & M SP-9010. 1972. A live album.
The Bitter End Years USA Roxbury RX3-300. 1976. Live material.

Mike Oldfield

Before joining Kevin Ayers, and well before *Tubular Bells,* Mike Oldfield and his sister Sally had been a duet called Sallyangie.

SALLYANGIE *Two Ships*/B side unknown. UK Big T BIG-126. 1968.
SALLYANGIE *Children Of The Sun* UK Transatlantic TRA-174 and USA Warner WS-1783. 1968. The album was re-issued in Britain in 1976 in an almost identical form.

British singles

Hergest Ridge Excerpts. Virgin one-sided white label promo, number unknown. 1974.
Ommadawn Excerpts. Virgin twelve-inch promo VDJ-9. 1975. One of the first British twelve-inchers.
Blue Peter With alternate ending. Virgin one-sided promo VSDJ-317. 1979.

British albums

Tubular Bells Quad mix. Virgin QV-2001. 1975.
Ommadawn Quad mix. Virgin QV-2043. 1975.
Boxed Virgin VBOX-1. 1976. This has the first three albums, plus a bonus album *Collaborations* and a book.
Tubular Bells Virgin picture disc VP-2001. 1978. If people bothered to actually take the record out of the sleeve and play it they would have discovered that this is the stereo re-mix of the quadraphonic version. This stereo from quad version first appeared in the boxed set.
Impressions Tellydisc, number unknown. 1980. A mail order double album compilation.

American singles

Sampler EP. Virgin promo PR-196. 1973.
Tubular Bells 7:30 version. Virgin promo PR-199. 1973.
Guilty Possibly the same track on both sides. Virgin ten-inch promo, number unknown. 1978.
Five Miles Out/Family Man Epic-Virgin twelve-inch promo AS-1240. 1982.
Family Man Long and short versions. Epic-Virgin promo 14-02877. 1982.

American albums

Hergest Ridge Banded for radio play. Virgin promo VR13-109. 1974.

Tubular Bells   Quad mix.   Virgin QR13-105.   1974.
Ommadawn   Quad mix.   Virgin PZQ-33913.   1975.

Odds and sods

The Exorcist   Film soundtrack.   UK/USA Warner.   1974.   This features a badly edited version of the *Tubular Bells* theme.
Royal Philharmonic Orchestra conducted by David Bedford   *The Orchestral Tubular Bells*   UK Virgin V-2026.   1975.   This also features Oldfield on guitar. A promo sampler single was made to promote it on UK Virgin promo VDJ-1.

Yoko Ono

As well as her own solo recordings Yoko has more often than not occupied John Lennon's B sides.

John Lennon singles with Yoko Ono on the B side:

American singles

Remember Love   (Give Peace A Chance)   Apple 1809.   1969.
Don't Worry Kyoko   (Cold Turkey)   Apple 1813.   1970.
Who Has Seen The Wind   (Instant Karma)   Apple 1818.   1970.
Listen The Snow Is Falling   (Happy Christmas)   Apple 1842.   1972.
Sisters O Sisters   (Woman Is The Nigger Of The World)   Apple 1848.   1973.
Kiss Kiss   (Starting Over)   Geffen GEF-49604.   1980.
Beautiful Boys   (Woman)   Geffen GEF-49644.   1981.
Yes I'm Your Angel   (Watching The Wheels)   Geffen GEF-49695.   1981.

American solo singles

Now Or Never   Long and short versions.   Apple promo, number unknown.   1973.
Walking On Thin Ice/It Happened/Hard Times   Geffen twelve-inch promo PROA-934.   1981.
Walking On Thin Ice   Long and short versions.   Geffen promo PROS-935.   1981.
No No No/Dogtown   Plus one other.   Geffen twelve-inch promo PROA-975. 1981.
My Man/Let The Tears Dry   Polydor twelve-inch promo PRO-192.   1982.

American album

Innerview   Radio Series.   Series 18, programmes 2 & 3.   1982.

British singles

All USA John Lennon B sides featuring Yoko correspond to their UK equivalent, with the exception of *Woman Is The Nigger Of The World* which was withdrawn from release in Britain.

Walking On Thin Ice/It Happened/Hard Times Are Over Geffen cassette K-79202-M. 1981. The last track was not included on the regular vinyl single.
Walking On Thin Ice Edited/*It Happened* Geffen promo K-79202-DJ. 1981.

British album

Season Of Glass Geffen K-99164. 1981. The initial pressings came with a free single *Walking On Thin Ice*. This is the same as the regular shop copies including the lyric sheet.
It's Alright (Watching Rainbows) Polydor POLD-5073. 1983. Promo copies came with the *My Man* single as well as a twelve-inch white label.

Odds and sods

Welcome (The Many Sides Of Yoko Ono) Japan Apple promo PRP-18026. c.1974. This contains sixteen previously unreleased songs, including many with John.

Orchestral Manoeuvres in the Dark

British singles

Electricity/Almost Factory FAC-6. 1980. This was later re-issued by DinDisc Records.
Souvenir Accidentally appeared on the A side of the Human League's *Love Action* single in 1981. Thirty-five copies were recalled from the batch of forty that were made.
OMD DinDisc DEP-2. 1981. This EP of early songs was given away with first pressings of the *Organisation* album.
Pretending To See The Future/NASH THE SLASH *Swing Shift* 'Smash Hits' magazine flexi, no number. 1981.

American singles

Enola Gay/Messages Epic-Virgin twelve-inch promo, number unknown. 1981.
Georgia Plus three. Epic-Virgin twelve-inch promo, number unknown. 1981.
New Stone Age/Bunker Soldiers Epic-Virgin flexi, number 1. 1982. This was given away with *Trouser Press* magazine.

American album

A Constructive Conversation With OMD Epic-Virgin promo AS-1408. 1982. This is an interview album with Richard Skinner.

Odds and sods

Street To Street, A Liverpool Album UK Open Eye OELP-501. 1979. This includes a track by ID who later became OMD.
DinDisc 1980 UK DinDisc DONE-1. 1980. This includes an alternate version of *Electricity*.
Urgh A Music War UK A & M AMLX-64692. 1981. This has live material.

Robert Palmer

Before going solo Palmer had recorded with The Alan Bown Set, Dada and Vinegar Joe.

American singles

Johnny And Mary   One-sided.   Island twelve-inch promo PROA-903.   1979.
ROBER PALMER/JETHRO TULL   *What's It All About!*   Radio Series MA-1785.   1980.

American albums

Live In Boston   Warner Brothers Music Show promo WBMS-111.   1979.
Secrets   Island promo picture disc, number unknown.   1979.
Robert R. Klein Radio Series, number 3.   c.1980.
ROBERT PALMER/TALKING HEADS   King Biscuit Radio Series   (Dated 3.80).
NBC *Source*   Radio Series   (Dated 11.80).

Odds and sods

RUPERT HINE   *Living In Sin*   UK A & M AM-111.   1982.   This has Palmer on vocals on the A side of this single only. (Also on twelve-inch).

Graham Parker and The Rumour

British singles

Kansas City/Silly Thing   Vertigo GPS-1.   1977.   This single was given away with the *Howlin' Wind* album in a limited edition of 5,000. Both tracks are taken from the *Marble Arch* album which was recorded live. There are two versions of this single. One has a red label, while the other is beige.
Hold Back The Night   Vertigo promo PARKDJ-001.   1977.   A one-sided promo single to promote *The Pink Parker* EP.
Hey Lord/Watch The Moon Come Down   Vertigo twelve-inch promo JUMBO-005.   1978.
Love Without Greed/Mercury Poisoning   Live version.   Stiff BUY-82.   1980. Some copies have an envelope-type sleeve with a flap at the top.

British albums

Live At Marble Arch   Vertigo promo GP-1.   1977.   Recorded at a Phonogram conference at a hotel in London's Marble Arch area in 1977, just after their signing to Vertigo. 500 copies were made, although it has been counterfeited.
The Up Escalator   Stiff cassette ZCSEEZ-23.   1981.   The tape version has an extra track *Women In Charge*.

American singles

Soul Shoes   Edited.   Same on both sides.   Mercury promo MDJ-463.   1977.

The Pink Parker Mercury EP twelve-inch promo MK-28. 1977
The Pink Parker Vertigo EP PARK-001. 1977. The pink vinyl single which was available in Britain was actually made in America and exported to the UK.
Mercury Poisoning One-sided. Arista grey vinyl twelve-inch promo SP-41. 1979. There is no real label identification on this, but it appeared just after they had signed with Arista. Copies came into Britain through Stiff records and were given to chart return shops as promotion, although some collectors' shops seemed to get copies from Stiff as well. Side two of this disc had a pattern cut into the vinyl to discourage bootleggers from copying it. It didn't.
I Want You Back/Local Girls Arista twelve-inch promo SP-54. 1979.
Mercury Poisoning/I Want You Back Arista AS-0439. 1979. The A side makes its only official appearance here on this blue vinyl 33rpm single.
Temporary Beauty/No More Excuses (Version). Arista twelve-inch promo SP-118. 1982.
You Hit The Spot/Habit Worth Forming Arista twelve-inch promo, number unknown. 1982.

American albums

Live Sparks Arista promo SP-63. 1979. This is an excellent promo-only live album. It also includes the studio cuts *Mercury Poisoning* and *I Want You Back*. It has also been pirated as *Local Girls*.
GRAHAM PARKER/BRAND X *Rock Around The World* Radio Series. 1979.
GRAHAM PARKER/DIRE STRAITS BBC *Rock Hour* Radio Series, number 138. 1980.
The Parker Treatment Modern Music Radio Series. 1980.
Innerview Radio Series. Series 18, programme 3. c.1981.
GRAHAM PARKER/SPARKS King Biscuit Radio Series (Dated 11.7.82).
BBC *Rock Hour* Radio Series, number 321. 1982.

Odds and sods

A Bunch Of Stiffs UK Stiff SEEZ-2. 1977. Graham Parker and The Rumour perform *Back To Schooldays,* but they get no credit due to contractual problems, etc.
The Honky Tonk Demos UK Oval OVLM-5003. 1979. The track here is a Parker solo track. It was recorded as a demo and sent to Charlie Gillett's radio show *Honky Tonk* in 1975 before The Rumour had been formed.
There were also two USA promo radio spots singles.
Squeezing Out Sparks USA Arista (Dated 18.4.79).
The Up Escalator USA Arista (Dated 11.6.80).

Peter and Gordon

British albums

I Go To Pieces Columbia export issue SCXC-25. 1965.
Woman Columbia export issue SCXC-29. 1965.

Lady Godiva   Columbia export issue SCXC-33.   1966.
These were similar to the American versions.

American singles

Interview plus three songs.   Capitol promo PRO-2681/2.   1964.
Paul McCartney introduces Peter and Gordon   *I Don't Want To See You Again*
Capitol promo PRO-2720.   1964.   The B side has John Lennon introducing
Cilla Black.
Wrong From The Start/B side unknown.   Capitol Creative Productions number
51.   Date unknown.

Odds and sods

Devant Toi Je Suis Sans Voix   French Columbia EP ESRF-1726.   c.1966.
These four songs were all sung in French.

Although Gordon Waller made a solo career after they split in 1968, Peter
Asher didn't.
The following are GORDON WALLER on his own:
Speak For Me/Little Nonie   USA Capitol 5886.   1966.
Everyday/B side unknown.   USA Capitol 2346.   1968.
Rosecrans Boulevard/B side unknown.   UK Columbia DB-8337.   1968.   This may
be the other side to *Everyday*.
. . . And Gordon   USA ABC ABCS-759.   1971.   His only album.

Tom Petty and the Heartbreakers

Before becoming a solo artist Petty was with a band called Mudcrutch who released
one single.   *Depot Street/Wild Eyes*   USA Shelter SR-40357.   c.1975.   This single
has been counterfeited.

American singles

Breakdown   2:42 version.   Mono and stereo mixes.   Shelter promo SR-62006.
1977.   Apparently this only got as far as the promo stage as it was never released.
When it was eventually released a longer version was used. This was on Shelter
SR-62008. A twelve-inch promo was also pressed of the full version.   Shelter
twelve-inch promo SPDJ-27.   1977.
Listen To Her Heart/I Don't Know What To Say To You   Shelter twelve-inch
promo SPDJ-37.   1978.
The Waiting   Same both sides.   MCA-Backstreet twelve-inch promo, number
unknown.   1981.
You Got Lucky   Same both sides.   MCA-Backstreet twelve-inch promo
L33-1785.   1982.
Change Of Heart   Studio and live versions.   MCA-Backstreet twelve-inch promo,
number unknown.   1982.

American albums

The Official Bootleg   Shelter promo 12677.   1977.
You're Gonna Get It   Shelter red vinyl promo DA-52029.   1978.
TOM PETTY/BE BOP DELUXE   *Rock Around The World*   Radio Series.   1978.
TOM PETTY/SAMMY HAGAR   *Rock Around The World*   Radio Series, number 184.
(Dated 2.78).
King Biscuit Radio Series   (Dated 13.4.80).
King Biscuit Radio Series   (Dated 2.11.80).
Inside Tom Petty   DIR Broadcasting network.   A radio show album.   1981.
Robert W. Morgan *Special Of The Week*   Radio Series   (Dated 12.12.81).
Retrorock   Radio Series   (Dated Feb. 1982).   Recorded in 1978.

British singles

*American Girl/*B side unknown.   Shelter WIP-6377.   1977.   His first release went
without notice.
American Girl/Luna   Live.   Shelter seven-inch WIP-6403 and twelve-inch
WIP12-6403.   1977.   This was released in late 1977, and is the easier of the two
versions to get.
Listen To Her Heart/I Don't Know What To Say To You   Shelter WIP-6455.
1978.   Most people have gone for the twelve-inch of *Listen To Her Heart* which
included two live tracks recorded in Boston on side two. The B side of the seven-
inch has a new non-album studio track.
Don't Do Me Like That/Century City   MCA-Backstreet MCA-596.   1980.   The
first 15,000 copies came with a free single *Something Else/Stories We Could Tell*
MSAM-4. Both tracks were recorded in London for King Biscuit.
Straight Into Darkness   Edited/*A Wasted Life*   MCA-Backstreet promo
MCADJ-805.   1983.

British albums

The Official Bootleg   Shelter promo IDJ-24.   1977.   The UK version has an extra
track *Wild One Forever* which for some reason isn't on the USA edition.
Hard Promises   MCA-Backstreet MCF-3098.   1981.   This has a different cover
from the American version. The USA version shows Petty standing next to a rack
of singles, while the British version has a black and white photo with titles at the top
and at the bottom.

Odds and sods

STEVIE NICKS   *Stop Draggin' My Heart Around*   USA Modern 7336.   1981.   This
single has both Petty and The Heartbreakers backing the Fleetwood Mac starlet on
the A side only. Nicks repaid the compliment on the track *Insider* from the *Hard
Promises* album.
Damn The Torpedoes   Canada MCA Masterphile audiophile MCA-5105.   1980.
Hard Promises   Canada MCA Masterphile audiophile pressing BSR-5162.   1981.

Pink Floyd

British singles

Arnold Layne/Candy And The Current Bun   Columbia DB-8156.   1967.   This came with a very rare picture sleeve.

Apples And Oranges/Paintbox   Columbia DB-8310.   1968.   Promo copies came with a picture sleeve.

Money   One-sided Harvest pink vinyl promo HAR-5217.   1981.   It's possible that this was considered as a single. It came in a picture sleeve similar to the *A Collection Of Great Dance Songs* album.

Run Like Hell   Harvest.   1980.   Withdrawn from release, but acetates exist.

Not Now John   Edited.   Harvest promo PSR-533.   1983.   This may have been a one-sided disc.

British albums

Piper At The Gates Of Dawn   Mono mix.   Columbia SX-6157.   1967.   The mono mix is different to the stereo version. There are now four different label designs for this album. The first was a black label with the word *Columbia* and its logo in blue. Then shortly after, in 1968, this changed to a black label with silver parallel lines and a white boxed logo. In 1979 this changed to a beige label with a dark brown *Columbia* at the top, with the logo on the right side just below. Then, in 1983, the Fame label, EMI's cheapo line, re-issued the album with a cream label having red lines across it; any mention of Columbia was relegated to a tiny logo at the bottom.

A Saucerful Of Secrets   Columbia SX-6258.   1968.   The mono mix may be different to the stereo.

Atom Heart Mother   Quad mix.   Harvest Q4SHVL-781.   1973.

The Dark Side Of The Moon   Quad mix.   Harvest Q4SHVL-804.   1973.

Wish You Were Here   Quad mix.   Harvest Q4SHVL-814.   1975.

The First XI   Harvest PF-11.   1979.   This was a boxed set of the first eleven albums in their original sleeves. The exceptions were *The Dark Side Of The Moon* and *Wish You Were Here* which were included as picture discs.

American singles

See Emily Play/Scarecrow   Tower 356.   1967.

Arnold Layne/If   Tower, number unknown.   1967.

Flaming/Gnome   Tower 378.   1968.   *Gnome* is an alternate version which only appears here.

Let There Be More Light/Remember A Day   Tower 440.   1969.   All these Tower releases are rare.

One Of These Days   Same on both sides.   Capitol promo PRO-6378.   1972.

The Dark Side Of The Moon   Sampler EP.   Harvest promo SPRO-6746/7.   1973. This rarity included *Money/Us And Them/Time/Breathe*.

Money   Censored version.   Harvest promo PRO-6669.   1973.   When the original promo was sent round to radio stations several banned it because of the word 'bullshit' in the lyrics. So Capitol pressed up a new version with the offending profanity taken out. (It may have been mixed out). It also came with a note telling DJ's to disregard the earlier promo.

Pink Floyd At Pompeii   Radio spots EP.   Promo single with 12 adverts.

Run Like Hell/Don't Leave Me Now   Columbia twelve-inch promo AS-777. 1980.

Comfortably Numb   6:12 and 3:59 versions.   Columbia promo 1-11311.   1980.

Money/Another Brick In The Wall Part Two   Columbia twelve-inch pink vinyl promo AS-1334.   1981.

When The Tigers Broke Free/Bring The Boys Back Home   Columbia twelve-inch promo AS-1541.   1982.

Not Now John   Censored version.   Same on both sides.   Columbia promo AE7-1653.   1983.

It Would Be So Nice   Columbia one-sided promo, number unknown.   1983.

American albums

Pink Floyd   Tower T-5093 mono, ST-5093 stereo.   1967.   Essentially *Piper At The Gates Of Dawn,* but has *Arnold Layne* and *See Emily Play* instead of *Flaming* and *Astronomy Domine.*

Tour '75   Capitol promo SPRO-8116/7.   1975.   A compilation album.

Animals   Banded and possibly edited for radio play.   Columbia promo JC-34474.   1976.

Off The Wall   Edited sampler from *The Wall.*   Columbia promo AS-756.   1979.

Innerview   Radio Series.   Series 17, programme 6.   1979.   Roger Waters and David Gilmore talk about *The Wall.*

BBC *Rock Hour*   Number 46.   1980.

Wish You Were Here   Columbia-Masterworks half speed HC-33453.   1981.

The Final Cut   Banded for radio play.   Columbia promo QC-38243.   1983.

Odds and sods

Tonight Let's Make Love In London   Film soundtrack.   UK Instant INLP-002. 1968.   This features an alternate version of *Interstellar Overdrive.* A French EP, released in 1968, also included an alternate *Interstellar Overdrive.* This may be the same as the above.

Zabriskie Point   Film soundtrack.   UK MGM 2354 040.   1970.   Floyd contribute about a third of the soundtrack of this hippie/biker movie.

Picnic   UK Harvest SHSS-1/2.   1971.   This double album sampler from EMI's progressive label featured the previously unreleased Floyd track *Embryo.* Apparently this track wasn't in a completed state. Floyd were annoyed. This track was re-issued in 1983 on the *Works* compilation from USA Capitol.

The Dark Side Of The Moon   Japan Mobile Fidelity audiophile pressing MFSL-1-017.   1980.   A limited edition of 5,000 copies pressed on thicker pure vinyl UHQR series was made in 1982.

A Collection Of Great Dance Songs   USA Columbia Masterworks audiophile series HC-47680.   1982.

Robert Plant

Before his first brief solo career he was with the band Listen who cut one single.
You'd Better Run/Everybody's Gonna Say   UK CBS 202456 and USA Columbia
4-43967.   1965.

British singles
Our Song/Laughing Crying Laughing   CBS 202656.   1966.
Long Time Coming/I've Got A Secret   CBS 202858.   1966.   Both of these singles
are now in the £50 bracket.
In The Mood   Long and short versions.   Es Paranza promo SAM-179.   1983.

British albums
Pictures At Eleven   Interview album.   Swansong promo SAM-154.   1982.
Interviewed by Alan Freeman.
The Principal Of Moments   Interview album.   Es Paranza promo SAM-169.
1983.   Another 'Fluff' Freeman interview.

American single
Big Log   Plus two.   Es Paranza twelve-inch promo PR-518.   1983.

American albums
King Biscuit *Inside Track*   Radio Series   (Dated 7.82).
NBC *Source*   Radio Series.   Retrospective.   1982.   A six-album set.

The Police

British singles
Fall Out/Nothing Achieving   Illegal ILL-001.   1977.   After having borrowed
money from an airline pilot to make their first record it appeared on the newly
formed Illegal label. The band put the first 5,000 copies into the picture bags
themselves. There are three different versions of this single. The first has a black
and white photo sleeve, while the record has a red label with black graphics. The
second has an altered photo but now in either purple or green tint. It also had an
entirely new back cover. The label was grey and white with a red logo looking like a
rubber stamp. The third version used the first picture sleeve with the second disc.
Roxanne/Peanuts   A & M AMS-7348.   1978.   The original sleeve had a telephone
design on the front and a live photo on the back. This version was used in the *Police
Six Pack* set in 1980. In addition there was also a very rare twelve-inch pressing of
the telephone cover AMSP-7348.
I Can't Stand Losing You/Dead End Job   A & M AMS-7381.   1978.   There are
three different blue vinyl pressings of this. When the single was re-issued in 1979

more colours appeared. White, red, yellow and green vinyl copies added to the confusion.

I Can't Stand Losing You/No Time This Time A & M AMS-7381. c.1980. This is a mispress. The B side of this re-issue should have been *Dead End Job.*

The Police Six Pack Sampler. A & M twelve-inch promo SAMP-5. 1980. This includes the six A sides from the six pack.

Spirits In The Material World/Low Life A & M AMS-8194. 1981. Although the poster sleeve that came with this isn't rare, it also had a badge which didn't come with all copies.

Every Breath You Take/Murder By Numbers A & M AM-117. 1983. 3,000 copies came with a free single. *Truth Hits Everybody* re-mix/*Man In A Suitcase* live. A & M AM-01. Most of these turned up in chart return shops. The package came in a gatefold sleeve with a black and white photo in the centrespread. A twelve-inch of *Every Breath You Take* was announced, but never materialised. It may have included the four songs from the double single. A & M AMX-117.

Wrapped Around Your Finger/Someone To Talk To A & M AM-127. 1983. There are three picture discs for this. Each one had a photo of either Sting, Stewart or Andy on side one and the same group photo on side two. There are 10,000 copies of the Sting, but only 1,000 each of the other two.

Synchronicity 2/Once Upon A Daydream A & M AM-153. 1983. Promo copies came with a gatefold sleeve in addition to the regular cover.

British albums

Outlandos D'Amour A & M AMLH-68502. 1978. The first batch were pressed on blue vinyl.

Police Enquiry A & M promo, SAMP-13. 1981. Capital Radio DJ Roger Scott interviews The Police.

Synchronicity A & M cassette CXM-63735. 1983. This tape version includes an extra track *Murder By Numbers.*

American singles

Roxanne/I Can't Stand Losing You A & M promo badge shape picture disc 2096/2147. 1979. This was later given a full release.

Message In A Bottle Studio/live. A & M star-shaped picture disc PR-4400. 1980. This live version wasn't made available in Britain until 1983.

Message In A Bottle Studio/live/*Landlord* A & M twelve-inch promo SP-17122. 1979.

Voices Inside My Head/When The World Is Running Down A & M twelve-inch promo SP-17137. 1979.

De Doo Doo Doo De Da Da Da Spanish and Japanese language versions. A & M 25000. 1980. Neither of these versions has appeared in Britain.

THE POLICE/RUPERT HOLMES *What's It All About?* Radio Series 519/520. c.1980.

Don't Stand Too Close To Me/De Doo Doo Doo . . . A & M star-shaped picture disc SP-3720. 1981. This was originally planned as a twelve-inch circular picture disc with a coloured stripe design. Twenty-five copies were made as test pressings and came complete with plastic cover and a sticker on the front.

One World/Too Much Information A & M twelve-inch promo SP-17173. 1981.
Secret Journey/Darkness A & M twelve-inch promo SP-17182. 1981.
THE POLICE *I Burn For You/*STING *Only You* A & M twelve-inch promo SP-17216. 1982.
THE POLICE/JETHRO TULL *What's It All About?* Radio Series 577/8. c.1982.
*Every Breath You Take/*Other tracks unknown. A & M twelve-inch promo SP-17230. 1983.

American albums

Regatta De Blanc A & M SP-3713. 1979. A double ten-inch album set with poster.
Police Inquiry A & M promo, number unknown. 1980. The Roger Scott interview may have been made available in the USA.
Ghost In The Machine A & M picture disc set, number unknown. 1981. This was a special issue limited to ten only. It was a picture disc with LED lights in red, set into the vinyl and powered by four small batteries. I don't know if this was ever intended for public release, but the copies that are in existence are probably test runs.
Interview From State Prison Details are unknown.
BBC *Rock Hour* Radio Series, number 207. (Dated 15.2.81).
The Police Tapes ABC Supergroups *In Concert* Radio Series (Dated 3.81). This is the best radio show album, compiled by Miles Copeland. It has interviews as well as live music recorded in Melbourne, Australia.
Westwood One *Off The Record* Radio Series. 1981.
King Biscuit *Inside Track* Radio Series. 1981.
Robert R. Klein Radio Series, number 33. 1981.
BBC *Rock Hour* Radio Series. (Dated 13.12.81).
Retrorock Radio Series, number 82.12. (Dated 15.3.82).

Odds and sods

EBERHARD SCHROENER *Video Flashbacks* UK Harvest SHSM-2030. 1978. The three members of the band were featured on this concept album. A single was also released *Video Magic/*B side unknown. UK Harvest HAR-5196.
Propaganda, No Wave Volume 2 UK/USA A & M. 1981. This has some session tracks recorded for an American radio station.
Urgh, A Music War UK/USA A & M. 1981. This has live material.
Brimstone And Treacle UK/USA A & M. 1981. This soundtrack has new tracks specially recorded.
Zenyatta Mondatta Japan Nautilus audiophile pressing NR-19. 1981.
Ghost In The Machine Japan Nautilus audiophile pressing NR-40. 1982.
Synchronicity A & M. 1983. This has thirty-six different sleeves world-wide, six of which are available on UK A & M. They all vary in colour and photo co-ordination.

All three members by the end of 1983 had released solo or duet albums and singles. In addition to pre-Police activities with other groups, devoted fans have to be pretty devoted to have everything.

Iggy Pop

Before becoming a Stooge, Iggy had played drums with The Iguanas who released one, rare, single in 1965. *Mona/I Don't Know Why* details about label etc., are unknown, but it was released in America only. The band who recorded for RCA with the same name have nothing to do with Iggy's band.

American singles

I Got A Right/B side unknown.   Siamese 001.   c.1974.   A rare independent release.
Knockin' 'Em Down/Ambition/Loco Mosqitio   Arista twelve-inch promo SP-81.   1979.
Bang Bang/Pumpin For Jill/Houston Is Hot Tonight/Time Won't Let Me Arista twelve-inch promo SP-115.   1981.

American albums

IGGY AND THE STOOGES *Metallic K.O.* Skydog-Import IMP-1015. 1980. Originally released as a bootleg in France, but given the thumbs up by Iggy for an official USA release.
The Stooge Turns Pop   *Rock Around the World*   Radio Series, number 143. (Dated 9.5.77).

British single

Zombie Birdhouse Extracts/STIFF LITTLE FINGERS   *Now Then* Excerpts.   UK Chrysalis flexi, number unknown.   1983.

Elvis Presley

American singles

Obviously all the Sun 45s and 78s are rare, but everybody knows about them. do you know about these?

TV Guide Presents Elvis Presley RCA-Custom promo GBMW-8705. 1956. This was made to promote that particular week's edition of TV Guide which had a cover story on Elvis.
Love Me Tender/Anyway You Way You Want Me RCA 47-6643. 1956. There are three different coloured sleeves for this single, white, pink and green.
Blue Christmas RCA one-sided promo HO-0808. 1957.
I Want You, I Need You, I Love You/My Baby Left Me RCA 47-6440. 1956. The promo copies came with a picture sleeve.
Old Shep RCA one-sided promo CR-15. 1956.
Wear My Ring Around Your Neck/Don't RCA promo SP45-70. 1958.

Stuck On You/Fame And Fortune   RCA stereo issue 61-7740.   1960.
It's Now Or Never/A Mess Of Blues   RCA stereo issue 61-7777.   1960.
It's Now Or Never   With alternate ending/J. P. MORGAN   *I Walk The Line*   USAF 125.   1960.
I'll Be Back   RCA promo one-sided SP33-513.   c.1966.
Are You Lonesome Tonight/I Got To Know   RCA stereo issue 61-7810.   1960.
Surrender/Lonely Man   RCA 33rpm issue 37-7850.   1961.   These were made for stereo juke boxes.
I Feel So Bad/Wild In The Country   RCA 33rpm issue 37-7880.   1961.
His Latest Flame/Litte Sister   RCA 33rpm 37-7908.   1961.
Good Luck Charm/Anything That's A Part Of You   RCA 33rpm issue 37-7992.   1962.
Good Luck Charm/Anything That's Part Of You   RCA 47-7992.   1962.   There are two different coloured sleeves for this. The first is brown and lavender, while the second is blue and pink.
King Of The Whole Wide World/Home Is Where The Heart Is   RCA promo SP45-118.   1962.
Roustabout/One Track Heart   RCA promo SP45-139.   1964.
Follow That Dream   DJ preview single.   RCA promo 4368.   1964.
Aloha From Hawaii   Sampler.   RCA promo, number unknown.   1971.   Made for Chicken Of The Sea. (No I don't know who they are either).
My Boy/Loving Arms   RCA export issue RCA-2453.   1974.   Made for Britain.
What's It All About?   Radio Series, number 555/6.   1980.
Let Me Be There   Mono and stereo mixes.   RCA promo JH-10951.   1978.   This single only got as far as the promo stage, and was never released.
Impossible Dream/American Trilogy   RCA JH-13302.   1982.   This was a special pressing, limited to 500, made for fans visiting Tupelo, Mississippi on the 16 August 1982, the fifth anniversary of Elvis' death. The single had a black and white graphic cover and had a yellow promo label.
Little Sister/Rip It Up   RCA twelve-inch promo, number unknown.   1983.
My Boy   Mono and stereo versions.   RCA promo JH-10191.   1975.   Promo copies came with a picture sleeve.
Guitar Man   Mono and stereo versions.   RCA promo red vinyl JH-12158.   1981.
The Elvis Presley Medley   Long and short versions.   RCA promo gold vinyl, number unknown.   1982.

American EP's

Elvis Presley   RCA EPA-747.   1956.   This was issued in two different sleeves. The first was a picture sleeve, while the second was a plainer design, made as a replacement while more picture sleeves were being made.
Blue Suede Shoes   RCA juke box issue EPB-1254.   c.1956.

An alternate version of *Heartbreak Hotel* was included in a seven-single set and given to members of RCA staff attending a sales conference in Miami in 1956. RCA promo SPD-19.   1956.

Elvis Presley   RCA promo SP45-15.   1956.   This featured *That's All right/Baby*

Let's Play House/Mystery Train/I Forgot To Remember To Forget.
*Love Me Tender/Anyway You Want Me/*JEAN CHAPPEL Two songs. RCA promo DJ-7. 1956.
*Too Much/Playin' For Keeps/*DINAH SHORE Two songs. RCA promo DJ-56. 1957.
Elvis Presley RCA 599-9122. 1957. This was a part of a three-EP set, numbered SPD 22, given away by RCA when customers bought an RCA victrola. I don't know whose recordings were on the other two EP's. There was another similar set which was a triple EP with just Elvis and no other acts. RCA SPD-23. 1957. Again, this was given away by RCA with their victrola.
Elvis Presley RCA SPA7-27. c.1957. This is a ten-track EP set.
By Request Flaming Star RCA double-EP set LPC-128. 1963.
Aloha From Hawaii Via Satelite RCA juke box issue DTFO-2006. 1970.

American albums
Elvis RCA-Victor LPM-1382. 1957. There are two particularly weird mis-pressings of this album. One version has the same song (although I don't know what it is) six times on one side. The other version has all the songs un-banded, so it gives the impression of being one continuous track.

I've decided to group certain items together to avoid confustion.

Soundtrack specials
Jailhouse Rock MGM Air View series promo, number unknown. 1957. This red vinyl album included an interview with Leiber and Stoller.
Girls Girls Girls Radio and Lobby Spots. Paramount promo SP-2017. 1962.
It Happened At The World's Fair Ten Radio Spots. Donahue one-sided promo 129994. 1963. This also includes *One Broken Heart For Sale.*
Fun In Acapulco Nine Radio Spots. Paramount promo SP-2180. 1963.
Viva Las Vegas Five Radio Spots. MGM promo ten-inch SP-2314. 1964.
Roustabout Ten Radio Spots. Paramount promo SP-2406. 1964.
Roustabout Lobby Spots. Paramount promo SP-2414. 1964.
Tickle Me Radio Spots. More details unknown. 1964.
Girl Happy Radio Spots. More details unknown. 1965.

Promo only issues
Special Palm Sunday Programming album. RCA promo SP33-461. 1967. This has extracts from the *How Great Thou Art* album.
1967 Christmas Show RCA seven-inch open reel EPC-1. (Dated 3.12.67).
Elvis At Madison Square Garden Banded for airplay. RCA SP33-571. 1970.
The International Hotel, Las Vegas, Presents Elvis Presley 1970 RCA LSP-6020. 1970. A limited edition of 50 copies of this boxed set version was made for the Vegas hotel which played host to Elvis while he was recording the *From Memphis To Vegas, From Vegas To Memphis* album. this special set included a pocket calendar, a record catalogue, a menu, plus the *Kentucky Rain* single in a picture sleeve.

Pure Elvis RCA DJL 1-3455. 1980. One of the most sought after Elvis items of all time. It featured familiar Elvis tracks with new instrumental backing tracks. This was a dummy run for the *Guitar Man* album in 1981. 400 copies were made.
Elvis Aaron Presley 25th Anniversary 37 excerpts. RCA DJL 1-3729. 1980.
Elvis Aaron Presley 25th Anniversary 12-track sampler. RCA DJL 1-3781. 1980.

Record club issues
World Wide Gold Award Hits Volume 1 & 2 RCA R-213690. 1974.
Aloha From Hawaii RCA R-213736. 1974.
World Wide Gold Award Hits Volumes 3 & 4 RCA R-214657. 1974.
Country Classics RCA R-233299. Date unknown.
From Elvis With Love RCA R-234340. 1978.
Legendary Concert Performance RCA R-244047. 1978.
Concert Memories RCA R-244069. 1978.

TV advertised and company sponsored items
Singer Presents Elvis Singing Flaming Star RCA Special Products PRS-279. 1968.
Elvis Presley Brookville SP-0056. c.1972.
Elvis In Hollywood Tee Vee TV-1 (RCA DPL 2-0168). c.1973.
The Greatest Show On Earth Brookville SP-0348. c.1974.
The Elvis Presley Story Tee Vee SP5-0263. c.1974.
Michelin Presents Highlights Of Elvis Presley ABCO-810. More details are unknown.
Legendary Recordings Of Elvis Presley Candlelite Music SP6-0412 (RCA LPL 6-0412). c.1976.
Memories Of Elvis Candelite Music DPL 1-0347. c.1974.

Quadraphonic issues
Live In Memphis RCA APD 1-0606. 1973.
Promised Land RCA APD 1-0873. 1974.
Elvis Today RCA APD 1-1039. 1975.

Unauthorised issues
Elvis, His First And Only Press Conference Current Audio 0249. c.1972. Buddah Records distributed this interview album which also had Mick Jagger on side two. RCA stepped in and stopped production.
Having Fun With Elvis On Stage Boxcar Records, number unknown. 1971. This obscure label released this unusual album of Elvis larking about and asking for water an awful lot. Again, RCA stopped it, only to release their own version soon after!

Radio show albums
There is really only one worth knowing about.
The Elvis Presley story Watermark Inc EPS-1-A13-B. 1977. This is a

thirteen-album set:
1. *The Early Years.*
2. *Sun Records.*
3. *Presleymania.*
4. *Presleymania 2.*
5. *Elvis The Pelvis Goes To War.*
6. *The Homecoming.*
7. *The Movie Era.*
8. *The Movie Era 2.*
9. *Elvis Meets The Beatles and Marriage.*
10. *Changes.*
11. *The King Of The Strip.*
12. *Good Times, Bad Times.*
13. *A Tribute.*

Each album is twenty-five minutes long.

British singles

Like the American Sun singles, all the British HMV singles with both gold and silver labels are collectable. So I won't go into details as most people would be aware of them.

All Shook Up/That's When Your Heartaches Begin   HMV export issue, no number. 1957.
Mystery Train/I Forgot To Remember To Forget   HMV export issue 7MC-42. 1957.
*Jailhouse Rock/*Track by another artist.   Decca vinyl promo 78rpm, number unknown.   1958.   This is not a mispress.
*The Wonder Of You/*Track by other artist.   RCA-Record Year LB-1.   c.1979. Introduced by Noel Edmonds.
Jailhouse Rock/The Elvis Presley Medley   RCA picture disc RCAP-1028.   1983. There are two different versions of this. The initial batch didn't credit *Hound Dog* as part of the medley. This was corrected on later pressings.
I Can Help   Long and short versions.   RCAPRO-369.   1983.

Flexis, etc.

The Truth About Me   *Weekend Mail* magazine five-inch 78rpm hard vinyl disc. 1957.
The Truth About Me   *Rainbow* magazine 78rpm flexi.   1957.
Speaks In Person   *Rainbow* magazine 78rpm flexi.   1957.
Greatest Hits   Reader's Digest flexi.   1973.   Introduced by Brian Matthews.

British EP's

Again, all his EP's are collectable.
G.I. Blues, The Alternate Takes   RCA RCX-1.   1982.   This was given with *The Elvis Presley EP Collection* set.
G.I. Blues, The Alternate Takes, Volume Two   RCA RCX-2.   1983.

Collectors Gold   RCA RCX-3.   1983.

The two above were taken from the *Elvis Presley EP Collection, Volume 2* set in 1983.

British albums
Rock 'N' Roll Number 2   HMV CLP-1105.   1957.   Initial pressings include the movie soundtrack version of *Old Shep* rather than the regular studio take. This was later corrected.
The Sun Collection   RCA HY-1001.   1975.   This has two different back covers.

Odds and sods
Singles
Torna A Surrento   *(Surrender* sung in Italian)/*Lonely Man*   Italian RCA 1160 and German RCA 47-7850.   1960.
O Sole Mio   (The original *It's Now Or Never)*/B side unknown.   German RCA 47-9314.   1961.

Albums
From Elvis In Memphis   Quad mix.   Japan RCA Quadradisk R4P-5005.   1973.
Elvis On Stage 1970   Quad mix.   Japan RCA Quadradisk R4P-5009.   1973.
That's The Way It Is   Quad mix.   Japan RCA Quadradisk R4P-5029.   1974.
Madison Square Gardens   Quad mix.   Japan RCA Quadradisk R4P-5032.   1974.
The Evolution Of Rock   USA 65 album radio series set.   Date unknown.   This set features a live version of *Heartbreak Hotel* (possibly from the Ed Sullivan TV show).
Elvis The Legend   RCA compact disc set, number unknown.   1983.   Country of origin probably Germany. This is a sixty track, three disc set and was limited to five thousand world-wide.

The Pretenders

Before Chrissie Hynde formed The Pretenders she had made a single with a band called The Moors Murderers. *Free Myra Hyndley* caused many British tabloids to errupt in 'disgust' at this 'degrading punk nonsense'. Even Hughie Green got his oar in by spouting on his British TV 'talent' show 'Opportunity Knocks' when the record was released in 1977. (This was one of the things that eventually got his show taken off the air in 1977). Chrissie Hynde was a freelance photographer at the time of this record's release.

British singles
The Pretenders   Sampler EP.   Real promo SAM-117.   1980.   A six-track sampler from the first album. All copies were autographed.
Talk Of The Town/THE DETROIT SPINNERS   Unknown track.   Real ARE-12.   1980.

A mispress. The B side should have been *Cuban Slide*.
I Go To Sleep Real promo, number unknown. 1981. Apparently some promo copies play at 33rpm.
I Go To Sleep/Louie Louie/English Roses Real ARE-18S. 1981. This was a special limited edition three-track version. The two B side tracks were taken from an American live radio show in 1981. The B side of this version plays at 33rpm, whereas the regular version with just *English Roses* on the B side plays at 45rpm.
Kid/Stop Your Sobbing Real cassette single, number unknown. 1981.
Talk Of The Town/Brass In Pocket Real cassette single, number unknown. 1981. Both of these were virtually ignored when released and deleted quickly.
Whatcha Gonna Do About It/Stop Your Sobbin Demo version. Flexipop 006 (Lyntone LYN-9650). 1981.
The Adultress Real promo, number unknown. 1981. Made to promote their second album.
2000 Miles/Fast Or Slow Real ARE-20-F. 1983. This came with a limited edition Christmas card type gatefold sleeve.

British album
The Pretenders Real RAL-3. 1980. 200 copies came autographed.

American singles
Brass In Pocket/Mystery Achievement/Precious Sire twelve-inch promo PROA-855. 1980.
Message Of Love/Talk Of The Town Sire promo PROS-942. 1981.
Back On The Chain Gang Same on both sides. Sire twelve-inch promo PROA-1085. 1982.

American albums
Westwood One Radio Series, number 82-11. 1982.
THE PRETENDERS/THE JIM CARROLL BAND King Biscuit Radio Series (Dated 3.5.81 and 15.2.81).

Odds and sods
Concerts For Kampuchea UK/USA Atlantic. 1981. This has some live tracks.
The Pretenders Japan Nautilus audiophile pressing, number unknown. 1981.

The Pretty Things

British albums
In the late '70s interest grew in the band culminating in their re-formation in 1980. Several companies issued previously unreleased material. The DeWolfe label issued five albums, but due to legal reasons the Pretty Things name couldn't be used. So the albums were credited to THE ELECTRIC BANANAS:

The Electric Banana   DeWolfe DWSLP-3280.   1980.
More Electric Banana   DeWolfe DWSLP-3281.   1980.
Even More Electric Banana   DeWolfe DWSLP-3282.   1980.
The Return Of The Electric Banana   DeWolfe DWSLP-3283.   1980.
Hot Licks   DeWolfe DWSLP-3284.   1980.

The Butt label also issued two Pretty Things albums:
The Seventies   Butt NOTT-001.   1980.
The Sixties   Butt NOTT-003.   1980.

Parachute   GI Records WAX-6.   1982.   This was a limited edition (1,000 only)
pressings taken from EMI's masters.
All of the above were only available for a very short while.

American single
Talkin' 'Bout The Good Times/Walkin' Through   Laurie LR-3458.   1968.   This
was their rarest American single taken from a UK Columbia single.

American album
THE PRETTY THINGS/MEDICINE HEAD   BBC *Rock Hour*   Radio Series, number
54.   1973.

Procal Harum

Before evolving into Procal Harum they had already hit the charts as THE
PARAMOUNTS, who were a Southend based R & B unit. They released six singles and
one EP. All are British unless noted:
Poison Ivy/I Feel So Good All Over   Parlophone R-5093.   1963.   This was given
an American release on Liverpool Records 903 in 1964.
A Certain Girl/Little Bitty Pretty One   Parlophone R-5107.   1963.
I'm The One/It Won't Be Long   Parlophone R-5155.   1964.
Bad Blood/Do I   Parlophone R-5187.   1964.
Blue Ribbons/Cuttin' In   Parlophone R-5272.   1964.
You've Never Had It So Good/Don't Ya Like My Love   Parlophone R-5351.
1965.
THE PARAMOUNTS   Parlophone EP GEP-8908.   1963.   This has the first two singles
back-to-back.
A Whiter Shade Of R & B   Edsel ED-112.   1983.   A compilation of singles.

British singles
Whiter Shade Of Pale/Conquistador   Cube twelve-inch black vinyl LBUG-77, and
twelve-inch white vinyl HBUG-77.   1979.   The white vinyl version was issued
shortly after the black version was released. Both were very limited, and
disappeared quickly.
A Whiter Shade Of Pale/Other artist.   RCA-Record Year LB-6.   c.1979.

American singles

Homburg EP. A & M promo AMX-2. 1969.
A Souvenir Of London/Fires Which Burn Warner promo PRO-562. 1973.
Bringing Home The Bacon Long and short versions. Chrysalis promo CHS-2011. 1973.
Grand Hotel Long and short versions. Chrysalis promo CHS-2013. 1973.

American albums

Lives A & M promo SP-8053. 1972. An interview album to promote their live album.
Innerview Radio Series. Series 12, programme 2. c.1980.
Retrorock Radio Series, number 82-17. 1982. Recorded in 1973 with the London Symphony Orchestra.

Odds and sods

Il Tuo Diamante/Fortuna Both sung in Italian. Italian IL Records IL-9005. c.1969.

Psychedelic Furs

British singles

Sister Europe Long and short versions. CBS promo 8179-DJ. 1979.
Dumb Waiters/Dash CBS A-1166. 1981. Some copies came with a playable sleeve. This was achieved by a thick coating of clear vinyl on the front cover. The track was actually a compilation of tracks from the *Talk Talk Talk* album with commentary.

British album

Forever Now CBS cassette 40CBS-85909. 1982. The tape version has an extra track, but CBS never identify what it is.

American singles

Sister Europe/We Love You Columbia twelve-inch promo AS-879. 1980.
Pretty In Pink/No Tears Columbia promo AE7-1235. 1981. This also had the playable sleeve, like the British.
Love My Way/Forever Now/President Gas/Angels Columbia twelve-inch promo AS-1538. 1982.

American albums

Interchords Columbia promo AS-1296. 1981. An interview album.
THE PSYCHEDELIC FURS/THE ENGLISH BEAT NBC *Source* Radio Series. 1982.

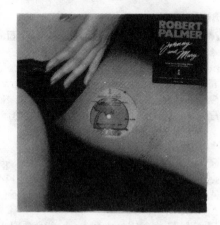

12-inch Promos
Top (left to right) MADNESS *Swan Lake;* ELVIS COSTELLO *Man Out Of Time.* Middle (left to right) BOB DYLAN *Renaldo and Clara;* FLEETWOOD MAC *Sara.* Bottom (left to right) GRAHAM PARKER *Mercury Poisoning;* ROBERT PALMER *Johnny and Mary.*

Queen

Before forming Queen, Brian May and Roger Taylor were in a band called SMILE who released one single in America:
Earth/Step On Me USA Mercury 72977. 1969. Counterfeits on red vinyl exist.
An album, *Getting Smile,* was released in Japan in 1983. This contains all the tracks they recorded.
Shortly before the first official Queen release, Freddie Mercury issued a one-off solo single under the name of LARRY LUREX (Freddie Mercury to a T!):
I Can Hear Music/Going Back UK EMI 2030 and USA Anthem AN-204. 1973.

British singles
Keep Yourself Alive/Son And Daughter EMI 2036. 1973. This rare single features an alternate version of the A side to that which appeared on their first album.
Bohemian Rhapsody/I'm In Love With My Car EMI 2375. 1975. There may be two different coloured vinyl pressings of this. The first is a run of 200 on blue vinyl in 1975, while the second version, a run of 300 in purple, was made when EMI was awarded the Queen's award to industry in 1978. Some early copies of the 1975 regular pressing have the wrong number on the label, 2378 instead of 2375.
Queen's First EP EMI 2623. 1977. There may be a two-track promo sampler for this.

Now for the weird stuff! At a record fair in 1983 I saw a Queen white label test pressing single. It was possibly an alternate version of *Lazing On A Sunday Afternoon.* The reason I say 'possibly' is that the Biro scribbling on the label was almost unreadable. It was a one-sided disc; it was also twenty quid!

British albums
News Of The World EMI. 1976. The promo version came as a boxed set.
A Night At The Opera EMI EMTCP-103. 1979. Another weird one. The number denotes that this is a picture disc, but it was never released in this format. The only Queen picture disc that I know of is the *Jazz* album from France.
Greatest Hits EMI EMTV-30. 1981. Some copies have *Anne Murray's Greatest Hits* on side two by mistake.

American singles
Bicycle Race and *Fat Bottomed Girls* segue/*Fat Bottomed Girls* and *Bicycle Race* segue. Elektra twelve-inch promo AS-11401. 1977.
Another One Bites The Dust Same on both sides. Elektra twelve-inch promo AS-11461. 1980.
Flash's Theme Same on both sides. Elektra twelve-inch promo AS-11481. 1981. This is a re-mix which hasn't appeared in Britain.
Calling All Girls Long and short versions. Elektra twelve-inch promo, number unknown. 1982.

Body Language   Same on both sides.   Elektra twelve-inch promo, number unknown.   1982.
Staying Power/Back Chat   Elektra twelve-inch promo 06754.   1982.

American albums

Rock Around The World   Radio Series, number 176.   (Dated 18.12.77).
Nightbird and Co.   Radio Series, number 267.   1977.   Hosted by Alison Steele.
Rock Around The World   Radio Series, number 132.   (Dated 21.7.77).   *An Audience With Queen.*
QUEEN   Six tracks/CON FUNK SHUN   Tracks.   American Forces Radio and Television Service P-17261,   c.1977.
Westwood One Radio Series, number 82-24/5.   1982.
QUEEN/THE BEACH BOYS.   *Sounds Of Solid Gold*   Radio Series, number 24.   1982.

Odds and sods

EDDIE HOWELL   *The Man From Manhattan*   UK Warner K-16701.   1976.   Queen appeared on the A side of this excellent single.
GRANDMASTER FLASH   *The Adventures Of Grandmaster Flash And The Wheels Of Steel*   UK Sugarhill twelve-inch SHL-557.   1981.   This features excerpts from Queen's *Another One Bites The Dust.*

Rainbow

Before joining DEEP PURPLE Ritchie Blackmore had not only been a member of THE OUTLAWS, but had cut a solo single: *Little Brown Jug/Getaway*   UK Oriole CB-314.   1964.
He was also a member of Green Bullfrog who released one self-titled album on USA Decca DL-75269 in 1973. A single from the album was issued:
*My Baby Left Me/*B side unknown.   USA Decca 32831.

British single

RITCHIE BLACKMORE'S RAINBOW   *Man On The Silver Mountain/Snake Charmer*   UK Oyster OYR-103.   1974.   The only single issued under this name.

American singles

Long Live Rock 'n' Roll   4:25 and 2:58 versions.   Polydor promo PD-14481.   1976.
I Surrender   Same on both sides.   Polydor twelve-inch promo PRO-147.   1980.
Stone Cold   Same on both sides.   Mercury blue vinyl twelve-inch promo, number unknown.   1981.
Power   Same on both sides.   Mercury twelve-inch promo, number unknown.   1981.

American albums

Innerview Radio Series. Series 16, programme 5. c.1981.

Rainbow Live At The Orpheum, Boston/PAT TRAVERS. King Biscuit Radio Series. (Dated 7.2.82).

Westwood One Radio Series, number 82-25. 1982.

Odds and sods

Rainbow On Stage German Polydor promo, number unknown. 1978. This is a special radio play version with interviews, etc.

Masters Of Rock UK/USA Polydor. 1980. This has live tracks recorded live in 1980 at the Castle Donington festival live.

The Ramones

American singles

Ramona/I Can't Give You Anything Sire, number unknown. c.1978. A withdrawn single.

Road To Ruin Sampler. Sire twelve-inch promo PROA-756. 1978.

Rock 'n' Roll High School Sire twelve-inch promo PROA-805. 1979. This may have the same track on both sides.

Pleasant Dreams Sampler. Sire twelve-inch promo PROA-966. 1981.

The Ramones Are Here And There EP. Sire promo, number unknown. 1983.

American albums

The Ramones Leave Home Sire SA-7528. 1977. This included the track *Carbona Not Glue*. When Warner Brothers re-issued the album in 1978 they replaced this track with a new AM radio re-mix of *Sheena Is A Punk Rocker*.

Beat From The Street The Ramones live at The Roxy, L.A./Martha Velez live at Papa's Place. *Rock Around The World* Radio Series, number 109. c.1978.

British singles

Road To Ruin Sampler. Sire promo PROMO-1. 1978. Joey Ramone introduces tracks from the album.

Baby I Love You/Don't Come Close Sire cassette single, number unknown. 1981.

British album

The Ramones Leave Home Sire 9103 254. 1978. The original Phonogram pressings feature *Carbona Not Glue*. Carbona was the brand name of a solvent and they decided to sue for bringing their name into disrepute. (See also CLASH *Combat Rock* album for similar story). When WEA took over distribution of the album in 1978 *Carbona Not Glue* was missing, lost in action.

214

Odds and sods

THE PALEY BROTHERS *Come On Let's Go* UK Sire SIR-4005. 1978. The Ramones guest on this A side.

THE RATTLERS *Livin' Along/On The Beach* USA Ratso records R-401. c.1980. Again, The Ramones are heard on this.

It's Alive Japan Warner, number unknown. 1979. This appeared as a single album in Japan, whereas it was a double album everywhere else.

Rock 'n' Roll Highschool Film soundtrack. UK/USA Sire album. 1979. The Ramones are the stars of this movie. In the film they sing a new Paul McCartney song *Did We Meet Somewhere Before,* but this is not on the soundtrack album.

Psychothereapy Sire. 1983. This album was ditched in favour of the *Subterranean Jungle* album. The first version includes the track *1234* which features Petula Clark on background vocals.

The Rascals

American singles

THE YOUNG RASCALS *Groovin'* Atlantic juke box EP LLP-190. 1968.

THE YOUNG RASCALS *I've Been Lonely Too Long/A Girl Like You* Ford-Philco Hip Pocket HP-18. c.1968.

Once Upon A Dream Atlantic EP. EP-1005. 1968.

Once Upon A Dream Atlantic juke box EP SD7-8169. 1968.

American albums

Freedom Suite Edited version. Atlantic promo TLST-137. 1969.

Freedom Suite Narration Atlantic promo, number unknown. 1969. An interview album.

24 Greatest Hits Warner Special Products SP-2502. c.1971.

Odds and sods

*Sentirai La Pioggla/*B side unknown. Italian Atlantic NP-3124. c.1968. Sung in Italian.

Groovin' Had been recorded in both Spanish and Italian. More details are unknown.

Otis Redding

American singles

Shout Bamalama/Fat Gal Confederate Records, number unknown. 1961. This was his first single.

Shout Bamalama/Fat Gal Bethlehem 3083. 1961. This label took up national distribution for the record shortly after its first release.

Shout Bamalama/Fat Gal   King 45-6149.   1961.   This label then took over from Bethlehem.

Shout Bamalama/Fat Gal   Orbit Records, number unknown.   1962.   This was probably the last issue.

*You Left The Water Running/*B side unknown.   Stone 209.   1962.   This was withdrawn. Apparently only 200 copies exist of this, which would have been his second single.

She's All Right/Tuff Enough   Finer Arts Records 2016.   1966.   This single was actually recorded in 1962, probably for Stone, but not released until 1966.

Shake/Fa Fa Fa Fa Fa   Ford-Philco Hip Pocket HP-13.   c.1968.

Otis Redding At The Whiskey A Go Go   Atco juke box EP SD37-265.   1968.

Higher And Higher   EP.   Atco EP-4539.   1968.   A rare EP release.

Dock Of The Bay   Juke box EP.   Volt SD37-419.   1968.

American album

OTIS REDDING/KING CURTIS.   Sampler album.   Atco promo TLST-131.   c.1968.

British singles

Shout Bamalama/Fat Gal   Sue WI-362.   1966.   This was the Confederate single's only UK release.

Gettin' Hip/Tuff Enough   Evolution E-2442.   1966.   This obscure label released this at the height of his success.

Odds and sods

Apollo Saturday Night   UK London/USA Stax.   1964.   This magnificent live album features Otis live with his Stax stablemates.

Live In Monterey   UK Atlantic and USA Reprise.   1968.   This was on Atlantic in Britain because of Redding's contract, and on Reprise in America because of Jimi Hendrix's contract. (Hendrix co-starred in the film of the concert).

Live In London   USA Stax-Volt SD-721.   1966.

Live In Paris   USA Stax-Volt SD-722.   1966.   Two albums of the Stax European package tour including Otis. In 1982 these two albums were edited down to one cassette *Hit The Road Stax* and made available through the NME.

Lou Reed

Reed was in several recording bands before joining THE VELVET UNDERGROUND in 1966.

THE PRIMITIVES   *The Ostrich/Sneaky Pete*   USA Pickwick City 9001.   c.1963.

THE BEACH NUTS   *Someday Soon/Out In The Sun*   USA Bang B-504 and UK London HL-9988.   1965.

Soundsville   USA Design DLP-187.   1965.   This cheapo compilation featured THE BEACH NUTS   *Cycle Annie*.   The album also had a track by THE ROUGHNECKS,

You're Driving Me Insane.   Lou Reed is thought to be on this as well.
He also recorded with THE SHADES and THE CAROL LOU TRIO, but details of releases
aren't known, as these are top-grade rarities.

American singles

Sweet Jane/Lady Day   RCA export issue APBO-0238-EX.   1974.   This was made
for Britain.
Street Hassle   Sampler.   Arista twelve-inch promo SP-14.   1976.
Walk On The Wild Side/Coney Island Baby/Satellite Of Love   Arista twelve-
inch promo SP-36.   1978.
Disco Mystic/I Want To Boogie With You   Arista twelve-inch promo SP-56.   1978.
Growing Up In Public   Sampler.   Arista twelve-inch promo SP-84.   1979.
Underneath The Bottle/Average Guy/Sweet Jane   RCA twelve-inch promo DJL
1-4345.   1982.

American albums

The Blue Mask   Interview album.   RCA promo DJL 1-4266.   1981.
Retrorock   Radio Series.   (Dated 12.7.82).   This was recorded in 1975.
Metal Machine Music   Quad mix.   RCA CPD 2-1101.   1975.

Odds and sods

No Where At All   One-sided.   RCA France PB-9135.   Date unknown.   This odd
single featured an non-album track.
Take No Prisoners   Although released by Arista in America, on both red and blue
vinyl, it appeared on RCA in Britain due to contractual problems.

Keith Relf

This is really a list of his work after leaving The Yardbirds in 1968.

British singles

Mr Zero/Knowing   Columbia DB-7920.   1966.
Shapes In My Mind/Blue Sands   Columbia DB-8084.   1966.

American singles

Mr Zero/Knowing   Epic 5-10044.   1966.
Shapes In My Mind/Blue Sands   Epic 5-10110.   1966.   The promo copy not only
came in a picture sleeve, but in red vinyl as well.

RENAISSANCE   *Renaissance*   UK Island/USA Elektra.   1969.   This album not only
features Keth Relf and his sister Jane, but Jim McCarthy as well.
REIGN   *Line Of Least Resistance/Natural Lovin' Man*   UK Regal-Zonophone
RZ-3028.   1970.   A one-off single by Relf and McCarthy.   This was a folksy-type

duo release. The two of them then changed the name to Together, but no releases were made.

JANE RELF   *Without A Song From You/Make My Time Pass By*   UK Decca F-13231.   1971.   It's highly likely that Keith Relf was involved here.

MEDICINE HEAD   *The Dark Side Of The Moon*   UK Dandelion 2310 066.   1972. Keith Relf had joined this band by this time. Two Relf-produced singles were also released, *Kum On,* and the hit, *Pictures In The Sky.*

ARMAGEDDON   *Armageddon*   UK/USA A & M.   1973.   This was his last band appearance.   A promo interview album may also exist in America. A band called Armageddon released one single in America in 1973.   *Get Yourself Together* USA Capitol 3142.   I'm not sure if this is the Keith Relf group of the same name.

Just before Keith died he was rehearsing with his sister Jane, with the idea of putting a new band together.

Renaissance

The band RENAISSANCE who released *Mary Jane* on British Polydor in the '60s have nothing to do with this band.

British singles

Islands/The Sea   Island WIP-6079.   1970.   Their first, and rarest, single.
Northern Lights/Opening Out   Sire export issue picture disc SRE-1022.   1978.
Jekyll And Hyde/Forever Changing   Sire SIR-4019.   1979.   This was withdrawn on Sire, but eventually released on Warner.

British albums

Illusion   Private pressing, label, etc. unknown.   1971.   This was to be the second album featuring the Relf-McCarthy line-up, but it was never released. Island Records had planned to release the album just after Keith Relf had died in 1976. Island HELP-27. Again, this was withdrawn. Jim McCarthy and Jane Relf later went on to form a band called ILLUSION which made one album for Island in 1978.
Prologue and *Ashes Are Burning*   Sovereign double-album set CAPACK-3.   1979. A very limited edition of the two albums, wrapped together in their original gatefold sleeves.
Camera Camera   Illegal ILP-008.   1981.   There are two different versions of this album. The second edition includes an extra track *Bonjour Swansong* (which was a single at the time). These copies have a silver sticker on the front cover.

American singles

Midas Man   Plus two.   Sire twelve-inch promo DM-3.   1976.
Northern Lights   4:06 and 3:29 versions.   Sire promo SRE-1022.   1978.
Northern Lights   4:06 and 3:29 versions.   Sire promo SRE-1041.   1978.   Issued a few months after the first version.

American albums

Renaissance Elektra EKS-74068. 1970. There are two different covers for this in America. The first has an embryo on the back cover, while the second version has a group cover photo.
Novella Sire SA-7526. 1977. The American cover has a brown graphic design instead of the green cover on the British version.
In existence is a sampler album which features an un-released live version of *Kiev*. More details are unknown.

Odds and sods

NEVADA *In The Bleak Midwinter/Pictures In The Fire* UK Polydor POSP-203. 1982. On this a few members of Renaissance perform under a pseudonym.

Paul Revere and the Raiders

American singles

My Steady Girl/B side unknown. Brunswick 55090. c.1958. Is this the same Paul Revere and The Raiders that recorded for Columbia?
Beatnik Sticks/Orbit The Spy Gardenia G-106. 1961.
Unfinished Fifth/B side unknown. Gardenia G-115. 1962.
Sharon/Like Long Hair Gardenia G-116. 1962.
Midnight Rider/Like Charleston Gardenia G-118. 1962.
All Night Long/Groovy Gardenia G-124. 1963.
Shake It Up Parts one and two Gardenia G-131. 1963.
Dardenella/What Time Is It? Liberty 55393. c.1963.
These were all pre-Columbia issues. There may be more.
In The Beginning Jerden juke box EP 7004. c.1965.
SS 396./THE CYRKLE *Camero* Columbia Special Products CSM-466. c.1967.
Something's Happening Columbia juke box EP 7-9665. c.1968.
Powder Blue Mercedes Queen 3:05 and 2:38 versions. Columbia promo 4-45601. 1972.
Love Music 3:42 and 3:18 versions. Columbia promo 4-45759. 1972.
What's It All About Radio Series, number 112. c.1973.
This band had a few coloured vinyl promos in the mid '60s.
Steppin' Out Same on both sides. Columbia red vinyl, and blue vinyl, promo 4-43375. 1965.
Just Like Me Same on both sides. Columbia red vinyl promo 4-43461. 1965.
Kicks Same on both sides. Columbia red vinyl promo 4-43556. 1966.
Hungry Same on both sides. Columbia red vinyl promo 4-43678. 1966.

American albums

Paul Revere And The Raiders Sande 1001. c.1960. Rarer than rare.
Like Long Hair Gardenia G-1000. c.1961.

In The Beginning   Jerden JAL-7004.   c.1965.   A cash-in album.

In The Beginning   Jerden-Capitol Record Club T-90709.   c.1966.

Paul Revere And The Raiders   Sears SPS-493.   Date unknown.   This may be the Gardenia material again.

Going To Memphis   Columbia Special Products P-13512.   c.1973.   A limited edition re-issue.

Indian Reservation   Quad mix.   Columbia CQ-30768.   c.1973.

Your Navy Presents   Radio Series.   Navy NP-70.   Date unknown on this rarity.

Paul Revere And The Raiders   Etiquette, number unknown.   c.1979.   This is a limited edition re-release of the Sande label album.

Midnight Ride With Paul Revere And The Raiders   Columbia LE-10170.   c.1979. Another limited edition re-release of a 1966 album.

British singles

Sharon /Like Long Hair   Top Rank JAR-557.   1962.   Their only original Gardenia release in the UK.

Sharon/Like Long Hair   Sue WI-344.   1966.   A re-issue, albeit a strange one as they never had any success in Britain.

The Rezillos and The Revillos

British singles

THE REZILLOS   *I Can't Stand My Baby/Good Sculptures*   Sensible FAB-1.   1977. This is a mispress, as the B side should have been *I Wanna Be Your Man.*

My Baby Does Good Sculptures/Flying Saucer Attack   Sensible FAB-2.   1977. This was withdrawn at the last minute as Sire records bought the licence.

I Can't Stand My Baby/I Wanna Be Your Man   Sensible FAB-1 (MARK-2). 1979.   A re-issue to cash in on their Sire records success.   The original had a green cover and white label, whereas the re-issue had a red cover and yellow label.

Top Of The Pops/Destination Venus   Sire cassette single, number unknown. 1981.

Cliff Richard

British singles

Gee Whiz It's You/I Cannot Find A True Love   Columbia export issue DC-756. 1961.

What'd I Say/Blue Moon   Columbia export issue DC-758.   1963.

With the Cast Of Aladdin *This Was My Special Day/*B side unknown.   Columbia DB-7435.   1965.   Withdrawn.

Razzle Dazzle/Angel   Columbia export issue DC-762.   c.1966.

Finders Keepers   EMI one-sided promo PSR-304.   1967.
Nothing To Remind Me/The Leaving   EMI promo, number unknown.   c.1967.
Unknown track/THE SHADOWS   *Magical Mrs Clamp*   EMI promo PSR-316. c.1968.
Every Face Tells A Story   Sampler.   EMI promo PSR-410.   1977.
40 Greatest Hits   Double single sampler.   EMI promo PSR-414/5.   1977.
Singles Sampler   EMI twelve-inch promo PSLP-350.   1981.   This was made to promote the fourteen singles re-released by EMI in new picture sleeves.

Flexis

Cliff's Rock Party   Serenade magazine blue vinyl flexi.   Number and date unknown.
'Boyfriend' magazine flexi.   More details are unknown.
Music From America   'Rainbow' magazine flexi.   More details are unknown.
With others   *Star Souvenir Greetings*   New Spotlight/208 Radio Luxembourg. Date unknown.
With others who included two of the Shadows   *The Sound Of The Stars*   'Disc and Music Echo' flexi (Lyntone LYN-995/6).   1967.
The Cliff Richard Story   Sampler with interview.   Lyntone LYNSF-1218.   1973. Made for the World Record Club.

British albums

Summer Holiday   Original soundtrack versions. Elstree Studios private pressing, number unknown.   1962.   Made as a souvenir for stars and staff who worked on the movie.
Wonderful Life   Original soundtrack versions. Elstree Studios private pressing. 1963.   Details as above.
How Wonderful To Know   World Record Club ST-643.   c.1964.
Cliff Richard   World Record Club STP-1051.   1966.
Good News   Columbia export issue JSX-6167.   1968.   The number denotes that this is in mono. This may not have been released in mono in Britain.
The Cliff Richard Story   World Record Club SM-255/260.   c.1972.   A six-album boxed set with book.
The Music And Life Of Cliff Richard   EMI cassette only issue TC-EXSP-1601. 1974.   A very limited edition six-tape boxed set.
Dressed For The Occasion   Banded for airplay.   EMI promo PSLP-372.   1983.

American singles

It's Wonderful To Be Young/The Young Ones   Dot promo DGT-029-X.   1962. The American title for *The Young Ones* was *It's Wonderful To Be Young*.
Two A Penny   Interview single.   World Wide promo PR-1.   c.1968.
Two A Penny/I'll Love You Forever Today   Light promo L-601.   c.1968.
We Don't Talk Anymore   Long and short versions.   EMI-America twelve-inch promo SPRO-9252.   1979.   The long version is a disco re-mix which hasn't yet appeared in Britain, although it was released as a twelve-inch in Holland.

American EP's

It's All In The Game Epic juke box issue ST5-26089. 1961.
Two A Penny UNI promo EP-001. c.1968.

American albums

Cliff Richard interviewed by Bill McCord in Houston, Texas, 1962. Label unknown. Exists in metal master disc form only.
Two A Penny Film soundtrack. Light LS-5530. 1968.
Two A Penny Film soundtrack. UNI S-1087. 1968. For some reason two different labels had the rights to this album.
All My Love MFP 1420. 1971. An export issue made for Britain by Capitol.

Foreign language issues
Singles

Schon Wie Ein Traume Sung in German. German Columbia C-21843.
Pote Lippen Soll Man Kussen/Let's Make A Memory German Columbia C-22503. The A side is sung in German.
Ich Traume Deine Traume Sung in German. German Columbia.
Man Gratuliert Mir Sung in German. German Columbia.
Ein Girl Wiedu Sung in German. German Columbia C-23510.
Du Bist Mein Erster Gedanke Sung in German. German Columbia.
Gut Dasses Freunde Gibt Sung in German. German Electrolia.
Maria No Mas/Tus Besos Both sung in Spanish. Dutch Columbia.
Power To All Our Friends Sung in Spanish. Spanish EMI.
Non Dimenti Care Chitiama Sung in Italian. Italian HMV.
Non L'Ascoltare Sung in Italian. Italian HMV.
Non L'Ascoltare Sung in Italian. Italian Columbia SCMQ-1860. It appears that this is on two different labels.

EP's

Un Saludo De Cliff All sung in Spanish. Spanish HMV 13.955.
Cliff En Espania All sung in Spanish. Spanish HMV.
O Mio Signore EP. Portugese Columbia 2221. Date unknown. All four songs sung in Italian.

Albums

My Italian Friends Probably all sung in Italian. Italian Columbia CCMQ-8024.
Per Un Bacio Diamour Probably all sung in Italian. Italian Columbia CCMQ-8081.

Apologies for any omissions. It's difficult to date these releases without having the records themselves. Needless to say they'd be impossible to get nowadays.

Odds and sods

Jack Good's Oh Boy! UK Parlophone PMC-1072. 1958. This legendary soundtrack album to the ABC-TV show of the late '50s features Cliff and others live.

With OLIVIA NEWTON JOHN *Suddenly* UK Jet 7002. 1980. Cliff duets on this A side.

With PHIL EVERLY *She Means Nothing To Me* UK Capitol CL-276. 1983. Another duet single.

With SHEILA WALSH *Drifting* UK DJM SHEIL-1, and SHEILP-1 picture disc. 1983. Again, he only appears on the A side.

Singles

Living Doll/Apron Strings Norway Columbia DB-4306. 1959. Pressed in yellow vinyl.

Please Don't Tease/Where In My Heart Norway Columbia DB-4479. 1960. Pressed in yellow vinyl.

Glaub Nur Mir/B side unknown. German Columbia C-23103. Date unknown.

Ein Girl Wie Do/Bilder Von Dir German Columbia. Number and date unknown.

Johnny Rivers

American singles

Your First And Last Love/White Cliffs Of Dover Dee Dee 239. c.1960.

Your First And Last Love/That's My Babe Coral 9-62425. 1960. I don't know if the versions of the A side on these are the same takes.

The Customary Thing/B side unknown. MGM K-13266. c.1961. A one-off flop.

Blue Skies/That Someone Should Be Me Chancellor C-1096. 1961.

Darling Talk To Me/B side unknown. Cub 9047. c.1961.

The Customary Thing/Answer Me My Love Cub 9058. c.1961.

Baby Come Back/Long Long Walk Gone 5026. c.1962.

Call Me/B side unknown. Era 3037. c.1962.

Baby Come Back/Long Long Walk Roulette R-4565. 1962.

Long Black Veil/B side unknown. Capitol 4850. 1963. This was re-issued on Capitol 5232 when Rivers was having hits on Imperial.

If You Want It You Got It/B side unknown. Capitol 4913. 1963.

All the above were pre-Imperial releases.

Johnny Rivers At The Whiskey A Go Go Imperial juke box EP LP4-2264. c.1964.

Here We A Go Go Again Imperial juke box EP LP4-2274. 1964.

Realization Radio Spots EP. Imperial promo JRC-1. 1965.

Message from Johnny Rivers and song excerpts/Boots Randolph. Rowe Juke Box Company promo 1008. Date unknown.

Johnny Rivers Rocks The Folk Imperial juke box EP LP4-2293. c.1966.

A Touch Of Gold Radio Spots. Imperial promo SP-9. 1967.

Voters registration spots. United Artists promo SP-77. c.1972.

American albums

The Sensational Johnny Rivers Capitol ST-2161. 1963. His first album.
Swinging' Shindig Coronet 246. c.1965.
Swinging' Shindig Premier 9037. c.1965.
That's Rock 'n' Roll Guest Star GS-1482. c.1966.
Discoteque A Go Go Design DLP-194. c.1966.
Mr Teenage Sears SP-417. c.1967.
Groovin' Sears SP-487. c.1968.
The above were cheapo compilations of Rivers tracks mixed in with filler material by other, unknown, artists.

Go Johnny Go Capitol Record Club ST-90813. c.1966.
Home Grown Armed Forces Issue RL-102. 1971.
La Reggae Armed Forces Issue RL-193. 1973.

Tom Robinson

Before forming TRB Robinson was in a band called Cafe Society who released one album *Cafe Society* on UK Konk records KONK-102 in 1975. A single, *Whitby Two Step,* was also released. Konk KOS-5.

British singles

Don't Take No For An Answer/Glad To Be Gay EMI juke box issue, number unknown. 1978. These two tracks were taken from the *TRB Rising Free* EP.
Too Good To Be True Edited/*Power In The Darkness* Edited. EMI promo EMI-2847-DJ. 1978.
All Right All Night/Black Angel EMI 2946. 1978. Withdrawn.
Live In Hamburg Panic records flexi, number unknown. 1982. This flexi was given away at certain record shops.
War Baby/Hell Yes Panic NIC-2. 1983. There are two different sleeves, one with a purple tint, and one with a grey tint.

American single

Now Martin's Gone/Looking For A Bonfire IRS-Panic twelve-inch promo, number unknown. 1982.

American albums

Pre-album sampler. Harvest promo SPRO-8791. 1978.
Power In The Darkness Harvest STBO-11778. 1978. This is a double album version of his first album. The second one was a compilation of single tracks that weren't on the first.

Odds and sods

Secret Policeman's Ball Music mini album. UK Island 12WIP-6598. 1980. This has two live tracks.

224

Coming Out, Ready Or Not   UK Jane, number unknown.   1983.   This has a live version of *War Baby*.

Rockpile

British singles

Wrong Way/Now And Always   F-Beat yellow vinyl XX-9-C.   1980.   One of the last releases in the coloured vinyl spree of the late '70s.
Dave Edmunds And Nick Lowe Sing The Everly Brothers   F-Beat BEV-1.   1980. A four-track EP recorded originally at Capital radio in London for the excellent Roger Scott afternoon show. This was given away with their album. *Heart*/B side unknown.   F-Beat XX-14.   1980.   Withdrawn.

American singles

Dave Edmunds and Nick Lowe Sing The Everly Brothers   Columbia AE7-1219. 1980.   Again, this was given away with their *Seconds Of Pleasure* album.
Little Sister   (featuring ROBERT PLANT) plus two others by WINGS and THE WHO. Atlantic twelve-inch promo, number unknown.   1981.

Odds and sods

CARLENE CARTER   *Musical Shapes*   UK F-Beat XXLP-3.   1980.   ROCKPILE provide backing on this album and the two singles that were taken from it.
Concerts For Kampuchea   UK/USA Atlantic.   1981.   ROCKPILE play live here.

The Rolling Stones

British singles

Poison Ivy/Fortune Teller   Decca F-11742.   1963.   Withdrawn.
I Want To Be Your Man/Stones   Decca F-11764.   1963.   This is a misprint on the label. It should have read 'Stoned'.
Satisfaction/Under Assistant West Coast Promotion Man   Decca F-12220.   1965. Some early copies have this as the B side instead of *The Spider And The Fly*.
Rocks Off/All Down The Line   Rolling Stones promo SAM-3.   1971.
Happy/Shine A Light   Rolling Stones promo SAM-4.   1971.   These two were taken from the *Exile On Main Street* double album.
Excerpts From 'Exile On Main Street'/FANNY AND CURVED AIR tracks.   Rolling Stones flexi SFI-107.   This was given away with the NME in April 1972.   It also included a piano linking track by Jagger.
Brown Sugar/Happy/Rocks Off   Rolling Stones K-19107.   1973.   This may have actually appeared with an Atlantic label. It was made in conjunction with Radio Luxembourg, and is their rarest '70s issue.

It's Only Rock 'n' Roll/Through The Lonely Night Rolling Stones promo RS-19114-DJ. 1974. This features special DJ versions of both sides. They may have been edited.

I Don't Know Why/Try A Little Harder Decca F-13584. 1975. The first 1,000 copies credit the composers as Jagger and Richard instead of Stevie Wonder.

Beast Of Burden/Everything Is Turning Gold Rolling Stones, number unknown. 1978. Withdrawn.

Emotional Rescue Long and short versions. Rolling Stones promo RSR-105-DJ. 1981.

Single Stones Decca BROWS-1. 1981. This was a boxed set of twelve singles with new picture sleeves. In addition there was a mail order only box set with poster and badge.

Waiting On A Friend Edited. Rolling Stones promo RSR-109-DJ. 1982. This may have been a one-sided disc.

Let's Spend The Night Together/Start Me Up Rolling Stones promo RSR-112-DJ. 1982. This was made to promote the concert movie of the same name.

Fan club single. Rolling Stones R-83 70/1. 1983. A great interview disc with members re-calling their past, etc. A hard vinyl double-sided single.

Under Cover (Of The Night) Edited. Rolling Stones promo one-sided RSR-113-DJ. 1983.

British albums

Out Of Our Heads Decca LK-4725 mono, SKL-4725 stereo. 1965. This version had a colour cover and included the tracks *Satisfaction* and *The Last Time*. The album was quickly re-issued without these two tracks in a black and white cover. Decca LK-4733 mono and SKL-4733 stereo. The first version was later used for export purposes.

Could You Walk On The Waters Decca, number unknown. 1966. This was withdrawn. Decca flatly refused to have anything to do with an album with this title. The track listing was to be *19th Nervous Breakdown, Sad Day, Take It Or Leave It, Think, Mothers Little Helper, Going Home* (which was reportedly eleven minutes long), *Sitting On The Fence, Don't You Bother Me, Ride On Baby* and *Looking Tired*. It had a gatefold sleeve with ten pages of colour photos in the middle. All tracks were recorded in Los Angeles. In addition there was to be an EP released which featured the Italian language version of *As Tears Go By*. Again, this was withdrawn.

Let It Bleed Decca promo RSM-1. 1969. This is a promo compilation made to accompany their last official Decca album. It was given a full release in Australia in 1979.

Still Life Edited highlights. Rolling Stones picture disc CUNP-39115. 1982. There is a mispress version which has the wrong tracks on it. It's thought that only three copies exist.

Under Cover Rolling Stones CUN-1654361. 1983. Initial copies came with stickers on the sleeve covering the woman's body. These were printed onto later copies.

The Great Years Reader's Digest, number unknown. 1983. A five-album boxed set.
The First Eight Studio Albums Decca ROLL-1. 1983. A boxed set of eight albums and a 192 page book *The First Twenty Years*.

Export issues
Singles
Heart Of Stone/What A Shame Decca F-22180. 1964. This coupling was an early American single.
Satisfaction/West Coast Promotion Man Decca F-12220. 1965. This American coupling may have made its way into British shops before its official British release. The gap between the release in the USA and Britain was about three months. The idea was that the record would not be released in the UK until it had got to number one in the USA. Of course, it worked.
Get Off Of My Cloud/I'm Free Decca F-22265. 1965.
She's A Rainbow/2000 Light Years From Home Decca F-22706. 1967.
Street Fighting Man/No Expectations Decca F-22825. 1969. The A side of this is heavily re-mixed, with the vocal track lost somewhere under the bass.
Little Queenie/Love In Vain Decca F-13126. 1971.

All the above have blue and silver Decca labels like the regular UK releases. There are also some black label singles made for the export market.

I Wanna Be Your Man/Stoned Decca AT-15005. 1963.
Not Fade Away/Little By Little Decca At-15008. 1964.
Tell Me/Come On Decca AT-15032. 1964.
Empty Heart/Around And Around Decca AT-15035. 1964.
Time Is On My Side/Congratulations Decca AT-15039. 1965.
Little Red Rooster/Off The Hook Decca AT-15040. 1965.

EP's
The Rolling Stones, Volume Two Decca SDE-7501. 1964.
Got Live If You Want It Decca SDE-7502. 1964.
Got Live If You Want It Decca DFE-8620. 1964. This has a red label instead of a blue label.
Title unknown. Decca SDE-7503. 1965.

Albums
Out Of Our Heads Decca LK-4725 mono and SKL-4725 stereo. 1964.
Have You Seen Your Mother Baby Live LK-4838 mono and SKL-4838 stereo. 1965.
Flowers Decca LK-4888 mono and SKL-4888 stereo. 1966.

American singles
I Wanna Be Your Man/Stoned London LON-9641. 1964. Withdrawn because of the B side title.
Satisfaction/Under Assistant. . . London promo LON-9766-DJ. 1965. It's

possible that this is either edited or censored because of the 'tryin' to make some girl' line which got them banned on several radio stations, and bleeped on the TV show 'Shindig'.

MARY WELLS *Dear Lover* Atco 45-6392. 1965. Some copies had The Stones' *19th Nervous Breakdown* on the A side by mistake.

Street Fighting Man/No Expectations London LON-909. 1969. The picture sleeve which came with this was withdrawn very quickly. It showed a riot scene.

Brown Sugar Mono and stereo versions. Atco promo RS-19100. 1971. The Rolling Stones logo may not have been ready for Atlantic when they sent out these promos in 1971.

Wild Horses Long and short versions. Rolling Stones promo RS-19101. 1971.

Hot Stuff Long and short versions. Rolling Stones promo RS-19304. 1976.

Hot Stuff/Crazy Mama Rolling Stones twelve-inch promo DSKO-70. 1976. This was pressed in black and blue streaked vinyl.

Heart Of Gold/What A Shame London LON-9725. 1965. The first pressings came with purple and silver labels. This was later changed to the more familiar blue and white.

THE ROLLING STONES/JANIS IAN *What's It All About?* Radio Series, number 218. c.1976.

Beast Of Burden/When The Whip Comes Down Rolling Stones RS-19309. 1978. The picture sleeve was withdrawn very quickly.

Miss You Same on both sides. Rolling Stones twelve-inch promo DSKO-119.

Beast Of Burden Long and short versions. Rolling Stones promo RS-19309. 1978.

THE ROLLING STONES/THE BEACH BOYS *What's It All About?* Radio Series MA-1790 (507/8).

Shattered 3:46 and 2:44 versions. Rolling Stones promo RS-19310. 1978.

Time Waits For No One Rolling Stones promo PR-228. c.1978.

Love You Live Sampler. Rolling Stones promo PR-287. 1978.

Angie/Brown Sugar/Bitch Rolling Stones promo PR-237. c.1978.

THE ROLLING STONES/CHICAGO *What's It All About?* Radio Series 3024. Date unknown.

Emotional Rescue Long and short versions. Rolling Stones promo RS-20000. 1981.

Emotional Rescue Same on both sides. Rolling Stones twelve-inch promo PR-367. 1981.

She's So Cold Radio version/album version. Rolling Stones promo RS-21001. 1981. The radio version excludes the word 'Goddamn'.

If I Was A Dancer Vocal and instrumental versions. Rolling Stones promo twelve-inch DMD-253. 1981. The instrumental version has never been released commercially.

Start Me Up Same on both sides. Atlantic twelve-inch promo PR-397. 1982.

Under Cover (Of The Night) Edited. Rolling Stones promo, number unknown. 1983.

American EP's

All of these are juke box issues.
12×5 London SBG-23. 1964.
The Rolling Stones Now! London SBG-34. 1965.
Out Of Our Heads London SBG-37. 1965.
December's Children London SBG-43. 1965.
Their Satanic Majesties Request London SBG-54. 1967.
Exile On Main Street Rolling Stones CO7-22900. 1972.
Goat's Head Soup Rolling Stones CO7-59101. 1973.

American albums

It's Here Luv, The Ed Rudy Interview Album Label unknown, LL-1003. c.1965.
Their Satanic Majesties Request London open reel 70141. 1967. This tape version came with the famous 3-D postcard on the box, like the British and American vinyl album.
Let It Bleed London promo RSD-1. 1969. This is the American version of the British special promo album which came with their, then, new album.
Greatest Hits RCA Special Products SP-0268. c.1972.
Songs Of The Rolling Stones ABKCO promo MPD-1. c.1973. A publisher's sampler.
Robert W. Morgan Radio Series. (Dated 30.6.79).
BBC *Rock Hour* Radio Series, number 133. 1979.
Ron Wood interview for the Rolling Stone magazine news service. This is a seven-minute interview on a five-inch open reel tape. c.1980.
Rock 'n' Religion Radio Series RR-105/6. 1980. This apparently features some unreleased music.
Rolling Stone (magazine) *Continuous History Of Rock 'n' Roll* Radio Series. 1982. A three-album set.
DIR/King Biscuit Inside Track Radio Series. (Dated 16.3.82). A three-album set.
Westwood One Radio Series. Part one. (Dated 12.4.82).
Westwood One Radio Series. Part two. (Dated 19.4.82).
ABC *Supergroups In Concert* Radio Series. (Dated 10.82). This has live music from 1974, 1975 and 1978 as well as an interview recorded in 1981 at a farm somewhere in Massachusetts where they were rehearsing for their mammoth USA tour.
The Rolling Stones Past And Present Mutual Broadcasting Co. 1982. A twelve-album boxed set featuring unreleased live tracks.
A Profile Of The Rolling Stones Rolling Stone (magazine) Radio Special. (Dated 1.9.82). A three-album set.
Twentieth Anniversary Special. Toby Arnold Associates Inc. 1982. An eight-album set.
THE ROLLING STONES/BUDDY HOLLY Sounds Of Solid Gold, number 6. 1982.
Rock 'n' Roll Never Forgets Radio Series made by Westwood One. 1982. This five-album set looks at the career of Brian Jones.

Odds and sods
Singles

Con Le Mie La Crime/Heart Of Stone Italian Decca F-22270. 1965. The A side is *As Tears Go By* sung in Italian.
The Last Time/Play With Fire Canada London blue vinyl promo LON-9741. 1965.
Paint It Black/Stupid Girl Canada London blue vinyl promo LON-901. 1966.
Let's Spend The Night Together/Ruby Tuesday Canada London green vinyl promo LON-904. 1967.
Jumpin' Jack Flash/Child Of The Moon Canada London stereo green vinyl promo LON-908. 1969.
THE ROLLING STONES *Let It Rock*/JAMMING WITH EDWARD *Blowin' With Ry* German Rolling Stones promo RS-19102-X. 1971. The A side is the live at Leeds version.

Albums

The Andrew Loog Oldham Orchestra *The Rolling Stones Songbook* UK Decca LK-4796 mono only. 1966. This doesn't include the Stones, but Oldham was, of course, their producer.
The Rolling Stones Beat German Decca ten-inch fan club issue 60368. 1966.
Sticky Fingers Spanish Rolling Stones 100 064 063616. 1971. This had a different cover from the UK version. It showed a woman sticking her fingers into a tin of treacle. The track listing also changed, replacing *Sister Morphine* with *Let It Rock*.
The Rolling Stones French Decca boxed set, number unknown. c.1976. This has a tee-shirt as a freebie.
Their Satanic Majesties Request French Decca re-issue 75064. c.1980. This is a re-issue with the original 3-D sleeve.
The First Ever Rolling Stones Picture Disc French Decca 361 30010. 1980. A limited edition picture disc of hits.
Sticky Fingers Japan Mobile Fidelity audiophile MFSL 1-060. 1981.

Mick Jagger and Keith Richards have yet to maintain a steady solo career (like Bill Wyman's for example). So their releases are few and far between.

Mick Jagger

Tonight Let's Make Love In London Film soundtrack. UK Instant INLP-002. 1968. This album has a Jagger interview.
Memo From Turner/JACK NITZSCHZE *Natural Magic* UK Decca F-13067. 1970. This single was taken from the *Performance* soundtrack.
Performance Film soundtrack. UK/USA Warner. 1970. The movie starred Jagger and Edward Fox as well as Anita Pallenberg.
Ned Kelly Film soundtrack. USA United Artists UAS-5213. 1970. This has Jagger crooning *Wild Colonial Boy*.
Mick Jagger (with Elvis Presley on side two) interview album. USA Current Audio Magazine from Buddah records 0249. c.1971. This was withdrawn very quickly by RCA because of the Elvis material.

Mick Jagger interviewed by Tom Donahue. USA Rolling Stones promo PR-164. 1971. Jagger gets a whole album to himself here.

PETER TOSH AND MICK JAGGER *Don't Look Back* UK Rolling Stones EMI-2895 seven-inch and 12EMI-2895 twelve-inch. Also USA RS-19308 and twelve-inch promo DSKO-130. 1978. Jagger sings on the A side only.

The Mick Jagger Special USA BBC *Rock Hour* Radio Series. 1982.

Jagger talks about the movie 'Let's Spend The Night Together'. French magazine flexi. 1983. More details are unknown.

Keith Richards

Run Rudolph Run/The Harder They Come UK Rolling Stones RSR-102 and USA Rolling Stones RS-19311. 1979.

Before They Make Me Run/Interview. USA Rolling Stones promo PR-316. 1979.

Westwood One Radio Series. Part one. (Dated 15.6.81).

Westwood One Radio Series. Part two. (Dated 22.6.81).

Brian Jones

Brian Jones Present The Pipes Of Pan In Joujouka UK Rolling Stones COC-49100. 1972. This was an album of pipe music on side one with an electronically treated version on side two.

Westwood One Radio Series. *Rock 'n' Roll Never Forgets* USA Radio album. 1982. A five-album set.

Various Stones have contributed songs and musical know-how to other people's records over the years. Everyone from Jimmy Tarbuck to Ry Cooder have had at least one Stone on their records.

Linda Ronstadt

Before going solo Ronstadt had recorded with a folk-rock outfit THE STONE PONIES:

The Stone Ponies
American singles

All The Beautiful Things/Sweet Summer Blue And Gold Capitol 5838. 1966.

One For One/Evergreen Capitol 5910. 1967.

So Fine/B side may be by other artists. Sidewalk 937. 1967.

Different Drum/I've Got To Know Capitol 2004. 1967.

Up To My Neck In Muddy Water/Carnival Bear Capitol 2110. 1968.

Some Of Shelley's Blues/B side unknown. Capitol 2195. 1968.

American albums

The Stone Ponies Capitol ST-2666. 1966.

The Stone Ponies Volume Two. Evergreen   Capitol ST-2763.   1967.
The Stone Ponies And Friends Volume Three   Capitol ST-2863.   1968.
Stoney End   Pickwick SPC-3298.   1973.
The Stone Ponies Featuring Linda Ronstadt   Capitol ST-11383.   1974.

Linda Ronstadt

Blue Bayou/Lago Azul   (*Blue Bayou* sung in Spanish)   Asylum blue vinyl twelve-inch promo AS-45431.   1976.
The Linda Ronstadt Hit Kit   Asylum-Spun Gold promo boxed set, no number. c.1978.   A boxed set of four re-issue singles.

American album

LINDA RONSTADT/ELTON JOHN   Playboy Silver Anniversary Radio Series, number 5. (Dated 23.11.78).

Odds and sods

CHRISTMAS SPIRIT   *Christmas Is My Time Of Year/Will You Still Believe Me*   USA White Whale WW-290.   c.1967.   This is members of THE TURTLES, LINDA RONSTADT and GRAM PARSONS making a Christmas record.
Celebration At Big Sur   Soundtrack album.   UK/USA Ode 70.   1971.   This has an early solo live appearance by Ronstadt.
Music From Free Creek   UK Charisma CADS-101.   1973.   This is a strange double-album jam session featuring the likes of Keith Emerson, Todd Rundgren and many others. Ronstadt's contribution was *He Darkened The Sun* which has also been pirated on a red vinyl Capitol twelve-inch. The double album version was reduced to a single album re-titled *Summit Meeting*   UK Charisma CS-3. 1976.
The NAPA Presents A Concert. Behind Prison Walls   USA Pointed Star, number unknown.   Date unknown.
F.M.   Film soundtrack.   UK/USA MCA.   1978.   This has some live tracks.
Simple Dreams   Japan Nautilus audiophile pressing, number unknown.   1982.
The Pirates Of Penzance   Film soundtrack.   USA Asylum VE-601.   1982.   She makes her opera debut here.

Roxy Music

Before Brian Ferry's mob started recording there was an American band called Roxy who released one album for Elektra in 1970. This has nothing to do with the early '70s art-rock darlings.

British singles

Do The Strand/B side unknown.   Island WIP-6308.   1976.   This single was withdrawn just as EG records, which own the licence, was changing distribution from Island to Polydor. I don't know if copies exist.

Trash Parts 1 & 2. Polydor-EG twelve-inch promo POSPX-32. 1978.

Over You/Eight Miles High Polydor-EG twelve-inch promo POSPX-93. 1980. The B side of the regular version was *Manifesto*.

Oh Yeah! Edited. Polydor-EG one-sided promo, number unknown. 1980.

Jealous Guy Polydor-EG one-sided twelve-inch promo ROXYX-2. 1981.

British albums

Manifesto Polydor-EG picture disc EGPD-001. 1979. There are some copies which have GORDON GILTRAP'S *Fear Of The Dark* on one side by mistake.

The First Seven Albums Polydor-EG EGBS-1. 1982. This is a grey cloth-covered box with no freebies.

American singles

Virginia Plain Mono and stereo versions. Reprise promo RPS-1124. 1972. Eno's synth' solo is twice as long on this single than on the album and the British single versions. This may be on the regular copies of the single as well.

Angel Eyes Same on both sides. Atco twelve-inch promo DSKO-198. 1979.

Oh Yeah Long and short versions. Atco promo 7210. 1980.

Jealous Guy Long and short versions. Atco promo, number unknown. 1981.

Take A Chance On Me Long and short versions/*More Than This/Avalon* Warner-EG twelve-inch promo PROA-1056. 1982.

American albums

Country Life Atco SD36-106. 1975. Some copies of this American version have the original British sleeve with the two women. This was quickly changed to a photo of the background foliage.

Manifesto Atco promo picture disc, number unknown. 1979. This is the same as the regular British release.

BBC *Rock Hour* Number 330. (Dated 25.7.82).

Odds and sods

THE DUMBELLES *Giddy Up*/B side unknown. EG, number unknown. 1976. This is Roxy Music using an alias for a Christmas record. It was re-issued in 1977 at Christmas time.

The Rumour

British singles

Frozen Years/All Fall Down Stiff promo RUM-1. 1979. A special pre-release for shop use only.

THE DUPLICATES *I Want To Make You Very Happy/Call Of The Faithful* Stiff BUY-54. 1980. An alias release.

Todd Rundgren

Before going solo Todd was a member of The Nazz (see Nazz).

American singles

We Got To Get You A Woman/Baby Let's Swing Ampex X-31001. 1970. This was also pressed as a twelve-inch single playing at 45rpm! The first twelve inch? This was credited to Runt.

I Saw The Light Mono and stereo versions. Bearsville blue vinyl promo BSS-0003. 1972. Beware of counterfeits.

Something Anything Bearsville juke box EP SB-2066/LLP-236. 1972.

International Feel This may have the same track on both sides. Bearsville promo PRO-562. 1973. This is from the *Premier 3* pack of three Warner promo singles.

Wolfman Jack/Breathless Bearsville BSS-0301. 1974. This obscure single had a new re-mixed A side featuring the Wolfman himself on co-lead vocals.

It Wouldn't Have Made Any Difference 4:37 and 3:41 versions. Bearsville promo BSS-0335. 1978.

UTOPIA *The Very Last Time* Long and short versions. Bearsville promo BSS-49247. 1980.

Time Heals/Tiny Demons Bearsville BHS-3522-EP. 1981. This was a free single given with the *Healing* album. It was eventually released on it's own BSS-49696.

American albums

RUNT *Runt* Ampex A-10105. 1970. There are at least two different versions of this album. The first had twelve tracks and appeared with a blue Ampex label. When *We Gotta Get You A Woman* became a hit the album was re-issued on a brown Bearsville label, but this time with only ten songs. To add to the confusion, I've heard of copies on Bearsville that are only missing one song.

Something Anything Bearsville red and blue vinyl promo 2BR-2066. 1972. A £100 plus item. This was a double album with one red album and one blue album.

The Todd Rundgren Radio Show Bearsville promo PRO-524. 1972. This was made to accompany *Something Anything*. It contains Todd joshing about, plus two previously unreleased Nazz tracks.

The Todd Rundgren Radio Show Bearsville promo PRO-597. 1974. This was made to accompany the *Todd Rundgren's Utopia* album. Again, more jibing as well as the track *The Ikon* on side two.

Back To The Bars Sampler. Bearsville promo PROA-788. 1978. This, in addition to live music, has a Patti Smith interview.

UTOPIA *Deface The Music* Sampler. Bearsville promo PROA-908. 1980.

Rock Around The World Radio Series, number 146. 1978. This also has Pablo Cruise.

Rock Around The World Radio Series, number 188. 1979.

UTOPIA King Biscuit Radio Series. (Dated 19.4.81).

NBC Source Radio Series. (Dated 10.81)

Rolling Stone magazine *Continuous History Of Rock 'n' Roll*   Radio Series, number 29.   1982.

UTOPIA   King Biscuit Radio Series.   (Dated 4.4.82).   This actually has Todd solo in Boston for twenty minutes and Utopia playing live in Akron, Ohio for forty minutes. (But not at the same time).

Retrorock   Radio Series.   1982.   Recorded in Atlanta 1973.

BBC *Rock Hour*   Radio Series, number 336.   1982.   A brilliant performance at The Venue in London, May 1982. I was there, I was there!

The Music Special Radio Service   Number 22.   Date unknown.

British singles

I Saw The Light/Marlene   Bearsville K-15502.   1972.

I Saw The Light/Black Maria/Long Flowing Robe   Bearsville K-15506.   1972.   The first version was replaced by the second about three or four months afterwards.

Wolfman Jack/Breathless   Bearsville K-15519.   1974.   This was very quickly deleted.

You Cried Wolf/B side unknown.   Bearsville.   1978.   Withdrawn. Acetates exist.

UTOPIA   *Set Me Free/Umbrella*   Bearsville WIP-6581.   1980.   The first few thousand copies credit the B side as *Umbrella*. This was later corrected to *Umbrella Man* which is the correct title.

UTOPIA   *I Just Want To Touch You*   Bearsville one-sided promo IEP-12-DJ.   1980. A one-track sampler from the *Meet Utopia* EP.

Time Heals/Tiny Demons   Bearsville PSR-455.   1981.   Given with the *Healing* album.

UTOPIA   Epic-Network XPS-166.   1982.   This five-track EP came with the *Utopia* album.

Bang The Drum All Day/Drive   Lambourghini LMG-1.   1983.   Issued in a very rare picture sleeve.

British albums

RUNT   *Runt*   Bearsville K-45505.   1972.   Although credited to Runt in the USA it was credited to Todd Rundgren in Britain.

The Ballad Of Todd Rundgren   Bearsville K-44506.   1972.   Again credited to Todd Rundgren. I've yet to see British copies of these.

A Wizard A True Star   Bearsville K-45513.   1973.   The British copies came in a square sleeve printed in Holland as opposed to the die-cut shaped American sleeves.

UTOPIA   *Another Live*   Bearsville K-55508.   1975.   Another different cover to the American. The UK version has a live photo on the front with a lyric insert, while the American copy has an ugly cartoon sleeve (worthy of a typical bootleg) with no lyric insert.

UTOPIA   *Utopia*   Epic-Network cassette EPC40-25207.   1982.   This contains the five tracks on the EP.

The Ever Popular Tortured Artist Effect   Avatar-Bearsville.   1983.   This was planned for a January 1983 release, but eventually turned up in September on the new Lambourghini label.

Odds and sods

National Association Of Progressive Radio Announcements *1972 Vote PSA's.* USA United Artists promo SP-79. 1972. This album also features The Beach Boys, Frank Zappa, Flo and Eddie, America and others.

1972 Vote PSA's. Warner promo (from USA) PRO-534. 1972. Another album featuring The Beach Boys, Flo and Eddie, Arlo Guthrie among others. 14 radio spots in all.

Opus '72 Made by USA Pams Inc. 1972. An odd promo item. It has special 'winter warm' radio jingles as well as excerpts from the top 100 singles, which I suppose is where Todd comes into it.

Music From Free Creek UK Charisma CADS-101. 1973. Todd appears on this odd jam session album. It was reduced to a single album version called *Summit Meeting* in 1976.

Hello It's Me Japan Warner P-8410-W. c.1977. His only compilation so far. This may be promo only.

Party At The Palladium USA King Biscuit Radio Series. (Dated Nov. 1981). This features not only Todd but also Southside Johnny, Ian Hunter, Hall and Oates and Ellen Foley.

Rush

American singles

Trees/Prelude -Circumstances Mercury twelve-inch promo MK-75. 1977.

Spirit Of The Radio/Trees/Working Man Mercury twelve-inch promo MK-125. 1979.

Passage To Bankok Mercury twelve-inch promo, number unknown. 1981.

Entre Nous 4:37 and 3:45 versions. Mercury twelve-inch promo MK-137. 1981.

RUSH AND MAX WEBSTER *Battlescar/Blue River Liquor Shine* Mercury twelve-inch promo MK-159. 1981.

Vital Signs/New World Man Mercury twelve-inch promo MK-216. 1982.

Subdivisions Long and short versions. Mercury promo, number unknown. 1982.

Rush 'n Roulette Mercury twelve-inch promo, number unknown. 1982. This has to be one of the greatest gimmicks of all time, besides being a bloody expensive one. The six tracks on this Rush sampler are cut, not in the regular order one after the other from tracks one to six, but are cut with the six tracks running simultaneously, like the M dual groove *Pop Musik* twelve-inch. The tracks are listed on the label, but when you place the stylus on a groove you don't know which track you're getting until you hear it. DJ's must have thought this was hiliarious!

American albums

Everything You Always Wanted To Hear Mercury promo MK-32. c.1975. A sampler album.
Rush Through Time Mercury promo picture disc 001. c.1978.
RUSH/BRAM TCHAIKOVSKY Robert R. Klein Radio Series. (Dated 21.6.81).
RUSH/IAN HUNTER King Biscuit Radio Series. (Dated 18.10.81).
NBC Source Radio Series, number 82-10. 1982.

British single

Vital Signs Edited. Mercury one-sided promo VITAL7DJ-1. 1980.

Odds and sods

The Signals Radio Special Mercury promo SPE-012. 1981. Country unknown, although it may be British. It's made up of two twelve-inch singles.
BOB AND DOUG McKENZIE *Great White North* UK/USA Mercury. 1982. This single features Geddy Lee on vocals.

Leon Russell

American singles

LEE RUSSELL *Rainbow At Midnight/Honky Tonk Woman* Roulette R-4049. c.1962.
LEON RUSSELL *Talking About The Young/It's Alright* Dot 45-16771. c.1963.
Misty/Cindy A & M 734. c.1967. This may have only got to the promo stage. *Misty* appeared on the *A & M Bootleg Album* compilation.
She Smiles Like A River Mono and stereo versions. Shelter promo SPRO-6246. 1971.
Sweet Emily/The Ballad Of Mad Dogs And Englishmen Shelter promo SPRO-6247. 1971.
Elvis And Marilyn Same on both sides. Paradise twelve-inch promo PROA-758. 1978.

American album

Leon Russell Shelter SHE-1001. 1968. This is the original independent pressing which featured the track *Old Masters* which was removed when Capitol re-pressed the album in 1970.

Odds and sods

ASYLUM CHOIR *Look Inside* USA Smash SRS-67107. 1967. The original sleeve showed a toilet with the lid up, this was changed when Mercury re-issued the album in the '70s.
ASYLUM CHOIR *Asylum Choir Two* USA Shelter SW-8910. 1969. This was the second album by Leon Russell together with Marc Benno.

Mad Dogs And Englishmen Film soundtrack. UK/USA A & M. 1970. This was a document of the Joe Cocker and Leon Russell with The Shelter People concerts in 1970.

HANK WILSON *Hank Wilson's Back* USA Shelter SW-8923. 1972. This album is a tribute to the early country stars like Hank Williams, Hank Snow and others. Three singles were also released under this alias.

WILLIE NELSON AND LEON RUSSELL *One For The Road* USA Columbia KC2-36064. 1979. Russell also help out on Nelson's 1973 album on Atlantic *Shotgun Willie*. *Concerts For Bangla Desh* UK/USA Apple. 1971. Russell appears on at least two tracks here.

Mike Rutherford

British single

Time And Time Again/At The End Of The Day Charisma CB-364. 1979. The first 6500 copies were pressed with the wrong B side *Overnight Job*. However, regular copies with the right B side are harder to get.

American singles

Working In Line/Moonshine Passport PS-7919. 1979. This has a new mix of the B side.
Maxine/Halfway There Atlantic-Duke twelve-inch promo PR-455. 1982.
Maxine Long and short versions. Atlantic-Duke promo 7-89981. 1982.

Odds and sods

Beyond An Empty Dream (Songs For A Modern Church) UK Charisma CAS-1101. 1976. This includes the track *Take This Heart* by Charterhouse which is Rutherford and ex-Genesis member Anthony Philips.
Masterpieces UK Charisma SS-6. 1979. A compilation made for Sounds music paper and features the American mix of *Moonshine*.

The Rutles

American single

The Rutles Sampler. Warner yellow vinyl twelve-inch promo PROA-723. 1978. A beautiful item.

American album

I Want To Hold Your Rut Modern Music Radio Series. 1978. This has an in-depth interview with Dirk and Nasty as well as live music.

Odds and sods

The Rutland Weekend Album   Soundtrack.   UK BBC and USA Passport.   1976.
The pre-fab four made their debut here on this album which was taken straight
from the original TV soundtrack.
DIRK AND STIG   *Ging Gang Goolie/Mr Sheene*   UK EMI 2852.   1979.   This
momentous re-union was captured on kahki vinyl.

Santana

American singles

Santana 3   Columbia juke box EP 7-30595.   1971.
Welcome   Columbia juke box EP 7-32445.   1973.
Well All Right   Long and short versions.   Columbia twelve-inch promo AS-517.
1978.
Stormy   Long and short versions.   Columbia twelve-inch promo AS-538.   1978.
One Chain   Long and short versions.   Columbia twelve-inch promo AS-585.
1979.
Winning/E Papa Ne   Columbia twelve-inch promo AS-937.   1981.
The Sensitive Kind   Long and short versions.   Columbia twelve-inch promo
AS-1266.   1982.
Hold On/Nowhere To Run   Columbia twelve-inch promo   AS-1513.   1983.

American albums

Abraxas   Quad mix.   Columbia CQ-30130.   1974.
Third   Quad mix.   Columbia CQ-30595.   1974.
Caravanserai   Quad mix.   Columbia CQ-31610.   1974.
Welcome   Quad mix.   Columbia CQ-32445.   1974.
Greatest Hits   Quad mix.   Columbia PCQ-33050.   1974.
Borboletta   Quad mix.   Columbia PCQ-33135.   1974.
Amigos   Quad mix.   Columbia PCQ-33576.   1975.
The Solo Guitar Of Devadip Carlos Santana   Sampler.   Columbia promo AS-573.
1979.
BBC *Rock Hour*   Radio Series, number 339.   (Dated 17.5.81).
King Biscuit Radio Series   (Dated 16.8.81).
Westwood One Radio Series   1981.
NBC *Source*   Radio Series   (Dated Oct. 1981).
SANTANA/BO DIDDLEY   *Sounds Of Solid Gold*   Radio Series, number 41.   1982.
King Biscuit Radio Series   (Dated 31.10.82).
Retrorock   Radio Series, number 82-45/6.   1982.

British single

Samba Par Ti   Long and short versions.   CBS promo 2561-DJ.   1973.

'A' Label Promos
Top (left to right) BILLY J KRAMER *Little Children;* SQUEEZE *Cool For Cats.* Middle (left to right) ELTON JOHN *Lucy In The Sky;* FRANK ZAPPA *Joe's Garage.* Bottom (left to right) PAUL McCARTNEY *Coming Up;* CLASH *I Fought The Law.*

British albums

Abraxas   Quad mix.   CBS Q-64087.   1974.
Third   Quad mix.   CBS Q-69015.   1974.
Caravanserai   Quad mix.   CBS Q-65299.   1974.
Welcome   Quad mix.   CBS Q-69040.   1974.
Greatest Hits   Quad mix.   CBS Q-69081.   1974.
Borboletta   Quad mix.   CBS Q-69084.   1974.

Odds and sods

Woodstock   UK Atlantic/USA Cotillion.   1970.   Santana play live here.
SANTANA AND CHICAGO   Unknown tracks.   USA Columbia Special Products flexi
CSM-1671.   c.1972.   Made for Young And Free (which is otherwise unknown).
WILLIE NELSON AND CARLOS SANTANA   *San Antone*   UK CBS.   1983.   Santana plays
on the A side of this single.

Boz Scaggs

American singles

I'll Be Long Gone   Long and short versions.   Atlantic promo 2692.   1971.
You Make It So Hard   Long and short versions.   Columbia promo 4-46025.   1973.
The Feel Of Silk Degrees   Sampler.   Columbia promo AE7-1100.   1976.
Hard Times   Long and short versions.   Columbia promo 3-10606.   1977.
Breakdown Dead Ahead   Same on both sides.   Colbumia twelve-inch promo
AS-759.   1978.
Jo Jo   Same on both sides.   Columbia twelve-inch promo AS-786.   1978.
Miss Sun   Same on both sides.   Columbia twelve-inch promo, number unknown.
1979.

American albums

Boz Scaggs   Ten-song sampler.   Columbia promo AS-203.   1974.
Still Falling For You   Columbia, number unknown.   1978.   Withdrawn. This
eventually became *Two Down, Then Left*.

British single

Simone/Look What You've Done To Me   CBS promo XPS-107.   1978.

Odds and sods

Boz   Swedish Polydor LPHM-46253.   1966.   A Sweden only release. His first
album.

Brinsley Schwarz

British singles

THE HITTERS *Hypocrite/Version* United Artists UP-35530. 1973.
THE KNEES *Day Tripper/Slow Down* United Artists UP-35773. 1975.
THE LIMELIGHT *I Should Have Known/Tell Me Why* United Artists UP-35779.
1975.

These were released under pseudonyms as their own name brought them no success
whatsoever.

Odds and sods

Greasy Truckers Party UK United Artists UDX-203/4. 1974.
Glastonbury Fayre UK Revelation REV-1. 1974.
Live At The Paradiso UK United Artists, number unknown. 1974.

The above three all feature live Brinsley's tracks.

Stardust Film soundtrack. UK Ronco/USA Arista. 1975. This has an
ELECTRICIANS' track, which was another alias that they used.

The Searchers

British singles

Four Strong Winds/Can't You Just See Me
Don't Make Promises/Just Around The Corner
These two singles were privately made by the band in the late '70s and were
probably made as demos to send to record companies. Label details are unknown.
Acetates exist of both of them.

British albums

The Searchers Private pressing, label and number unknown. 1962. This was
made as a demo, but some may have been sold at pubs and clubs to raise funds, etc.
It cost the band £40 to make, but it paid off when they got a deal with Pye Records
in 1963. A version of *Sweets For My Sweet* was included on the album and it was
this that got the attention of record producer Tony Hatch.
The Searchers File Pye PFS-002. 1976. This was quickly re-issued with the
number FILD-002.
The Searchers Sire SRK-6082. 1979. This was the first version of this album with
a colour cover of silver Concorde-like planes against a blue and purple background.
The Searchers Sire SRK-6086. 1980. This was the second version, this time with a
black and white photo of the band and a silver title on the front cover. The most
notable change was that the track listing was different. A new Bob Dylan song
Coming From The Heart which was included on the first version was now replaced

by three new songs *Back To The Wars, Oh Silver* and *Love's Melody*.

The Searchers Reader's Digest, number and date unknown. This is proably just Pye label material.

American singles

Sweets For My Sweet/It's All Been A Dream Mercury 72172. 1963.
Sugar And Spice/Saints And Searchers Liberty 55689. 1963.

Both of the above releases were pre-British invasion, and sold very poorly.

American EP

This Is Us Kapp juke box issue KB-5985. 1965.

American albums

Hear Hear Mercury MG-20914 mono and SR-60914 stereo. 1964.
The Searchers Meet The Rattles Mercury MG-20994 mono and SR-60994 stereo. 1964.

Both of these Mercury albums feature material recorded at The Star Club in Hamburg in 1963.

THE SEARCHERS/THE MOODY BLUES *Sounds Of Solid Gold* Radio Series, number 26. 1982.

Odds and sods

*Tausend Nadelstiche/*B side unknown. German Vogue 14130. 1963.
*Süb Ist Sie/*B side unknown. German Vogue 14116. 1963.
These were two German language singles.
Needles And Pins (sung in German) German Ariola. 1964.
Needles And Pins (sung in French) French Pye. 1964.

Mike Pender sung lead on both of these instead of Tony Jackson who handled vocals on the English original. More details on these two are unknown.

Twenty Flashback Greats Of The Sixties UK K-Tel NE-494. 1975. This album has an alternate Pye recorded take of *Don't Throw Your Love Away*.
Anos Dorados (Goodbye My Love) Spanish PRT single. 1982. This is a Spanish medley of four songs.
The Searchers French Mode Records green vinyl 9039. Date unknown. An odd album.

John Sebastian and The Lovin' Spoonful

American albums

THE LOVIN' SPOONFUL *Spoonful Of Lovin'* Verve V6-5034-X. 1966. This was the first album, then they quickly moved to Kama Sutra.

JOHN SEBASTIAN *Live* MGM SE-4720. 1970. This was withdrawn and then bootlegged on Bassoon Records.
THE LOVIN' SPOONFUL *Sounds Of Solid Gold* Radio Series, number 13. 1982.

Odds and sods
What's Shakin' USA Elektra EKS-74002. 1966. This session jam album features The Lovin' Spoonful among others. There was also a promo EP issued in America EK-1.
Woodstock UK Atlantic/USA Cotillion. 1970. John Sebastian appears on the first volume only.
The Bitter End Years USA Roxbury RX3-300. 1976. This triple album has some John Sebastian tracks.

Neil Sedaka

American singles
Ring A Rockin'/B side unknown. Legion 133. c.1957. This was then picked up for national distribution and released on Guyden 2004.
Laura Lee/B side unknown. Decca 9-30520. 1958.
Beautiful You 3:35 and 2:45 versions. Kirshner promo SP45-370. 1971.

American EP's
The Diary RCA juke box EP LOC-105. 1960. This also has the title *Neil's Best* on some copies.
Little Devil RCA juke box EP LOC-135. 1961.

The Seeds

American singles
Daisy Mae/Can't Seem To Make You Mine GNP-Crecendo 354. 1966.
Can't Seem To Make You Mine/I Fell Myself GNP-Crecendo 354. 1966. These two singles have the same number for some reason.
900 Million People Daily Long and short versions. GNP-Crecendo promo 408. c.1968.
Pushin' Too Hard/Can't Seem To Make You Mine Ford-Philco Hip Pocket HP-26. c.1968.
Shuckin' And Jivin'/B side unknown. AJ Records 11. Date unknown. An obscurity.

American albums
A Web Of Sound Capitol Record Club issue ST-91224. c.1969.
Heavenly Earth Sunbow Records. More details are unknown. It could be a bootleg, but I'd hate to accuse anyone!

Bob Seger

American singles

BOB SEGER AND THE LAST HEARD *East Side Story*/B side unknown. Hideout 1013.
1966. His first release. All his Hideout and Cameo releases are credited to Bob
Seger And The Last Heard.
Chain Smokin'/Persecution Smith Hideout 1014. 1966.
East Side Story/B side unknown. Cameo C-438. 1966. The Philadelphia-based
Cameo label took up national distribution rights on his Hideout recordings as well
as taking up the option on future recordings.
Sock It To Me Santa/Florida Time Cameo C-444. 1966. *Florida Time* was
originally recorded by The Beach Bums on Are U Kidding Me Records 1010 in
1965. Their lead singer was Bob Seger. (The B side of The Beach Bums single was
The Ballad Of The Yellow Beret).
Chain Smokin'/Persecution Smith Cameo C-465. 1967. The other Hideout
re-issue.
Heavy Music Parts 1 & 2. Cameo C-494. 1967.
Vagrant Winter/Very Few Cameo, number unknown. 1967. This was his last
release for Cameo. The previous release *Heavy Music* was the last before they went
bankrupt. It's possible that *Vagrant Winter* was issued by the receiver to re-coup
losses incurred by Cameo. Alan Klein later bought the whole Cameo-Parkway
empire and released two Seger Cameo singles on the ABKCO label in 1974.
Midnight Rider/B side unknown. Reprise promo PRO-571. 1974.
Travellin' Man/Beautiful Loser Capitol promo PRO-8433. 1975.
Hollywood Nights Long and short versions. Capitol promo P-4618. 1977.
Old Time Rock 'n' Roll/Sunspot Baby Capitol twelve-inch promo SPRO-9086.
1977.
We've Got Tonight Same on both sides. Capitol twelve-inch promo SPRO-8987.
1978.
What's It All About? Radio Series, number 434. 1978.
Trying To Live My Life Long and short versions. Capitol twelve-inch promo
SPRO 9687. 1981.
Trying To Live My Life/Nine Tonight/Hollywood Nights Capitol twelve-inch
promo, number unknown. 1981.
Let It Rock Live and studio versions. Capitol twelve-inch promo SPRO-9717.
1981.

American albums

Smokin' O.P.'s Palladium P-1006. 1972. A rare independent release.
It was later picked up by Reprise Records.
Robert W. Morgan Radio Series   (Dated 7.7.79).
Innerview Radio Series. Series 8, programme 2. 1980.
Innerview Radio Series. Series 13, programme 8. 1981.
The Bob Seger Story Capitol promo, number unknown. 1981.

British singles

Main Street/Come To Poppa   Capitol twelve-inch promo PSLP-193.   1976.
Even Now/Little Victories   Capitol CL-284.   1982.   This came with a free single
We've Got Tonight/Brave Strangers.   A cassette single with these four tracks was
also released TC-CL-284.

British album

Seger Classics   Capitol promo PSLP-271/2.   1977.   This double album
compilation was limited to a thousand numbered copies.

Odds and sods

Night Moves   Japan Mobile Fidelity audiophile MFSL-1-034.   1980.

The Sex Pistols

British singles

Anarchy In The UK/I Wanna Be Me   EMI 2566.   1976.   This initially came in a
plain black bag, and when these ran out a normal EMI bag was used.
God Save The Queen/No Feeling   A & M AMS-7284.   1977.   Withdrawn by A &
M just before the Queen's Silver Jubilee celebrations. There are some bogus copies
in existence – these are Virgin label copies with A & M labels stuck on each side. As
both Virgin and A & M are pressed by CBS, it becomes easy to bootleg. The easy
way of distinguishing the A & M copy from the Virgin is to look at the run-off
groove; if it has the A & M number you have a winner – although you'll have to pay
about a £100 (currently) for the privilege. A picture sleeve for the A & M copy was
prepared, but most copies that turn up seem to have just the regular A & M bag.
Check the inner gatefold of *The Great Rock 'N' Roll Swindle* album for a peek of
this rarity.
*Belsen Was A Gas/*B side unknown.   Virgin, number unknown.   1977.   This was
to be the follow up to *God Save The Queen,* but not even Virgin would touch this
one. Acetates exist.
Submission   Virgin one-sided VDJ-24.   1977.   Given away with the first copies of
the *Never Mind The Bollocks* album. The track was included on later copies of the
album. For some reason side two has an anti-clockwise groove, but it has nothing
on it whatsoever.
Holiday In The Sun/Satellite   Virgin VS-191.   1977.   Several thousand picture
sleeves had already been printed before the police seized them. A travel firm
claimed that Rotten and Co. had ripped off their holiday brochure to provide
artwork for their new single. Virgin, however, got their own back by getting
someone to whip over the wall of the courtyard where the singles sleeves were boxed
up and 'borrow a few' back. These were then put back into circulation as a limited
edition.
*My Way/*THE MOTORS   *Airport*   Virgin mispress.   1978.

*The Biggest Blow/*Ronnie Biggs interview/*My Way*   Virgin VS-220-12.   1978.
Only the first few thousand have the Biggs interview.
Silly Thing/Frigging In The Rigging   Virgin VS-240.   1978.   Another mispress.
The A side should have been *Something Else.*
The Great Rock 'N' Roll Swindle/Rock Around The Clock   Virgin VS-290.   1978.
This has the now famous American Express credit card sleeve. The said credit card
company objected to having one of their cards defaced by those cuddley spikey tops
and demanded that they change it. They didn't.
The Sex Pistols Six Pack   Virgin SEX-1.   1980.   A plastic wallet of six singles
including one new single: *Black Leather/Here We Go Again*   Virgin SEX-16.

British albums

Spunk   This was a pre-release cassette given to fans who couldn't wait for the
album. It featured tracks and mixes which didn't appear on the *Bollocks* album.
Inevitably, it has been bootlegged.
Never Mind The Bollocks, Here's The Sex Pistols   Virgin V-2086.   1977.   There
are several different sleeves for this album. One has a totally blank white back cover
as Virgin weren't sure about the track listing. Some copies come with the
Submission single. To celebrate the release Virgin flouted the Sunday trading laws
and opened up their Notting Hill Record store to sell nothing but this album.
Apparently they had more records stolen than sold.
The Heydays   Factory cassette, number unknown.   1980.   This is a documentary-
style tape featuring an interview with Malcolm McLaren's granny.

Odds and sods

*Anarchy Pour La UK/*B side unknown.   French Barclay-Matrixbest, number
650105.   1977.   A French language version.
Troublemakers   USA Warner PROA-857.   1981.   This compilation double album
has two live tracks, *Anarchy In The USA* and *No Fun* recorded at their last concert
at the San Fransisco Winterland in 1977. As Rotten said, 'If you can take this, you
can take anything'.

The Shadows

Before joining up with Cliff Richard, Hank Marvin and Bruce Welch had already
recorded one song with The Five Chestnuts: *Jean Dorothy/Teenage Love*
UK Columbia DB-4165.   1958.

The Shadows who had singles released on UK HMV are nothing to do with Hank
Marvin & Co.

British singles

THE DRIFTERS   *Feelin' Fine/Don't Be A Fool With Love*   Columbia DB-4263.   1959.
THE DRIFTERS   *Jet Black/Driftin'*   Columbia DB-4325.   1959.

These were the two singles that they released before they had to change their name to avoid confusion with the Atlantic R & B group.

THE SHADOWS   *Los Shadows*/B side unknown.   Columbia export issue, number unknown.   1964.
The Rise And Fall Of Flingel Blunt   Columbia DB-8261.   1964.   Some copies have the A side on both sides by mistakes.
Thunderbirds Are Go   EMI one-sided promo PSR-305.   1967.
Maroc Seven   With talking intro.   EMI one-sided promo PSR-304.   1967.
Chelsea Boot/Jigsaw   EMI promo PSR-310.   1967.
Naughty Nippon Nights/Let Me Take You There   EMI promo PSR-313.   1967.
Magical Mrs Clamps/CLIFF RICHARD track.   EMI promo PSR-316.   1968.
The Shadows   World Record Club flexi LYN-10099.   1972.   This sampler was to plug the mail order boxed set.
Twenty Golden Greats   Sampler.   EMI promo, number unknown.   1977.

British EP

Los Shadows   Columbia SEG-8278.   1964.   This has four different sleeves.

British album

Twenty Golden Greats   EMI EMTV-3.   1977.   Some copies have Pink Floyd's *Animals* on side two by mistake.

So far I've not seen an American discography of The Shad's as they didn't exactly set the charts alight there, so here goes:

American singles

THE DRIFTERS   *Feeling Fine/Don't Be A Fool With Love*   Capitol F-4220.   1959.
THE FOUR JETS   *Jet Black/Driftin'*   Capitol, number unknown.   1959.   After giving the first single The Drifters name Capitol had no choice but to re-name them for the American market.
THE SHADOWS   *Apache/Quatermass Stores*   ABC-Paramount 45-10138.   1960.
ABC tried desperately to plug this as the 'original version' when Sweden's Jorgen Ingmann beat them to it and reached number two with his cover version on Atco.
FBI/B side unknown.   Atlantic 2111.   1961.   Atlantic thought that this group might be worth investing in because of *'Apache'* on Atlantic's sister label Atco. They started by editing the A side of this single.
Man Of Mystery/Kon-tiki   Atlantic 45-2135.   1961.
Wonderful Land/Stars Fell On Stockton   Atlantic 45-2146.   1961.
Guitar Tango/What A Lovely Tune   Atlantic 45-2166.   1962.
Dance On/The Rumble   Atlantic 45-2177.   1962.
The Rise And Fall Of Flingel Blunt/Lovers   Atlantic 45-2235.   1963.
Rhythm And Greens/The Miracle   Atlantic 45-2257.   1964.
Mary Anne/Chu Chu   Epic 5-9793.   1965.
Don't Make Me Blue/My Grandfather's Clock   Epic 5-9849.   1965.
I Met A Girl/Late Night Saturday   Epic 5-10020.   1966.

American albums

Surfin' With The Shadows Atlantic SD-8089. 1962.
The Shadows Know Atlantic SD-8097. 1963.

Sham 69

British singles

I Don't Wanna/Ulster/Red London Step Forward SF-4. 1977. This twelve-inch originally came with a black and white photo sleeve. When it was re-issued in 1979 a new coloured graphic sleeve was used.
Song Of The Streets No label. 1978. A one-sided concert freebie.
What Have We Got Polydor one-sided promo, number unknown. 1978.
If The Kids Are United/Borstal Breakout Polydor 2812 095. 1979. This was a twelve-inch given away with the *Adventures Of The Hersham Boys* album.
Live EP. Polydor SHAM-1. 1980. This seven-inch EP was given away with their *The First The Best And The Last* compilation album.

Del Shannon

American singles

Runaway '67/He Cheated Liberty 55993. 1967.
*Runaway/*B side unknown. Eric 189. c.1972. The only stereo version recorded in the early '60s.
*Runaway/*B side unknown. Twirl 4001. Date unknown.
*Runaway/*B side unknown. Terrific 5000. Date unknown.

The above two may be yet more re-recordings.

*Runaway/*B. BUMBLE AND THE STINGERS *Nut Rocker* Polydor 2040 109. 1978. This version may have been recorded for K-Tel originally.
Runaway/Hats Off To Larry Gusto GT4-2035. 1979. This time he gave both songs the country treatment.

In addition to the original version I make that possibly seven different versions of the same song. Has he finished the song yet?

British single

Runaway/The Snake London HLK-9317. 1961. This is a mispress as the B side should have been *Jody*.

Odds and sods

Never Thought I Could/Show Me Philippines Liberty LB-20324. 1966.
Lightning Strikes/Hey Little Star Philippines LB-20361. 1967.

The Letter/Silently   Philippines Liberty LB-20376.   1967.
These three were Philippino only releases.
Oh How Happy/The Ghost   Australian Interfusion 5439.   1975.   An Australian only single.
Rock Rools OK?   USA K-Tel RL-001.   1976.   This has new recordings of '60s hits by Del and other artists.

The Shoes

American singles
Heads Or Tails   EP.   Private pressing.   c.1974.   More details are unknown.
I Don't Wanna Hear It/Now And Then   Elektra twelve-inch promo AS-11440.   1981.

American albums
Un Dans Versailles   Private pressing.   c.1974.   More details are unknown.   This is one of the rarest, and subsequently the most sought-after, albums of the pre-new wave era.
Black Vinyl Shoes   Black Vinyl Records S-51477.   1977.   Another rarity, but at least this one was re-released.   The original cover had the title written on a blackboard type background.

This band is not to be confused with the band who recorded for Polydor in Britain in the late '60s. When asked why they chose the name The Beatles, Paul McCartney replied: 'We could have been called The Shoes for all you know!'

Paul Simon

American singles
Pre-CBS releases
TRUE TAYLOR   *True Or False/*B side unknown.   Big records 614.   c.1958.
TICO AND THE TRIUMPHS   *Motorcycle/I Don't Believe Them*   Madison M-169.   c.1960.
TICO AND THE TRIUMPHS   *Motorcycle/I Don't Believe Them*   Amy 835.   c.1960.

The same as the above single, but taken up by the Amy for national distribution.

TICO AND THE TRIUMPHS   *Wild Flower/Express Train*   Amy 845.   c.1960.
TICO AND THE TRIUMPHS   *Cry Little Boy Cry/Get Up And Do The Wobble*   Amy 860.   c.1961.   Do the wobble?! Paul Simon?!
TICO   *Card Of Love/Noise*   Amy 876.   1961.
JERRY LANDIS   *The Lonely Teen Ranger/Lisa*   Amy 875.   1961.
JERRY LANDIS   *Cards Of Love/Noise*   Amy 876.   1961.   A re-issue of the Tico single.

JERRY LANDIS *Lone Teen Ranger/Lisa* Jason Scott Records 22. c.1962.

JERRY LANDIS *I'm Lonely/I Wish I Weren't In Love* Can-Am 130. 1962.

JERRY LANDIS *Just A Boy/Shy* Warwick 552. 1962.

JERRY LANDIS *I Want To Be The Lipstick On Your Collar/Just A Boy* Warwick 588. 1962.

JERRY LANDIS *Play Me A Sad Song/It Means A Lot* Warwick 619. 1962.

JERRY LANDIS *Anna Belle/Loneliness* MGM K-12822. c.1962.

PAUL KANE *Carlos Diminquez/He Was My Brother* Tribute 1746. 1963.

This final pseudonym release showed how far Simon had come with his songwriting. The first True Taylor single is truly horrific, while *He Was My Brother* showed promise of what was to come later with Art Garfunkel.

Carlos Diminquez/He Was My Brother Tribute 128. Date unknown, but possibly issued as a cash-in during the mid-'60s. Some copies with this number are also credited to Paul Kane.

American Tune Same on both sides. Columbia promo AE7-1105. 1972.

Stranded In a Limousine Same on both sides. Columbia promo AE7-1158. 1977.

Late In The Evening Possibly the same track on both sides. Warner twelve-inch promo PROA-889. 1980.

What's It All About? Radio Series (with Foreigner on side two). MA-1788. 1981.

PAUL SIMON/PAT BENETAR *What's It All About?* Radio Series, number 583/4. 1981.

American albums

Paul Simon made no official albums until the British *Paul Simon Songbook* album in 1965. Any pre-CBS material are just on compilations.

Paul Simon Plus MCP 8027. 1966. This compilation album also features Neil Sedaka and The Four Seasons.

Early Songs Crest Records promo EBM-7172. Date unknown. This is probably a publisher's sampler made by Edward B. Marks who also issued the Tribute label singles.

Paul Simon Solo Music 166. Date unknown. It's anyone's guess as to what this could be.

There Goes Rhymin' Simon Quad mix. Columbia CQ-32280. 1974. There may be more quads.

PAUL SIMON/JACK BRUCE King Biscuit Radio Series (Dated 23.11.81).

Still Crazy After All These Years Columbia-Masterworks audiophile pressing HS-43540. 1981.

British singles

JERRY LANDIS *Carlos Diminquez/He Was My Brother* Oriole CB-1390. 1962. It's possible that this single was actually recorded in Britain while he was working the folk clubs and pubs.

PAUL SIMON *I Am A Rock/Leaves That Are Green* CBS 201797. 1965. This was the single taken from his first solo album.

Kodakchrome/B side unknown. CBS 1545. 1973. Withdrawn. It was replaced as the A side by *Take Me To The Mardi Gras*. The BBC objected to the original choice because of the advertising factor.

The Sound Of Silence Long and short versions. CBS promo 2349-DJ. 1973.

Something So Right Long and short versions. CBS promo 2822-DJ. 1976.

British albums

The Paul Simon Songbook CBS SBPG-62579. 1965. Recorded in London, this album made very little impact at the time. Paul Simon must have disliked his early work as he asked CBS to delete the album in the late '70s. In reality he had nothing to be ashamed of as it's not a bad album at all.

Paul Simon Quad mix. CBS Q-69007. 1973.

There Goes Rhymin' Simon Quad mix. CBS Q-69035. 1973.

Still Crazy After All These Years Quad mix. CBS Q-86001. 1975.

Odds and sods

DOTTY DANIELS *I Wrote You A Letter* USA Amy 885. c.1961. Produced by Jerry Landis.

DOTTY DANIELS *Play Me A Song* USA Amy, number unknown. c.1962. Written by Eddie Simon and Jerry Landis. Produced by Jerry Landis.

JACKSON C. FRANK *Jackson C. Frank* UK Columbia 33SX-1788. 1965.

JACKSON C. FRANK *Blues Run The Game/Can't Get Away From Love* UK Columbia DB-7795. 1965. Paul Simon produced the album and single for this UK-based folk singer.

ART GARFUNKEL, JAMES TAYLOR AND PAUL SIMON *Wonderful World* USA Columbia and UK CBS. 1977. Simon sung on this single A side.

THE NOT READY FOR PRIME TIME PLAYERS *Saturday Night Live* Soundtrack. USA Arista AL-4107. 1978. Simon makes a brief appearance here in a non-singing role. He made an appearance on the TV show once with George Harrison singing a duet on *Bye Bye Love*.

RANDY NEWMAN *The Blues* UK/USA Warner. 1983. Simon sings duet with Newman on this single A side, also taken off Newman's *Trouble In Paradise* album.

Simon and Garfunkel

American singles
Tom and Jerry

Pre-CBS releases. Credited to TOM AND JERRY (Tom Graph and Jerry Landis):

Hey Schoolgirl/Dancin' Wild BT Records 103. c.1957.

Hey Schoolgirl/Dancin' Wild   Big Records 613.   1957.   This was the version that was nationally available.
Don't Say Goodbye/B side unknown.   Big 618.   1957.
Our Song/Two Teenagers   Big 619.   1958.
Baby Talk/B side unknown.   Big 621.   1958.
That's My Story/Tijuana blues   Hunt 319.   1959.
Hey Schoolgirl/B side unknown.   King 45-5167.   1960.
Surrender Please Surrender/Fightin' Mad   ABC-Paramount 45-10363.   1962.

Simon and Garfunkel

The Sound Of Silence   Same on both sides.   Columbia red vinyl promo 4-43396. 1965.
I Am A Rock   Same on both sides.   Columbia red vinyl promo 4-43611.   1966.
That's My Story/Tijuana Blues   ABC 45-10788.   1966.   An old single re-issued as a cash-in on their CBS success.
Silent Night – Seven O'Clock News   Same on both sides.   Columbia promo JZSP-116469.   1967.
Baby Talk/RONNIE LAWRENCE   *I'm Going To Get Married*   Bell 45-120.   c.1967. Another cash-in single.
America/Keep The Customer Satisfied   Columbia promo AE-43.   1972.   Made to promote the *Greatest Hits* album.

American EP's

Parsley, Sage, Rosemary And Thyme   Columbia juke box EP SONE-70007.   1967.
Bookends   Columbia juke box EP 7-9529.   1967.
Bridge Over Troubled Water   Juke box EP 7-9914.   1970.

American albums

Wednesday Morning 3 AM   Columbia CL-2249 mono and CS-9049 stereo.   1964. The first album by Simon and Garfunkel made no impact whatsoever when first released. One track, however, *The Sound Of Silence* was later overdubbed with session musicians by producer Tom Wilson and released as a single. This was done without the permission of Paul Simon, who had since split from Art Garfunkel and was sharing a flat in London with another folk singer of the time, Al Stewart. By the time the record had got to number one in Boston, Simon felt he had to get back together with Art Garfunkel, so he left Britain. The album wasn't released in Britain until 1968.
The Hit Sounds Of Simon And Garfunkel   Pickwick SPC-3059.   1966.   An album of the really rotten pre-CBS tracks like True Taylor's *True Or False* among others. A shameful cash-in.
The Tom And Jerry Sessions   Offshore 725.   Date unknown.   A bootleg?
Simon And Garfunkel   Sears SP-435.   Date unknown.   More pre-CBS grot.
Bridge Over Troubled Water   Quad mix.   Columbia CQ-30995.   c.1972.

The Complete Collection   Columbia Special Products TV-2002.   c.1974.
A TV-advertised boxed set of their five albums.
Bridge Over Troubled Water   Columbia-Masterworks audiophile HC-49914.
1981.

British single

TOM AND JERRY   *Baby Talk*/B side unknown.   Gala GSP-806.   Date unknown.
Their only official British release using this name.

British albums

The Hit Sounds Of Simon and Garfunkel   Allegro ALL-836.   1966.   This is the
same as the American Pickwick label album.
Bridge Over Troubled Water   Quad mix.   CBS Q-63699.   1973.

Odds and sods

DAVID WINTERS   *Bye Bye*   USA Rori 703.   Date unknown.
RITCHIE CORDELL   *Tick Tock*   USA Rori Records 707.   Date unknown.
Simon and Garfunkel did back-up vocals on both of these singles.
Voices Of Vista   Radio Series, number 46.   1966.   An American album.

Voices Of Vista   Radio Series, number 58.   1967.   Another American album.
Both of these feature contributions from Simon and Garfunkel.

Greatest Hits   Japan CBS-Sony audiophile pressing 30AP-2259.   1980.

Siouxsie and the Banshees

British singles

Hong Kong Garden/Voices   Polydor 2059 052.   1977.   Some early copies came
with a gatefold sleeve.
Fireworks/Coal Mind   Polydor POSPG-450.   1982.   Another limited edition
gatefold sleeve.
Dear Prudence/Tattoo   Wonderland SHE-4.   1983.   This also had a limited
edition triple foldout sleeve in green.
Fan Club Single   More details unknown.

British album

The Singles Album   Polydor, number unknown.   1982.   This was to be the original
compilation album put together by Polydor. The cover showed all the singles
sleeves with the group name at the top and the album title at the bottom. Initial
copies of the album were to have included a free single with two previously
unreleased tracks. Typically, this never turned up. What we did get though was
Once Upon A Time.

Odds and sods

Mittagessen/Love In A Void German Polydor 2059 151. 1978. Although an import, this did get into the chart. This record has never been pressed in Britain, although the sleeve states *Made In The United Kingdom*.

THE CREATURES *Mad Eyed Screamers/So Unreal* Polydor promo PODJ-354. 1981. This is a two-track promo from the *Wild Thing* double single.

Slade

Before forming Slade, Noddy Holder had already recorded several singles:

STEVE BRETT AND THE MAVERICKS *Wishing/Anything That's A Part Of You* UK Columbia DB-7470. 1965.

Chains Of My Heart/Sugar Shack Columbia DB-7794. 1965.

Sad Lonely And Blue/Candy Columbia DB-7581. 1965.

I don't know if The Mavericks were the other members of Slade.

THE 'N' BETWEENS *You Better Run/Evil Witchman* UK Columbia DB-8090. 1966. This is basically Slade.

British singles

AMBROSE SLADE *Genesis/Roach Daddy* Fontana TF-1015. 1969.

AMBROSE SLADE *Wild Winds Are Blowing/One Way Hotel* Fontana TF-1056. 1969.

AMBROSE SLADE *Shapes Of Things To Come/C'mon C'mon* Fontana TF-1079. 1970.

None of the above sold, so Fontana let them go after three singles and one album.

SLADE *Hear Me Calling*/B side unknown. Polydor promo 2814 008. 1970. This may have been withdrawn, since all the copies that have turned up so far are promos playing at 33rpm.

Know Who You Are/Dapple Rose Polydor 2058 054. 1971. This was their last flop single before *Get Down And Get With It*.

The Whole World's Gone Crazy Music Scene magazine flexi SFI-122. 1973.

Unknown tracks. *19* magazine flexi LYN-2797. 1973.

Far Far Away Smith's crisps flexi. 1974.

Gypsy Road Hog Mono re-mix/B side unknown. Barn promo, number unknown. 1977.

British albums

AMBROSE SLADE *Beginnings* Fontana STL-5492. 1969.

SLADE *The Beginnings Of Ambrose Slade* Contour, number unknown. 1973.

The two above are virtually the same album. The second version was a cheapo cash-in, but was withdrawn due to legal problems.

American single

Merry Christmas Everybody/Don't Blame Me   Polydor export issue 2058 419. 1973.

American album

AMBROSE SLADE   *Ballzy*   Fontana SRF-67598.   1969.   This re-titled version of *Beginnings* is easier to find than the UK version.

Odds and sods

THE 'N' BETWEENS   *Take A Heart*   EP.   French Barclay 2017.   1966.   Contains tracks which didn't appear in the UK.
Get Down And Get With It/Gospel According To Rasputin   Italian Polydor 2058 112.   1971.   Issued in pink vinyl.
THE DUMMIES   *When The Lights Are Out*/B side unknown.   UK Cheapskate FWL-1.   1979.
THE DUMMIES   *Didn't Know It Used To Be You*/B side unknown.   UK Cheapskate CHEAP-003.   1979.

Both of these singles are Slade using an alias in a desperate attempt to get some radio play.

Grace Slick

Before joining Jefferson Airplane, Slick was a member of The Great Society who, in 1965, had cut the original version of *Somebody To Love* on the San Francisco-based Northbeach label. They then went to Columbia and made one single and an album.

American singles

GRACE SLICK AND PAUL KANTER   *China/Starfighter*   Grunt promo SP45-303.   1972.
Dreams   Long and short versions.   RCA twelve-inch promo JD-12042.   1979.

American albums

GRACE SLICK AND PAUL KANTNER   *Manhole*   Banded for radio use.   Grunt promo DJL 1-0347.   1973.
And Through The Hoop With Grace Slick   Interview album. RCA promo DJL 1-3544.   1979.
Welcome To The Wrecking Ball   Interview album.   RCA promo DJL 1-3922. 1981.

The Small Faces

Steve Marriott had already cut a few records before joining The Small Faces.
Give Her My Regards/Imaginary Love UK Decca F-11619. 1964.
THE MOMENTS *You Really Got Me*/B side unknown. USA World Artists 1032.
1965. This band featured Marriott.

British albums

The Small Faces New World NW-6000. 1971. A cheapo album with Immediate
material.
The Small Faces And The Amen Corner New World NW-6001. 1971. More
Immediate label material.
Ogden's Nut Gone Flake Charly export issue CR-300015. 1977.
The Small Faces Charly export issue CR-300025. 1977.

American singles

Runaway/B side unknown. Pride 1006. 1969. This MGM label issued this
obscure release.
Around The Plynth/Wicked Messenger Warner 7393. 1969.
Had Me A Real Good Time/Rear Wheel Skid Warner 7442. 1970.
Had Me A Real Good Time 3:59 and 2:50 versions. Warner promo 7442. 1970.

These Warners singles were actually The Faces, but credited to The Small Faces.

Patti Smith

American singles

Hey Joe/Piss Factory Mer 601. 1974. This was made during her Patti Hearst
lookalike period, and was released on her own label as no one else would touch it.
Ask The Angels Same on both sides. Arista promo SP-4. 1975.
Frederick Studio version/Live version. Arista twelve-inch promo SP-62. 1978.

American albums

PATTI SMITH/MARTIN MULL Crawdaddy Radio Revue Series, number CR2-76. 1976.
Rock Around The World Radio Series. 1977. Recorded live in Cleveland.

Soft Cell

British singles

Mutant Moments EP. Big Frock Records ABF-1. 1980. A local release which
has never been re-released complete.

Memorabilia/A Man Can Get Lost   Some Bizarre Label seven-inch HARD-1. 1981.
Memorabilia/Persuasion   Some Bizarre Label twelve-inch HARD-12.   1981.

These two made up their first nationally available release, but both are still hard to get hold of. Apparently some copies of the seven-inch have an alternate vocal version of *A Man Can Get Lost*.

The Twelve-Inch Singles   Some Bizarre Label CELBX-1.   1982.   A boxed set of six twelve-inchers.
Martin/Jimi Hendrix Medley   Some Bizarre Label APART-12.   1982.   This twelve-inch was given away with the *Art Of Falling Apart* album.
Mr X   Flexipop 12 (Lyntone LYN-10410).   1982.   This was a track from their *Mutant Moments* EP.
Numbers   Edited.   Some Bizarre Label one-sided promo BXSDJ-17.   1983.
Soul Inside/You Only Live Twice   Some Bizarre Label BZS-20/20.   1983.   The first few thousand came with a free single *Loving You, Hurting Me/007 Theme*.

American singles

Sex Dwarf/Entertain Me/Seedy Films   Sire twelve-inch promo PROA-1021.   1981.
Where Did Our Love Go/Tainted Love/Where Did Our Love Go   Sire promo PROS-1028.   1981.
What/Insecure Me   Sire twelve-inch promo PROA-1037.   1982.

American album

Non Stop Ecstatic Dancing   Sire 1-23694.   1982.   This American version has *Insecure Me* instead of *Chip On My Shoulder*.

Odds and sods

The Some Bizarre Album   UK Some Bizarre Label BXLP-1.   1981.   This has some early tracks.
MARC ALMOND AND FRIENDS   *Discipline*   UK Flexipop 23 (Lyntone LYN-12505). 1982.

Both members of Soft Cell have also worked with Vicious Pink Phenomina, Psychic TV and others.

Sparks

Previous to re-naming themselves Sparks they had already cut one album using the name HALFNELSON   *Halfnelson*   USA Bearsville BV-2048.   1972.   This album was re-issued as Sparks a year later along with the *Woofer In A Tweeter's Clothing* album.

American albums

Introducing Sparks   Columbia red vinyl promo PC-34901.   1976.
SPARKS/GRAHAM PARKER   King Biscuit Radio Series   (Dated 11.7.82).
BBC *Rock Hour*   Radio Series, number 324.   (Dated June 1982).

Spirit

American single

Holyman/Looking Into Darkness   Mercury, number unknown.   1977.   This may
have been withdrawn.

American album

Potatoland   Interview album.   Rhino one-sided promo, number unknown.   1981.

British singles

Midnight Train/Potatoland Theme   Illegal SFI-326.   1978.   This flexi was given
away with Dark Star magazine.
Nature's Way/Stone Free   Illegal IL-007.   1978.   This has two different label
designs. The first was red with black titles, while the second was grey and white with
red and black titles.

British albums

Highlights Of Spirit Of '76   Mercury promo 001.   1976.   Edited highlights on one
album.
Potatoland   Beggars Banquet BEGA-23.   1981.   A limited edition came with a
great cartoon book. This didn't come with the American version.

Odds and sods

ED CASSIDY   *Jakaranda/Same Old Way*   USA Epic 5-10808.   c.1972.
RANDY CALIFORNIA   *Kaptain Kopter And The Twirly Birds*   USA Epic E-31755.
1972.   A single was also released from this album *Walkin' The Dog/Live For
The Day*   USA Epic 5-10927.   1972.
RANDY CALIFORNIA   *Euro-American*   UK Beggars Banquet BEGA-36.   1982.
RANDY CALIFORNIA   *Shattered Dream/Magic Wind*   UK Beggars Banquet RAN-1.
1982.   This seven-inch single was given away with the above album.
RANDY CALIFORNIA   *Hand Guns/This Is The End*   UK Beggars Banquet BEG-76.
1982.
Reading Rock '82   UK Mean Records MNLP-82.   1983.   This live double set
features California and his band, but not Spirit.
SPIRIT   Re-Union   Japan Nautilus audiophile.   1981.   This album was never
released to my knowledge.

Dusty Springfield

British singles

DUSTY SPRINGFIELD *O Holy Child*/THE SPRINGFIELDS *Jingle Bells* Philips BF-1381. 1964. This was a special charity single.

TOM AND DUSTY SPRINGFIELD *Morning Please Don't Come* Philips BF-1835. 1970. Dusty only appears on the A side.

That's The Kind Of Love/Sandra   Mercury twelve-inch promo, number unknown. 1978.

Baby Blue   Single version/re-mixed version.   Mercury twelve-inch promo JUMBO-14. 1979.

British EP's

The Hits Of Dusty Springfield Philips cassette MCP-100. c.1968.

The Hits Of The Walker Brothers And Dusty Springfield   Philips cassette MCP-1004. c.1968.

British albums

Dusty Springfield World Record Club ST-848. c.1967.

Star Dusty Philips Audio Club Of Great Britain 6850 002. c.1972.

Sheer Magic Philips Audio Club Of Great Britain 6860 020. c.1973.

American singles

The Look Of Love Philips juke box EP PL-2700. 1966.

The Six Million Dollar Man Theme ABC promo, number unknown. c.1976.

That's The Kind Of Love Same on both sides. United Artists twelve-inch promo SP-178. 1978.

Donnez Moi Same on both sides.   Casablanca twelve-inch promo, number unknown. 1983.

American albums

Dusty In Memphis and *Climb Aboard Led Zeppelin* Atlantic promo TLST-135. 1969.

Longings Dunhill DSX-50186. 1973. Withdrawn.

Odds and sods

Warten Und Hoffen (*Wishing And Hoping* sung in German)/B side unknown. German Philips, number unknown. 1964.

Bruce Springsteen

American singles

Circus Song Columbia promo AE-52. 1972. As luck would have it, this is one of the two live tracks to appear on CBS, and it's promo only.

Blinded By The Light Same on both sides. Columbia red vinyl promo 4-45805.
1973. This rarity also came with a nice picture sleeve.
Blinded By The Light/Rosalita/Growin' Up Columbia promo AE7-1088. 1974.
Another impossible to find promo. All tracks are the regular studio versions.
Devil In A Blue Dress (medley)/JACKSON BROWNE *Stay* and *The Load Out* Asylum
twelve-inch promo AS-11442. 1978. Taken from the *No Nukes* soundtrack
album.
Fade Away/Held Up Without A Gun/Be True Columbia twelve-inch promo
AS-830. 1980.
Fade Away Same on both sides. Columbia twelve-inch promo AS-928. 1980.
Santa Claus Is Coming To Town Same on both sides. Columbia twelve-inch
promo AS-1329. 1981.
Santa Claus Is Coming To Town Same on both sides. Columbia promo
AE7-1332. 1981. This is the other live CBS track, taken from the *In Harmony 2*
album.

American albums

Born To Run Columbia PC-33795. 1975. Some early copies came with a slightly
different sleeve, with the front titles in script print rather than the capital print
which appears on most copies.
Darkness On The Edge Of Town Columbia acetate. 1978. This acetate has an
extra song *Don't Look Back* which never appeared on the final copies.
As Requested On Tour Around The World Columbia promo AS-978. 1981.
This is an excellent 'greatest hits' compilation to promote his 1981 world tour. It
also has a great black and white photo sleeve with Bruce in full flight.
Darkness On The Edge Of Town Columbia promo picture disc, no number.
1978.
Born To Run Columbia-Masterworks audiophile HC-33795. 1981.
Darkness On The Edge Of Town Columbia-Masterworks audiophile HC-
45318. 1981.

British single

Sherry Darling/Independence Day CBS promo, number unknown. 1980.
Open All Night Mono and stereo versions. CBS promo A-2969. 1982. An odd
British promo.

Odds and sods

No Nukes UK/USA Asylum. 1978. This triple has some great live material from
Bruce.
In Harmony 2 UK/USA CBS. 1981. The money from this album went to a
children's charity and included Bruce's *Santa Claus Is Coming To Town*.
The Last American Hero Japan CBS-Sony promo YAPC-95. 1979. This is a
compilation album.
The River Australian CBS promo flexi disc 84623. 1980.

Springsteen has, of course, been associated with acts like Gary US Bonds,
Southside Johnny, Ronnie Spector and Graham Parker, among others.

Squeeze

British singles

Take Me I'm Yours/No Disco   BTM SBT-107.   1977.   Scheduled for release in January 1977, but was withdrawn.

Packet Of Three   EP Deptford Fun City DFC-01.   1977.   The original seven-inch sleeve was white with a blue tinted photo and red titles. The back cover credits the keyboard player as Julian Holland instead of Jools, and Harry Kukdulli instead of Harry Kukulli. When the seven-inch was re-released in 1979, not only was the sleeve different, but only one track was credited on the B side label instead of two. The first 500 copies of the twelve-inch came with a poster.

Goodbye Girl/Saints Alive   A & M AMS-7398.   1978.   Some copies came with a 'lumpy' sleeve. Features on the cartoon front cover like muscles, faces, etc., have been moulded to give a three-dimensional effect.

Cool For Cats/Model   A & M AMS-7426.   1979.   This has three different coloured vinyl runs. The first was in bright pink, limited to 5,000. The next was whiteish pink, limited to 100,000. The last was in red, possibly only 1,000 were made in this colour. In addition there was a very limited white-pink twelve-inch pressing AMSP-7426.

Wrong Way   Smash Hits magazine flexi made by Lyntone.   1980.   This song was given to Rockpile.

East Side Story   Sampler EP.   A & M twelve-inch promo SAMP-9.   1981.

Black Coffee In Bed   Long and short versions.   A & M promo AMS-8219-DJ. 1982.

I'm At Home Tonight   A & M one-sided single SAMP-17.   c.1982.   This is either a fan club record or a concert freebie. It came with a picture sleeve.

Singles 45's And Under   A & M one-sided promo, number unknown.   1982.   This is actually the *Squabs On Forty Fab* medley which appeared on the B side to *Labelled With Love*.

British albums

Cool For Cats   A & M AMLH-68503.   1979.   There are two different sleeve designs for this. The original cover was purple and had green streaks on the front as well as raised figures. The back was also purple with a palette-shaped black and white photo showing the line-up of the band that recorded the album (including Harry Kakulli). When the title track had become a hit the album was re-issued with a new sleeve. Although the basic design of the front cover was the same, it was now available in different colours such as yellow, blue, green, etc. The most noticeable difference was in the back cover. It was now a yellow and red tinted photo showing John Bently (who never played on the album) instead of Harry Kukulli (who did). Musically, both versions are the same.

Sweets From A Stranger   A & M promo cassette, number unknown.   1982.   This includes an interview on side two.

American singles

If I Didn't Love You   4:10 and 3:25 versions.   A & M promo 2229-S.   1980.
Tempted/Messed Around/Is That Love   A & M twelve-inch promo SP-17158.
1981.
Black Coffee In Bed/I've Returned/I Can't Hold On   A & M twelve-inch promo
SP-17193.   1982.

American albums

UK SQUEEZE   *UK Squeeze*   A & M SP-4687.   1978.   This had to appear under this
name because of an American band called Tight Squeeze. The first copies came on
red vinyl.
Six Squeeze Songs Crammed On To One Ten Inch Record   A & M SP-3719.
1980.   This mini album wins the award for the worst packaging ever, as it is almost
impossible to get the disc in or out of the sleeve without damaging it. On the good
side, some versions and re-mixes are included which haven't appeared in Britain.
Singles 45's And Under   A & M, number unknown.   1982.   This American version
has *If I Didn't Love You* instead of *Labelled With Love.*
King Biscuit Radio Series   (Dated 26.7.81).
BBC *Rock Hour*   Radio Series, number 239.   (Dated 27.8.81).
Retrorock   Radio Series.   1982.   Recorded in 1979.

Odds and sods

JOOLS HOLLAND   *Boogie Woogie '78*   EP UK Deptford Fun City DFC-03.   1978.
This features other members of Squeeze including Tilbrook and Difford.
ELVIS COSTELLO   *From A Whisper To A Scream*   UK F-Beat XX-14.   1980.   This
had Glen Tilbrook on co-lead vocals.
HELEN SHAPIRO   *Straighten Up And Fly Right*   UK Oval OVLP-507.   1983.   This
album features one track, *Where Or When,* which has Glen Tilbrook on co-lead
vocals.
THE LONG HONEYMOON   *The Amazoon*   3 versions.   UK A & M twelve-inch
AMX-106.   1982.   This was taken from the musical *Labelled With Love.*
Propaganda UK/USA A & M.   1980.   This compilation features *Wrong Way* and
an alternate version of *Goodbye Girl.*

Ringo Starr

British singles

Only You/Ringo interviewed by Bob Mercer.   EMI promo, number unknown.
1974.
Lipstick Traces/Old Time Revolvin'   Polydor 2001 782.   1978.   Withdrawn.

British album

Ringo's Rotogravure   Polydor 2302 040.   1977.   Initial copies came with a free
plastic magnifying glass.

American singles

Beaucoup Of Blues/Choochy Choochy Apple 2969. 1970. Some copies were pressed with the number 1826.

A Dose Of Rock 'N' Roll Long and short versions. Atlantic promo 3361. 1976.

Drowning In A Sea Of Love 5:08 and 3:39 versions. Atlantic promo 3412. 1977.

Drowning In A Sea Of Love Same on both sides. Atlantic twelve-inch promo DSKO-93. 1977.

White Christmas/Some Disco, Some Don't Atlantic test pressing. 1977. Withdrawn.

RINGO STARR/ROBIN WILLIAMS *What's It All About?* Radio Series 567/8. 1979.

American albums

Ringo Apple SWAL-3413. 1973. Some early pressings have a longer version of *Six O'Clock*.

Goodnight Vienna Quad mix. Apple eight-track cartridge 8XT-3417. 1974.

Robert W. Morgan Radio Series (Dated 28.10.78).

RINGO STARR AND CATHERINE BACH Interviewed by Merv Griffin. Merv Griffin Productions promo 102781. c.1980.

Odds and sods

GUTHRIE THOMAS *Lies And Alibies* USA Capitol ST-11519. 1976. Ringo wrote, played drums on and sang on *Band Of Steel*. This album was not released outside America.

Scouse The Mouse Soundtrack. UK Polydor 2480 429. 1978. Ringo plays the part of the mouse stuck in a pet shop in Liverpool while Donald Pleasance, Barbara Dickson, Adam Faith and others help out. This album sold poorly and was quickly deleted.

Richard Perry Super Producer USA Radio Show album (Dated 10.3.79). Ringo talks about Perry on this album.

Old Wave German Boardwalk 260 16 029. 1983. This album was also released by RCA in Japan and Canada, but not released in the UK or USA.

Status Quo

This band had recorded a few singles before changing their name to Status Quo.

THE SPECTRES *I Who Have Nothing/Neighbour Neighbour* UK Piccadilly 7N-35339. 1966.

THE SPECTRES *Hurdy Gurdy Man/Laticia* UK Piccadilly 7N-35252. 1966.

THE SPECTRES *We Ain't Got Nothin' Yet/I Want I* UK Piccadilly 7N-35368. 1967.

THE TRAFFIC JAM *Almost But Not Quite There/Just A Minute* UK Piccadilly 7N-35386. 1967.

British singles

Roundhouse Blues/BLACK SABBATH   *Children Of The Grave*   Phonogram promo DJ-005.   c.1976.
Don't Waste My Time   EMI-Disc acetate.   1974.   This is the version included on the *Reading Festival '73* album, and was considered as a single at one time.
Down Down Down   Lyntone flexi LYN-3154/5.   c.1976.   This was given away by Smith's crisps.
In My Chair   Pye flexi QUO-1   (SFI-434).   1979.   A concert freebie.

British album

Back To Back   Edited highlights.   Vertigo white label promo one-sided VERH-10. 1983.

American single

Mean Girl   Long and short versions.   Pye promo 65017.   1971.

Odds and sods

Reading Festival '73   UK GM Records GML-1008.   1974.   Live material.
All This And World War Two   UK Riva/USA 20th-Century Fox.   1976.   Status Quo sing The Beatles.
Intergalactic Touring Band   UK Charisma/USA Passport.   1977.   This features several members on this concept album.

Steely Dan

Walter Becker and Donald Fagen had already recorded one soundtrack album before forming Steely Dan.   *You Gotta Walk It Like You Talk It*   USA Spark 02. c.1971.

American singles

Dallas/*Sail The Waterway*   ABC 45-11323.   1972.   The rarest Steely Dan item. The A side was included on the British MFP compilation *Spirit Of Rock* and was credited on the sleeve as being from the *Can't Buy A Thrill* album, which it wasn't.
Countdown To Ecstacy   ABC juke box LLP-225.   1973.
East Saint Louis Toodle Oo   ABC one-sided promo SPDJ-20.   1974.
Pretzel Logic   Quad mix.   ABC quad juke box EP LLPQD-255.   1974.
Aja   Long and short versions.   ABC twelve-inch promo SPDJ-26.   1977.
Deacon Blues   Long and short versions.   ABC twelve-inch promo SPDJ-33.   1978.
Josie   Long and short versions.   ABC twelve-inch promo SPDJ-36.   1978.
Here In The Western World   ABC one-sided twelve-inch promo SPDJ-47.   1979. This was the new track from the *Greatest Hits* album.

American albums

Can't Buy A Thrill ABC-Command quad mix CQD-40009. 1974.
Pretzel Logic Quad mix. ABC-Command CQD-40015. 1975.
Rock Around The World Radio Series, number 198. (Dated 21.5.78).
Robert R. Klein Radio Series, part one. (Dated 14.12.80).
Robert R. Klein Radio Series, part two. (Dated 22.2.81).

British single

Dallas ABC one-sided promo, number unknown. 1978. Made to promote the *Plus Fours* EP.

Odds and sods

Can't Buy A Thrill Canada ABC, number unknown. 1972. This has a gatefold sleeve with lyrics.
Aja Japan Mobile Fidelity audiophile MFSL 1-034. 1980.
Gaucho Canada MCA Masterphile audiophile MCA-6102. 1980.

Jim Steinman

American singles

Rock 'n' Roll Dreams Come Through/The Storm Epic AE7-1232. 1981. This single was given away with the *Bad For Good* album.
Bad For Good/Love And Death/Stark Raving Love/Out Of The Frying Pan/Surf's Up/Dance In My Pants Epic twelve-inch promo AS-914. 1981. This is very nearly the whole damn album!!
Rock 'n' Roll Dreams/Coral Reprise/Rock 'n' Roll Dreams/Love And Death/Stark Raving Love Epic twelve-inch promo AS-967. 1981.

American albums

BBC *Rock Hour* Radio Series (Dated 16.8.81).

British singles

Rock 'n' Roll Dreams/The Storm Epic XPS-117. 1981. Given away with the *Bad For Good* album.
Rock 'n' Roll Dreams/Love And Death/The Storm Epic blue vinyl twelve-inch EPCA13-1236. 1981. A very limited edition release.

Cat Stevens

British album

Cats And Dogs Deram, number unknown. 1967. Scheduled for release on the 24 February 1967, but eventually it was replaced by *Matthew And Son* later in the year.

American singles

Teaser And The Firecat   A & M juke box EP LLP-163.   1971.
Foreigner   A & M juke box EP LLP-4391.   1973.
Was Dog A Doughnut/Sweet Jamaica   A & M promo twelve-inch SP-8440.   1977.

American albums

Foreigner   Quad mix.   A & M SPQU-54391.   c.1974.
Saturday Night Live   A & M promo, number unknown.   c.1975.   A live album.
Numbers   Extracts/THE FOUR SEASONS   *Who Loves You*   Extracts.   American
Forces Radio and Television Service P-15690.   c.1976.

Odds and sods

Tea For The Tillerman   Japan Mobile Fidelity audiophile MFSL 1-035.   1980.

Al Stewart

British singles

Elf/Turn To Earth   Decca F-12467.   1966.   His first single, which flopped, is now
available again on the *Lost And Found* compilation on Decca.
Year Of The Cat   Long and short versions.   RCA promo RCA-2771-DJ.   1976.

British album

Bedsitter Images   CBS, number unknown.   1967.   This album was re-issued in
1972 with a new track listing and title   *The First Album (Bed Sitter Images)*
CBS-64023.

American EP

The Early Years   Janus juke box issue, number unknown.   1977.

American albums

The Al Stewart Concert   Arista promo SP-40.   1977.
Modern Music Radio Series.   c.1979.   A live album.
Robert W. Morgan *Watermark*   Radio Series SWB-80111.   c.1980.

Odds and sods

Year Of The Cat   Japan Mobile Fidelity audiophile MFSL 1-009.   1980.
24 Carrots   Japan Nautilus audiophile, number unknown.   1981.

Rod Stewart

British singles

Good Morning Little Schoolgirl/I'm Gonna Move   Decca F-11996.   1964.   His
first solo release.

The Day Will Come/Why Does It Go On   Columbia DB-7766.   1966.
Shake/I Just Got Some   Columbia DB-7892.   1966.
These two Columbia singles have as yet not been re-issued in Britain.

Little Misunderstood/So Much To Say   Immediate IM-060.   1967.   His first decent record. His version of this Mike D'Abo song should have been a hit.
It's All Over Now/Jo's Lament   Vertigo 6059 002.   1970.   The only pre-*Maggie May* Phonogram release and is quite rare.
Reason To Believe/Maggie May   Mercury 6052 097.   1970.   The original copies have *Maggie May* as the B side.
Tonight's The Night/The First Cut Is The Deepest   Riva 3.   1977.   Withdrawn.
Do You Think I'm Sexy/Dirty Weekend   Riva twelve-inch promo SAM-92. 1978.
*You're Insane/*B side unknown.   Riva twelve-inch promo, number unknown. 1980.

British albums

ROD STEWART AND THE FACES/RORY GALLAGHER   BBC Transcription Service 130320.   1972.   Both are taken from the *Radio One In Concert* series.
Reason To Believe St Michael, number unknown. c.1979. A cheapo album made for a department store. These albums are usually hard to find as they're not always advertised, so obviously not many people would know about them.

American singles

Good Morning Little Schoolgirl/I'm Gonna Move   Press PRE-9722.   1964.
By Popular Request   EP.   Mercury promo MEPL-3.   c.1970.
Italian Girls/Twisting The Night Away   Plus one.   Mercury promo MEPL-28. 1972.
It's All Over Now   Mono and stereo versions.   Mercury promo MDJ-252.   1972. This may not have been released commercially.
The Killing Of Georgie   Probably the same track on both sides.   Warner blue vinyl twelve-inch promo PROA-680.   1977.   This plays at 45rpm which is unusual for an American twelve-inch.
Hot Legs   Same track on both sides.   Warner twelve-inch promo, number unknown.   1978.
Do You Think I'm Sexy/Scarred And Scared   Warner twelve-inch WBSD-8727. 1978.   The A side is a special re-recording which wasn't released in Britain.
Passion   5:29 and 4:45 versions.   Warner seven-inch promo WBS-49617.   1981.
Passion   7:30 and 5:35 versions.   Warner twelve-inch promo PROA-921.   1981.
Young Turks   Long and short versions.   Warner twelve-inch promo PROA-989. 1982.
How Long   Long and short versions.   Warner promo WBS-50051.   1982.

American albums

The Rod Stewart Album   Mercury SR-61237.   1969.   This was the American title for the *An Old Raincoat Will Never Let You Down* album.

ROD STEWART/THE MOODY BLUES *Rock Around The World* Radio Series. c.1978.
Innerview Radio Series. Series 8, programmes 12 and 13. 1980.
Spotlight Radio Special. c.1980.
Innerview Radio Series. Series 10, programmes 11 and 12. 1981.
Mellow Yellow Radio Series. 1981. This was a four-album set of live material
and interview. One album was re-called due to profanities and later replaced.
Westwood One Radio Series. Part one, number 82-1. 1982.
Westwood One Radio Series. Part two, number 82-2. 1982.

Odds and sods – singles

LONG JOHN BALDRY *Up Above My Head* UK United Artists UP-1056. 1964.
Stewart sings on this B side.
JIMMY POWELL *Been Watching You* UK Pye, number unknown. 1964. Another
vocal contribution on this single.
THE SHOTGUN EXPRESS *I Could Feel The Whole World Turn 'Round* UK Columbia
DB-8025. 1966. Although Stewart was a member of this trio, he only sang on this
A side. This track was re-released on a ten-inch EP on UK Charly CYM-2 in 1983.
JEFF BECK *Tallyman/Rock My Plimsoul* UK Columbia DB-8227. 1968. The B
side was re-issued on the *Hi Ho Silver Lining* EP in 1972.
JEFF BECK *I've Been Drinking* UK Columbia DB-8369. 1968. This was the B side
to *Love Is Blue* and appeared as an A side on Rak Records in 1972.
PYTHON LEE JACKSON *In A Broken Dream* UK Young Blood YB-1002. 1970.
Stewart's best non-Faces vocal from this period. Apparently his fee for the session
was a set of seat covers for his car! This single was given a re-issue in 1972 on Young
Blood International, in 1978, on Lighting and, in 1981, in twelve-inch form on
Young Blood. In America it first appeared on Eurogram 5001 in 1970, and then on
GNP-Crecendo 449 in 1972.
PYTHON LEE JACKSON *Rod's Blues* USA GNP-Crecendo 462. 1972.
LONG JOHN BALDRY *Iko Iko* UK/USA Warner. 1972. Rod and his mate
Elton sing on this A side.
LONG JOHN BALDRY *Mother Ain't Dead* USA Warner 7617. 1972. Another vocal
track for Rod.
Maggie Mae UK Mercury BRAUN-3. Date unknown. This EP was a giveaway.

Albums

JEFF BECK *Truth* UK Columbia/USA Epic. 1967.
JEFF BECK *Beck Ola* UK Columbia/USA Epic. 1968.
Stewart was the singing member of The Jeff Beck Group at the time.
PYTHON LEE JACKSON *Python Lee Jackson* USA GNP-Crecendo 2066. c.1972.
Again, Stewart is included here.
Tommy UK/USA Ode. 1973. This London stage cast version includes Stewart.
History Of British Rock, Volume Two USA Sire SASH-3705/2. 1974. This
includes an alternate version of *Little Missunderstood*.
STEAMPACKET *The First Supergroup* UK Charly CR-30020. 1975. An album of
previously unreleased material of one of Stewart's old groups.
A similar album was released in America.

Rod Stewart And Steampacket   USA Springboard SPB-4063.   1973.
Scotland Scotland   UK Polydor 2383 282.   1974.   This album was made to raise money for the Scotland World Cup team of 1974.   Rod Stewart and footballer Dennis Law sang a duet *Angel* on this album.
All this And World War Two   UK Riva/USA 20th Century Fox.   1978.

Stiff Little Fingers

British singles

Suspect Device/Wasted Life   Rigid Digits SRD-1.   1978.   There are two different pressings of this.   The first has a yellow label with a picture sleeve, while the second has a red label without a picture sleeve.
Listen   Long and short versions.   Chrysalis promo, number unknown.   1982.
Now Then/IGGY POP   *Zombie Birdhouse*   Chrysalis flexi, number unknown.   1982. Given with *Melody Maker* magazine.
Listen/Two Guitars Clash   Chrysalis juke box issue CHSDJ-2580.   1982.

Stephen Stills

American singles

Hide It So Deep/Fallen Eagle   Atlantic promo PR-172.   1973.
Stephen Stills   Atlantic juke box EP SD7-7206.   1972.
Stephen Stills 2   Atlantic juke box EP LLP-157.   1973.

Odds and sods

STILLS, KOOPER AND BLOOMFIELD   *Supersession*   USA Columbia/UK CBS.   1971. This was re-mixed for quad in 1973.   USA Columbia CQ-30991.

The Stranglers

British singles

Choosie Suzie/Peasant In The Big Shitty   United Artists FREE-3.   1977.   This single was given away with the first 5,000 copies of the *Rattus Norvegicus* album.   It was re-issued by EMI in Japan in 1979 and given away with the *X Rated* album.
Peaches/THE BUZZCOCKS   *Oh Shit*   United Artists.   1978.   A mispress.
Peaches/Go Buddy Go   United Artists UP-36248.   1977.   The picture sleeve which came with initial copies was hurriedly withdrawn.   It showed a group photo with Sex

Pistols type newspaper printed titles. When the single was re-issued in 1979 it came with a new sleeve.

Peaches   Edited version.   United Artists one-sided promo FREE-4.   1977.   This version has altered lyrics for radio use.

No More Heroes/In the Shadows   United Artists UP-36300.   1978.   Some early copies came with a floral wreath label design, which was quickly changed.

No More Heroes   Probably edited.   United Artists one-sided promo FREE-8. 1977.

Walk On By/Tits/Mean To Me   United Artists FREE-9.   1978.   A white vinyl single given away with the *Black And White* album.

Walk On By   Edited version.   United Artists one-sided promo, number unknown. 1978.

Don't Bring Harry   United Artists one-sided promo STR-1-DJ.   1978.   A one-track sampler from their Christmas EP.

Who Wants The World/The Men In Black   United Artists BPX-355.   1980.   This was a limited edition run sold at 75p. Later copies sold at full price. This cheaper version was identified by a red corner on the sleeve.

Tomorrow Was The Hereafter/Bring On The Nubiles   Stranglers Information Service SIS-001.   1980.   This was intended as their first single release in 1976, but not released until 1980, and then only by their fan club.

Golden Brown/Love Thirty   Liberty BP-407.   1981.   This came in two different sleeves. The first had gold titles on the front, while the second version had white titles.

European Female   Long and short versions.   Epic promo EPCA-2893-DJ.   1982.

Aural Sculpture   Epic one-sided XPS-167.   1983.   This was given away with initial copies of the *Feline* album.

JEAN JAQUES BURNEL   Interview.   Label details unknown.   1983.   A picture disc pressing, limited to 1,200. This isn't a fan club issue.

British albums

The Raven   United Artists UAG-30262.   1980.   Some early copies came with a 3-D photo sleeve.

The Gospel According To The Men In Black   EMI test pressing.   1981.   This white label features an alternate mix of *Second Coming*.

The Old Testament   Liberty, number unknown.   1982.   Withdrawn. This was a twenty-track greatest hits compilation which was replaced by . . .

The Stranglers Singles Collection 1977-1982   Liberty LBG-30353.   1982.   The original proof covers have a different design. It was the sleeve which was released in Europe which has a dark cover with the titles in the middle.

Feline   Epic cassette EPC40-25237.   1982.   This tape edition has an extra track *Aural Sculpture*.

American singles

Totally Suitable For Airplay   EP.   A & M promo, number unknown.   c.1978.

Do The European/Choosie Suzie/White Room/Straighten Out   IRS SP-70952. 1979.   Given away with the *Stranglers VI* compilation album.

Midnight Summer's Dream   Epic twelve-inch promo, number unknown.   1983.
Paradise   Epic twelve-inch promo, number unknown.   1983.

American album
BBC *Rock Hour*   Radio Series.   1980.   Recorded at The New York Ritz.

Odds and sods
CELIA AND THE MUTATIONS   *Mony Mony/Mean To Me*   UK United Artists UP-36262.   1977.
CELIA AND THE FABULOUS MUTATIONS   *You Better Believe Me*/CELIA AND THE YOUNG MUTATIONS *Round And Around*   UK United Artists UP-3618.   1977.   Most people seem to think these two records are The Stranglers using an alias and that Celia doesn't exist. She does! Her name is Celia Gollin and she was discovered by a friend of the band working a London bar singing Dietrich songs.
The Hope And Anchor Front Row Festival   UK Warner-Albion K-66077.   1978. This double album set, recorded in 1977, features two live Stranglers tracks. *Hanging Around* and *Straighten Out.*
Sverge (Jag Ar Insnoad Pa Ost Fronten) *(All Quiet On The Eastern Front* sung in Swedish)/*In The Shadows*   Swedish United Artists UP-36459.   1978.
N'Emmenes Pas Harry/B side unknown.   French United Artists, number unknown.   1979.   The A side is a French version of *Don't Bring Harry.*

The Strawbs

British album
Heartbreak Hill   Arista, number unknown.   1979.   Withdrawn.

Odds and sods
THE STRAWBS AND SANDY DENNY *All Our Own Work*   UK Pickwick SHM-813.   1973. This features demos recorded as The Strawberry Hill Boys in the mid '60s.
The King Of Elfland's Daughter   UK Chrysalis CHR-1137.   1975.   This concept superstars album featured The Strawbs.   A promo sampler single from this album exists, number LO-1, but I don't know if this features The Strawbs.

The Stray Cats

American singles
Rock This Town/Runaway Boys/Built For Speed/Stray Cat Strut   EMI-America twelve-inch promo SPRO-9793/4.   1982.
She's Sexy And Seventeen/Lookin' Better Every Beer   EMI-America BB-8169. 1983.   The initial copies came with a free single, *Cruisin'/Lucky Charm.*

American albums

Built For Speed   EMI-America SW-17070.   1982.   Although, obviously, the album itself isn't exactly rare it does, however, contain some material which was specially re-mixed for America only.
King Biscuit Radio Series.   1983.

Odds and sods

DAVE EDMUNDS AND THE STRAY CATS   *The Race Is On*   UK/USA Swansong.   1981.

The Style Council

British singles

THE MONEY GO ROUND   Re-mix/dance mix.   Polydor twelve-inch promo TSCDM-2.   1983.
A Long Hot Summer/The Paris Match   Polydor promo TSCDJ-3, and juke box issue TSCD-3.   1983.
The Paris Match   Polydor one-sided promo TSCDJ-3.   1983.
A Long Hot Summer/re-mix.   Polydor twelve-inch promo TSCDM-3.   1983.

Styx

American singles

Soul Flow/Promised Land   Paramount PAA-0104.   c.1972.   Their first release.
Almost Grown/B side unknown.   Paramount, number unknown.   1972.
The Grand Illusion   Sampler.   A & M twelve-inch promo SP-17021.   1976.
Come Sail Away   Long and short versions.   A & M promo 1977-S.   1977.
Fooling Yourself   5:29 and 3:35 versions.   A & M promo 2007-S.   1978.
Renegade   4:13 and 3:39 versions.   A & M promo 2110-S.   1978.

American albums

Styx   Wooden Nickel WNS-1008.   1972.   This was the original independent issue before RCA took up distribution in 1974.
Styx 2   Wooden Nickel WNS-1012.   1973.   Again, this was re-issued by RCA in 1974.
The Styx Radio Show   A & M promo SP-8431.   c.1976.
The Styx Radio Special   A & M promo SP-17053.   1977.
Robert W. Morgan Radio Series   (Dated 21.10.78).
Cornerstone   A & M SP-3711.   1979.   A limited edition of 2,000 silver vinyl pressings made for their fan club.
Innerview   Radio Series.   Series 16, programme 10.   1980.
NBC *Source*   Radio Series, number 82-17.   1982.

Westwood One Radio Series, number 82-13.   (Dated 29.3.82).
Rolling Stone Continuous History Of Rock 'N' Roll   Radio Series, number 46. 1982.

British album

A Collection Of Styx   A & M promo, number unknown.   1979.   A boxed set of three albums, *Pieces Of Eight, The Crystal Ball* and *The Grand Illusion*.

Odds and sods

The Grand Illusion   Japan Mobile Fidelity audiophile MFSL 1-026.   1980.   The Nautilus audiophile label from Japan have also released the following albums: *Pieces Of Eight, Cornerstone* and *Paradise Theatre*.

Supertramp

Some members of Supertramp had previously been in the group Argosy who had released one single   *Mr Boyd*   USA Congress CG-6013.   c.1969.

American singles

Ain't Nobody But Me   5:15 and 3:36 versions.   A & M promo 1814.   1977.
Take The Long Way Home   Long and short versions.   A & M promo 2193.   1979.
It's Raining Again/Waiting So Long   A & M twelve-inch promo SP-17212.   1982.

American albums

Profiles In Rock   Radio Series PRB-801-1.   (Dated 16/17.2.80).
BBC *Rock Hour*   Number 147.   (Dated Sept. 1980).
NBC *Source*   Radio Series   (Dated Dec. 1980).
SUPERTRAMP/PAT METHANY   Robert R. Klein Radio Series, number 42. (Dated 21.8.81).
Innerview   Radio Series.   Series 15, programme 13.   1981.
BBC *Rock Hour*   Radio Series, number 343.   (Dated 24.10.82).

Odds and sods

All of their albums, except the first two, have been released on one audiophile label or another over the years.

The Supremes

Before re-naming themselves The Supremes they had already cut one single as THE PRIMETTES: *Tears Of Sorrow/Pretty Baby*   USA Lupine 120.   1960.   These two tracks and others that The Primettes had recorded for others were included on *Looking Back With The Primettes*   UK Ember EMBS-3398.   1968.   This album was re-issued on Windmill Records in the early '70s.

American singles

I Want A Guy/Never Again   Tamla T-54038.   1962.
Who's Loving You/Buttered Popcorn   Tamla T-54045.   1962.
Their two pre-Motown label releases are gold-dust nowadays.
Twinkle Twinkle Little Me   Same on both sides.   Motown red-vinyl promo M1085.   1964.
Where Did Our Love Go   Motown juke box EP MT-60621.   1964.
A Bit Of Liverpool   Motown juke box EP MT-60623.   1964.
Sing Holland Dozier And Holland   Motown juke box EP MT-60650.   1965.
The Only Time I'm Happy/Interview.   George Alexander-Motown Special Products promo M-1079-XS-1.   c.1965.
The Happening   Excerpts.   Colgems promo, no number.   1967.
Dr Goldfoot And The Bikini Machine/B side unknown.   American International Records, number unknown.   c.1967.   The Supremes sang the theme for this memorable movie.

There were also a series of cardboard picture discs made in the late '60s, but more details are unknown.

Things Are Changin'   This was a special single made for the Equal Employment Opportunities unit in 1967.
THE SUPREMES AND THE FOUR TOPS   *Dynamite*   Motown juke box EP LLP-134.   1972.
Medley   Same on both sides.   Motown twelve-inch promo PR-69.   1980.

American albums

Meet The Supremes   Motown MS-606.   1964.   The early copies came in a sleeve with a picture of The Supremes sitting on barstools. This was quickly withdrawn.
THE SUPREMES AND NEIL DIAMOND   *It's Happening*   Decca-MCA Special Products DL-734727.   c.1969.   This has The Supremes on one side and Diamond on the other.

Odds and sods

Things Go Better With Coke   EP (with others).   German Coca-Cola CC-10542.   c.1965.
Thank You Darling/Johnny Und Joe   Dutch Tamla-Motown GO-42609.   1967.   The B side is sung in German.
L'Amore Verra/Se Il Filo Spezzerai   Both sung in Italian.   Italian Tamla-Motown TM-8004.   c.1966.
Could This Be You/B side unknown.   USA Kitten 6969.   Date unknown, but from the '60s.   The Supremes?
Moonlight And Kisses/Baby Bay Wo Ist Unsere Liebe   Dutch Tamla-Motown GO-42625.   1967.   Another German language B side.
Greatest Hits   Quad mix.   Japan Tamla-Motown 7095.   c.1973.
Glow/You And Me   USA Grog 500.   Date unknown, but from the '70s.   Again, this is probably not The Supremes.
THE TEMPTATIONS AND THE FOUR TOPS   have also recorded foreign language singles for the European markets.
Many of The Supremes' European albums have alternate versions and mixes.

The Sweet

Members of the band had already recorded before forming The Sweet.
BRIAN CONNELL AND THE ROUND SOUND *Just My Kind Of Loving/Something You've Got* UK Mercury MF-956. 1966. This was Brian Connolly.
MAYFIELD'S MULE *Double Dealin' Woman/Drinking Moonshine* UK Parlophone R-5817. 1968.
MAYFIELD'S MULE *We Go Rollin'/*B side unknown. UK Parlophone R-5858. 1968. Andy Scott was a member.

British singles

The Juicer/All You'll Ever Get From Me Parlophone R-5826. 1969.
Get On The Line/Lollipop Man Parlophone R-5848. 1969.
*Slow Motion/*B side unknown. Fontana, number unknown. 1970.
Teenage Rampage/Own Up RCA LPBO-5004. 1974. Some early copies were pressed at the wrong speed due to a foul-up at the mastering stage. The disc sounded too fast.

British album

The Sweet And The Pipkins MFP 5248. 1973. This was a cash-in album featuring their Parlophone tracks.

American singles

The group The Sweet who recorded for Smash Records in 1966 have nothing to do with the glam teeny rock band.
The Juicer/All You'll Ever Get From Me Paramount PAA-0044. 1969. A rare release.
*It's Lonely Out There/*B side unknown. 20th Century TC-2033. 1973. More Parlophone material?
Love Is Like Oxygen/Short 'n' Sweet Plus one other. Capitol twelve-inch promo SPRO-8849. 1978.
Mother Earth 6:27 and 3:55 versions/*Discophony* Capitol twelve-inch promo SPRO-9123. 1978.
*Air On A Tape Loop/*B side unknown. Capitol twelve-inch promo, number unknown. 1979.

American albums

For AOR Radio Only Capitol promo, number unknown. c.1975. A compilation.
Level Headed Music Modern Music Radio Series. 1978.

Odds and sods

Saturday Scene UK Philips, number unknown. 1975. This has an interview with the group.

ANDY SCOTT *Lady Starlight/Where Do Ya Go* UK RCA 2629. 1975.
BRIAN CONNOLLY *Hypnotised/Fade Away* UK Polydor, number unknown. 1981.
ANDY SCOTT *Krugerrands/Face/Krugermetal* UK Statik TAK-10-12. 1983. This is the twelve-inch version.

Rachel Sweet

American singles
Faded Rose/Country Style Premier 2310. c.1972.
Paper Airplane/We Live In Different Worlds Derrick 1000. c.1974.
*All The Love We Have/*B side unknown. Derrick 109. c.1974.
*I Believe What I Believe/*B side unknown. Derrick 111. c.1975.
Overnight Success/Bluer Than The Dress Derrick 115. c.1975. I have to guess at these dates as they're all pretty obscure.
I Go To Pieces/Who Does Lisa Like Stiff-Columbia twelve-inch promo AS-611. 1979.
Spellbound 4:26 and 2:47 versions. Stiff-Columbia promo 1-11272. 1979.

British album
Fool Around Stiff SEEZ-12. 1978. A limited edition of 2,000 were pressed in black vinyl.

Odds and sods
Be Stiff Tour UK Stiff promo ODD-2. 1978. This includes Sweet's version of Devo's *Be Stiff*.
Can't Start Dancing UK Stiff SOUNDS-3. 1979. This album was given away with *Sounds* magazine. It includes a new Rachel Sweet track *I'll Watch The News*.

Talking Heads

American singles
Uh Oh Love Comes To Town/Don't Worry About The Government Sire promo PRO-696. 1977.
I Zimbra/Air/Life During Wartime Sire twelve-inch promo PROA-846. 1979.
Cross Eyed and Painless 4:56 and 3:16 versions. Sire twelve-inch promo PROA-903. 1980.
Once In A Lifetime Long and short versions*/Born Under Punches/Houses In Motion* Sire twelve-inch promo PROA-930. 1980.
Psycho Killer/Life During Wartime/Take Me To The River/Houses In Motion Sire twelve-inch promo PROA-1033. 1982. These are the live versions from their *The Name Of This Band Is Talking Heads* album.

American albums

Live At The Roxy Warner Brothers Music Show promo WBMS-104. 1979. This excellent live album is probably the most counterfeited album of its kind. TALKING HEADS/ROBERT PALMER King Biscuit (Dated March 1980).

British singles

Take Me To The River/Found A Job Sire SIR-4004. 1979. The first 10,000 copies with a free single, *Psycho Killer/Loves Goes To Building On Fire* SAM-87. 1979.
Psycho Killer/New Feeling Sire SAM-108. 1979. This single came with the initial copies of the *Fear Of Music* album.
Speaking In Tongues Sire cassette 92-3883-4. 1983. This includes longer versions of the tracks as well as re-mixes. This was probably released in America as well.

Odds and sods

Speaking In Tongues Sire 92-3883-1. 1983. A special edition, limited to 50,000 worldwide, was made featuring a clear vinyl album with plastic wheels in front and behind, housed in a plastic case. These wheels were able to rotate, so that the colours on them would make patterns.

James Taylor

Before going to England and recording for Apple, Taylor had made one single with THE ORIGINAL FLYING MACHINE. *Night Owl* did nothing and the band split up, but an album of rehearsals was released in 1972. *Rainy Day Man* USA Euphoria EST-2 was credited to James Taylor And The Original Flying Machine. A single was also released, *Knockin' 'Round The Zoo/Brighten Your Night With My Day* USA Euphoria 45-201. The album has been re-issued in America by Trip and Springboard, while in Britain, DJM had the rights.

American singles

Carolina In My Mind/Taking It In Apple 1805. 1968. Withdrawn.
Sweet Baby James Radio Spots. Warner promo PRO-379. 1970.
Mud Slide Slim Radio Spots. Warner promo PRO-483. 1971.
Mud Slide Slim Warner Juke box EP LLP-150. 1971.
Handy Man/Bartender's Blues Columbia twelve-inch promo ASF-358. 1977.
Bartender's Blues Long and short versions. Columbia promo 3-10557. 1977.

American albums

James Taylor Apple SKAO-3352. 1968. This issue has the title in black, whereas the 1971 re-issue has an orange title on the front.
One Man Dog Quad mix. Warner BS4-2660. 1974.
Gorilla Quad mix. Warner BS4-2866. 1975.

Odds and sods

CARLY SIMON *Mockingbird* USA/UK Elektra. 1973. Taylor sings a duet on this single.

The Bitter End Years USA Roxbury RX3-300. 1976. This has live material.

ART GARFUNKEL, JAMES TAYLOR AND PAUL SIMON *Wonderful World* USA/UK CBS. 1977. Their version of this Sam Cooke Classic was released as a single.

KATE TAYLOR *It's In His Kiss* USA Columbia 3-10596. 1978. Another duet single

CARLY SIMON *Devoted To You* USA/UK Elektra. 1980. More duets yet! A single release.

THE DOOBIE BROTHERS, JOHN HALL AND JAMES TAYLOR *Power* UK Asylum K-12463. 1978. Taken from . . .

No Nukes USA/UK Asylum. 1978. A triple album with live material.

Gorilla Japan Nautilus audiophile, number unknown. 1980.

Teardrop Explodes

British singles

Sleeping Gas/Camera Camera/Kirby Workers Dream Fades Fast Zoo Records CAGE-003. 1979.

Bouncing Babies/All I Am Is Loving You Zoo CAGE-005. 1979.

Treason/Read It In Books Zoo CAGE-008. 1980.

These three were released on the independent Zoo label. All three were deleted when they signed to Phonogram in 1980.

Ha Ha I'm Drowning/Poppies In The Field Mercury TEAR-4. 1981. Initial copies came with a free single *Bouncing Babies/Read It In Books* TEAR-44. Both single and double versions were withdrawn from release in Britain. All copies that were made were sent to Europe, but some came back to Britain.

You Disappear From View/Suffocate Mercury TEAR-8. 1983. Again, initial copies came with a free single, *Soft Enough For You/Ouch Monkeys/The In Psycho Peadia* TEAR-88. The twelve-inch version included all five tracks, but used an alternate version of *Suffocate*.

Tiny Children Live version/B side unknown. Mercury white label twelve-inch, number unknown. 1983. This may have come with some copies of the twelve-inch *You Disappear From View*.

British album

Kilamanjaro Mercury 6359 035. 1981. The first version had a colour group photo on the cover.

Kilamanjaro Mercury 6359 035. 1981. The second version was issued only four or five months later. Not only did it have a new cover of Mount Kilamanjaro and sundry wild animals, but the record also included the hit *Reward*. Apparently the band wanted the cover changed, but Phonogram would only agree if the hit single was included somewhere. So they put the track at the end of side one.

Odds and sods

On The Shores Of Lake Placid UK Zoo ZOO-4. 1982. This compilation album featured some of their single tracks.

Ten C.C.

Everyone by now would know that in a previous life Ten CC were Hotlegs, but between *Neanderthal Man* and *Donna* a band comprising the four members of Ten CC had cut one single for Apple. The B side of which was *Donna*. I don't know what the name of the band was at that time, although it's possible that it may still have been Hotlegs. I'd love to know what the A side of this single was. Maybe acetates exist?

British singles

The Worst Band In The World Radio version. UK Records promo UK-57. 1974. This version has altered lyrics. The 'up yours, up mine' line had suddenly become 'I'm yours, I'm mine'. Also at the beginning of the song the line 'we don't give a . . .' changed to 'we don't give up'. The BBC insisted that they change the lyrics or face a ban.
I'm Not In Love Long and short versions. Mercury promo 6008 014. 1975.

British albums

The Original Soundtracks Mercury half-speed cut edition HS-9102 500. 1982.
Greatest Hits Mercury half-speed cut edition HS-9102 504. 1982.

American singles

Art For Art's Sake 3:37 Edited version, same on both sides. Mercury promo MDJ-444. 1976.
For You And I Long and short versions. Polydor promo PD-14528. 1978.
For You And I Same on both sides. Polydor twelve-inch promo PRO-062. 1978.

Odds and sods

Donna by Ten CC, plus three other artists. USA UK records promo EP UK-101. 1972. A rare promo EP.
Music For 5AM UK Mercury YARD-005. 1978. This EP was given away by Yardley's perfume and included *I'm Not In Love*.
I'm Not In Love EP. UK Mercury BRAUN-1. Date unknown. This EP was a freebie, but may have tracks by other artists.

Thin Lizzy

British singles

Dublin/Remembering Part Two/Things Ain't Working Out/Old Moon Madness
Decca F-13208. 1972. This, their first single, went without notice.
Vagabonds Of The Western World. EP. Decca promo, number unknown. 1973.
Chinatown Long and short versions. vertigo promo LIZZYDJ-006. 1978.
Bad Reputation/Are You Ready Vertigo promo LIZZYDJ-8. 1979.
Hollywood Vertigo one-sided promo LIZZYDJ-10. 1981. This may be edited. In
addition there have been two double singles.
Killer On The Loose/Chinatown Vertigo LIZZY-77. 1979. The free single was
Don't Play Around/Got To Give It Up.
Cold Sweat/Bad Habits Vertigo LIZZY-1111. 1982. The free single here was
Angel/Don't Believe A Word.
Song For Jimmy Plus three tracks by other artists. Flexipop 010 (Lyntone
LYN-10138/9). 1981.

British album

Thunder And Lightning Vertigo cassette VERLC-3. 1983. The tape version
includes four extra tracks.

American singles

Wild One Same on both sides. Vertigo promo VEDG-205. 1975.
Showdown Same on both sides. Vertigo promo VEDJ-7. 1975.
Dancing In The Moonlight/Bad Reputation Mercury twelve-inch promo
MK-36. 1977.
The Boys Are Back In Town Same on both sides. Warner twelve-inch promo
PROA-754. 1978.

American albums

Fighting Vertigo SRM 1-1107. 1975. This has a different sleeve to the UK
version – a group photo in colour.
Innerview Radio Series. Series 8, programme 11. 1980.

Thirteenth Floor Elevators

American singles

You're Gonna Miss Me/Tried To Hide Hanna Babera HBR-492. 1966.
You're Gonna Miss Me/Tried To Hide International Artists IA-107. 1966.
There are, in addition, two different label designs for this.
You're Gonna Miss Me/B side unknown. Contact 5269. 1966. I really don't
know what order these come in!

Thunderclap Newman

American single

Something In The Air   Long and short versions.   MCA promo 60132.   c.1975.

American albums

Hollywood Dream   Track SD-8264.   1969.   This cover has the band members behind a camera.
Peter Townshend Talks To, And About, Thunderclap Newman   Track promo PR-160.   1969.   An interview album to promote *Hollywood Dream*.
Hollywood Dream   MCA-Track MCA-354.   1974.   This re-issue has a new cover with John 'Speedy' Keen in cardboard cut-out form overlooking Hollywood.

Pete Townshend

British singles

Let My Love Open The Door/Classified/Greyhound Girl   Atco K-11486.   1980.
A limited edition was sold at 60p and this was indicated by an irremovable sticker.
Uniforms/Dance It Away   Atco twelve-inch picture disc K-11751-PT.   1982.
Most people would know about the seven-inch, but a very limited twelve-inch was also made with a different design. Musically it was the same as the seven-inch.

British albums

The Townshend Tapes   Atco promo SAM-121/2.   1980.   This was a double album of Pete introducing tracks from the *Empty Glass* album. Quite a few copies were autographed.
Pete's Listening Time   Atco promo SAM-150.   1982.   Similar format to the above, but for *All The Best Cowboys Have Chinese Eyes*. Again, many copies were autographed.

American singles

PETE TOWNSHEND/PAUL WILLIAMS *What's It All About?*   Radio Series, number 3048.
Date unknown.
PETE TOWNSHEND/REO SPEEDWAGON   *What's It All About?*   Radio Series, number 643/4.   c.1981.

American album

Pete Townshend Talks To, And About Thunderclap Newman   Track promo PR-160.   1969.   See Thunderclap Newman for details.

Odds and sods

MEHA BABA *Happy Birthday* UK Universal Spiritual League USL-001. 1970.
This features six tracks by Townshend. This was reissued in 1975 as *The All Time
Star Of The Silent Screen . . . Meha Baba* UK MBO 1. This version didn't have
the inserts.
I Am UK Universal Spiritual League USL-002. 1973. This has five new
Townshend songs. Again this was re-issued in 1975 on MBO-2 without the inserts.
With Love UK Universal Spiritual League USL-003. 1974. The final charity
album has three new songs by Townshend. This has not been re-released.
Glastonbury Festival UK Revelation REV-1. 1973. This has the track *Classified,*
but not the version on the *Let My Love Open The Door* single.
PETE TOWNSHEND AND ROGER DALTREY Interviewed about the *Tommy* movie.
USA Rolling Stone News Service five-inch open reel tape lasting ten minutes.
1975.
ANGIE *Peppermint Lump*/ANGIE'S ORCHESTRA *Breakfast In Naples* UK/USA Stiff.
1979. This dreadful single has Townshend on the front cover, as well as producing
the record.
The Secret Policeman's Ball UK Island mini-alarm 12WIP-6598. 1980. This has
three brilliant tracks recorded live.
PETER TOWNSHEND AND JOHN WILLIAMS *Won't Get Fooled Again* UK Island one-
sided promo SPB-1. 1981. Taken from the above mini-album.
MUSIC AND RHYTHM UK WEA K-68045. 1982. This double album has one track by
Townshend – *Assencion Two.*
Classic Rock UK K-Tel. 1981. One of these hideous albums features Peter
Townshend singing *See Me Feel Me.*
My Generation/Pinball Wizard USA Evatone square flexi 623827 X 2. 1982.
This was given away with the *Maximum R & B* book written by Richard Barnes.
Both these tracks are home-made demos and are not included on *Scoop!*

Toyah

British singles

It's A Mystery/War Boys Safari promo and juke box issue TOY-1. 1980. A two-
track sampler from the *Four From Toyah* EP.
Stand Proud Safari flexi FLX-215. 1981. This was given with the *Thunder
In The Mountains* single.
Sphinx/For You Flexipop 008 (Lyntone LYN-9899). 1981.
Good Morning Universe/In The Fairground Safari promo and juke box issue
TOY-2. 1981.

Odds and sods

Urgh, A Music War UK/USA A & M. 1981. This has some live material.

Traffic

British singles

Gimmie Some Lovin'   Island one-sided promo, number unknown.   1971.
Welcome To The Canteen.   Sampler EP.   Island promo, number unknown.   1971.
Empty Pages   Same on both sides.   Island white label promo, number unknown.   1974.
Hole In My Shoe/Paper Sun   Island promo IEP-7-DJ.   1978.
Hole In My Shoe/Paper Sun   Island juke box issue IEP-7-JB.   1978.
Hole In My Shoe   EP.   Island IEP-7.   1978.   A very obscure, and limited picture disc issue.
Hole In My Shoe   Island one-sided promo IEP-7-DJ.   1978.

American single

Walking In The Wind   Long and short versions.   Asylum-Island promo E-45207. 1974.

American album

BBC *Rock Hour*   Radio Series, number 50.   c.1979.   Recorded in 1969.
BBC *Rock Hour*   Radio Series, number 216.   (Dated April, 1981).

Odds and sods

Here We Go 'Round The Mulberry Bush   Film soundtrack.   UK/USA United Artists.   1967.   Traffic contribute to the soundtrack.

The Troggs

British single

My Girl/Girl In Black   Page One POF-022.   1967.   This was either withdrawn or a mispress.

American singles

Wild Thing/From Home   Fontana F-1548.   1966.
Wild Thing/With A Girl Like You   Atco 6415.   1966.   These two were released almost simultaneously on two different labels. So far, this is the only record to get to number one in America on two different labels at the same time!
I Can't Control Myself/Gonna Make You Mine   Fontana F-1557 and Atco 6444.   1966.
Live At Max's Kansas City   Ram twelve-inch promo, number unknown.   1979.

American albums

Wild Thing   Fontana MGF-27556 mono and SRF-67556 stereo.   1966.
Wild Thing   Atco SD33-193.   1966.   A duplicated album release.

Live At Max's Kansas City   Ram, number unknown.   1979.   Not released in Britain.

Odds and sods
Three For All   UK DJM DJF-20448.   1976.   Although this film soundtrack features The Troggs, I don't know if it's new material.
Troggs On 45/Save The Last Dance For Me/I Do   French New Rose twelve-inch, number unknown.   1982.
Blackbottom   French New Rose, number unknown.   1982.   This, their most recent album, has not been released in Britain.

The Tubes

American singles
White Punks On Dope   Censored version.   Mono and stereo mixes.   A & M promo 1733-S.   1976.
Get Off   Radio Spots.   A & M promo, no number.   c.1977.   This is a PSA single to persuade kids to kick the drug habit.
Prime Time   Plus two others.   A & M twelve-inch promo SP-17068.   1979.
Sports Fans/Gonna Get It Next Time   Capitol twelve-inch promo SPRO-9728.   1982.
Sports Fans   Long and short versions.   Capitol twelve-inch promo SPRO-9740.   1982.

American albums
The Tubes First Clean Album   A & M promo SP-17012.   1978.   This is a single album of edited highlights from the *What Do You Want From Live* set.
THE TUBES/BLONDIE   *Rock Around The World*   Radio Series, number 194.   (Dated April 1978).
BBC *Rock Hour*   Radio Series, number 235.   (Dated 3.8.81).   Recorded at the Hammersmith Odeon in London.
NBC *Source*   Radio Series   (Dated 4.8.81).
King Biscuit Radio Series   (Dated 23.8.81).

British singles
Prime Time/No Way Out   A & M AMS-7423.   1979.   This was available in seven different coloured vinyl pressings. These were also obtainable in a promo only boxed set complete with a bonus picture disc.
Talk To You Later and *Succi Girl*/BILLY SQUIER   Two tracks.   Capitol twelve-inch promo PSLP-338.   1981.

Odds and sods
Prime Time/No Way Out   German A & M square picture disc, number unknown.   1979.

The Turtles

Before becoming The Turtles they had been a surfing band – THE CROSSFIRES. They had cut two singles in the early '60s.
One Potato, Two Potato/That'll Be The Day USA Lucky Token LT-112. 1964.
Fibreglass Jungle/Dr Jekyll And Mr Hyde Capco 104. 1964.

American singles

Outside Chance/We'll Meet Again White Whale WW-237. 1966.
Making My Mind Up/Outside Chance White Whale WW-237. 1966.
Two different singles with the same number, the first version being the easier of the two to find. The second version was only released in the Seattle area.
House On The Hill/Come Over White Whale WW-306. 1967. Withdrawn. This was released without the band's permission, so it was withdrawn a few days after its issue. There are a lot of promos around with just the A side.
Is It Love You Want/Losin' One Capitol 2018. 1967. Is this THE TURTLES?
Mystery Train/B side unknown. RCA 47-6356. Date unknown. Another question mark hangs over this one. The Elvis re-issue on RCA is 47-6357, one number after the Turtles' single. Is this a wind-up, or what?!
The Turtles Collectable Records EX-7. 1981. This is a neat boxed set of seven singles in clear vinyl. There is also in existence a ten-inch EP with eight hits on it from the Lost Nite label, also pressed in clear vinyl. This is a pirate.

British singles

It Ain't Me Babe/Almost There Pye International 7N-25320. 1966.
Let Me Be/Your Mama Said You Would Pye International 7N-25341. 1966.
You Baby/Wanderin' Kind Immediate IM-031. 1966.
These are all pre-London releases.

British EP

It Ain't Me Babe Pye International NEP-44089. 1966. This has the two Pye singles back to back.

British albums

The Turtles Present The Battle Of The Bands London SHU-8376. 1968. This has a single sleeve, as opposed to the American gatefold cover which has photos of all the bands taking part.
Happy Together Again, The Turtles Twenty Greatest Hits Philips 9299 425. 1976. This was reduced to a single album in Britain, while in America it was a double set with twenty-eight tracks, including some unreleased material.

Odds and sods

CHRISTMAS SPIRIT *Christmas Is My Time Of Year/Will You Still Believe In Me* USA White Whale WW-290. 1966. This is The Turtles with Linda Ronstadt and Gram Parsons.

THE DEDICATIONS *Teardrops*/B side unknown.   USA White Whale WW-340. 1967.   The Turtles use an alias on this authentic sounding doo-wop song. All the following are credited to The Rhythm Butchers.
The Legendary Rhythm Butchers Sampler USA Rhino RNFE-100.   1980.
Meat The Rhythm Butchers USA Rhino RNFE-101.   1980.
The Rhythm Butchers Return USA Rhino RNFE-102.   1980.
Invasion Of The Rhythm Butchers USA Rhino RNFE-103.   1981.
The Rhythm Butchers Sing For Young Lovers USA Rhino RNFE-104.   1981.
The Rhythm Butchers vs. The Zanti Misfits USA Rhino RNFE-105.   1982.

All these EP's are sub-titled *The Turtles Backstage,* which gives some indication of what these are all about. After a hard night onstage, our heroes would return to their hotel room lusting for blood. Their only satisfaction was to mutilate songs from their past, a ritual repeated out of habit. Showing no mercy, more can be expected. All of these EP's are mail order only, and limited to a thousand copies. The early ones were autographed.

Judie Tzuke

British singles

TZUKE AND PAXO *These Are The Laws*/B side unknown.   Good Earth GD-12. 1976.   Paxo is Tzuke's writing partner, Mike Paxman.
ZOOKIE *Judie Judie Hold On*/B side unknown.   DJM DJS-10796.   1977.
JUDIE TZUKE *For You/Sukarita* Rocket ROKN-541.   1978.   This is the original EMI pressing.
For You/Sukarita Rocket XPRES-2.   1978.   This was re-issued by Phonogram very quickly.
Love On The Border Edited.   Chrysalis one-sided promo CHS-2600-DJ.   1982.
For You/B side unknown.   Chrysalis promo JUD-102.   1982.   Taken from the live album.
For You/Black Furs/Come Hell/Hunter   Chrysalis twelve-inch promo JUD-12-103.   1982.   More live tracks. What is JUD-101?

American single

Stay With Me Till Dawn Mono and stereo versions.   Rocket blue vinyl promo PIG-41133.   1979.

American album

Stay With Me Till Dawn Rocket PIG-27001.   1979.   This is more or less the *Welcome To The Cruise* album with a different title.

Rare LPs

Top (left to right) UTOPIA *Deface The Music* sampler; *The Recorder* (with Peter Gabriel). Middle (left to right) BEACH BOYS Interview LP; *Troublemakers* (compilation inc. SEX PISTOLS). Bottom (left to right) ELP Radio special; SQUEEZE *Cool For Cats* (back cover).

UFO

British singles

Come Away Melinda/B side unknown. Beacon BEA-165. 1970.
Boogie For George/B side unknown. Beacon BEA-172. 1970.
Prince Kajuku/B side unknown. Beacon BEA-181. 1970.

These are all pretty rare, to say the least. The Beacon label was a tiny outfit operating from a shed in a builder's yard in North London. These were deleted very quickly as Beacon went out of business in 1972.

Call My Name   Chrysalis one sided promo UFODJ-1. 1981.

British albums

UFO 1   Beacon BES-12. 1970.
Flying   Beacon BES-19. 1971.
Like their Beacon singles these were deleted very quickly, and as yet they've not been re-released in Britain.

American albums

UFO 1   Rare Earth RS-524. 1970. Their only USA Beacon release.
Force It   Chrysalis CHR-1074. 1975. This has a slightly different sleeve in America – it doesn't show the two people in the shower.
UFO/PAT TRAVERES   King Biscuit Radio Series. (Dated 8.7.81).
BBC *Rock Hour*   Radio Series, number 316. (Dated April 1982).
UFO/SAXON   King Biscuit Radio Series. (Dated 25.4.82).
Reading Rock '82   UK Mean MNLP-82. 1983. This has some live material.

Ultravox

Before Ultravox they had been TIGER LILY and had cut one single. *Ain't Misbehavin'*/*Monkey Jive* UK Gull GULS-12. 1975. This was re-issued on UK Dead Good DEAD-11. 1980.

British singles

Quirks/*Modern Love* Island WIP-6417. 1978. This was given away with the *Ha Ha Ha* album.
Systems Of Romance Sampler EP. Island twelve-inch promo UV-1. 1978.
ULTRAVOX/MICHAEL SCHENKER GROUP   Chrysalis twelve-inch promo, number unknown. 1981. This is a four-track EP.
So far most, if not all, their Chrysalis singles have been released in clear vinyl.

British album

ULTRAVOX *Rage In Eden*/SPANDAU BALLET *Diamond* Sampler album. Chrysalis promo, number unknown. 1982.

American singles

Sleepwalk   Same on both sides.   Chrysalis twelve-inch promo 22-PDJ.   1980.
Vienna   Long and short versions.   Chrysalis promo CHS-2481.   1981.
The Voice   Same on both sides.   Chrysalis twelve-inch promo 35-PDJ.   1982.

The Undertones

British singles

Teenage Kicks   EP.   Good Vibrations GOT-4.   1978.   Pressed in Ulster, but distributed in Britain by Rough Trade. Most copies came with a poster.
Teenage Kicks/B side unknown. Sire promo, number unknown.   1978.   This was a two-track sampler from the above. A ten-inch promo single dated from around this time is also in existence, limited to a thousand copies. It's possible that this is the *Teenage Kicks* EP yet again.
The Hypnotised Apatizer   Sire twelve-inch promo SAM-120.   1979.   This has six tracks from their second album.
The Love Parade   Edited.   Ardeck one-sided promo ARDS-11-DJ.   1982.

British albums

The Undertones   Sire SRK-6071.   1978.   The first issue came with a white cover and a black and white photo of the band sitting on a wall. This version has not been re-released.
The Undertones   Sire SRK-6081.   1979.   This second version not only had a new colour cover, but *Get Over You* was added to the track listing. This version was re-issued by Ardeck in 1983.

American album

BBC *Rock Hour*   Radio Series.   c.1981.   Recorded at Reading University.

U2

British singles

I Will Follow   Edited. Island one-sided promo WIP-6650-DJ.   1980.
Fire/J. Swallo   Island WIP-6679.   1981.   The initial copies came with a free live single *11 O'Clock Tick Tock/The Ocean/The Cry/The Electric Co.*   Island UWIP-6679.
New Year's Day/Treasure   Island WIP-6848.   1983.   Early copies again came with a free single *Fire/I Threw A Brick/A Day Without Me*   Island UWIP-6848. The free single featured more live tracks.
Two Hearts Beat As One/Endless Deep   Island IS-109.   1983.   The free single with this had two USA re-mixed hits *Two Hearts Beat As One/New Year's Day*   Island ISD-109.

British album

Under A Blood Red Sky Interview Album   Island promo U2-1-PR.   1983.

American singles

I Will Follow/Out Of Control Island IS-49716. 1981. The B side was recorded for WBCN-FM radio in Boston, and has not been released in Britain. Some promo copies come with a poster.
New Year's Day   Same on both sides.   Island promo twelve-inch DMD-604. 1983.
Two Hearts Beat As One   Three versions.   Island twelve-inch promo DMD-643. 1983.

American albums

Boy Island ILPS-9646. 1981. This American version has a different sleeve from the British. Instead of the photo of the boy it has as a stretch drawing of the band which has to be viewed from the side edge of the sleeve to make any sense.
Two Sides Live Warner Brothers Music Show promo, no number. 1981. This brilliant album was recorded for WBCN-FM in Boston and has not been given a full release, although several of the tracks have been released on British B sides, etc. Beware of clear vinyl copies, they're counterfeits.
U2/DEVO King Biscuit Radio Series. (Dated 31.2.82).
U2/BERLIN Westwood One Radio Series. 1982.
BBC *Rock Hour* Radio Series. 1982. Recorded at the Hammersmith Odeon.

Odds and sods

An Cat Dubh Appeared on the *Dancin' Master* cassette from the NME in Britain. NME-001. 1981. This track was taken from the American live promo album.
Gloria Studio/*I Will Follow* Live in Holland. Dutch Island, number unknown. 1981. I don't know if this is the same live B side which appeared on the British B side.
U2 Four Play Irish CBS, no number. 1982. This is a set of four singles pressed in yellow vinyl and housed in a plastic wallet. The four singles were *Out Of Control* CBS-7951, *A Day Without Me* CBS-8306, *11 O'Clock Tick Tock* CBS-8687 and *I Will Follow* CBS-9065. Later copies were pressed in black vinyl.

Velvet Underground

American singles

What Goes On/Jesus MGM promo K-14057. 1966. Probably withdrawn from a full release like the Verve label singles.
Sunday Morning/Femme Fatale Verve promo VK-10466. 1966.
White Light White Heat/Here She Comes Now Verve VK-10560. 1967.

I Heard Her Call My Name/Here She Comes Now   Verve promo VK-10560.
1967. This has the same number as above.
Loop   Aspen magazine flexi.   1967.
Index   Index magazine flexi.   1967.

Odds and sods
The Electric Newspaper USA ESP-Disk ESP-1034.   1967. This includes the track
Noise.

So far there have been two of Velvet's compilations from the Australian Plastic
Inevitable label. Both *Etc* and *And So On* can be regarded with a certain amount of
suspicion as far as their legality is concerned. There is also a British set which is very
similar in content. *Everything You've Ever Wanted To Know About The Velvet
Underground* is a three-album boxed set with a book, and the Nico Immediate label
single thrown in for good measure.

Gene Vincent

American single
Slow Times/Grease   Plus one other.   Kama Sutra promo SSP-19.   1969.

British single
Rip It Up/High Blood Pressure   Capitol promo CL-15307.   1963.   When the
record reached the shops the A side was now *Crazy Beat*.

British EP's
Rainy Day Sunshine   Stars records RD-1.   1979.   This was a very limited edition
release made by Second Time Around Records. It was given a re-release by
Magnum Force records in 1980.
Vintage Vincent Capitol PSR-458.   1981.   This was given with the *Singles Album*.

Odds and sods
It's Trad Dad   Film soundtrack.   UK Columbia SX-1412.   1962.   This includes
Vincent's *Spaceship From Mars*.

Rick Wakeman

British single
Spider/Danielle   WEA K-18354.   1981.   Apparently only 2,000 copies were made.

British album
Piano Vibrations   Polydor 2460 135.   1971.   This was a musak album and was
deleted very quickly.

Juke Box Only issues
Top (left to right) TRAFFIC *Paper Sun;* KATE BUSH *On Stage.*   Middle (left to right) STYLE COUNCIL *Long Hot Summer;* TODD RUNDGREN *Something Anything* EP.   Bottom (left to right) GENESIS *Paperlate;* STIFF LITTLE FINGERS *Listen.*

American albums

The Six Wives Of Henry The VIII Quad mix. A & M QU-54361. 1974.
The Myths And Legends Of King Arthur Quad mix. A & M QU-54515. 1974.

Odds and sods

Wagner's Dream/Love's Dream/Count Your Blessings A & M Lyntone flexi LYN-3176. 1975. This flexi, featuring Wakeman and others, was given away with '19' magazine.

We Give A Damn UK A & M AMLX-3804. 1976. This compilation album was available through 'Melody Maker'. It included a new Wakeman track *Babylon*.

Scott Walker

American singles

SCOTT ENGEL *When A Boy Is A Man/Steady As A Rock* RKO-Unique 386. c.1961.

THE DALTON BROTHERS *I Only Came To Dance With You/Without Love* Martay 2001. c.1963.

SCOTT ENGEL *Devil Surfer/*B side unknown. Martay 2004. c.1963.

SCOTT ENGEL *Devil Surfer/*B side unknown. Challenge 59206. c.1963. This was the nationally available version.

SCOTT ENGEL WITH COUNT DRAC AND HIS BOYS *The Livin' End/Good For Nothin'* Orbit 506. c.1964.

SCOTT ENGEL *Charlie Bop/All I Do Is* Orbit R-511. c.1964.

SCOTT ENGEL *Paper Doll/Blue Bell* Orbit R-521. c.1964.

SCOTT ENGEL *The Golden Rule Of Love/Sunday* Orbit R-537. 1964.

SCOTT ENGEL *Comin' Home/I Don't Want To Know* Orbit R-545. 1964.

SCOTT ENGEL *Mr Jones/Anything Will Do* Liberty 55312. Date unknown.

SCOTT ENGEL *Forever More/Anything Will Do* Liberty 55428. Date unknown.

SCOTT ENGEL AND JOHN STEWART *I Only Came To Dance With You/Greens* Tower 218. 1964.

As you can doubtless see I'm taking pot shots at these dates as they're all extremely rare.

American album

SCOTT ENGEL AND JOHN STEWART *I Only Came To Dance With You* Tower ST-5026. 1965.

British single

SCOTT ENGEL AND JOHN STEWART *I Only Came To Dance With You/Greens* Capitol CL-15440. 1965.

British EP

SCOTT ENGEL *Scott Engel* Liberty LEP-2261. 1966.

British album

SCOTT ENGEL   *Looking Back With Scott Engel*   Ember EMB-3393.   1967.

Joe Walsh

American singles

The Smoker You Drink . . .   Dunhill juke box EP.   LLP-256.   1974.
Turn To Stone   Same on both sides.   ABC twelve-inch promo SPDJ-46.   1977.

American albums

The Smoker You Drink The Player You Get   Quad mix.   ABC-Command COQ-40016.   1974.
NBC *Source* Radio Series.   (Dated July 1981).
King Biscuit Radio Series.   (Dated 11.10.81).
King Biscuit Radio Series.   (Dated 11.4.82).

Whitesnake

British singles

DAVID COVERDALE   *Hole In The Sky/Blind Man*   Purple PUR-133.   1977.
DAVID COVERDALE   *Breakdown/Only My Soul*   Purple PUR-136.   1977.
These were two pre-Whitesnake singles.

WHITESNAKE   *Long Way From Home/Trouble*   United Artists promo   BP-324-DJ. 1981.   A two-track sampler from an EP.
Take Me With You   Liberty one-sided twelve-inch promo, number unknown. 1982.
Victim Of Love/Love 'n' Affection   Liberty BP-418.   1982.   Withdrawn.
Here I Go Again   Long and short versions.   Liberty promo BP-416-DJ.   1982.

British albums

DAVID COVERDALE   *Whitesnake*   Purple TPS-3509.   1977.
DAVID COVERDALE   *Northwinds*   Purple TPS-3513.   1977.
DAVID COVERDALE'S WHITESNAKE   *Trouble*   EMI-International   INS-3022.   1978.
When United Artists re-issued this album in 1980 the sleeve had been changed.

American album

In The Heart Of The City   Mirage, number unknown.   1981.   Not only was this reduced to a single album, but it was also re-mixed for the American market.

Odds and sods

Reading Festival '82   UK Mean MNLP-82.   1983.   This has some live tracks.

The Who

The High Numbers

I'm The Face/Zoot Suit UK Fontana TF-480. 1964. One of the most famous rarities in the world. It apparently sold less than 300 copies. *I'm The Face* reappeared on the *Odds And Sods* album in 1974, and on the B side of *Long Live Rock* in 1979. Both sides were given a full re-release in 1979 during the height of the mod revival. This was released on Back Door Records BACK-1 originally, but changed very quickly to DOOR-4. It was given an airing in America in its entirety for the first time in 1980, but you had to buy an album to get it. It was pressed as a single, on Mercury MDJ-570, with a slightly different picture sleeve, and given away with the *Thru The Back Door* compilation album. A second High Numbers single was planned. *The Kids Are Alright* was shelved, although test pressings on Fontana exist.

The Who
British singles

I Can't Explain/Bald Headed Woman Brunswick 05926. 1965. The first press ran to 1,000 only as Decca, who owned the label, weren't too sure if this new band would sell. All copies seem to mis-spell 'Townsend'.
Anyway, Anyhow, Anywhere/Daddy Rolling Stone Brunswick 05935. 1965. The first 1,000 copies came with a colour pop art pic sleeve.
My Generation Decca one-sided promo AD-1001. 1965. A special pre-release pressing.
My Generation/Shout And Shimmy Brunswick 05944. 1965. The first 200 came with a group photo picture sleeve.
*Circles/*B side unknown. Brunswick, number unknown. 1966. Withdrawn. This was scheduled for release 18 February 1966.
Substitute/Instant Party Reaction BM-591001. 1966. Released on 4 March 1966, it was immediately withdrawn. The reason being the B side. *Circles,* the withdrawn Brunswick single, and *Instant Party* were the same track, but re-titled for legal reasons. Shel Talmy claimed that the track had been recorded as their last Brunswick single. So Decca pressed up a new single.
A Legal Matter/Instant Party Brunswick 05956. 1966. The A side must a been a joke!
*Substitute/*THE WHO ORCH *Waltz For A Pig* Reaction 591001. 1966. The second version of their first Reaction single had a new B side. The Who Orchestra were The Graham Bond Organisation plus others. Was the title aimed at Talmy? The instrumental was used because The Who couldn't come up with a new track in time.
Substitute/Circles Reaction 591001. 1966. This third issue settles the argument for once and for all!
I'm A Boy/In The City Reaction 591004. 1966. This A side version with John Entwistle on vocals has not appeared in Britain on any album for years as both

Direct Hits and *The Story Of The Who* are now deleted.
The Last Time/Under My Thumb Track 604 006. 1967. This was made to help
Jagger and Richards' court costs during their respective drugs trials.
Magic Bus/Dr Jekyll And Mr Hyde Track 604 024. 1968. This version of *Magic Bus* was not the one that appeared on the *Meaty Beaty Big And Bouncy* album.
Tommy Singles boxed set. Track promo. 1969. This is a set of four singles given
to radio stations to promote the album.
*I'm Free/*B side unknown. Track PRO-1.
Sally Simpson/Go To The Mirror Track PRO-2.
Acid Queen/1921 Track PRO-3.
Christmas/Tommy Overture Track PRO-4.

All of these singles have the regular Track label design, but have 'promotional only,
not for sale' under the Track logo.

Won't Get Fooled Again Track one-sided white label promo A-4112. 1971.
Join Together/Baby Don't You Do It Track export issue 2094 102. 1972. This
was specially made for Spain and came with a picture sleeve.
Who Are You Polydor promo WHODJ-2. 1978. This may be one-sided, but I
don't know if it's edited.
Who Are You Polydor blue label one-sided promo WHODJ-3. 1978. Again, I
don't know if this is edited for radio or not.
Who Are You? Radio version/*I've Had Enough* Polydor promo WHO-1-DJ.
1978. This masks the line 'who the fuck are you?'. It also came in a discreet brown
paper bag.
Athena/Won't Get Fooled Again/Why Did I Fall For That? Polydor twelve-inch
picture disc WHOPX-6. 1982. This is a mispress, as the last track should have
been *A Man Is A Man.*
Eminence Front/Athena/Dangerous Polydor twelve-inch promo WHOX-6.
1982.

British albums

A Quick One Reaction 592 002 mono, 593 002 stereo. 1966. Mono and stereo
mixes are different.
The Who Sell Out Track 612 002 mono, 613 002 stereo. 1967. Again, the mono
and stereo mixes are different. Some early copies came with a poster.
Tommy. Part One Track 613 013. 1969.
Tommy. Part Two Track 613 014. 1969.

These two were released in single sleeves and didn't contain any music which wasn't
on the double album version.

The Who And Jimi Hendrix Backtrack 4 (Track 2407 004). 1970. This cheapo
album had a side for each act.
My Generation Coral, number unknown. 1970. Withdrawn due to pressure from
Track. Coral were planning to re-issue the album in its original sleeve for 99p.
Who Did It? Track 2856 001. c.1971. This probably originates from a record
club. It has a side each from *A Quick One* and *The Who Sell Out.*

The Best From Tommy   Track, number unknown.   c.1972.   Withdrawn.
The Who Story   BBC Transcription Service 134736.   c.1974.   A radio show on three albums.
Odds And Sods   Track 2406 116.   1974.   Only the early copies came with the braile message on the back. What does it say?
The Who By Numbers   Polydor 2490 129.   1976.   Early copies came individually numbered.
Filling In The Gaps   Polydor promo WHOT-1.   1981.   This was a double interview set to promote the *Face Dances* album.
Phases   Polydor 2675 216.   1981.   A boxed set of albums from *My Generation* to *Who Are You* with no freebie.

American singles

Substitute/THE WHO ORCHESTRA   *Waltz For A Pig*   Atco 45-6509.   1966.   Atco released this thinking that they had the rights because of their tie-up with UK Polydor. American Decca thought otherwise. The result was that this was their only Atco release.
I Can See For Miles/Mary Anne With The Shaky Hand   Decca 32206.   1967. For about fifteen years this was their most sought after American single as this contained a B side which didn't appear in Britain. That was until it appeared on *Rarities. Volume One* in 1983.
Tommy   Singles boxed set.   Decca promo.   1969.   This set of four singles came in a special gold box with gold sleeves. Unfortunately, I don't have full details. The singles were numbered 34610-34613.
Go To The Mirror/Tommy Can You Hear me   Decca 34611.
I'm Free/B side unknown.   Decca 34613.
Substitute/Young Man's Blues   Decca 32737.   1970.   Withdrawn.   Both tracks are from the *Live At Leeds* album.
Who Are You   6:11 and 3:22 versions.   MCA promo MCA-40948.   1978.
I've Had Enough   Same on both sides. MCA promo S45-1809.   1978.   This was the B side of *Who Are You,* but was flipped by MCA.
Long Live Rock   Long and short versions.   MCA promo MCA-41053.   1979.
Long Live Rock   Same on both sides.   MCA promo picture disc 41053.   1979. There are several different versions of this. One side has a group photo and is the same on all copies, but the other side shows the symbol of various record stores like Pamida, Musicland, Narm, National Record Mart and others.
What's It All About?   Radio Series.   Number and date unknown.
You Better You Bet   Long and short versions.   Warner twelve-inch promo PROA-938.   1981.
Athena   Same on both sides.   Warner twelve-inch promo PROA-1065.   1982.
Eminence Front   5:35 and 4:05 versions.   Warner promo 7-29814.   1982.
Eminence Front   5:35 and 4:05 versions.   Warner twelve-inch promo PROA-1087. 1982.

American albums

The Who Sing My Generation   Decca DL-4664 mono and DL-74664 stereo.   1966.

This last version claims to be in stereo, but it's mono-reprocessed. It also has the famous photo of Big Ben overlooking the band on the front cover. Musically the only difference is that *Circles* replaces *I'm A Man*.

Happy Jack   Decca DL-4892 mono and DL-74892 stereo.   1966.   This is more or less *A Quick One* with *Happy Jack* instead of *Heatwave*.

The Who Sell Out   Banded for airplay.   Decca promo DL-4950 mono.   1967.

Magic Bus, The Who On Tour   Decca promo DL-5064 mono.   1968.   The mono version was promo only.   This is not a live album as the title suggests, but another compilation album.

THE WHO AND THE STRAWBERRY ALARM CLOCK   *Double Star Series*   MCA-Philco DL-734586.   1970.   A cheapo album from certain stores only.

Who Are You   Interview album.   MCA promo, number unknown.   1978.

Who Are You   Promo version.   MCA promo L33-1987.   1978.   This includes the 'clean' version of the title track.

THE WHO/KISS   *Rock Around The World*   Radio Series, number 225.   (Dated 11.12.78).

Robert W. Morgan *Profiles*   Radio Series.   1980.

Filling In The Gaps   Warner Brothers Music Show promo WBMS-116.   1981.   This red interview album has the red sleeve and red labels.

Filling In The Gaps   Warner promo PROA-944.   1981.   This version has a black and white paint by numbers sleeve in a similar style to the *Face Dances* sleeve. Both of these albums have the same material, namely an interview album to promote *Face Dances*.

Who Are You?   Superdisk audiophile pressing SD-166108.   1981.

Who Are The Who? The Hooligans Radio Special   MCA promo open-reel Radio Show.   1981.   This was made to promote the *Hooligans* compilation.

The Who Special   BBC *Rock Hour*   Radio Series.   (Dated April 1982).   A three-album set.

It's Hard   Warner promo Quiex II pure vinyl pressing 23731-1.   1982.

Westwood One *Off The Record*   Radio Series.   (Dated 8. and 15.11.82).   A four-album set.

Who Dunnit?   DIR Broadcasting Radio Show.   (Dated 17.12.82).   A six-album set.

The Great Lost Who Tapes   Westwood One Radio Series.   (Dated Dec. 1982). This double-album set was hosted by Bill Wyman and included rare B sides, one previously unreleased live track as well as alternate takes, etc. A great set.

Odds and sods
Singles

I'm Free/Overture   UK Ode ODS-66302.   1973.
I'm Free/Underture   USA Ode 66040.   1973.
*Underture/*B side unknown.   UK Ode ODS-66303.   1973.
Tommy   Sampler.   UK Ode promo TOMMY-1.   1973.
Tommy   Sampler.   USA Ode promo EP-10/T-2.   1973.
Tommy Overture/Listening To You/See Me Feel Me   UK/USA Polydor.   1975. This is the movies soundtrack version.

Sister Disco/Tracks by Rockpile and Wings.   USA Atlantic twelve-inch promo, number unknown. 1981.

Albums

Woodstock USA Cotillion/UK Atlantic.   1970.   They only appear on the first volume.
Top Of The Pops.   (Dated 20.2.71).   UK BBC Transcription Service album, number unknown. This has a live version of *Heaven And Hell*.
Won't Get Fooled Again/I Don't Know Myself Italian Polydor 2121 057.   1971. Pressed in pink vinyl.
Tommy Stage version. UK/USA Ode. 1973.
Tommy Film soundtrack. UK/USA Polydor. 1975.
The Making Of Tommy Interview album. USA Polydor promo SA-010. 1975.
Roger Daltrey And Pete Townshend Talk About Quadrophenia Interview album. USA Polydor promo PRO-114.   1979.
Concerts For Kampuchea UK/USA Atlantic. 1981.

Steve Winwood

American single

Still In The Game Same on both sides.   Island twelve-inch promo PROA-1034. 1982.

American albums

Innerview Radio Series.   Series 15, programme 12. 1981.
NBC *Source* Radio Series.   (Dated 15.12.81).
STEVE WINWOOD AND JUDAS PRIEST   Rolling Stone magazine guest DJ radio series. 1982.

Odds and sods

THE ANGLOS *Incense/You're Fooling Me* UK Fontana TF-589. 1966. This single fooled a lot of people into thinking that it was some American band using a British-type name. It was in fact Steve Winwood and others (possibly The Spencer Davis Group?) A great record. So good in fact that it was re-issued at least three times over the next eighteen months. Brit WI-1004, Sue WI-4033 and Island WIP-6061. So how about re-issuing it now?
JOHN MAYALL AND STEVE ANGLO *Long Night* This was featured on the compilation album *Raw Blues*. UK Ace Of Clubs/USA London. 1967. Steve Anglo was of course, Steve Winwood.
What's Shakin UK/USA Elektra. 1967. This compilation album again featured Steve Anglo, along with Eric Clapton's Powerhouse.

Steve Winwood has appeared on over thirty albums by other people during his career.

Wishbone Ash

British single
Come In From The Rain/Lorelei MCA PSR-431. 1977. This was given away with the *No Smoke Without Fire* album.

American albums
An Evening Program With Wishbone Ash Decca promo, number unknown. 1972. Probably a sampler album.
Live From Memphis MCA promo L33-1922. 1974. A live album recorded for WMC-FM in Memphis.
BBC *Rock Hour* Radio Series, number 301. (Dated January 1982). Recorded at the Hammersmith Odeon in London.

Wizzard

British single
I Wish It Could Be Christmas Everyday/Rob Roy's Nightmare Warner K-16336. 1973. Withdrawn. Re-issued on Harvest HAR-5079 as they owed one more single to EMI. As Warner had already pressed and distributed some copies of the record with the gatefold sleeve, EMI bought these from Warner and put a Harvest sticker over the Warner logo, appropriately covered in snow. The old Warner copies occasionally turn up.

American singles
See My Baby Jive/Bend Over Beethoven United Artists UA-XW 272-W. 1973.
See My Baby Jive/Got A Crush On You United Artists UA-XW 272-W. 1973. Two versions of the same single.
See My Baby Jive Long and short versions. United Artists promo UA-XW 272-W. 1973.
Are You Ready To Rock/Marathon Man Warner export issue K-16497. 1974.

Odds and sods
Dynamite UK K-Tel. TE-298. 1973. This features an edited version of *Angel Fingers*.

Roy Wood

British album
The Singles Album Speed 1000. 1982. This was quickly re-issued with an extra track *I Wish It Could Be Christmas Everyday*.

American album

On The Road   Warner BSK-3247.   1980.   This album was never released in Britain.

Odds and sods

GERRY LEVINE AND THE AVENGERS   *Dr Feelgood/Driving Me Wild*   UK Decca F-11815.   1964.

MIKE SHERIDAN AND THE NIGHTRIDERS   *Oh What A Sweet Thing That Was/Fabulous* UK Columbia DB-7302.   1964.

MIKE SHERIDAN AND THE NIGHTRIDERS   *Here I Stand/Lonely Weekend*   UK Columbia DB-7462.   1965.

MIKE SHERIDAN'S LOT   *Take My Hand/Make Them Understand*   UK Columbia DB-7677.   1965.

MIKE SHERIDAN'S LOT   *Don't Turn Your Back On Me/Stop Look And Listen*   UK Columbia DB-7798.   1965.

Roy Wood was a member in all these bands.

DANNY KING'S MAYFAIR SET   *Pretty Things/Youngblood*   UK Columbia DB-7456. 1965.   He may have appeared on this as a session man.

ANNIE HASLAM   *Annie In Wonderland*   UK Warner/USA Sire.   1978.   Roy Wood plays all the instruments on this album and is seen on the cover.

ANNIE HASLAM AND ROY WOOD   *I Never Believed/*B side unknown.   UK Warner K-17028.   1978.   This was the single from the album.

THE ROCKERS   *We Are The Boys*   Long and short versions/*Rockin' On The Stage* UK CBS twelve-inch TA-3929.   1983.   This included Roy Wood with others.

Bill Wyman

British singles

BILL WYMAN AND MARIA MULDUA   *Tenderness/Merche D'Amour*   Polydor, number unknown.   1981.

Je Suis Un Rock Star   Radio version/Regular version.   A & M promo AMS-8144-DJ.   1981.   This changes the line 'she smoked marajuana' to 'she was a disco dancer'.

British album

Green Ice   Film soundtrack.   Polydor POLS-1031.   1981.   This soundtrack was written by Wyman and included a track *Si Si* which eventually became *Je Suis Un Rock Star* when lyrics were added.

American singles

BILL WYMAN   *The Lantern/*THE ROLLING STONES   *In Another Land*   London LON-907.   1968.   This was pushed as a new Stones single.

Je Suis Un Rock Star/Rio De Janeiro   A & M twelve-inch promo SP-12041.   1981.

American albums

Monkey Grip Quad mix. Rolling Stones QD-79100. 1974.

NIGHTBIRD AND CO. Radio Series, number 265. c.1978.

XTC

British singles

*Science Friction/*B side unknown. Virgin VS-188. 1977. Withdrawn. This was taken from the *3-D EP* twelve-inch.

Go Plus EP. Virgin VS-23312. 1978. This twelve-inch dub EP was given away with the *GO 2* album.

Chain Of Command/Limelight Virgin VDJ-30. 1979. This was given away with the *Drums And Wires* album.

Making Plans For Nigel/Bushman President/Pulsing, Pulsing Virgin VS-282. 1979. Initial copies came with a free board game.

Generals And Majors/Don't Lose Your Temper Virgin VS-365. 1980. The first 15,000 came with a free single *Smokeless Zone/The Somnambulist*.

*Ten Feet Tall/*THE SKIDS *The Olympian* Smash Hits flexi HIT-002. 1981. This was a magazine freebie.

Towers Of London/Set Myself On Fire Virgin VS-372. 1981. Another free single came with this *Batterey Wives/Scissor Man*.

Senses Working Overtime/Blame The Weather/Tissue Tigers Virgin VS-462. 1982. This comes with a limited edition fold-out sleeve.

Looking For Footsteps Flexipop 016 (Lyntone LYN-11032). 1982.

Wonderland/Jump Virgin picture disc VSY-606. 1983. An extremely limited release.

Love On A Farmboy's Wages/In Loving Memory Of A Name Virgin VS-613. 1983. Initial copies came with a free single *Desert Island/Toys*.

American singles

Limelight/Chain Of Command Virgin PR-344. 1979. Given away with the *Drums And Wires* album.

Senses Working Overtime/Ball And Chain Epic-Virgin twelve-inch promo AS-1405. 1982.

Blame The Weather/Tissue Tigers Epic-Virgin flexi number 4. 1982. Given away with *Trouser Press* magazine.

American album

BBC *Rock Hour* Radio Series, number 212. (Dated 22.3.81).

Odds and sods

Traffic Light Rock UK Virgin, no number. 1978. This was included on a hard vinyl EP given away with *Record Mirror*. (Also included are three other Virgin artists). This track was recorded live in 1977.

The Hope And Anchor Front Row Festival UK Warner-Albion K-66077. 1978. This has two live tracks.

Are You Receiving Me/This Is Pop Australian Virgin, number unknown. 1979. Both tracks are recorded live, and as yet haven't appeared in the UK.

Times Square UK/USA RSO. 1980. This is the soundtrack album to a really bad film about street cred' punkos, but it did include one new, and excellent, XTC track *Take This Town*. This track was also released as a single in Britain on RSO.

Towers Of London/Set Myself On Fire Dutch Virgin, number unknown. 1980. The A side has a different introduction to the British version.

THE COLONEL *I Need Protection/Too Many Crooks* UK Virgin VS-380. 1981. This is Colin Moulding using an alias.

Five Senses Canada Virgin twelve-inch, number unknown. 1981. This EP has some re-mixes.

Urgh A Music War UK/USA A & M. 1981. More live material.

Music And Rhythm UK WEA K-68045. 1982. This has a new studio track *It's Nearly Africa*.

THE THREE WISE MEN *Thanks For Christmas* UK Virgin VS-642. 1983. This is an excellent pseudonym single.

The Yardbirds

British singles

Good night Sweet Josephine/Think About It Columbia DB-8368. 1968. This was withdrawn, but promos exist.

Goodnight Sweet Josephine EMI-Disc acetate. 1968. An alternate take.

British albums

Having A Rave Up With The Yardbirds Columbia export issue SCXC-28. 1966. Similar to the American version, but with the regular black and blue label.

Roger The Engineer Mono and stereo mixes. Edsel cassette EDC-116. 1983. This tape has the two versions back to back.

American singles

I Wish You Would Same on both sides. Epic red vinyl promo 5-9709. 1964.

For Your Love/Got To Hurry Epic 5-9790. 1965.

For Your Love/I Wish You Would Epic 5-9790. 1965. This definitely has two different B sides.

Shapes Of Things/I'm Not Talking Epic 5-9891. 1966.

Shapes Of Things/New York City Blues Epic 5-10006. 1966. The first version was very quickly deleted.

Ha Ha Said The Clown/Tinker Tailor Epic 5-10204. 1968.

Ten Little Indians/Drinking Muddy Water Epic 5-10248. 1968.

7-inch Picture Discs
Left column, top to bottom CARS *Double Life;* JOHN ENTWHISTLE *Too Late The Hero;*
RENAISSANCE *Northern Lights.* Right column POLICE *Wrapped Around Your Finger* set
of three discs.

The two above were American only releases. Mickie Most was brought in to produce them in a vain attempt to get them back into the charts. It didn't work, and they split in mid-1968.

Goodnight Sweet Josephine/Think About It Epic 5-10303. 1968. This single was given a full release in America, but beware of counterfeits. These have the matrix number on the run-off groove, hand written instead of stamped.

American albums

Five Live Yardbirds Epic LN-24201. 1964. Withdrawn.
Live Yardbirds Featuring Jimmy Page Epic E-30615. 1971. Recorded in Chicago in 1968, but not released for three years, and only then to cash in on the success of Led Zeppelin. This album was withdrawn about a week after its release. Beware of imitations!! The original copies have a colour sleeve, whereas the counterfeits have black and white covers.
Live Yardbirds Featuring Jimmy Page Columbia Special Products P-13311. c.1974. A limited edition re-release with the colour cover.
THE YARDBIRDS/JEFF BECK *Rock Around The World* Radio Series, number 117. 1978.
Rolling Stone Continuous History Of Rock 'n' Roll Radio Series. 1982.
Retrorock Radio Series (Dated 7.9.81). This was the Anderson Theater, Chicago show from 29.3.68 which was used for the withdrawn album.
THE YARDBIRDS/THE ANIMALS *Retrorock* Radio Series (Dated 20.9.82).

Odds and sods

Face And Place New Zealand Direction records, number unknown. 1964. This has live material recorded at Government House, Auckland in 1964.
Paf Bum/Questa Volta Italian Ricordi International records SIR-20010. 1966.
San Remo '66 Spanish MRL 6050. 1966. This album has *Questa Volta* live.
PHILAMORE LINCOLN *The North Wind Blew South* US Epic BN-26497. 1967. This album features The Yardbirds.
Blow Up Film soundtrack. UK/USA MGM. 1968. This has *Stroll On* and *Psycho Daisies*.

Also in existence is a Japanese double album which features four previously unreleased tracks. Typically the album disappeared very quickly and I haven't a clue what it's called!

Yes

British singles

Sweetness/Something's Coming Atlantic 584 280. 1969. This rare single features a non-album B side.
Interview single. Atlantic promo SAM-7. 1972. This lasts for about ten minutes.

Five songs with a fourteen-minute interview. Lyntone flexi LYN-2536. Date unknown. This also came with an 80pp songbook. Origin unknown, although it may be a fan club item.

Going For The One/Parallels Atlantic seven- and twelve-inch K-10985. 1977. Withdrawn. The twelve-inch featured longer versions of both tracks.

Into The Lens Atlantic one-sided twelve-inch promo SAM-125. 1980. Some copies come with a printed note explaining line-up changes within the band.

Roundabout/Your Move Atlantic SAM-141. 1981. These two live tracks were featured on a single given away with the *Classic Yes.*

British albums

Fragile Atlantic 2400 019. 1971. Original copies come with a colour book in the gatefold.

Going For The One Atlantic boxed set edition DSK-50379. 1977. This consists of three twelve-inch singles. WEA used these plates to press two regular twelve inchers *Wonderous Stories* and *Going For The One.*

Classic Yes Atlantic withdrawn version. 1980. Test pressings of this 1980 version have different sleeves.

Classic Yes Atlantic cassette K-450842. 1981. This has the two tracks from the free single.

American singles

Your Move Special 2:54 radio edit, same on both sides. Atlantic promo 2819. 1971.

Roundabout Mono and stereo versions. Atlantic yellow vinyl promo 2854. 1972.

Yessongs Radio spots single. 1975. Label details, etc. are unknown. This was made to plug the movie.

Owner Of A Lonely Heart Atco one-sided twelve-inch promo PR-529. 1983.

Owner Of A Lonely Heart Long and short versions. Atco promo 7-96881. 1983.

American albums

Yes Atlantic SD-8243. 1969. The American version has a different cover to the British. It was a colour photo of the band in a garden.

Time And A Word Atlantic SD-8273. 1970. Another different sleeve. This has a colour photo of the group with the titles on the right.

Fragile Atlantic (Record Club edition) SD-7211. 1971.

Relayer Banded for radio play. Atlantic promo SD-18122. 1975.

Rock Around The World Radio Series, number 225. (Dated 3.12.78).

Innerview Radio Series. Series 4, programme 1. c.1979.

Robert W. Morgan *Profiles* Radio Series. c.1980.

Innerview Radio Series. Series 15, programme 1. 1981.

Retrorock Radio Series. (Dated Oct. 1981). Recorded c.1973.

YES/ELP *Retrorock* Radio Series. (Dated 13.9.82).

Odds and sods

Yes Solos USA Atlantic promo PR-260. 1976. A compilation of tracks from the, then, new albums by their solo members.

Neil Young

His first recording was:

DANNY AND THE MEMORIES *Can't Help Lovin' That Girl*/B side unknown. USA Valiant 6049. c.1965.

American singles

Everybody Knows This Is Nowhere Same on both sides. Reprise promo 0819. 1969. This promo is an alternate version.
Everybody Knows This Is Nowhere Sampler EP. Reprise promo PRO-334. 1969.
Harvest Reprise juke box EP, number unknown. 1972.
Comes A Time/Motorcycle Mama Reprise promo picture disc, number unknown. 1978. One of the most sought after late '70s collectables.
NEIL YOUNG AND BILL MURRAY *Buffalo Stomp/Ode To Wild Bill* Backstreet twelve-inch promo L33-1878. 1979.
Hawks And Doves/Union Man Reprise blue vinyl twelve-inch promo PROA-901. 1980. These are mono re-mixes.
Southern Pacific/Motion City Reprise triangular red vinyl RPSP-49870. 1981. Very peculiar!
Opera Star/Joe And Moe The Sleaze Reprise twelve-inch promo PROA-1014. 1981. This is edited and censored for radio play.

American albums

Neil Young Reprise RS-6317. 1968. The initial copies didn't have Young's name on the cover. When the album was re-released in the early '70s Young's name was at the top of the front cover in large black letters. The album had also been re-mixed.
After The Goldrush Reprise RS-6383. 1971. This had an edited *Southern Man* (the British album version being slightly longer).
Chrome Dream Reprise test pressing, number unknown. 1976. This eventually became *American Stars And Bars*.
Decade Reprise 3RS-2257. 1976. Some early sleeves have a different track listing as Neil changed his mind just after the first batch had been printed.
Gone To The Wind Reprise test pressing MSK-2266. 1978. The title was later changed to *Comes A Time*.
A Conversation With Neil Young Warner Brothers Music Show promo, number unknown. 1980.
Robert W. Morgan Radio Series. c.1980.

Rolling Stone News Service Radio Series. c.1980. A twelve-minute interview on a five-inch open reel.
Human Highway Film soundtrack. 1982. More details are unknown. Not an official Neil Young album.
Trans Geffen promo Quiex II pure vinyl pressing GHS-2018. 1982. Like the regular copies the inner sleeve credits the track *If You Got Love* which isn't on the album.
Everybody's Rockin' Geffen promo Quiex II pure vinyl pressing, number unknown. 1973.

Odds and sods
Where The Buffalos Roam Film soundtrack. Backstage BSR-5126. 1979. Neil Young contributes to this soundtrack album.
The Last Waltz UK/USA Warner. 1979. He makes an appearance here.
Harvest Japan Nautilus audiophile pressing, number unknown. 1981.

The Youngbloods

JESSE COLIN YOUNG *Youngblood* USA Mercury MG-21005. c.1965. This was the album which started the whole thing off.

American singles
*Wine Wine/Sometimes/*JOE COCKER Two tracks. Mercury promo EP-97. c.1968.
Get Together Long and short versions. RCA promo SP45-199. 1969.

American albums
The Youngbloods RCA LSP-3724. 1969.
Get Together RCA LSP-3724. 1969. A re-issue of the above.
Retrorock Radio Series. (Dated Nov. 1981).

Odds and sods
The Young Rascals, The Youngbloods And The Isley Brothers USA Design DLP-253. c.1967. A cheapo compilation featuring Mercury material.
Se Qualcuno Mi Dira/Qul Con Noitradi Noi Italian RCA-Italiana, number unknown. c.1970. Both sung in Italian.

Frank Zappa

Before forming THE MUTHAS in 1965 Zappa had already produced and appeared on many records. He has continued this productive role thoughout his career.

These are some of the records he was responsible/irresponsible for. All listed are American unless noted.

THE MASTERS   *Breaktime*   Emmy Records.   1961.

BRIAN LORD   *Big Surfer/Not Another One*   Vigah Records.   1964.   Taken up by Capitol for national distribution. Capitol 4981.

LOS PERSUADERS   *El Grunion/Tijuana Surf*   Mexico Gamma 528.   1964.

THE HOLLYWOOD PERSUADERS   *Grunion Run/Tijuana Surf*   Original Sound OS-39. 1964.

MR CLEAN   *Mr Clean/Jesse Lee*   Original Sound OS-40.   1964.

THE PENGUINS   *Memories Of El Monte*   Original Sound.   c.1964.

CLIVE DUNCAN AND THE RADIANTS   *To Keep Our Love*   Dootone 451.   Date unknown.

THE HOGS   *Loose Lip*   Hanna-Barbera HBR-511.   1966.

THE SONICS   *Anyway The Wind Blows*   UNI 55039.   1967.

BURT WARD   *Boy Wonder I Love You/Orange*   MGM K-13632.   1967.   Burt Ward was, of course, Robin The Boy Wonder from the TV series Batman.

DWEEZIL   *My Mother Is A Space Cadet/Crunchy Water*   Barking Pumpkin WS4-03366.   1982.   Frank brought his son to the microphone for the first, and, hopefully, the last time here.

American singles

All the Verve and early Reprise singles are rare and contain tracks and mixes which aren't available on albums.

Hot Rats   Radio Spots.   Reprise promo PRO-366.   1971.

Cosmic Debris/Uncle Remus   Discreet promo PRO-586.   1974.

Dancin' Fool/Baby Snakes   Zappa twelve-inch promo MK-83.   1979.

Joe's Garage/Central Scrutinizer   Zappa twelve-inch promo MK-107.   1980.

I Don't Wanna Get Drafted   Same on both sides.   Zappa promo ZRP-21AM. 1980.   Possibly an AM radio edited version.

FRANK ZAPPA/DAVID BOWIE   *What's It All About?*   Radio Series 547/8.   1981.

Valley Girl   Long and short versions.   Zappa promo AE7-1490.   1982.

Valley Girl   Long and short versions.   Zappa twelve-inch promo AS-1495.   1982.

Man From Utopia Meets Mary Lou Medley/We Are Not Alone   Barking Pumpkin twelve-inch promo, number unknown.   1983.

Barking Pumpkin Goes Digital   EP.   Barking Pumpkin twelve-inch promo AS-1594.   1983.

American albums

Again, all the Verve albums are rare as no one has bothered to give them a full re-release.

Apostrophe   Quad mix.   Discreet DS4-2175.   1974.

Overnite Sensation   Quad mix.   Discreet DS4-2149.   1974.

Live In New York   Discreet 2DS-2290.   1977.   Early copies included the track *Punky Whips* which was deleted on later copies.

Clean Cuts From Shiek Yabouti   Zappa promo MK-78.   1980.

Welcome To Joe's Garage   Zappa promo MK-129.   1981.

Clean Cuts From Tinseltown Rebellion   Barking Pumpkin promo AS-995.   1981.

Clean Cuts From You Are What You Is   Barking Pumpkin promo AS-1294. 1981.

Sampler   Barking Pumpkin promo AS-1569.   1982.   Probably from *Ship Arriving Too Late To Save A Drowning Witch.*
Innerview   Radio Series.   Series 4, programme 2.   c.1980.
King Biscuit Radio Series.   (Dated 28.6.81).

British singles
Like America, both Verve and early Reprise singles are rare.
You Are What You Is   Radio version/Regular version.   CBS promo A-1622-DJ. 1981.   This changes the line 'I ain't no nigger no more' to 'I ain't no . . . no more'. The gap in the line is filled in with echo.
The Frank Zappa EP   CBS XPS-147.   1982.   This is a sampler for the three-album boxed set *Shut Up And Play Yer Guitar* and was given away with the *Ship Arriving . . .* album.
Man From Utopia   Sampler EP.   CBS promo XPS-180.

British albums
Freak Out   Verve SVLP-9154.   1966.   This was a single album as opposed to the American double album.
Uncle Meat   Transatlantic TRA-197.   1970.   This was the first Reprise album in America, but they weren't taking any chances in Britain. So the indie label Transatlantic took up their option to release it.
Live In New York   Discreet K-69204.   1977.   Early British copies have *Punky Whips.*

Odds and sods
Zapped   US Reprise-Bizarre promo PRO-368.   c.1972.   This is a collection of Zappa proteges and productions.
Keep Your Teeth   USA American Dental Association PSA's promo.   c.1974. This 33rpm single also has other artists.
REUBEN AND THE JETS   *For Real*   USA Mercury SRM 1-659.   1975.   Although the name Reuben And The Jets originates from Zappa, this band have nothing to do with him.

Warren Zevon

Before going solo Zevon had been a member of The Brothers who had cut two American singles.

*Today Is Today/*B side unknown.   USA White Whale WW-250.   c.1966.
*The Girl's Alright/*B side unknown.   USA White Whale WW-255.   c.1966.

American singles
Werewolves Of London/Roland   Asylum twelve-inch promo picture disc AS-11886.   1979.   This has to be one of the best uses of a gimmick of all time. It

shows some fool in a werewolf mask. Zevon perhaps!

Nightime In The Switching Yard Same on both sides. Asylum promo twelve-inch promo AS-11395. 1980.

American albums

Wanted Dead Or Alive Imperial LPS-12456. c.1967. His first album. I don't know if any singles were released from this.

Wanted Dead Or Alive Pickwick SPC-3715. c.1975. A re-issue in a new sleeve.

WARREN ZEVON/WILLIE NILE King Biscuit Radio Series. (Dated 11.5.81).

WARREN ZEVON/NOVA COMBE King Biscuit Radio Series. 1981.

COMPILATIONS ▰
AND SOUNDTRACKS ▰

Listed by title.

Featuring previously unreleased or rare material.

A Bunch Of Stiffs   UK Stiff SEEZ-2.   1977.   Including Nick Lowe, Dave Edmunds, Tyla Gang plus one uncredited Graham Parker and The Rumour track.
All This And World War Two   UK Riva/USA 20th-Century Fox.   1976. Including Elton John, Leo Sayer, The Bee Gees, Brian Ferry, Roy Wood, Keith Moon, Rod Stewart, The Four Seasons, Jeff Lynne, Status Quo, Peter Gabriel and others performing Beatles songs.
Almost Summer   UK/USA MCA.   1978.   This is a movie soundtrack featuring Mike Love's band Celebration.
The Astrology Album   USA Columbia CS-2689.   c.1967.   This odd album features contributions from David Crosby, Chad and Jeremy and others talking about their beliefs in the stars.
The Beat Merchants   UK United Artists UDM-101/2.   1976.   This is an essential compilation of British beat groups from 1963 and 1964. It features the likes of Wayne Fontana, The Zephyrs, The Escorts, The Big Three, The Paramounts, The Pirates, The Downliners Sect, Mike Sheridan and The Nightriders, The Roulettes, The Mojo's and many more who contributed, in a modest way, to Britain pitching its state in rock and roll history. Many of the people in these bands, like Roy Wood, Russ Ballard, Gary Brooker, Rod Stewart and others, later went on to greater fame.
Beserkley Times   German Beserkley 6.28457.   DP.   1978.   This is the soundtrack to a televised Rockpalast concert in Hamburg 1977. It featured one side each from The Greg Kihn Band, The Rubinoos, The Tyla Gang and Earthquake on this live double album.
Big Sound For A Small World   UK London/Big Sound SHY-8527.   1979.   A compilation from the American Big Sound label. It featured a couple of tracks of Mick Farren, including his version of *Play With Fire* which is better than the Stones' version anyday.

The Bitter End Years   USA Roxbury RX3-300.   1976.   This is a three-album document of the Bitter End Cafe in New York, which during the '60s became the meeting place for the newly emerging singer-songwriter brigade. Among those included are John Sebastian, Van Morrison, James Taylor, Dion, The Everly Brothers, Phil Ochs and many others live. A one-album collected of edited highlights was released in the UK by Chelsea Records.

Blue Collar   USA/UK MCA.   1978.   This movie soundtrack features Captain Beefheart's *Hard Workin' Man,* plus contributions from Ry Cooder, as well as incidental music from Jack Nitzsche.

Brimstone And Treacle   UK/USA A & M.   1982.   This has new material from Sting and The Police as well as previously released tracks from Squeeze and The Go Go's.

Christmas At The Patti   UK United Artists UDX-205/6.   1973.   A recording of the Christmas party held at The Patti Pavillion in Swansea given by members of Man. In addition to the Man clan, Ducks DeLuxe, Dave Edmunds and others came along. It came in the unusual form of a ten-inch double album.

Concert For Bangladesh   UK/USA Apple.   1971.   This famous concert, which was also filmed, featured George Harrison, Ringo Starr, Bob Dylan, Leon Russell, Eric Clapton and the usual accompanying crowd. Although the album was on Apple, it was distributed by CBS because of Bob Dylan. A video version was also released in 1983, but only in an edited form.

Concerts For Kampuchea   UK/USA Atlantic.   1981.   Another charity album recorded at The Dominion Theatre in London over the Christmas period 1979 and featured the last live appearance of Paul McCartney. It also featured great sets by The Who, Queen, The Clash, The Specials, Ian Dury, Elvis Costello, The Pretenders, Rockpile with Robert Plant, as well as probably the last public appearance of John Bonham.

Doctor Rhino And Mister Hyde   UK Beggars Banquet BEGA-35.   1981.   This had a live track by Love which didn't appear on the *Live Love* album. *Time Is Like A River* was recorded at the reunion in 1978. The rest of this album is made up of the usual Rhino renegades.

The Exorcist   USA/UK Warner.   1973.   This film soundtrack features a horribly mucked about version of Mike Oldfield's *Tubular Bells.*

Fundamental Frolics   UK BBC REB-435.   1982.   Another charity show, this time with music and comedy. Unfortunately Mel Smith from Not The Nine O'Clock News provides the music, while Elvis Costello provided the comedy with *Hungarian Suicide Song.* It also featured Ian Dury, John Anderson, Alan Price, Neil Innes and others.

Glastonbury Fayre   UK Revelation REV-1.   1973.   This infamous album desperately needs to be re-released as it contains many artists who appeared at this open-air festival, including Bowie, The Grateful Dead, Marc Bolan, Gong, Brinsley Schwarz, Mighty Baby and Pete Townshend. Copies now fetch in excess of £35. The three-album set came in a clear plastic sleeve, complete with posters and books.

Greasy Truckers   UK Greasy Truckers GT-4997.   1973.   A double-album live set had a side each from Gong and Camel.

Greasy Truckers Party UK United Artists UDX-203/4. 1974. The follow-up to the above featured Brinsley Schwarz among others.

Hard Up Heroes UK Decca DPA-3009/10. 1975. An odd set made up of mainly obscure Decca tracks from the archives, recorded by artists who went on to greater things. Like Steve Marriott, The Big Three, Alexis Korner and Cyril Davies, The Warriors (featuring John Anderson), Andrew Loog Oldham, The Mighty Avengers, Joe Cocker, The Poets, The Rockin' Vicars, The Birds and many others.

Heroes And Villains UK Dakota OTA-1001. 1982. This collection of legends and has beens were collected by Dave Dee. As well as raising money for charity this concert coincided with the fifteenth anniversary of Radio One in September 1982. The cast included Sandie Shaw, Wayne Fontana, Billy Fury, Dave Dee etc., Cliff Bennett, Chris Farlowe, The Swinging Blue Jeans, The Troggs, Carl Wayne and others.

Hitmakers UK Marble Arch MAL-1259. 1969. A compilation of artists who made it big after leaving Pye Records. David Bowie's wonderful *Can't Help Thinking About Me* is included here as well as tracks by John Paul Jones, The DC5, Otis Redding and others.

Hits Greatest Stiffs UK Stiff FIST-1. 1978. A compilation of the first ten or so Stiff singles, so it includes Elvis Costello's *Radio Sweetheart*.

The Honky Tonk Demos UK Oval OVLM-5003. 1980. This is a collection of demo tracks sent to Charlie Gillett's *Honky Tonk* Radio Show on Radio London during the mid-70s. Dire Straits *Sultans Of Swing* first appeared on this show. Others included here are Graham Parker, Darts, Leo Kosmin, Chas 'n' Dave and others. Although Elvis Costello made his radio debut on this show in 1976, he isn't on this set.

Hope And Anchor Front Row Festival UK Warner-Albion K-66077. 1978. Recorded in late 1977 at the famous pub at Islington. It features live tracks by The Stranglers, The Pirates, Steve Gibbons, Wilko Johnson, XTC, 999, The Pleasers, The Tyla Gang, X-Ray Spex, The Saints, The Only Ones, Steel Pulse, Dire Straits and others.

The Last Waltz USA/UK Warner. 1978. A triple-album soundtrack to Martin Scorcese's movie of The Band's last concert in 1977. Many friends turned up to see them off in style, including Bob Dylan, Ronnie Hawkins, Neil Young, Joni Mitchell, Dr John, Neil Diamond, Muddy Waters, Eric Clapton, Van Morrison, Ringo Starr, The Staple singers and many others. The movie was over long, but none the less worthy.

Light Up The Dynamite UK Magnum Force MFLP-006. 1982. A compilation of the Dutch label Dynamite with Shakin' Stevens and The Sunsets, Nick Lowe, Ducks DeLuxe and others.

Live At CBGB's USA CBGB's/UK Atlantic. 1977. The famous New York club in the Bowery played host to virtually all the early punk/new wave pioneers, but this album has none of them. It does however have The Shirts, Mink DeVille, The Laughing Dogs and a few others.

Lost And Found UK Decca DPA-3083/4. 1981. The companion to *Hard Up Heroes*. This also features rare single tracks by Bowie, Al Stewart, Marc Bolan, Denny Laine, Rod Stewart, Genesis, Kenny Everett and others.

Mersey Beat 1962-1964 UK United Artists USD-305/6. 1975. A double album re-issue of two old Oriole label compilations from the early '60s. this was the forerunner to *The Beat Merchants* album of the following year. This included all the important second division bands from the Mersey era like Farron's Flamingo's, The Merseybeats, The Searchers, The Big Three, The Undertakers, The Escorts, Kingsize Taylor and The Dominos, Rory Storm and The Hurricanes and many others. They may have been second division, but the second division in those days was much better.

Music And Rhythm UK WEA K-68045. 1982. All tracks were contributed by artists to raise money for the World Of Music Arts And Dance Festival at Shepton Mallet which was partly organised by Peter Gabriel. It brought together dance groups, musical groups and artists from all over the world. Several of the stars who contributed to this album were Peter Gabriel, XTC, Pete Towshend, David Byrne and others.

My Generation UK EMI NUT-4. 1977. Compiled by Colin Miles, this is basically a southern beat collection featuring Tomorrow, The Action, Terry Reid, Tony Rivers, The Gods, Rod Stewart and many others. Like other compilations of its kind, it's an essential look at British music from the '60s by lesser known artists, many of whom later became famous.

The New Age Of Atlantic UK Atlantic K-20024. 1972. The Led Zeppelin track *Hey, Hey What Can I Do* makes its album debut here.

Oh Boy! UK Parlophone PMC-1072. 1958. The soundtrack to Britain's first real rock 'n' roll TV show, produced by Jack Good for ABC-TV in the late '50s. Included on this album were Cliff Richard, The John Barry Seven and many others.

One More Chance UK Charisma CLASS-3. 1973. This Charisma label sampler has one rarity to offer. The Genesis track *Happy The Man* appears here in a re-mixed form.

Party, Party UK A & M AMLH-68551. 1982. Soundtrack to a British movie about a typical New Year's Eve party. The soundtrack featured cover versions of old hits by the likes of Midge Ure, Dave Edmunds, Bananarama, Altered Images, Bad Manners, plus Elvis Costello's theme song.

Peter And The Wolf UK RSO 2479 167. 1976. Guiding you through a young persons guide to the orchestra on this occasion was Viv Stanshall, Manfred Mann, Gary Brooker, Christ Spedding, Eno, Phil Collins, Cozy Powell and others.

Rare Tracks UK Polydor 2482 274. 1978. An ace collection of obscurities from the vaults of Polydor and MGM, again, all from the '60s. Included are goodies from The Soft Machine, Cream, Frabjoy and Runcible Spoon (Godley and Creme), Fairport Convention, Linda Lewis, Jethro Tull (both sides of their single), Nicky Hopkins, the High Numbers, Stu Brown and Bluesology (Elton John included), John's Children, Sly and The Family Stone, Jimi Hendrix and Alex Harvey's Soul Band. This album was released before it became fashionable to re-release rarities, so it was deleted very quickly. A bargain bin beauty! There was a second volume called *Medium Rare* in 1979, but it was a real let down.

Raw Blues UK Ace Of Hearts/USA London. 1967. Mike Vernon produced this all stars jam album at the height of the British blues boom. It featured contributions from Eric Clapton, Peter Green, Steve Anglo (Steve Winwood using an alias), and of course, John Mayall.

Reading Festival '73 UK GM GML-1008. 1974. Live tracks by Rory Gallagher, Greenslade, Status Quo, The Faces, Tim Hardin and more.

Reading Festival '82 UK Mean MNLP-82. 1983. This double set has live tracks by Whitesnake, Michael Schenker, Budgie, Marillion, UFO, Randy California and others.

The Recorder, Volume Two UK Bristol Recorder BROO-2. 1981. This is actually a fanzine with an album. The album contains three new tracks by Peter Gabriel recorded live.

Roadie USA/UK Warner. 1980. A movie soundtrack which features new stuff from Blondie, Cheap Trick, as well as two excellent tracks by Alice Cooper, Eddie Rabbitt, Steven Bishop, Roy Orbison, Jerry Lee Lewis and others. Although Meatloaf appears in the movie, he doesn't figure on the album.

Rock On The Road USA DIR Broadcasting/King Biscuit Radio Series. 1980. This five-album set features many 'great English groups'. It includes . . . John Lennon *(Come Together* recorded at Madison Square Garden, New York in 1970), five live cuts from the Rolling Stones, two live tracks by Eric Clapton, as well as many other rare live cuts by David Bowie, The Kinks, Rockpile, The Who, Elton John, Paul McCartney, Yes, Rod Stewart, Elvis Costello, Graham Parker, Joe Jackson and Queen, as well as interviews from Joe Cocker, Pete Townshend and Mick Jagger.

Rock On The Road, Volume Two Same details as above. American artists are included here. They kick off with two live Springsteen cuts from 1973 and 1978. It follows on with The Band (they're Canadian), Tom Petty, Linda Ronstadt, The Doobie Brothers, Pat Benetar, Lynyrd Skynyrd, James Taylor, The Blue Brothers, The Beach Boys, Blondie, Jackson Browne, Foreigner (most of them are British) and Jefferson Starship.

The Roxy, London, WC2 UK Harvest SHSP-4069. 1977. This excellent compilation sounds as through it was recorded on a Walkman stuck on top of a toilet cistern, but captures 'the punk scene', as EMI would call it, pretty well. Included are Slaughter And The Dogs, The Unwanted, Wire, The Adverts, X-Ray Spex, and The Buzzcocks, among others.

Scouse The Mouse UK Polydor 2480 429. 1978. This children's story featured Ringo Starr, Donald Pleasance, Adam Faith, Barbara Dickson and others.

Secret Policeman's Ball (The Music) UK Island mini-album 12WIP-6598. 1981. A charity album with a brilliant set from Pete Townshend, as well as Tom Robinson, Neil Innes and John Williams.

Secret Policeman's Ball (The Music Volume Two) UK Island-Springtime HAHA-6004. 1982.

The second music compilation features Phil Collins, Bob Geldof and Johnny Fingers, Jeff Beck and Eric Clapton, Donovan, and Sting.

Sgt. Pepper's Lonely Hearts Club Band UK A & M/USA RSO. 1978. This was probably the greatest insult The Beatles had to suffer. Behind this mess were The

317

Bee Gees, Peter Frampton, Earth Wind & Fire, Alice Cooper, Aerosmith and others including Frankie Howerd!!

Short Circuit, Live At The Electric Circuit UK Virgin VCL-5003. 1978. Recorded at the Manchester punkhaus. It included John Cooper-Clark, Joy Division, The Drones, The Fall, The Buzzcocks and Steel Pulse. A blue vinyl ten-inch.

The Some Bizarre Album UK Some Bizarre Label BZLP-1. 1981. This sampler album included Soft Cell, Depeche Mode, B Movie among others.

Songs Lennon And McCartney Gave Away UK EMI NUT-18. 1979. An essential companion to The Beatles own releases, this consists of the songs they gave to others to help launch their careers. Included are Billy J. Kramer, Tommy Quickly, The Fourmost, Peter and Gordon, Cilla Black, The Strangers, The Applejacks and P. J. Proby as well as ditties by Chris Barber, Carlos Mendes and *I'm The Greatest* by Ringo Starr.

Stardust UK Ronco, number unknown. 1975. The second and final part of the Jim MacLaine story, as played by David Essex, following on from *That'll Be The Day*. Sides one to three include the usual '60s oldies, but side four has some tasty stuff by Dave Edmunds and his fictitious band The Stray Cats. It also has a contribution from The Electricians (also known as Brinsley Schwarz).

Stars Sing Lennon And McCartney UK MFP 5157. 1971. The original inspiration for *Songs Lennon And McCartney Gave Away*. This features EMI-only material by Billy J. Kramer, The Fourmost, Peter And Gordon, Cilla Black as well as some more unusual artists like Kenny Lynch, and Bernard Cribbins.

Stiff Live Stiffs UK/USA Stiff. 1979. A record of the first Stiff package tour with Ian Dury, Elvis Costello, Nick Lowe, Wreckless Eric, Larry Wallis and a few crates on the back seat of the coach. Although the album was re-released by MFP in 1981 it edited Elvis Costello's set by fading him out early.

That'll Be The Day UK Ronco MR-2002/3. 1973. This was the first, and best, of the two part story of the career and fall of Jim MacLaine, as written by *Melody Maker* journalist Ray Connolly. The first three sides of this double album are '50s oldies, some of them are not the original versions either, but side four included some new material from Viv Stanshall and David Essex, as well as four tracks by Billy Fury, one of which, *Long Live Rock,* was specially written by Pete Townshend.

Tommy UK/USA Polydor. 1975. The film soundtrack version with The Who, Eric Clapton, Elton John, Tina Turner and Oliver Reed!!

Troublemakers USA Warner PROA-857. 1981. This is a wonderful double album of punkish items from Warner's catalogue. It was a mail-order only album. You pay $2 for the postage and you get the album for nothing. It included two previously unreleased Sex Pistols' live tracks, as well as unreleased John Cale and Modern Lovers cuts. It also included regular tracks by Nico, PIL, Wire, The Gang Of Four and many others. A beaut.

Urgh, A Music War UK/USA A & M. 1981. A double live album of acts with some connection to Miles Copeland's management agency, plus a few others. It's actually a fine soundtrack to a promo movie. Making an appearance are The Police, The Go Go's, Echo and The Bunnymen, XTC, OMD, Devo, X, Magazine,

318

The Gang Of Four, Pere Ubu, Wall Of Voodoo, Gary Numan, The Cramps, 999, Jools Holland, Athletico Spixx 80, Toyah, Steel Pulse, Joan Jett, John Otway and many other less notables. Surprisingly enough, there's no Squeeze.

War Of The Worlds UK CBS 96000. 1978. This musical adaptation of H. G. Wells' sci-fi masterpiece was arranged by Jeff Wayne and included Justin Hayward, Phil Lynott, Chris Thompson, Julie Covington and others. Richard Burton narrated the English version while Curt Jergens narrated the German translation. There may be other versions worldwide.

White Mansions UK A & M AMLX-64691. 1978. The American Civil War set to music featuring Waylon Jennings, Jesse Colter and Eric Clapton among others.

Woodstock, Volume One USA Cotillion/UK Atlantic. 1970. The hippies graveyard. Featuring performances from Joan Baez, Joe Cocker, The Butterfield Blues Band, Canned Heat, Country Joe, Crosby Stills Nash and Young, Arlo Guthrie, Ritchie Havens, Jimi Hendrix, Jefferson Airplane, Santana, Sha Na Na, John Sebastian, Sly and The Family Stone, Ten Years After and The Who.

Woodstock, Volume Two USA Cotillion/UK Atlantic. 1970. Anyone wishing to buy five albums of this were treated to volume two later in the year. Joan Baez, The Butterfield Blues Band, Canned Heat, Crosby Stills Nash and Young, Jimi Hendrix, Jefferson Airplane, Melanie and Mountain all had the dubious pleasure of finishing off the Woodstock saga.

FLEXIPOP

'Flexipop' was a glossy pop mag aimed at the more demented end of the youth market. Regular features included The Silly Chart, a compilation of some of the most ridiculous band names at the time, e.g., Two Fat Women Who Can't Add Up, The Entire Crew Of HMS Ark Royal, Lofter Socket Dextrous And The Ging Gang Gouley Gumby Fly Swotters, and myriad others. It also had a strip cartoon, Trunky The Toilet. As well as flashes of soft porn, the rag's most popular feature was stuck to the front. A free flexi disc with previously unreleased songs by current faves. This provided the only real selling point of the magazine, which is strange as they stopped giving away the freebies in early 1983 and, inevitably, the sales dropped. 'Flexipop' passed away quietly in the summer of '83. 'Bye 'bye Trunky.

This is a list of their flexis:

1 SELECTOR *Ready Mix Radio* (SFI-566). Nov. 1980.
2 THE JAM Pop Art Poem and *Boy About Town* (LYN-9048). Dec. 1980.
3 THE BOOMTOWN RATS *Dun Laoghaire*. Jan. 1981.
4 ADAM AND THE ANTS *A.N.T.S.* (LYN-9285). Feb. 1981.
5 BAD MANNERS *Just Pretendin'* and *No Respect*. Mar. 1981.
6 THE PRETENDERS *Whatcha Gonna Do About It* and *Stop Your Sobbin'* (LYN-9650). Apr. 1981.
7 MOTORHEAD *Train Kept A Rollin'*. May 1981.
8 TOYAH *Sphinx* and *For You* (LYN-9899). June 1981.
9 HAZEL O'CONNOR *Men Of Good Fortune* and *D Days*. July 1981.
10 GRAHAM BONNETT *Nigh Games*/THE POLECATS *We Say Yeah*/THIN LIZZY *Song For Jimmy*/WAY OF THE WEST *Monkey Love* (LYN-10138/9). Aug. 1981.
11 DEPECHE MODE *Sometimes I Wish I Were Dead*/FAD GADGET *King Of The Files* (LYN-10209). Sept. 1981.
12 SOFT CELL *Metro Mr X*/B MOVIE *Remembrance Day* (LYN-10410). Oct. 1981.
13 GILLAN *Higher And Higher* and *Spanish Guitar* (LYN-10599). Nov. 1981.
14 ALTERED IMAGES *Happy New Year, Real Toys* and *Leave Me Alone* (LYN-10795). Dec. 1981.

15 BLONDIE AND FREDDIE *Yuletown Throwdown*/THE BRATTLES *Christmas Song*/SNUKY TATE *Santa's Agent* (LYN-10840/1). Jan. 1982.

« 16 XTC *Looking For Footsteps* (LYN-11032). Feb. 1982. Musically this was the best disc they gave away.

17 HAIRCUT 100 *Nobody's Fool* (LYN-11175). March 1982. This wasn't the hit version, but a Nick Heyward demo.

18 BOW WOW WOW *Elimination Dancing* and *King Kong* (LYN-11358). March 1982.

19 MADNESS *My Girl* (LYN-11546). April 1982. This is a slow version.

20 THE ASSOCIATES *Even Dogs In The Wild* (LYN-11649). May 1982.

21 GENESIS *The Lady Lies* (LYN-11806). June 1982.

22 THE CURE *Lament* (LYN-12011). July 1982.

23 BAUHAUS *A God In Alcove* (LYN-12106). Aug. 1982.

24 MARC ALMOND AND FRIENDS *Discipline* (LYN-12505). Sept. 1982.

25 BUCKS FIZZ *Christmas Medley* (LYN-12468). Oct. 1982.

26 THE ANTI NOWHERE LEAGUE *World War Three*/THE DEFECTS *Dance*/THE METEORS *Mutant Rock* (LYN-12647). Nov. 1982.

Some flexis came with picture sleeves on the subscription copies. Hard vinyl white label pressings were made for radio station use. They all had the title scribbled in biro on the label. Only fifty copies of these were made. In addition there was a special album pressed on hard vinyl as a sampler. *The Flexipop Album* LYN-11966. Again, only fifty copies were made, but here's the scam. All the tracks were re-mixed specially for this album. Included on this album were The Jam, Soft Cell, Altered Images, Depeche Mode, Haircut 100, The Pretenders, etc.

SFX

This was a bold move by its makers – a music magazine on a good quality C60 cassette, available only from newsagents. Each tape came with an A4 size card attached to it for reference. Ex-NME staffer Max Bell edited the tape and the first copy hit the stands in November 1981. The public had not really seen anything like this before, although there had been fanzines with a cassette previously. With all new ventures like this the first edition had to be a bit special, so it sold for only 50p. The price from edition two onwards was 75p. Obviously, at that price they were soon going to go out of business, so they had to take in washing, so to speak. Advertising anything from movies to burgers became a regular feature on the tape, with the same advert appearing up to four or five times on each edition, as well as advertising on the index card attached. The real diet of SFX was news, reviews and interviews. The very fact that the public could actually hear what the subject was saying was almost a novelty. Mis-quotes didn't exist, so this must have been an immediate success with interviewers and artists alike. As the list below shows, many big artists gave their time to SFX. It's difficult to calculate how many copies were sold, but the sheer novelty value of such an idea, especially for the blind who can't read the NME (lucky them), proved popular – for a while. Novelties, being what they are, soon wear off, and SFX came to an abrupt end only nine months after its creation. The most important thing was that it really started something. As I said, a bold move. So bold in fact, that the NME, always willing to fight the hand that beat them to it, copied the idea in 1983 with what I consider as their awful 'Audio Supplement'.

Hopefully someone will again make use of this important creative medium. If someone does, please make it last.

1 Madness, Linx, Spandau Ballet, Bow Wow Wow, Soft Cell.   Nov. 1981.
2 Kim Wilde, ABC, Eurythmics, Virna Lindt, Annabelle Lewin's mum.   Dec. 1981.
3 Sting, Stray Cats, Julian Cope, Dave Wakeling, Rat Scabies, Lemmy, Kid Creole, Nona Hendrix, The Belle Stars.   Jan. 1982.

4 The Human League, Depeche Mode, OMD, Steve Strange, James Brown, A&R Men. Jan. 1982.

5 Phil Collins, Duran Duran, The Pretenders, Heaven 17, Suggs. Feb. 1982.

6 Paul Weller, UB 40, Ultravox, The Mobiles, Pete Shelley, Killing Joke. Feb. 1982.

7 Billy Connolly, Gary Kemp, Modern Romance, Gary Numan, Fashion Article. March 1982.

8 Hugh Cornwall, Hall & Oates, Holger Czukay, Alice Cooper, Fashion, Alexei Sayle, XTC. March 1982.

9 Lou Reed, Wah, Haircut 100, Rap, Bill Wyman, The Questions, Apocalypse, Pirate Radio, Toni Basil. April 1982.

10 The Fun Boy Three, Hoddle and Ardeles, The Thompson Twins, The Associates, Kirk Brandon, Indies, Brixton Fair Deal. April 1982.

11 Bob Geldof, Paul McCartney, The Impossible Dreamers, Dollar, Vic Goddard, Maze. April 1982.

12 Sandie Shaw, Paul McCartney part two, The Belle Stars, Bananarama, Swans Way, Hank Marvin, Jim Kerr, Girlschool, Gil Scott Heron. May 1982.

13 Meatloaf, Adam Ant, Steve Davis, King Trigger, Culture Club, The Group, Thomas Dolby, Paul Simon, James King. May 1982.

14 Altered Images, Echo & The Bunnymen, Biz International, Bart, Michael Palin, Saxon, Paula Yates meets Duran Duran. June 1982.

15 Queen, Yazoo, Pete Townshend, End Games, Still Life, Women In Rock, Todd Rundgren, Dalek 1. June 1982.

16 Peter Gabriel, Ry Cooder, The Three Courgettes, Why Not, Hairdressing, Joan Jett, Lindsay Anderson, Scritti Politti, Yello. July 1982.

17 Marc Almond, Mel Brooks, Laurie Anderson, Kissing The Pink, VDU's, Bekki Bondage, Peter Wolf, No Fixed Address. July 1982.

18 Clint Eastwood, Video promos, UB 40, Johnny Byrne, Reflex, Elvis Costello, Captain Sensible, Sheena Easton. Aug. 1982

19 Martin Rushent, Kevin Rowland, Toto Coello, Indies, The Young Ones, Martha Ladley, Peter Murphy, Garry Roberts, The Alarm, The The. Aug. 1982.

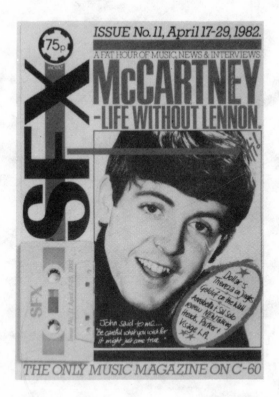

Cassettes
Upper left corner *SFX* No. 11.   Upper right corner *NME* 'Dancin' Master Compilation.
Middle right Madness Fan Club cassette.   Bottom (left to right) ELVIS COSTELLO
10 Bloody Mary's and 10 How's Your Fathers; YOKO ONO *Walking On Thin Ice.*

THE NME TAPES

In 1981 the NME decided to assemble a tape compilation together with Rough Trade Records. It was available through the NME only if you collected the required amount of coupons from the paper together with a charge of about £2. All the tapes featured previously unreleased tracks, as well as re-mixes, etc.

C 81 NME-Rough Trade COPY-001. 1981. THE SPECIALS *Raquel,* THE BUZZCOCKS *I Look Alone,* IAN DURY *Close To Home.* Plus Scritti Politti, The Beat, Wah Heat, Orange Juice, DAF, Robert Wyatt, Aztec Camera, Linx, Subway Sect and others.

Dancin' Master NME-001. 1981. THE JAM *When You're Young* Live version, IAN DURY *The Inbetweenies* Live version, U2 *An Cot Dubh* Live version. Kid Creole, Teardrop Explodes, Talking Heads, Junior, Grandmaster Flash, The Beat, Linx, The B52's, etc.

Jive Wire NME-002. 1982. THE BEAT *Stand Down Margaret* and *Get A Job* Live, KRAFTWERK *Das Model,* ALTERED IMAGES *Happy Birthday* Re-mix. Plus The Thompson Twins, Pigbag, Scritti Pollitti, The Gun Club, Theatre Of Hate, Suicide, etc.

Hit The Road Stax NME-003. 1982. Recorded in Paris and London 1966. Booker T and The MG's, Carla Thomas, Arthur Conly, The Markeys, Sam and Dave, Otis Redding.

Mighty Reel NME-004. 1982. Elvis Costello, Haircuit 100, Kid Creole, UB 40, Weekend, Fashion, Yello, Mari Wilson, Robert Wyatt, The Fun Boy Three, etc.

Pocket Jukebox NME-005. 1982. All taken from the Charly catalogue, including Robert Parker, Lee Dorsey, The Dixie Cups and a cast of thousands.

The Racket Packet NME-006. 1982. Getting thin on goodies here. MADNESS *Grey Day* Live. Plus Gregory Isaacs, Imagination, Lene Lovich and a lot of others not worth mentioning.

Stompin' At The Savoy NME-007. 1982. A collection of boppers from the Arista/Savoy catalogue from the '40s and '50s.

Mad Mix II NME-008. 1983. U2 *Two Hearts Beat As One* Re-mix, THE STYLE COUNCIL *Party Chambers,* plus others by Tom Waits, The Associates, Special AKA, Joboxers, etc.

NON-ALBUM TRACKS

The recordings are listed in date order under the name of the group or artist.

This is basically a list of tracks which haven't appeared on official albums. By 'official' I mean that no tracks from collections or greatest hits albums are included. This list only takes British released albums only. Some of these tracks may have appeared on albums in America, Europe, Lapland, etc. I've decided not to include promo only material like edits, or radio show albums but, by the same token, some of these tracks are extremely rare, like the Bowie Mercury singles for example. The titles in brackets are the source of the track (most of these are singles). Not all previously mentioned artists are featured here as they may not have any tracks which fall into this category. Most of the artists featured here are fairly recent, i.e. in the last ten years or so. The reason is that many artists from the '60s made albums as a matter of financial purpose. Doubtless many of them would rather have stuck to singles only. Plus many album tracks by The Dave Clark Five, The Yardbirds, Donovan, Peter and Gordon among others appeared in America only causing total confusion.

Abba

Ring Ring   Single re-mix from 1974.
Crazy World   *(Money Money Money).*
Happy Hawaii   *(Knowing You, Knowing Me).*
Summer Night City/Medley.
Lovelight   *(Chiquitita).*
A Man After Midnight.
I Have A Dream/Take A Chance On Me   Live versions.
Elaine   *(The Winner Takes It All).*
Should I Laugh Or Cry   *(One Of Us).*
The Day Before You Came/Cassandra.
Under Attack/You Owe Me One.
The version of *Chiquitita* on the *Music For UNICEF* album may be live.

Adam and the Ants/
Adam Ant

Young Parisians/Lady.
Whip In My Valise *(Zerox).*
Cartrouble Part Two/Kicks.
Press Darlings *(Kings Of The Wild Frontier).*
Physical *(Dog Eat Dog).*
Fall In *(Ant Music).*
Beat My Guest *(Stand And Deliver).*
Christian D'Or *(Prince Charming).*
Friends *(Ant Rap).*
A.N.T.S. (Flexipop giveaway).
Deutcher Girls, Plastic Surgery and *Nine To Five* *(Jubilee* album).
Friends *(The B Sides EP).*
Red Scab *(Goody Two Shoes).*
Juanito The Bandito *(Friend Or Foe).*
Why Do Girls Love Horses *(Desperate But Serious).*
Puss In Boots Long version/*Kiss Drummer* Seven- and twelve-inch.

The Beach Boys

Why Do Fools Fall In Love Edited USA single.
Do You Wanna Dance Re-mixed USA single.
Barbara Ann Edited.
You're Welcome *(Heroes And Villains).*
Do It Again Edited.
Bluebirds Over The Mountain/Never Learn To Love Both re-mixed.
Bluebirds Over The Mountain Dutch single mix.
Little Saint Nick With new sound effects. 1973 single.
Cuddle Up Re-mix *(You Need A Mess Of Help To Stand Alone).*
California Saga USA single re-mix.
Child Of Winter *(Suzie Cincinnatti)* Withdrawn single.
Rock 'n' Roll Music Re-mix.
Lady Lynda Edited. USA single.
It's A Beautiful Day *(Americathon* Soundtrack album).
Ten Years Of Harmony Album. This features a lot of re-mixes.
The Beach Boys Rarities Album. As well as odd mixes, this includes some previously unreleased tracks (all of which should have stayed in the can).

Blondie

Prototypes Demo EP.
Poet's Problem (Presence Dear).
Heart Of Glass Re-mix and instrumental versions. Twelve-inch.
Sunday Girl French version. Twelve-inch.
Heroes Live *(Atomic* twelve-inch).
Ring Of Fire From the *Roadie* soundtrack.
Call Me English and Spanish versions. (Spanish version on USA twelve-inch).
Yule Town Throwdown (Flexipop giveaway).

David Bowie

None of his Parlophone or Pye singles have appeared on official albums.
Rubber Band Re-mix (USA single).
Love You Till Tuesday Re-mix.
Space Oddity/The Wide Eyed Boy From Freecloud UK single re-mixes.
Space Oddity USA single re-mix on Mercury.
Ragazza Sola, Ragazza Solo (Italian single).
The Prettiest Star/Conversation Piece.
Memory From A Free Festival Parts 1 & 2 Re-mix.
Holy Holy Re-mix (Mercury version).
Jean Genie UK single re-mix.
Jean Genie USA single re-mix.
Rebel Rebel UK single re-mix.
Rebel Rebel USA single re-recording with *Hot Tramp I Love You So* at the beginning.
Holy, Holy (Diamond Dogs This is not the Mercury version).
Panic In Detroit (Knock On Wood).
Young Americans Edited.
Fame Edited.
Stay Edited (USA single).
Heroes Edited.
Heroes French and German versions.
John I'm Only Dancing 1975.
Ashes To Ashes Edited.
Crystal Japan (Up The Hill Backwards).
David Bowie In Baal EP.
Cat People Twelve-inch mix (MCA version) and BING CROSBY *Peace On Earth, Little Drummer Boy.*
Let's Dance Edited.
China Girl Edited.
Modern Love Edited/*Modern Love* Live version.
The Supermen On the *Glastonbury Fayre* album and QUEEN *Under Pressure.*

Kate Bush

Kate Bush On Stage   EP.
The Empty Bullring   (Breathing).
Ran Tan Waltz   (Babooshka).
Passing Through Air   (Army Dreamers).
December Will Be Magic Again/Warm And Soothing.
Lord Of The Reedy River   (Sat In Your Lap).
Dreamtime   (The Dreaming).
Ne T'en Fui Pas/Un Basir D'Enfant   French single release. The A side also turned up on the B side of the British *There Goes A Tenner* single.

The Clash

1977   (White Riot).
Complete Control/City Of The Dead.
Capital Radio/Interview/Listen   The NME freebie.
Clash City Rockers/Jail Guitar Doors.
White Man At Hammersmith Palais/The Prisoner.
1 2 Crush On You   (Tommy Gun).
Pressure Drop   (English Civil War).
The Cost Of Living   EP.
Armagideon Time/Justice Tonight/Kick It Over   (London's Burning   twelve-inch).
Time Is Tight   (USA *Black Market Clash*   ten-inch).
*Bankrobber/*MIKEY DREAD   *Rockers Galore, UK Tour*.
Bankrobber Dub   (USA *Black Market Clash*   ten-inch).
The Call Up/Stop The World.
Radio One   (Hitsville UK).
Magnificent Dance   (Magnificent Seven   re-mix on seven- and twelve-inch).
This Is Radio Clash/Radio Clash/Outside Broadcast/Radio Five   Twelve-inch.
First Night Back In London   (Know Your Rights).
Long Time Jerk   (Rock The Casbah).
Concerts For Kampuchea   Tracks.

Elvis Costello

DAY COSTELLO   *The Long And Winding Road/*B side.
Less Than Zero   Re-recording   (*A Bunch Of Stiffs*   album).
Radio Sweetheart   (Less Than Zero).

I'm Not Angry   (USA *Jem Import Collection* good luck!).
Alison   Re-mix   (USA single).
Watching The Detectives/Blame It On Cain/Mystery Dance.
Live Stiffs Live   Tracks.
Stranger In The House/Neat Neat Neat.
Big Tears   (Pump It Up).
Radio Radio/Tiny Steps.
Live At Hollywood High   EP.
Wednesday Week/Talking In The Dark   (Accidents Will Happen).
My Funny Valentine   (Oliver's Army).
Girl's Talk   (I Can't Stand Up For Falling Down).
Peace Love And Understanding   (NICK LOWE   *American Squirm).*
Getting' Mighty Crowded/Clowntime Is Over   (High Fidelity   twelve-inch) and
GEORGE JONES   *Stranger In The House.*
Dr Luther's Assistant/Just A Memory/Ghost Train   (New Amsterdam   EP
version).
Clean Money/Hoover Factory   (Clubland).
Crawling To The USA   (Americathon   Soundtrack album).
Psycho   (Sweet Dreams).
Cry Cry Cry/Wondering   (I'm Your Toy   seven-inch).
I'm Your Toy/Blues Keep Calling/Honky Tonk Girl/My Shoes   Twelve-inch
version.
Gloomy Sunday   (Fundamental Frolics album).
Concerts For Kampuchea   Tracks.
Big Sister/Stamping Ground   (You Little Fool).
Town Cryer/Imperial Bedroom   (Man Out Of Time   twelve-inch).
Man Out Of Time   Edited   (USA single).
From Head To Toe/The World Of Broken Hearts.
Party Party   (Single and soundtrack album).
With MADNESS   *Tomorrow's Just Another Day*   (Madness twelve-inch).
THE IMPOSTER   *Pills And Soap*   Long version.
Everyday I Write The Book   Re-mix/*Heathen Town/Night Time*   Twelve-inch.
Let Them All Talk   Re-mix/*The Flirting Kind*   Twelve-inch.

The Damned

Help   (New Rose).
Singalongascabies   (Neat Neat Neat).
Stretcher Case Baby/Sick Of Being Sick.
Suicide   (Love Song).
Burglar   (Smash It Up).
Ballroom Blitz/Turkey Song   (I Just Can't Be Happy Today).
White Rabbit/Rabid Over You/Seagulls.

I Believe The Impossible/Sugar And Spite *(History Of The World Part One* seven- and twelve-inch).
There Ain't No Sanity Clause.
Friday The Thirteenth EP.
Lovely Money/I Think I'm Wonderful/Lovely Money *(Disco).*
Lively Arts/Teenage Dream/So Bored.
Take That/Mine's A Large One Landlord/Torture Me *(Dozen Girls).*

Bob Dylan

Many of Dylan's rare tracks appear on the superb *Masterpieces* three-album set. Japan CBS-Sony S3BP-220502. 1978. This was also released in Australia.
Highway 61 Revisited Edited *(Can You Please Crawl Out Your Window).*
Rainy Day Women Numbers 12 and 35 Edited.
Just Like Tom Thumb's Blues Live version *(I Want You).*
Concert For Bangladesh Tracks.
Spanish Is The Loving Tongue *(Watching The River Flow).*
George Jackson Acoustic/big band versions.
Hurricane Edited part one.
Rita May/Stuck Inside Of Mobile Live version edited.
The Last Waltz Tracks.
Trouble In Mind *(Precious Angel).*
Heart Of Mine Edited/*The Groom's Still Waiting At The Altar* (USA single).
Angels Flying *(Union Sundown).*

These are in addition to his Blind Boy Grunt recordings and his appearances on the Newport Folk Festival albums.

Dave Edmunds

JILL READ *Maybe/Wang Dang Doodle.*
Jo Jo Gunne *(A Bunch Of Stiffs* Album).
Run Run Rudolph *(Christmas At The Patti* Album).
With MICKEY GEE *Pick Axe Rag* *(Born To Be With You).*
Stardust Soundtrack album. Fourth side.
Some Other Guy *(I Ain't Never* or *Stardust* Soundtrack album).
London's A Lonely Town *(Pebbles Volume Four* Album).
New York's A Lonely Town *(Where Or When).*
As Lovers Do *(Here Comes The Weekend* and *Crawling From The Wreckage).*
Television.
A 1 On The Jukebox/It's My Own Business.

Bad Boy   (Girl's Talk).
Boy's Talk   (Singing The Blues).
Queen Of Hearts   Live version   *(Me And The Boys)*.
True Love   Live version   *(From Small Things)*.
Live At The Venue   EP   *(DE 7th*   Freebie).
Run Run Rudolph   (USA single and *Party Party*   Soundtrack).

Peter Gabriel

Strawberry Fields Forever   (All This And World War Two).
Solsbury Hill   Edited.
D.I.Y.   Re-mix/*Teddy Bear*.
The Start/I Don't Remember   (Games Without Frontiers)   Both are different versions from the third album.
Biko   Re-mix/*Shozoloza/Jetz Kommt Die Flut*   Twelve-inch.
Biko   Edited   (Although this was a promo edit, this single could be found in newsagents, etc.).
Solsbury Hill   Live in New York.   Flexi.
Bristol Recorder   Tracks.
Shock The Monkey   Edited/*Soft Dog*   Seven-inch.
Across The River   (I Have The Touch and *Music And Rhythm* album).

Genesis

Happy The Man   (Single mix or *One More Time* album mix).
Watcher Of The Skies   (USA single or German *Rock Theatre* album).
I Know What I Like   Edited/*Twilight Alehouse*.
Counting Out Time   Re-mix.
The Waiting Room   Live version.   *(The Carpet Crawlers)*.
It's Yourself   (Your Own Special Way).
Spot The Pigeon   EP.
Follow You Follow Me   Re-mix   (USA single).
The Day The Light Went Out/Vancouver   (Many Too Many).
Go West Young Man   Edited   (USA single).
Open Door   (Duchess).
Evidence Of Autumn   (Misunderstanding).
Turn It On Again   Re-mix   (USA single).
Abacab   Edit.
Naminau   (Keep It Dark   Seven- and twelve-inch).
Submarine   (Man On The Corner).
3 × 3   EP.
Mama   Edited.
Firth Of Forth   Live version.   *(That's All*   Twelve-inch).

George Harrison

Bangladesh/Deep Blue.
Concert For Bangladesh Tracks.
Miss O'Dell (Give Me Love).
I Don't Care Anymore (Ding Dong).
It's What You Value Edited.

The Jam

All Around The World/Carnaby Street.
Sweet Soul Music/Back In My Arms Again (This Is The Modern World).
News Of The World/Aunties And Uncles/Innocent Man.
So Sad About Us/The Night (Tube Station).
Strange Town/The Butterfly Collection.
When You're Young/Smithers Jones.
See Saw (Eton Rifles).
Going Underground/The Dreams Of Children.
Live EP Freebie with the above.
Start/Lisa Radley.
Funeral Pyre/Disguises.
Absolute Beginners/Tales From The Riverbank.
A Town Called Malice Live version/*Precious* Long version. Twelve-inch.
Precious Edited *(A Town Called Malice* Seven-inch).
That's Entertainment Re-mix.
The Bitterest Pill/Poor, Poor Alfie/Fever.
Beat Surrender Twelve-inch EP.
Snap! Live EP.
Funeral Pyre (Fan club flexi). Recorded live in the studio.
Tales From The Riverbank (Fan club flexi).
When You're Young (Fan club flexi).
Pop Art Poem/Boy About Town (Flexipop giveaway).
Move On Up (Melody Maker flexi).
When You're Young (NME's Dancin Master Cassette).

Elton John

I've Been Loving You/Here's To The Next Time.
Lady Samantha/All Across The Heavens.
From Denver To L.A.

It's Me That You Need/Just Like Strange Rain.
Bad Side Of The Moon   (Border Song).
Rock 'n' Roll Madonna/Grey Seal.
Into The Old Man's Shoes   (Your Song).
Friends/Honey Roll.
Rocket Man.
Skyline Pigeon   New version   *(Daniel).*
Jack Rabbit/Whenever You're Ready   (Saturday Night's Alright).
Screw You   (Goodbye Yellow Brick Road).
Step Into Christmas/Ho Ho Ho.
Sick City   (Don't Let The Sun Go Down On Me).
Cold Highway   (The Bitch Is Back).
Lucy In The Sky With Diamonds/One Day At A Time.
Philadelphia Freedom.
House Of Cards   (Somebody Saved My Life Tonight).
Sugar On The Floor   (Island Girl).
Pinball Wizard   (Single version and soundtrack album version).
With KIKI DEE   *Don't Go Breaking My Heart/Snow Queen.*
Bite Your Lip   Twelve-inch re-mix.
Ego/Flintstone Boy.
I Cry At Night   (Part Time Love).
Loving   (Song For Guy).
The Goaldigger's Song.
The Thom Bell Sessions   EP.
Strangers   (Victim Of Love).
Johnny B. Goode   Long version/*Thunder In The Night*   Twelve-inch.
Conquer The Sun   (Little Jeannie).
White Man Danger/Cartier   (Sartorial Eloquence).
Tactics   (Dear God).
Steal Away Child/Love So Cold   (Freebie with above).
With JOHN LENNON   *28th November 1974*   EP.
Fools In Fashion   (Nobody Wins).
Can't Get Over Getting Over You   (Just Like Belgium).
Hey Papa Legba   (Blue Eyes).
Tortured   (USA Chloe).
Down To The Ocean   (Empty Garden).
The Retreat   (Princess).
LORD CHOC ICE   *Choc Ice Goes Mental   (I Guess That's Why They Call It The Blues).*
LORD CHOC ICE   *Earn While You Learn   (I'm Still Standing).*
I'm Still Standing   Re-mix   Twelve-inch.
Kiss The Bride   Long version/*Dreamboat*   Twelve-inch.

John Lennon

PLASTIC ONO BAND *Give Peace A Chance*/YOKO AND POB *Remember Love.*
Cold Turkey/YOKO *Don't Worry Kyoko.*
Instant Karma/YOKO *Who Has Seen The Wind.*
Instant Karma Phil Spector re-mix (USA single).
Power To The People/YOKO *Open Your Box.*
Happy Christmas/YOKO *Listen The Snow Is Falling.*
Move Over Mrs L (Stand By Me).
Give Peace A Chance (Shaved Fish Re-recording).
With ELTON JOHN *28th November 1974* EP.
Love Re-mix.

In addition John appears on the infamous Elastic Oz Band single.

Nick Lowe

TARTAN HORDE *Bay City Rollers We Love You/Rollers Theme.*
TARTAN HORDE *A La Rolla Part One* (Japanese single).
DISCO BROTHERS *Let's Go To The Disco/Everybody Dance.*
I Love My Label (A Bunch Of Stiffs Album).
Truth Drug/Keep It Out Of Sight (Dutch single).
Heart Of The City (So It Goes).
Bowi EP (The album mix of *Marie Prevost* is slightly different).
Halfway To Paradise/I Don't Want The Night To End.
Live Stiffs Live Tracks.
They Call It Rock (Breaking Glass).
Cruel To Be Kind (Little Hitler).
American Squirm/Elvis Costello and The Attractions using the name NICK LOWE
AND HIS SOUND *Peace Love And Understanding.*
Basing Street (Cracking Up).
Pet You And Hold You (My Heart Hurts).
Cracking Up/Peace Love And Understanding (Freebie given with the above).
Cool Reaction (Irregular Version) *(Ragin' Eyes* Twelve-inch).

Madness

Madness (The Prince).
Mistakes/Nutty Theme (One Step Beyond).
Stepping Into Line/In The Rain (My Girl).
Uno Paso Adalante (One Step Beyond in Spanish from Spanish EP).

Deceives The Eye/The Young And The Old/Don't Quote Me On That (Work Rest And Play EP).
The Business (Baggy Trousers).
Crying Shame (Embarrassment).
That's The Way To Do It/Swan Lake/My Girl (Return Of The Los Palmos Seven Twelve-inch).
A Town With No Name (Shut Up).
It Must Be Love/Shadows On The House.
Cardiac Arrest Long version/*In The City* Twelve-inch.
Don't Look Back (House Of Fun).
Animal Farm/Riding In My Car Alternate *(Driving In My Car* Twelve-inch).
Our House Warp mix/*Walking With Mr Wheeze* Twelve-inch.
Our House Edited warp mix.
Madhouse (Our House dub mix. Twelve-inch import).
Tomorrow's Just Another Day Warp mix/*Madness Is All In The Mind.*
With ELVIS COSTELLO *Tomorrow's Just Another Day* Twelve-inch.
Wings Of A Dove/Behind The Eight Ball.
Wings Of A Dove Re-mix/*One Second's Thought* Twelve-inch.
The Sun And The Rain/Fireball XL 5.
The Sun And The Rain Re-mix/*My Girl* Live. Twelve-inch.

Paul McCartney

Another Day/Oh Woman, Oh Why?
Give Ireland Back To The Irish/Version.
Mary Had A Little Lamb/Little Woman Love.
Hi Hi Hi/C Moon.
The Mess (My Love).
Live And Let Die/I Lie Around.
THE COUNTRY HAMS *Walking In The Park With Eloise/Bridge Over The River Suite.*
Helen Wheels/Country Dreamer.
Zoo Gang (Band On The Run).
Junior's Farm/Sally G.
Beware My Love Re-mix (French twelve-inch) good luck!
SUZY AND THE RED STRIPES *Seaside Woman/B Side To Sea Side.*
Mull Of Kintyre/Girl's School.
Goodnight Tonight Seven- and twelve-inch mixes/*Daytime Nightime Suffering.*
Wonderful Christmas Time/Rudolph The Red Nose Reggae.
Coming Up Live version/*Lunch Box, Odd Sox (Coming Up* Studio).
Check My Machine (Waterfalls).
Secret Friend (Temporary Secretary).
Concerts For Kampuchea Tracks.

Rainclouds/Ebony And Ivory Solo version *(Ebony And Ivory* Twelve-inch).
Take It Away Edited.
I'll Give You A Ring *(Take It Away)*.
Tug Of War Re-mix.
With MICHAEL JACKSON *The Girl Is Mine* (Also on Michael Jackson's *Thriller* album).
Say Say Say Re-mix long version/*Ode To A Koala Bear* Twelve-inch.

Graham Parker

I'm Gonna Use It Now *(Silly Thing)*.
Kansas City/Silly Thing *(Howlin' Wind* Freebie. Live versions).
Back To Schooldays *(A Bunch Of Stiffs* Album).
The Pink Parker EP.
The Bleep *(New York Shuffle)*.
Don't Ask Me Questions Live version *(Hotel Chambermaid)*.
I Want You Back Alive *(Protection* Seven- and twelve-inch).
Mercury Poisoning (USA twelve-inch) This was available at some shops under the counter.
Women In Charge *(Stupefaction)*.
Mercury Poisoning Live version *(Love Without Greed)*.
No More Excuses Version *(Temporary Beauty)*.

Tom Petty and The Heartbreakers

Fooled Again *(Anything That's Rock 'n' Roll* Seven- and twelve-inch).
Luna *(American Girl* Seven- and twelve-inch).
I Don't Know What To Say To You *(Listen To Her Heart* Seven-inch).
I Fought The Law and *Route 66* *(Listen To Her Heart* Twelve-inch).
Casa Dega and *Don't Bring Me Down* *(Here Comes My Girl* Twelve-inch).
It's Raining Again *(Refugee)*.
Century City *(Don't Do Me Like That)*.
Somethin' Else/Stories We Could Tell (Freebie given with the above).
Gator On The Lawn *(A Woman In Love)*.
Heartbreakers Beach Party *(Change Of Heart)*.
With STEVIE NICKS *Stop Draggin' My Heart Around*.

The Police

Fall Out/Nothing Achieving.
Dead End Job   (Can't Stand Losing You).
No Time This Time   (So Lonely).
Landlord   (Message In A Bottle).
Visions Of The Night   (Walking On The Moon).
Friends   (Don't Stand So Close).
A Sermon   (De Doo Doo Doo).
The Bed's Too Big Without You   Mono re-mix   (From the six pack).
De Doo Doo Doo   Spanish and Japanese.
Shamelle   (Invisible Sun).
Flexible Strategies   (Every Little Thing She Does Is Magic).
Low Life   (Spirits In The Material World).
Murder By Numbers   (Every Breath You Take).
Truth Hits Everybody/Man With A Suitcase   Live version   (Freebie given with the above).
Someone To Talk To/Message In A Bottle   Live version/*I Burn For You (Wrapped Around Your Finger*   Twelve-inch).
Propaganda, Urgh A Music War and *Brimstone And Treacle*   These albums also have new Police tracks.
Once Upon A Daydream   (Synchronicity Two).
Tea In The Sahara   (King Of Pain).

The Pretenders

Swinging London/Nervous But Shy   (Brass In Pocket).
Cuban Slide   (Talk Of The Town).
Porcelain   (Message Of Love).
In The Sticks   (Day After Day).
Louie Louie/English Roses   Live   *(I Go To Sleep).*
Precious   Live   *(The Pretenders*   USA mini-album).
Whatcha Gonna Do About It/Stop Your Sobbin'   (Flexipop giveaway).
Concerts For Kampuchea   Tracks.
Money   Live   *(2000 Miles*   Twelve-inch).

The Ramones

California Sun/I Don't Wanna Walk Around With You Both live. *(I Remember You)*.
I Don't Care (Sheena Is A Punk Rocker).
Let's Dance Live *(Swallow My Pride)*.
It's A Long Way Back To Germany (Do You Wanna Dance).
Needles And Pins Re-mix (USA single).
Rock 'n' Roll High School Tracks.

The Rolling Stones

I've only included post-Decca material here as they've all been re-issued and re-packaged over the years, as well as releasing rare and odd tracks on those early seventies Decca compilation albums.
Let It Rock Live *(Brown Sugar)*.
Through The Lonely Nights (It's Only Rock 'n' Roll).
Miss You Re-mix Twelve-inch.
Beast Of Burden Live *(Going To A Go Go)*.
If I Were A Dancer (Sucking In The Seventies Compilation).

Roxy Music

Virginia Plain/The Numberer.
Pyjamarama/Pride And Pain.
Hula Kula (Street Life).
Your Application's Failed (All I Want Is You).
Sultanesque (Love Is The Drug).
Both Ends Burning Edited/*For Your Pleasure* Live.
Trash Two (Trash One).
Dance Away Re-mix and edited.
Angel Eyes Re-mix. Twelve-inch.
South Downs (Oh Yeah).
Lover (Same Old Scene).
Jealous Guy.
Always Unknowing (Avalon).
The Main Thing Re-mix. *(Take A Chance On Me* Twelve-inch).
THE DUMBELLES *Giddy Up* Single.

Patti Smith

Hey Joe/Piss Factory.
Gloria Edited/*My Generation* Live version.
Godspeed (Because The Night).
Privilege EP.
Frederick Live *(Rock 'n' Roll Star).*
54321 Live *(Dancin' Barefoot).*

Spirit

She Smiles (USA *I Got A Line On You* Single).
1984/Sweet Stella Baby.
Red Light Roll On (Animal Zoo USA single).
Hand Guns (UK *We've Got A Lot To Learn).*
Turn To The Left Re-mix.

Bruce Springsteen

No Nukes Tracks.
Held Up Without A Gun (Hungry Heart).
Be True (UK *Sherry Darlin'*, USA *Fade Away).*
The Big Payback (Open All Night).
Santa Claus Is Coming To Town (In Harmony 2 Compilation album).

Squeeze

Packet Of Three EP.
Take Me I'm Yours Long version/*Night Nurse* Twelve-inch.
All Fed Up (Bang Bang).
Goodbye Girl Re-recording/*Saints Alive.*
Cool For Cats Edited/*Model.*
Up The Junction Re-mix.

Goodbye Girl and *Slap And Tickle* Re-mix (USA *Six Squeeze Songs* . . . Ten-inch mini-album. The first track is recorded live).
All's Well (Slap And Tickle).
Christmas Day/Going Crazy.
Pretty Thing (Another Nail).
Pulling Mussels From The Shell Re-mix/*What The Butler Saw*.
Trust (Is That Love).
Yap Yap Yap (Tempted).
Squabs On Forty Fab (Labelled With Love).
The Hunt (Black Coffee In Bed).
Elephant Girl (When The Hangover Strikes).
Annie Get Your Gun/Spanish Guitar.
Wrong Way (Smash hits flexi).
I'm At Home Tonight (Fan club single).

Ringo Starr

Choochy Choochy (Beaucoup Of Blues USA single).
It Don't Come Easy/Early 1970.
Back Of Boogaloo/Blindman (The version of *Back Off Boogaloo* on the *Stop And Smell The Roses* album is different).
Scouse The Mouse Tracks.

The Stranglers

Choosie Suzie/Peasant In The Big Shitty (Freebie with the first LP).
Go Buddy Go (Peaches).
Straighten Out (Something Better Change).
In The Shadows (No More Heroes).
Five Minutes/Rok It To The Moon.
Shut Up (Nice And Sleazy).
Walk On By/Tits/Mean To Me (Freebie with the *Black And White* album).
With GEORGE MELLY *Old Codger (Walk On By* Regular single).
Sverge (Swedish single).
Hope And Anchor Front Row Festival Tracks.
Fools Rush Out (Duchess).
Yellowcake UF6 (Nuclear Device).
In The Shadows Live *(Don't Bring Harry* EP).
N'Emmenes Pas Harry (French single).

Bear Cage Seven- and twelve-inch mixes/*Shah A Go Go.*
Who Wants The World/The Men In Black.
Tomorrow Was The Hereafter/Bring On The Nubiles.
Top Secret (Thrown Away).
Man In White (Just Like Nothing On Earth).
Vietnamerica (Let Me Introduce You To My Family).
Love 30 (Golden Brown).
Waltz In Black (La Folie).
Strange Little Girl/Cruel Garden.
Savage Breast (European Female).
Aural Sculpture (Freebie with the *Feline* album).
Midnight's Summer Dream Long version/*Vladimir And Olga* Twelve-inch.
Pawsher (Paradise Seven- and twelve-inch).

Talking Heads

Love Goes To Building On Fire/New Feeling.
Psycho Killer Acoustic version/*I Wish You Wouldn't Say That. (Psycho Killer).*
Psycho Killer Live (Freebie with the *Fear Of Music).*
Take Me To The River Edited (USA single).
Once In A Lifetime Edited.
Houses In Motion Re-mix/Live version. Twelve-inch.
Cities Live/*Artists Only* Twelve-inch.
Speaking In Tongues Cassette version.

Pete Townshend

Happy Birthday Six songs by Pete Townshend on this album.
I Am Five new Townshend songs here.
With Love Three new songs here.
Glastonbury Fayre Album. This has *Classified.*
Classified and *Greyhound Girl (Let My Love Open The Door).*
Secret Policeman's Ball Mini-album tracks.
Pinball Wizard/My Generation (Free flexi with *Maximum R & B* book).
Assencion Two (Music And Rhythm Compilation album).
See Me, Feel Me (A *Classic Rock* type album).

The Undertones

Teenage Kicks EP.
Really Really/She Can Only Say No (Get Over You).
Mars Bars (Jimmy Jimmy).
One Way Love/Top Twenty (Here Comes The Summer).
You Got My Number/Let's Talk About Girls.
Hard Luck Again/Don't Wanna See You (My Perfect Cousin).
Told You So (Wednesday Week).
Fairly In The Money Now (It's Gonna Happen).
Kiss In The Dark (Julie Ocean).
Beautiful Friend/Life's Too Easy.
The Love Parade Re-mix/*Like That/You're Welcome/Crisis Of Mine/Family Entertainment* Twelve-inch.
Got To Have You Back Seven- and twelve-inch mixes/*Turning Blue.*
Window Shopping For Clothes (Chain Of Love).

U2

Out Of Control (Irish *U2:3* Twelve-inch EP. This is a different version to the *Boy* album).
Touch 11 O'Clock Tick Tock.
Things To Make And Do (A Day Without Me).
Out Of Control Live version (USA *I Will Follow* single).
J. Swallo (Fire).
11 O'Clock Tick Tock/The Ocean/The Cry/The Electric Co. (Free single with the above).
An Cat Dubh Live version (NME's Dancin' Master cassette).
I Will Follow Live version *(Gloria).*
Trash, Trampoline And The Party Girl (A Celebration).
Treasure (New Year's Day).
Fire/I Threw A Brick/A Day Without Me (Free single with the above and on the twelve-inch).
Endless Deep (Two Hearts Beat As One).
Two Hearts Beat As One Re-mix/*New Year's Day* UA re-mix/*Two Hearts Beat As One* USA re-mix twelve-inch.

The Who

Many of The Who's rare singles and EP tracks have appeared on *Rarities Volumes One And Two,* but these didn't.
Bald Headed Woman   (I Can't Explain).
Daddy Rolling Stone   (Anyway Anyhow Anywhere).
Shout And Shimmy   (My Generation).
Waltz For A Pig   (Substitute).
I'm A Boy   Single version.
Happy Jack   Mono single version.
Pictures Of Lily   Mono single version.
Magic Bus and *I'm A Boy   (Meaty Beaty Big And Bouncy*   Album).
Woodstock Volume One   Tracks.
Concerts For Kampuchea   Tracks.

There are various other oddities on the *Odds And Sods* and *The Kids Are Alright* albums as well.

Yes

Something's Coming   (Sweetness).
Roundabout   Edited and re-mixed/*Long Distance Runaround*   Edited   (USA single).
America   Edited and re-mixed.
Going For The One   Edited.   Seven-inch.
Abalene   (Don't Kill The Whale).
Roundabout/Your Move   Both live   (Free single with *Classic Yes).*
Owner Of A Lonely Heart   Edited   (USA single).

Frank Zappa

Big Leg Emma.
Tears Began To Fall   Re-mix/*Junior Mintz Boogie.*
Joe's Garage   Re-mix.
I Don't Wanna Get Drafted/Ancient Armaments   Live version.

Notes for Your Own Collection

Notes for Your Own Collection

Notes for Your Own Collection

Notes for Your Own Collection